THE LAST YEARS OF
ROBERT E. LEE

T0159518

Reviews of *The Court Martial of Robert E. Lee* (an historical novel)

"I had always thought that Michael Shaara's *The Killer Angels* offered the finest fictional evocation of Robert E. Lee. I now believe that Savage presents an even more credible, more compelling portrait of Lee both as a commander, as a husband, and father. Savage's creativity, eye for detail, and flair for character development make the book an irresistible combination of history, biography, and courtroom drama." —Edward G. Longacre, author of *The Cavalry at Gettysburg*

"A brilliant premise, superb characterizations, fine historical research and setting. *Court Martial* is as good as *The Killer Angels*." —David Martin, author of *Regimental Strengths and Losses at Gettysburg*

"*Court Martial* is a remarkable accomplishment." —William Garrett Piston, author of *Lee's Tarnished Lieutenant: James Longstreet*

Reviews of *A Mouthful of Dust*

"Douglas Savage's writing is so compelling that Stephen Crane himself could have written *A Mouthful of Dust*." —David Halliburton, PhD, author of *The Color of the Sky: A Study of Stephen Crane*

"*A Mouthful of Dust* is an enticing read that explores the soul of a soldier, and of a writer. Highly recommended." —Midwest Book Review

"Powerful, and haunting. A tour de force, and a real treat." —Perry Lentz, PhD, author of *Private Fleming at Chancellorsville: The Red Badge of Courage*

"In Douglas Savage's novel *A Mouthful of Dust*, I found an old compañero—still burning himself out, still living, though barely, inside the 'story under his hand.' I loved the surprise ending in *A Mouthful of Dust* and I think Crane—who surely got through to Douglas Savage—would have, too." —Linda H. Davis, author of *Badge of Courage: The Life of Stephen Crane*

Review of *Cedar City Rendezvous*

"This is a compelling Western that achieves moments of mythic grandeur." —Booklist

Novels by Douglas Savage
The Glass Lady
The Court Martial of Robert E. Lee
Incident in Mona Passage
Highpockets
Cedar City Rendezvous
The Sons of Grady Rourke
A Mouthful of Dust

Nonfiction by Douglas Savage
Soldiers' Life in the Civil War
Civil War Medicine
Prison Camps in the Civil War
The Civil War in the West
Ironclads and Blockades in the Civil War
Rangers, Jayhawkers, and Bushwhackers in the Civil War
Women in the Civil War

THE LAST YEARS OF ROBERT E. LEE

From Gettysburg to Lexington

DOUGLAS SAVAGE

TAYLOR TRADE PUBLISHING
Lanham • Boulder • New York • London

TAYLOR TRADE PUBLISHING
An imprint of Rowman & Littlefield

Distributed by NATIONAL BOOK NETWORK

Copyright © 2016 by Douglas Savage

British Library Cataloguing-in-Publication Information Available

Library of Congress Cataloging-in-Publication Data Available

ISBN 978-1-63076-169-1 (paperback)
ISBN 978-1-63076-011-3 (e-book)

∞™ The paper used in this publication meets the minimum requirements of American National Standard for Information Sciences—Permanence of Paper for Printed Library Materials, ANSI/ NISO Z39.48-1992.

In memory of
Benjamin Abraham Silverman,
an old soldier,
314th Supply Company, Quartermaster Corps, AEF,
and
Sonia Little Silverman,
who loved him, and who loved all the rest of us

I am considered now such a monster that I hesitate to darken with my shadow the doors of those I love, lest I should bring upon them misfortune.

—Robert E. Lee

One

MEN AND BOYS, HOMESICK AND HUNGRY IN DIRTY SNOW, TURNED THEIR winter bivouac into one great tent revival.

Along the frozen Rapidan River, a religious revival swept the Army of Northern Virginia in winter camp in Orange County, Virginia, seventy-five miles northeast of Richmond and twenty-five miles west of Fredericksburg during a cold and dismal January, 1864. Nearly every brigade in Robert E. Lee's army built rough-hewn chapels from logs and mud. At least fifteen thousand Confederates were newly baptized in at least forty tiny churches and wrote home about being "converted" to Southern Christendom.

The religious fervor around him did not escape the general. Sunday, February 7, General Lee (West Point, '29) issued a Sabbath proclamation as General Orders Number 15: The commanding general declared that "he has learned with great pleasure that in many brigades convenient houses of worship have been erected, and earnestly desires that every facility consistent with the requirements of discipline shall be afforded the men to assemble themselves together for the purpose of devotion." Field inspections of the regiments by their officers were arranged to not interfere with chapel attendance.

The previous day, General Lee's weary mind turned to his crippled and ailing wife. "I am sorry to hear that you have been suffering," he wrote to Mother Lee at her new Richmond home, known as The Mess. "I fear you took cold in your rides." One week later, Robert Lee was overcome with winter loneliness and he wrote sadly to his wife, "The young men have no fondness for the society of the old general. He is too somber and heavy for them."

Not everyone was cold and grim beside a frozen river.

Everyone loved twenty-three-year-old Sandie Pendleton, and Lieutenant Colonel Pendleton loved Major General Jeb Stuart of the Confederate cavalry corps and the dead Lieutenant General Thomas Jonathan Jackson of Second Corps. When "Stonewall" died of wounds at Chancellorsville last May, 1863, his corps adjutant general Sandie Pendleton dressed Stonewall's one-armed body for burial in Lexington. In Second Corps, Sandie was proud to be known as Stonewall's Man. Old Jack would have liked that.

From Robert Lee's fifty-seventh birthday on January 19 through February 3, 1864, newlyweds Sandie Pendleton (Washington College; Lexington, VA, '57) and Kate Corbin Pendleton honeymooned in hungry Richmond. Then Sandie joined the staff of Lieutenant General Richard "Baldy" Ewell (West Point, '40) who had inherited the dead Stonewall Jackson's beloved Second Corps of the Army of Northern Virginia. Kate returned alone to the Moss Neck Plantation.

The long winter, which followed a disappointing summer and fall after Gettysburg, took its toll upon Robert Lee's spirits and upon his health. At fifty-seven, he felt old and weary.

General Lee's defeat on the blood-soaked green and rocky hillsides at Gettysburg ate at his military soul when his battered army retreated back to Virginia. His self-doubt gnawed at his failing heart for a month, from his July 5, 1863, retreat until August 8. What a relief when he decided what his duty demanded: that he resign from his command of the Army of Northern Virginia.

With dip pen and inkwell, he carefully composed a letter to President Jefferson Davis:

> *The general remedy for the want of success in a military commander is his removal . . . I have been prompted by these reflections more than once since my return from Pennsylvania to propose to Your Excellency the propriety of selecting another commander for this army . . . I sensibly feel the growing failure of my bodily strength. I have not yet recovered from the attack I experienced this past spring. I am becoming more and more incapable of exertion, and am thus prevented from making the*

personal examinations and giving the personal supervision to the oper-
ations in the field which I feel necessary. Everything, therefore, points
to the advantages to be derived from a new commander . . . A younger
and abler man than myself can readily be attained.

Jefferson Davis had few friends after living fifty-five years. His way
was to be chilly, reserved, and somber. Old Sam Houston who invented
Texas meant it when he said of Davis, "One drop of Jeff Davis's blood
would freeze a frog." Due to serious aches and pains, Davis suffered from
chronic insomnia, and he was a familiar sight on Richmond streets in the
middle of the night on the back of Kentucky, who would carry him for
lonely hours. But when it came to Robert Lee, President Davis had trust
absolute and even affection.

Four days after sending his letter of resignation, General Lee received
his president's comforting response:

Suppose, my dear friend that I were to admit, with all their impli-
cations, the points which you present, where am I to find that new
commander who is to possess the greater ability which you believe to be
required? . . . To ask me to substitute you by some one in my judgment
more fit to command, or who would possess more of the confidence of
the army . . . is to demand an impossibility.

With his president's unconditional confidence, Robert Lee returned
to business. On August 17, five days after the president's kind letter,
General Lee wrote to Davis to complain about desertions from his army
still recovering from the Gettysburg slaughter:

The number of desertions from this army is so great and still continues
to such an extent that, unless some cessation of them can be caused, I
fear success in the field will be seriously endangered. Nothing will
remedy this great evil which so much endangers our cause except the
rigid enforcement of the death penalty in the future in cases of con-
viction.

One week later, the general returned to his daily battle with Richmond to secure provisions for his hungry and barefoot divisions and their weakening animals.

"Nothing prevents my advancing now but for the fear of killing our artillery horses," Lee wrote to the president. "Some days, we get a pound of corn per horse and some days more, some days none. Our limit is five pounds per day per horse. You can judge of our prospects."

By early October, Lee wrote to General Alexander Lawton, the Confederacy's quartermaster general, that "The want of the supplies of shoes, clothing, overcoats, and blankets is very great."

Ten days later, the weary general had to vent his frustration to Mother Lee, writing that "Thousands were barefooted, thousands with fragments of shoes, and all without overcoats, blankets or warm clothing."

Robert Lee's failing heart did not help matters during the second half of 1863. His first attack of angina pain struck a month before the Chancellorsville victory last May. From April 6 to April 16, he managed his army from the back of an ambulance wagon. His second attack came the month after Gettysburg.

Depressed with his health, he wrote to Mother Lee on September 4 that "An attack of rheumatism in my back has given me great pain and anxiety. If I cannot get relief, I do not see what is to become of me."

Sixteen days later, angina chest and back pain again confined the general to an ambulance from September 20 until October 10. Yet another heart seizure put him down from October 31 through November 5.

By December 2, 1863, Robert Lee confided to one of his principal aides at winter camp, Lieutenant Colonel Charles Marshall: "I am too old to command this army."

But the old man's congestive heart disease was nothing when compared to a heart which was broken.

He dearly loved his son Rooney's fragile wife, Charlotte. Rooney and Charlotte had known each other as children and were distant cousins on the Lee side. Charlotte Wickham married Rooney in March, 1859, when Rooney was twenty-one and she was eighteen.

To General Lee, Charlotte was like another daughter. "Summer returns when I see you," he had written to her in June of '62.

Rooney and Charlotte buried two babies, one being Robert E. Lee III. She never recovered from those devastating losses and from Rooney becoming a prisoner of war the past June, just before Gettysburg. Only two months ago, so desperate was Charlotte's health that General Lee's eldest son, Custis, thirty-one, had offered the Federal authorities to take his brother Rooney's place in prison for forty-eight hours over Christmas so Rooney could be at Charlotte's deathbed. But the Yankees refused the exchange of prisoners of war.

Rooney had been first imprisoned at Fort Monroe, Virginia, on Chesapeake Bay. General Lee helped build it and son Custis was born there in September, 1832, when his father served the army Corps of Engineers.

Having been summoned to Richmond for a war council, General Lee could have enjoyed a warm Christmas with his wife and daughters. But he could not be comfortable when his beloved army was cold and hungry. He returned to winter camp at Orange Courthouse by Christmas Day to share their discomfort.

Wasted by grief and tuberculosis, Charlotte died on Christmas Day, 1863. She was buried beside her babies at Shockoe Hill Cemetery in Richmond. General Lee wrote to Mother Lee on Christmas Day, "I feel for her all the love I bear Fitzhugh . . . I loved them as one person." Fitzhugh was most often called Rooney to distinguish him from his first cousin, Major General Fitzhugh Lee. And two days later, the stricken father again wrote to Mother Lee: "Thus dear Mary is link by link of the strong chain broken that binds us to earth . . . I grieve for our lost darling as a father can only grieve for a daughter. I loved her with a father's love."

As icy February, 1864, dragged on under gray skies, neither last year's heart attacks nor December's heartbreak diverted General Lee's attention from the gripping crisis of filling the army's ranks. On February 15, he wrote to War Secretary James Seddon to request permission to send officers to the hospitals in Virginia, Georgia, and both Carolinas, to search for sick and wounded men who were strong enough to rejoin their regiments. The malingerers had to be rounded up before the spring campaigns.

During that mid-February, Sandie Pendleton managed a furlough from Baldy Ewell's side for a few days with Kate at Moss Neck. When Sandie returned to Second Corps, he left his son growing inside his

Katinka. From February 22 to 29, General Lee went to Richmond for consultations with President Davis. Upon his return, the men and boys beside the river welcomed General Lee's daily rides through camp aboard his warhorse, Traveller. Most often, his shivering soldiers simply uncovered their heads and stood in reverent silence when their "Uncle Robert" passed.

The winter order of the day was hunger. Only the lice were more common than hunger pangs. The daily ration per man in the Army of Northern Virginia was cut to four ounces of salted pork and one pint of cornmeal. The animals' rations were cut from ten pounds of corn and ten of hay to five pounds of corn and no forage at all. The horses which hauled the cannon, the wagons, and the bloodstained ambulances munched on tree bark and wastepaper. Half of Jeb Stuart's cavalry horses which dragged the artillery died of starvation. Faring no better than his thin troops, General Lee's dinner was usually nothing more than cabbage boiled in salt water. And the boisterous, young Jeb Stuart (West Point, '54) lost more than his vital horses: The hard winter and an outbreak of smallpox killed his devoted and legendary banjo picker, Sam Sweeney.

With James Longstreet's large First Corps still stationed in Tennessee, the army counted only 35,000 men in winter camp. It would number only 54,344 by late April. General Richard Ewell's Second Corps camped at Verdiersville, and A. P. Hill's Third Corps camped at Orange Courthouse. Jeb Stuart's cavalry mustered between 8,000 and 9,700 troopers on horses made of skin and bone.

The manpower crisis gripped the entire Confederacy. On February 17, President Jefferson Davis signed a new conscription law which lowered the minimum draft age from eighteen to seventeen, and raised the upper age limit on conscription from forty-five to fifty-five years. The whole Confederacy was down to only 126,000 draftable white men. Meanwhile, President Lincoln raised another 700,000 men to dress in Yankee blue.

What men and officers General Lee mustered beside the Rapidan were a shadow of the magnificent legion of the preceding year. Stonewall Jackson and dozens of other generals were dead, along with the thousands buried in unmarked graves beside Antietam Creek, the heights of Fredericksburg, the jungle around Chancellorsville, and the rocky green slopes at Gettysburg.

With the approach of spring, "Baldy" Ewell had only one leg with which to fill Stonewall's boots. And "Little Powell" Hill (West Point, '47) barely had the strength to command himself, let alone Third Corps. By March, Lieutenant General Hill's venereal disease had devastated him. His chronic prostatitis was crippling. He now suffered from rampant infection, kidney failure, and painful inability to urinate. The fragile Little Powell had to relinquish command altogether for a few weeks in March, and riding his gray charger, Champ, would be all but impossible throughout April.

March 10, General Lee returned to Richmond to plan the spring offensive with Jefferson Davis. James "Old Pete" Longstreet (West Point, '42) came east from Tennessee to join in half of the meetings.

The same day that Lee left for Richmond, Federal Major General George Meade (West Point, '35) received company at his winter head-quarters at Brandy Station on the north side of the Rapidan: Hiram Ulysses Grant had arrived in Virginia. An error in Grant's nomination to West Point misspelled his name as Ulysses S. Grant. He liked and kept his new name.

Fresh from his Federal victories in the west at Vicksburg, Mississippi, and Chattanooga, Tennessee, General Grant (West Point, '43) was finally the man for whom Mr. Lincoln had searched for thirty bloody months. After Federal Generals Irwin McDowell, George McClellan, John Pope, then McClellan again, Ambrose Burnside, "Fighting Joe" Hooker, and then George Gordon Meade, had all failed to destroy Robert E. Lee, President Lincoln and his Congress called for Grant. The prayerful Congress in Washington reinvented the rank of lieutenant general to bestow upon Ulysses S. Grant, like Moses anointing Aaron.

Although the Confederacy had always used the rank of lieutenant general for corps commanders, the Federals retained major general as their highest field rank. Congress re-created the rank in March, 1864, specifically for Grant, and confirmed him as Yankee general-in-chief. The last time that rank was awarded by the US Congress was upon George Washington. General-in-Chief Winfield Scott had been nominated for the rank but was never confirmed by Congress. Now Lieutenant General Grant would command all Federal armies in the field. He elected to retain Major General Meade as commander of the Army of the Potomac, camped opposite General Lee. But history would remember that army as General Grant's.

The Army of the Potomac under Meade's immediate command (on paper, anyway) was reorganized into three corps of infantry and one cavalry corps. The blue cavalry was commanded by General Phil Sheridan, who had graduated from West Point in 1853, one year behind Jeb Stuart. Sheridan would have graduated with the class of '52 had he not been suspended for one year for attacking a fellow cadet with a bayonet.

Though a ferocious fighter, Lieutenant General Grant was short, chomped an ever-present cigar, and had a remarkable voice. Those who knew him never forgot his strangely soft, almost lilting voice which always rang crystal clear, as if he had studied speech or opera.

Lieutenant Generals Grant and James Longstreet were friends for almost a lifetime. They had been close friends at West Point, where Cadet Grant had been one year behind Old Pete. After the Point, when both young officers were stationed at Jefferson Barracks, St. Louis, Longstreet had introduced Grant to Longstreet's cousin, Julia Dent, who became Mrs. Grant. Julia was related to Longstreet's mother, Mary Dent Longstreet. Old Pete knew his Federal kinsman well, and he warned his comrades in gray when Mr. Lincoln sent Grant to do battle with Lee: "We must make up our minds to get into line of battle and to stay there; for that man will fight us every day and every hour till the end of this war."

Two

General Grant's detachment to the Army of the Potomac was not the only homecoming noted by General Lee in March, 1864. On February 25, the Yankees finally issued a parole for William Henry Fitzhugh Lee (Harvard dropout, '57), known to friends as Rooney. The general's widower son returned from Federal prison to Richmond on March 14. Rooney's wife was three months dead, but his battlefield wounds were healed, and he rejoined Jeb's cavalry along with his first cousin, Major General Fitzhugh Lee (West Point, '56), the son of the Old Man's brother, Captain Sidney Smith Lee, CSN.

As Rooney made his way home and U. S. Grant unpacked at George Meade's winter headquarters, Mother Lee and the girls busied themselves, furiously knitting socks for the barefoot Army of Northern Virginia. On March 18, General Lee wrote to his wife, thanking her for the shipment of 103 pairs of socks, which the Old Man had sent over to the Stonewall Brigade, Old Jack's first command. Quite pleased with Mrs. Lee's skill at knitting double-heels on her socks, the weary father asked his wife, "Can you not teach Mildred that stitch?" Another 43 pairs of socks for the Stonewall Brigade arrived within days from The Mess on Franklin Street. On March 24, General Lee thanked Mother Lee for still another set of 17 pairs, which left only 300 men barefoot in the Stonewall Brigade. Letters from the Rapidan front on March 30, April 9, and May 2 acknowledged 392 pairs of socks made by the crippled fingers of Mother Lee and daughters Mary Custis, Agnes, and Mildred.

On Saturday, March 26, Lieutenant General Grant formally became general-in-chief, attached to Major General Meade's headquarters. Ten days later, General Lee, perhaps aware of Grant's presence across the Rapidan at Brandy Station, warned Jefferson Davis that "All the information I receive tends to show that the great effort of the enemy in this campaign will be made in Virginia." Two days later, April 7, he confided to Cousin Margaret Stuart that "A soldier's heart, you know, is divided between love and glory." And two days after that note, Robert Lee's heart felt the remnants of his earlier heart seizures again tighten his sore chest. He confided by letter to son Custis on April 9: "I feel a marked change in my strength since my attack last spring at Fredericksburg, and am less competent for my duty than ever." But even with the angina, the black eyes still glowed with fervor when he wrote to Mother Lee on the same day, saying, "I want for nothing but independence for our distracted country."

With his chest in pain and his army still hungry and barefoot, Robert Lee prepared for the coming spring offensive by the Federals. On April 11, General Longstreet, camped at Bristol, Tennessee, was ordered to come back to Virginia with First Corps. Old Pete reached Charlottesville by April 14.

While First Corps and Old Pete tramped eastward toward Virginia, General Lee again begged Richmond for food to prevent starvation before doing battle with Grant. "My anxiety on the subject of provisions for the army is so great," he wrote on April 12, "that I cannot refrain from expressing it. I cannot see how we can operate with our present supplies." And, he warned, "We have rations for the troops today and tomorrow."

Longstreet's First Corps trickled back to Virginia due to the South's poor railroads. The vital Virginia Central Railroad had but eight engines to haul First Corps back at the rate of only 1,500 men per day. When the Yankees destroyed miles of rails, the Confederates had to pirate rail from one line to lay it on another for repairs.

By April 16, General Lee's field intelligence predicted that Generals Grant and Meade would attack by crossing the Rapidan with simultaneous Yankee assaults into the Shenandoah Valley and at Drewry's Bluff on the James River. The same day, General Lee advised President Davis that "I am not yet able to call to me the cavalry or artillery. If I am obliged to retire from this line, either by a flank movement or the want of supplies, great injury will befall us." On Tuesday, April 19, General Lee wrote to his president: "We have now but one thing to do: to establish our independence. We have no time for anything else." When he wrote to his president, General Lee believed that his 64,000 men faced 75,000 Federals. He did not yet know that the Yankee force numbered 119,000.

On April 23, Rooney Lee was promoted to the rank of major general, befitting a division commander of Rebel cavalry. The next day, his father warned him, "If defeated, nothing will be left for us to live for." While the two great armies stirred from their long winter encampment with the coming of Virginia spring, General Grant perhaps felt the sudden weight of command upon his shoulders. April 27 was his forty-second birthday. "Getting old, am I not?" he wrote to wife Julia. The coming spring offensive fell with equal or greater weight upon Robert Lee across the Rapidan. "You must sometimes cast your thoughts on the Army of Northern Virginia and never forget it in your prayers," he wrote the day after Grant's birthday, to cousin Margaret Stuart. "It is preparing for a great struggle," he added.

First Corps returned to the Virginia front on the eve of the predicted Great Struggle.

On Friday, April 29, Robert Lee rode over to Gordonsville for a formal review of the returned First Corps of the Army of Northern Virginia. The thin and hard infantrymen had not seen their Uncle Robert since September. Ten thousand voices shouted hysterically and thousands of battered hats were tossed into the air at the sight of the stately general with the whitening beard. Regiment after regiment broke ranks to crowd around General Lee and to lay hands upon the gray sides of Traveller. A Rebel band blared out "Hail to the Chief" as tears streamed down the ruddy cheeks of First Corps' "Marse Robert." A Yankee band had played the same tune nine months earlier when George Gordon Meade looked down the hill at the bloodied heap which had been Pickett's Charge.

The proud Lieutenant General James Longstreet beamed as his hearty divisions trooped their colors for the commanding general. It was good to feel Virginia earth underfoot once again.

The day after First Corps returned to the army, Jefferson Davis's five-year-old son, Joseph, went climbing on a construction scaffold erected for repairs to the presidential mansion in Richmond. When Joseph slipped, he was dead by the second bounce. His mother, First Lady Varina, was seven months pregnant when she saw her dead child on the ground. The little boy would be buried in Hollywood Cemetery, where three of General Longstreet's children were buried within days of each other twenty-seven months earlier.

But life went on. The day after little Joseph Davis died in Richmond, the sickly A. P. Hill and his Dolly baptized their five-month-old daughter, Lucy, at Third Corps' winter camp at Orange Courthouse. Robert Lee stood beside the proud parents and the commanding general held the infant as her godfather. Both Little Powell and Old Pete Longstreet had bestowed upon General Lee the highest honor they could: the names of their newest children, Lucy Lee Hill and Robert Lee Longstreet.

The day after Lucy Hill's baptism, Robert Lee climbed to his observation post atop Clark's Mountain for the last time on May 2. The 1,100-foot-high ridge overlooked twenty Virginia counties and the melted Rapidan waters. Across the river were 102,000 Federals with 4,300 wagons of supplies. On this last lookout, General Lee had brought with him all three corps commanders, Longstreet, Hill, and Ewell, and at least eight division commanders. Rising clouds of dust from the visible Yankee encampment convinced General Lee that Grant and Meade were about to launch the spring assault upon Richmond by crossing the Rapidan at Ely's or Germanna Fords.

When the Federals crossed the Rapidan, General Lee had only half their number with which to stop them. The Confederates had First Corps with 10,000 men at Gordonsville, forty-two miles away. Baldy Ewell's Second Corps with 17,000 was thirty miles away at Verdiersville, and A. P. Hill's 22,000 men in Third Corps were nearby at Orange.

The springtime air was charged with the impending clash of two mighty armies. There was no doubt in Washington or in Richmond that the coming onslaught would be the death struggle of one or the other. With a massive engagement perhaps only hours away, Robert Lee climbed down from Clark's Mountain and jotted off a note to Mother Lee. He wrote her to send him a new set of suspenders for his trousers.

May 3, Lieutenant General Grant held a final staff meeting in the evening at Culpepper, A. P. Hill's hometown. Powell's brother, Baptist Hill, still had a home there.

After Grant's conference with his generals in blue, the mighty Army of the Potomac prepared to cross the Rapidan to do battle with Robert Lee. Grant had to race the Confederates through the jungle of thickets on the Rebel side of the river. General Lee had to stop the Yankees in the tangled mess before Grant could break out into open ground to maneuver his two-to-one, numerically superior force.

The gloomy target of both armies was known in Virginia as the Wilderness.

By ten p.m. on the night of May 3, the Federal 50th New York Engineer regiment was on station at Germanna Ford on the banks of the Rapidan. By three in the morning, Yankee cavalry had secured the Germanna beachhead. Within one hour, the engineers began construction of two pontoon bridges, which were finished by five-thirty in the morning. During the next twelve hours, two blue infantry corps totaling fifty thousand men crossed the river. The spring campaign had begun. General Grant crossed the river at noon. Another Federal corps crossed at Ely's Ford with Ambrose Burnside's independent IX Corps crossing the next morning, May 5, at Germanna.

Confederate scouts atop Clark's Mountain reported the Federals on the march within two hours of the Federal engineers' arrival at Germanna Ford. General Lee immediately issued orders for his Second and Third Corps to march eastward in pursuit of the Army of the Potomac. Longstreet's First Corps was ordered to march toward the Wilderness from Gordonsville for Todd's Tavern, a nothing crossroads four and a half miles southeast of Chancellorsville. First Corps was still one division short, since George Pickett's bloodied division remained behind to man the defenses around Richmond as the capital's home guard.

The mighty host in blue rumbled toward Richmond. Just the wagon train of supplies to feed and to arm the Federals was sixty-five miles long. As the blue divisions churned up clouds of dust with their 200,000 boots on the morning of May 4, twenty-eight-year-old Micah Jenkins was troubled by a dream. The young brigadier general from the gray

First Corps spoke softly about his fitful night to his friend, Colonel Asbury Coward. General Jenkins saw his whole short life laid out like a photograph album in his dream. But the lifeline went completely blank after the coming battle with the marching Federals. This troubled the brigadier, who had distinguished himself in every battle under General Longstreet's admiring eye.

It was no wonder that nightmares haunted the sleep of Brigadier General Jenkins. Since Chancellorsville last May, of twenty-eight brigades, only eleven brigadier generals remained with their brigades by April, 1864. The rest were promoted or transferred and five were dead with three more wounded.

Like two blind giants, the blue and gray armies stumbled toward their rendezvous inside the Wilderness. The Federals rolled southward, and Lee's divisions marched eastward to head them off. By nine-thirty on the morning of May 4, Winfield Hancock's blue II Corps had reached the old battlefield at Chancellorsville. His weary bluecoats were appalled to find Federal bones, skulls, and rotting limbs sticking out of shallow graves. Wind and rain had eroded the mass graves from the May, 1863 debacle when Stonewall Jackson had rolled up the Army of the Potomac.

South of the Rapidan, two narrow highways ran east and west: the Orange Turnpike and the Orange Plank Road. The Army of Northern Virginia clogged both roads in its eastward push. Jeb Stuart and the gray cavalry broke camp, which he cheerfully called "the Wigwam," near Orange Courthouse and followed the Orange Plank Road toward the Wilderness this Wednesday, May 4. They scouted the Federal position and joined Powell Hill's Third Corps.

The gray and butternut-brown army marching eastward faced difficult odds. General Lee could quickly muster only 28,000 infantry, some 8,400 cavalry, and 4,000 artillerymen. Another 20,000 men were either detached to Richmond or were with First Corps, well up the road at Gordonsville. General Lee led only three full divisions and parts of two others against Grant and Meade's 122,000 well-fed and well-clothed infantry, cavalry, and artillery. If the Yankees turned to fight, they could form a battle line two men deep and thirty miles long. General Lee's army would only stretch across a sixteen-mile front.

But Robert Lee had worries even bigger than manpower. As with every new campaign, he had many men with new field promotions who had not been tested in battle with the increased responsibility. Longstreet's First Corps had two of three divisions under newly promoted major generals: South Carolina lawyer Joe Kershaw, forty-two, and Charles Field (West Point, '49). Kershaw's division (formerly McLaws's division) had three new brigadiers, while Field's division (formerly Hood's) had two new brigadiers. Second Corps had three veteran division commanders, but four new brigade commanders. In Hill's Third Corps, Cadmus Wilcox (West Point, '45, and a groomsman at the 1848 wedding of U. S. Grant) was the newly minted commander of the dead Dorsey Pender's division, which had five new brigadiers. To General Lee's weary mind and painful heart, he carried too many newly promoted officers eastward to meet Grant and Meade.

A. P. Hill had received his marching orders by eleven in the morning this May 4. Third Corps would walk toward Verdiersville, eleven miles eastward from Orange Courthouse along the Orange Plank Road. Richard "Old Bald Head" Ewell's Second Corps followed the parallel Orange Turnpike, bound for camp at Locust Grove. Hill marched with two of his three divisions. General Richard "Dick" Anderson's division remained behind at Orange to guard the supply wagons. Their objective in the Wilderness was some twenty-five miles toward the northeast. Hill's marching divisions jammed the road with 14,500 men. Baldy Ewell marched with 13,500 troops. General Lee left Orange about noon to ride with Third Corps.

It was always the Old Man's way to ride close to the corps commander about whom he worried the most should the crunch come in a hail of musketry. So General Lee rode with Little Powell, whose gaunt face grimaced with each step of his warhorse, Champ.

Robert Lee with Third Corps planned to allow Grant and Meade to cross the Rapidan unmolested. Once First Corps arrived from Gordonsville, Lee would trap the Federals inside the prickly Wilderness, where the Yankees could not wield their horse-drawn cannon in the thick brambles and scrub trees.

Old Pete left Gordonsville at four in the afternoon with ten thousand men marching hard, forty miles southwest of Parker's Store, a widening in the dirt road. By late afternoon, Third Corps with Hill and General Lee were at Verdiersville, halfway between Orange Courthouse and Chancellorsville. Ewell's Second Corps had reached Locust Grove, six miles northeast of Lee's position.

Throughout May 4, the continent's two greatest armies converged on the Wilderness. At six o'clock in the evening, Lieutenant General Grant issued marching orders for May 5: The blue II Corps of General Winfield Hancock (West Point, '44) would march from Chancellorsville southwest, to Shady Grove Church; V Corps of General Gouverneur Warren (West Point, '50) would march from Wilderness Tavern southwest to Parker's Store; and "Uncle John" Sedgwick's (West Point, '37) blue VI Corps would tramp from Germanna Ford to Wilderness Tavern. Ambrose Burnside's IX Corps would stay behind to defend the ford.

General Lee also issued orders late on May 4. General Ewell's Second Corps would strike the Federals if they appeared to be moving down the Rapidan toward Fredericksburg. When General Longstreet sent word to Lee that First Corps should arrive at Verdiersville by noon on May 5, General Lee planned to destroy Grant inside the Wilderness maze on May 5 after Longstreet's timely arrival. At ten o'clock on the night of May 4, General Lee sent Baldy Ewell orders to delay attacking the mighty blue army until Longstreet's First Corps was on the field. Lee would wait to fight until Old Pete came up—just as he had paced and waited for Longstreet at Gettysburg. The one-legged Ewell now had two sets of conflicting orders from his commanding general.

By first light on May 5, the Federals had marched into the overwhelming gloom of the Virginia Wilderness. General Warren's V Corps of bluecoats headed down the Brock Road already made famous by Stonewall Jackson's outrageous flank march around Fighting Joe Hooker one year and three days earlier, during the Battle of Chancellorsville. The gray-clad Third Corps entered the Wilderness from the west at five in the morning by way of the Orange Plank Road. Jeb Stuart's cavalry led Powell Hill's corps. Baldy Ewell's Second Corps continued into the jungle along the Orange Turnpike. Near Verdiersville, General Lee remained at his field headquarters, awaiting Longstreet's First Corps, due any minute.

By seven-thirty on this Thursday morning, General Grant ordered Major General Meade as titular commander of the Army of the Potomac to strike the Rebel Second Corps, sighted along the turnpike. The pickets of Ewell's gray corps were spotted only three-quarters of a mile from the blue division of General Charles Griffin (West Point, '47).

Within half an hour of the gray advance pickets taking a few potshots at the Yankee pickets, Baldy Ewell nervously sent his son-in-law, Major Campbell Brown, off to General Lee to request clarification of Lee's earlier, wait-for-Longstreet orders. Lee repeated to Major Brown his order that Second Corps was not to get into a firefight until at least Hill's Third Corps could close the three-mile distance separating the two Confederate corps, filling the two parallel highways through the Wilderness. This conflicted with the first set of instructions Ewell had received from Lee the night before.

By ten o'clock in the morning, Lieutenant General Grant conferred with George Gordon Meade at the intersection of the Orange Turnpike (on which Ewell advanced from the west) and the Germanna Ford Road. Grant ordered Griffin's blue division to strike Ewell immediately, supported by John Sedgwick's entire VI Corps. In the cool Virginia morning, "Old Snapping Turtle" Meade reached over to button up General Grant's blue greatcoat like a doting grandfather.

Still uncertain about what to do with the blue horde massing a mile down the road, Lieutenant General Ewell at eleven a.m. sent his trusted, youthful chief of staff, Sandie Pendleton, to General Lee. The father-to-be found General Lee repeating his warning to avoid a major confrontation inside the suffocating Wilderness. General Lee told Sandie to have Richard Ewell withdraw from an assault by Grant.

Three

Baldy Ewell's indecision was resolved at noon when three Federal divisions slammed into Ewell's Second Corps. Because he'd lost a leg at Bull Run, Ewell sat strapped to his saddle on his gray horse, Rifle.

While General Lee, Jeb Stuart, and Powell Hill rode into the Wilderness, Ewell was no closer than two miles from A. P. Hill's reinforcements. The thick Wilderness restricted visibility to less than twenty yards, and the two miles of thickets between Second and Third Corps might just as well have been twenty miles. Ewell's seven brigades fought for their lives against 25,000 screaming Federals. The wild fighting quickly cost Confederate Brigadier General John Marshall Jones, forty-three, his life. Jones (West Point, '41) was two years ahead of Lieutenant General Grant at the Point. General Jones's nickname at the Point was simply "Rum."

By one p.m., Robert Lee found himself in the middle of his worst nightmare: His army was cut into three independent commands, two of which were suddenly fighting hard. Ewell's Second Corps fought desperately to the north at a bloody meadow called Saunders Field, along the turnpike, while Hill's Third Corps was jumped by bluecoats to the south along the Plank Road. Longstreet's First Corps was somewhere in the rear, and hopefully coming hard.

The Confederate Second Corps had been struck at Saunders Field by Griffin's blue division. A ferocious countercharge by the Stonewall Brigade pushed the Yankees back after Stonewall's successor at brigade command, James Walker, thirty-one, had shouted to his bloodied regiments, "Remember your name!" Twelve years earlier, Thomas Jackson had now-General Walker expelled from the Virginia Military Institute after Cadet Walker challenged Major Jackson to a duel. When another Federal charge broke the Second Corps line, Major General Jubal Early's nephew, Captain Robert Early, was shot dead. Leading Virginia lawyer "Old Jube's" (West Point, '37) division, Georgia lawyer General John Gordon charged to plug the break in the gray line. "All who are faint-hearted, fall out!" General Gordon cried. "We do not want anyone to go in but heroes!" The barefoot heroes countercharged and pushed the Federals back.

In the early-afternoon hailstorm of molten lead at Saunders Field, the thick brush between the dense trees of the Wilderness caught fire. The fire swept over the piles of bleeding wounded in blue and gray and ignited the gunpowder in the wounded men's cartridge boxes. Already wounded teenagers were blown apart when their belts exploded.

Baldy Ewell held Saunders Field at two-thirty as Uncle John Sedgwick's blue VI Corps arrived on the field. Half an hour later, three of General Sedgwick's brigades slammed into Ewell's shaky line from the north side of the Orange Turnpike. Neither side could see the other through the smoke and thick forest. The Federals advanced two hundred yards before Ewell's shattered line drove them back. What little artillery could maneuver within the dense tangle caused horrific damage. One Rebel shell plowed into Sedgwick's field headquarters. The ball tore off one bluecoat's head and the flying skull hit another officer in the face, knocking him down with a mouth full of gray and bloody brains.

While Baldy Ewell's men held onto Saunders Field with their finger-nails, Powell Hill had his hands full to the south.

Hill's Third Corps had been struck at one p.m. by Winfield Hancock's blue II Corps, which descended upon Hill from the north side of the Orange Plank Road along the Brock Road, where Old Jack had marched to glory last May. Hill sent the division of Cadmus Wilcox northward to attempt to link Third Corps with Ewell's line.

General Wilcox touched Ewell's line and joined Second and Third Corps into a north-south front by three o'clock. General Hancock sent three full blue divisions into the firestorm. For two hours, Hancock's brave boys were cut into bloody shreds. Along the Plank Road, the Confederates rolled dead Federals over, piled the bodies on top of each other, and used the blue-clad corpses as makeshift barricades and breastworks for cover. Among the Federal dead was Brigadier General Alexander Hays, who had attended Allegheny College in Meadville, Pennsylvania, before transferring to West Point. He had graduated from the Point in 1844 as a close friend of Cadet U. S. Grant. Brigadier General Hays had held the little stone wall at Gettysburg on the slope of Cemetery Ridge, where Pickett's Charge was pulverized. For his constant gallantry fighting for his bloodied country, Brigadier General Hays was promoted to major general after his death in the Wilderness.

Along the Orange Plank Road, Hill's battered corps was attacked at least five times by overwhelming forces. Henry Heth's gray division of Hill's command with 6,700 troops held off 30,000 Federals from four blue divisions. Heth's division fired 100,000 rifle rounds within ten minutes of bloodletting. The Yankees were finally driven back after their sixth charge.

With the Confederate lines now linked within the smoking Wilderness, the firing did not abate until after dark, at ten p.m. The blue and gray lines of bleeding and exhausted men were so close to each other in the darkness that men staggered into enemy lines when they searched for streams to fill empty canteens. The Army of Northern Virginia held its ground between the Orange Turnpike to the north and the Orange Plank Road to the south. James Longstreet's First Corps was still nowhere to be found in the smoky darkness, filled with the cries of the wounded.

While the Confederate Army struggled to avert destruction, the Federals nearly bagged a prize such as make and break nations. At three that afternoon, Robert E. Lee, A. P. Hill, and Jeb Stuart put their heads together in a council of war at the Widow Tapp's house along the Orange Plank Road. A Federal skirmish line of infantry suddenly appeared, coming toward the generals in gray. The Yankees marched in parade order to within two hundred yards of Robert Lee and half of his corps commanders. Well within pistol range of three soldiers with gold stars on all of their lapels, the Federals paused, executed an about-face, and returned to the cover of the Wilderness. Not a shot was fired in this brief moment, when General Grant had the chance to shake Robert Lee's hand for the first time since Mexico, seventeen years earlier.

As the armies dropped in the darkness to sleep upon their hot rifles, General Lee counted upon Old Pete to bring up First Corps during the night of May 5. Lee anticipated being able to strike Grant at dawn with his fresh, gray First Corps. But by five in the evening, First Corps was at a crossroads called Richard's Shop, at least ten weary miles behind Hill's bloodied Third Corps. General Longstreet's tired divisions had marched twenty-eight miles on May 5. Not knowing how far back Longstreet camped, Lee still planned to assault the blue army at five o'clock in the morning on May 6. When the Yankees beat Lee to the punch with their own dawn attack, Longstreet was still three miles away from the action. The Army of Northern Virginia could be exterminated before First Corps arrived.

After his army had barely escaped being cut in half and destroyed one corps at a time, and after nearly ending May 5 on a train to a Yankee prison camp, Robert Lee's problems were far from over. His divided army faced twice their number digging in under cover of darkness and Wilderness greenery.

After the ten-hour battle inside a jungle of pine and scrub brush, Lieutenant General A. P. Hill could hardly walk. The excruciating pain of his swollen prostate and backed-up kidneys made putting one foot in front of the other a greater effort than preserving Third Corps to fight another day. Only Little Powell's raw willpower kept him at his post.

In the darkness of the night of May 5, General Lee waited for Longstreet. After resting his men for five hours, Old Pete prodded his divisions back to the road shortly after midnight. First Corps then marched all night along the Orange Plank Road toward A. P. Hill's panting survivors.

At four in the morning on May 6, Ambrose Burnside brought up his detached IX Corps to reinforce the badly bruised Army of the Potomac. Within an hour, the red-eyed Federals again slammed into Robert Lee's army in the thick forest of bullet-riddled trees.

If Old Pete did not ride up the Orange Plank Road with First Corps just as the now-incapacitated Powell Hill had done at the last possible minute beside Antietam Creek, the Army of Northern Virginia could be finished during the first two days of the spring campaign of 1864.

The five a.m. attack was a full frontal assault by Hancock's blue II Corps. Little Powell Hill's two exhausted divisions were inundated by three Federal divisions with two more blue brigades supporting them. With the sun barely up in the eastern sky obscured by billowing sulfur clouds and burning brush, Hill's divisions of Generals Wilcox and Heth simply had to give way. Yard by yard and corpse by corpse, the graybacks fell back under the weight of the Yankee charges. With Baldy Ewell's Second Corps too far north in the Wilderness to help and with Longstreet's corps still on the march, Robert Lee looked squarely into the prospect of destruction as he had not done since Sharpsburg on the banks of the Antietam.

And just like at Antietam, at the last possible minute a dust cloud appeared far down the Orange Plank Road. With the gray Third Corps on the verge of collapse in the early morning shadows, mighty First Corps ran barefoot up the road.

Robert Lee had been pacing since three-thirty in the morning at the Widow Tapp's house. By six a.m., Third Corps was falling back under the weight of thirteen Federal brigades, which attacked in blue waves. Hill's two divisions were pushed backward over their own dead and wounded, three hundred yards from their front, secured during yesterday's bloodbath. In desperation, General Lee ordered a dozen Confederate cannon to fire double loads of the ghastly canister over the heads of the retreating Third Corps. The loads of iron marbles cut down rows of Federals like red stalks of corn at ranges as short as two hundred yards.

It was seven a.m. when the first of Old Pete's winded veterans ran past Robert Lee's field headquarters at the Tapp farm. Led by John Hood's old Texas Brigade, fourteen First Corps brigades formed up and let the fleeing Third Corps remnants file through their ranks. The worried Old Man was beside himself when the mud-caked First Corps ran past him.

"Hurrah for Texas!" Robert Lee cried into the melee. In a rare show of emotion and passionate relief, he waved his hat wildly at the Texans as the dawn breeze ruffled his thinning, white hair.

The bloodied Third Corps re-formed doggedly behind the fresh but weary First Corps. Powell Hill personally fed one of the cannon. His groin was as hot as his cannon, but he cheered First Corps along with his own shattered divisions.

Old Pete on horseback shouted above the crash of cannon and the roar of forty thousand rifles. "Keep cool, boys! Keep cool!" James Longstreet cried. When the Texas Brigade, now commanded by Texas lawyer and judge Brigadier General John Gregg, thirty-five, prepared to countercharge the Federals, Uncle Robert's blood was up.

General Lee on Traveller quietly rode to the front of Gregg's brigade. With the morning air full of Minié balls and cannon shot, General Lee prepared to personally lead Longstreet's last-ditch attack against 25,000 Federals. If the Army of Northern Virginia was to perish in the field, Robert Lee was not going to watch it from a distance.

The Texans shouted, "Lee to the rear!" with one hoarse voice.

When Lee would not budge, the Texans refused to attack with General Lee so exposed to hostile fire. The Old Man only turned around when Longstreet and Colonel Venable dragged Traveller from harm's way.

Longstreet's battle line was a mile wide, perpendicular to the Orange Plank Road. Joe Kershaw's division formed on the left (north) side and Charles Field's division lined up on the right. The blood-spattered survivors of Third Corps formed up with them.

Old Pete's boys attacked like Vikings. In a ferocious firefight, they drove the Yankees back into the Wilderness thickets. By 9:45 a.m., General Hancock's brave boys were pushed back to their original positions.

The rock-like Texas Brigade lost half its men in the holocaust of hot lead and burning trees.

Within half an hour, Longstreet's left flank joined Baldy Ewell's right flank, extending down from the north along the turnpike. The vital juncture was scouted by the frail Powell Hill, who personally led his regrouped divisions of Heth and Wilcox through the Wilderness to link First and Second Corps with Hill's Third Corps in the middle. When Hill had dismounted to study the dense landscape, a Federal patrol came within one hundred yards. Little Powell calmly led his staff in the opposite direction, avoiding capture for the second time in two days. At last, the Army of Northern Virginia was one united front, driving the Federals before it, just like old times.

By ten o'clock, after five hours of fearful slaughter in the Wilderness, the two wrecked armies paused to catch their collective breath in air so full of smoke that it burned the throat.

During the momentary lull, scouts reported to Longstreet that they had found an unfinished railroad bed well off to the south in the undergrowth. The railroad cut was a concealed path toward the Federals' left flank. Perhaps with memories of Old Jack's flank march through the Wilderness at Chancellorsville somewhere in his mind, General Longstreet dispatched his aide, Lieutenant Colonel Moxley Sorrel, a twenty-six-year-old railroad clerk, to lead four brigades into the railroad bed. The actual attack would be commanded by General Billy Mahone (VMI, '47).

At eleven o'clock, Sorrel moved out with his four brigades gathered from four different divisions. As the brigades disappeared in the Wilderness, Old Pete aligned his weary regiments for another countercharge to push the bloodied Federals still further.

Lieutenant Colonel Sorrel hacked his way through the trees and bushes for forty-five minutes. At 11:45 a.m., Mahone plowed into the surprised left end of the Yankee line. The startled bluecoats fell back and their left flank collapsed. As Sorrel and General Mahone hammered the Federals from the south, Old Pete drove his divisions into them from the west. Longstreet's First Corps attacked eastward along the Plank Road, with Hill's Third Corps right behind them. The Federals fell back, leaving their dead and wounded to burn.

When the elated General Lee watched Old Pete vanish up the Plank Road, did he see in James Longstreet's back his ghostly last glimpse of Stonewall Jackson in this same Wilderness, one year and four days earlier? "Well, go on," the Old Man had said, and Robert Lee never looked into Old Jack's fiercely blue eyes again.

The Federals were driven until two in the afternoon.

As the air still crackled with waning musketry, Lieutenant General Longstreet rode along the brambles of the front line with General Kershaw, Lieutenant Colonel Sorrel, and young General Micah Jenkins. It was Jenkins who had been troubled two days earlier about his dream, which had only a blank after the first clash with Grant on the south side of the Rapidan River.

In the wildly dense brush, Old Pete rode near the Brock Road. Billy Mahone's gray Fourth South Carolina regiment could only hear horsemen coming. Taking no chances after their nine-hour firestorm, the boys from Carolina opened fire with a wall of lead.

A Confederate bullet struck James Longstreet in the throat, passed through, and slammed into his right shoulder. He dropped like a stone. Another bullet blew Micah Jenkins's brains out.

When the stretcher bearers carried the limp Longstreet out of the woods, a soldier had laid Longstreet's bloody hat over the general's face. His beloved First Corps blinked wet eyes at his body.

"He's dead," the teenagers in butternut-brown said softly.

When Old Pete in his sudden delirium heard the grieving among the trees, he weakly lifted his hat with his good left arm and waved it at his boys. As First Corps cheered, its wounded commander ordered General Field to take charge of the corps.

With General Longstreet carried wounded, perhaps dead, from the forward lines, the First Corps advance stalled. Finally, at 4:15 p.m., General Lee took active field command and ordered a continuation of the progress made by Old Pete, whose boys had saved Robert Lee's divided army from extinction.

Thirteen Confederate brigades pushed eastward along the Orange Plank Road toward the Brock Road intersection. The harried Federals of General Hancock's iron-willed II Corps refused to budge easily. The bluecoats fought furiously for nearly four hours. At 5:30 p.m., in lengthening shadows, General Lee held a war council surrounded by the clatter of muskets and the boom of cannon. He conferred with Second Corps commander Baldy Ewell, division commander Jubal Early, and brigade commander John Gordon. General Gordon urged another flank attack against the Federal right.

Gordon led his brigade into the twilight, struck the exposed Federals, and rounded up six hundred blue prisoners. By six o'clock, the Wilderness underbrush was again burning, and the flames rolled without mercy over wounded boys, blue and gray. Old men would remember all their days the screams of the burning wounded. At least two hundred men and boys burned alive. By seven o'clock, the first Yankee line collapsed in the gloom, but their second line of defenses held. In the gathering darkness, the Confederate offensive had to retire.

Darkness brought a slackening of the firefight which had raged in the dense trees and bushes for fourteen hours since General Hancock's dawn assault.

Generals Lee and Grant assessed the grim cost of their two-day contest. The Federals had lost 17,666 men, killed, wounded, or missing, during the most vigorous offensive ever executed by Federal soldiers. The boys in blue had fought harder than ever before. Old Pete had been proven correct: Things would be different with his Cousin Ulysses in charge.

Cousin Ulysses agreed. He would remember of his first two days of fighting Robert Lee in the Wilderness: "More desperate fighting has not been witnessed on this continent than that of the 5th and 6th of May."

Four

EAST OF THE BLOODIED FEDERALS, ROBERT LEE TOOK STOCK. GENERAL Longstreet was now gravely wounded, perhaps fatally, in the same terrible place and by the same accident which had killed Stonewall Jackson. Of Lee's other two corps commanders, Little Powell Hill was practically incapacitated by exhaustion and disease. In addition to the wounded Longstreet, the Army of Northern Virginia had lost 8,949 men, killed or wounded, plus another 1,881, captured or missing. Some 7,000 of the Rebel casualties were from Hill's decimated Third Corps. Over 25,000 Americans, blue and gray, had been destroyed or captured within thirty-eight hours of Grant and Meade engaging Robert Lee on the south side of the Rapidan River.

During Friday night, May 6, the Confederate survivors entrenched in the Wilderness thickets, and General Lee hoped that Grant would assault his dug-in breastworks on Saturday. The bluecoats would have been slaughtered under these works like they had been sixteen months earlier at Fredericksburg—and like the Confederates had been ten months ago at Gettysburg. One mile of dead and wounded bodies separated the two armies in the darkness. Only the cries of the wounded and the crackling flames consuming them broke the sudden forest calm.

Lieutenant General Grant was not foolish. He chose not to lay siege to Lee's fieldworks on Saturday. Any other Federal commander would have turned his back on the fabled Robert E. Lee to retreat north. That is what Fighting Joe Hooker and Ambrose Burnside would have done. General Lee labored during Friday night to read Grant's mind. Lee knew how his predecessors thought; he did not yet know Grant—at least, not as well as the bleeding James Longstreet, who had a hole where his throat used to be.

On Saturday, Lieutenant General Grant issued marching orders: The blue army would not retreat. They would back out of the Wilderness and then head south toward a crossroads called Spotsylvania Courthouse. The march would be an all-night, forced march beginning at 10:30 p.m. on Saturday night, in an effort to beat Lee south. The little hamlet would have been less than insignificant, but like Gettysburg, its communications hub made Spotsylvania important overnight. It sat between the Virginia Central Railroad, which approached from the east, and the Richmond-Fredericksburg-Potomac line, both of which converged at the town of Hanover Junction, further south on the road to Richmond.

While trying to guess Grant's plans during Saturday morning, May 7, General Lee appointed Richard Anderson to take Old Pete's place at the head of First Corps. Major General Anderson was graduate number 40 in the West Point Class of 1842; his classmate, James Longstreet, had been graduate number 54. Anderson commanded one of Little Powell's Third Corps divisions, but he had also led a division in Longstreet's corps, and the men knew him and respected him. General Billy Mahone, who had commanded Moxley Sorrel's flank assault on Friday, was ordered to take over General Anderson's division. Moxley Sorrel, Longstreet's chief of staff, agreed with Lee's selection of General Anderson during a private early-morning meeting with the Old Man. When Dick Anderson rode over to First Corps to assume command, the boys of his old First Corps brigade threw their tattered hats into the air and gave Anderson a silent ovation. They were too close to the Yankee lines to cheer out loud. Richard Anderson cried.

While General Lee spent Saturday morning choosing Longstreet's successor and laboring to pierce the veil of General Grant's mind, most of the front was quiet except for isolated picket fire among advance units of both armies. Skirmishing flared when the Federals sent out a reconnaissance-in-force to pinpoint the location of the battered gray line.

Even with the pockets of musketry, by first light it was clear that the Yankees were about to move again, either retiring toward Fredericksburg, or continuing south in their spring drive toward Richmond, and victory.

At five-thirty on Saturday morning, General Early's division of Ewell's Second Corps sent out pickets to make contact with the Federal position obscured by the thick Wilderness. The scouts found the Federal VI Corps fortifications empty. Preliminary reports also suggested that the Federals were pulling out of their Germanna Plank Road defenses on the path to the Rapidan. If the Yankees were indeed changing their base, the critical question was their route of march. General Lee told General John Gordon that Grant was probably aiming for Spotsylvania, twelve miles to the southeast. But the Federals might still be aiming for a Fredericksburg retreat.

An hour later, at six-thirty, Lieutenant General Grant was cutting his marching orders. The blue II Corps would march toward Todd's Tavern and V Corps would move toward Spotsylvania. The Federal VI and IX Corps would spread out along the front.

By one o'clock Saturday afternoon, the Federals had moved their mobile pontoon bridges southward to Ely's Ford across the Rapidan River, downriver from Germanna Ford, where the pontoons were dismantled. By three o'clock, the orders from General Grant were posted over the signature of Robert Lee's old West Point friend, Seth Williams, now assistant adjutant general of the Army of the Potomac. The march to Spotsylvania required, in Grant's prairie English, "punctuality and promptitude."

Perhaps to keep an eye on the new general-in-chief, President Lincoln's assistant secretary of war, Charles Dana, arrived at Grant's headquarters this Saturday. Dana, a Harvard dropout, would stay on Grant's heels for two months.

While planning for his unprecedented decision not to turn his back on a thrashing by General Lee, Grant had to move more than his army southward: He also had to move his thousands of dead and wounded from the field of battle. He prepared a wagon train of agony bound for Federal hospitals. General Grant's pain train would number 488 horse-drawn ambulances supported by another 325 supply wagons, winding their way to Washington. Another 960 Union wounded would be left behind, since they were too seriously injured to move. These shattered men would be tended in Federal field hospitals—or in Confederate amputation tents.

At seven in the evening, General Lee thought that Grant would press south to Spotsylvania, but he still was not certain. A Fredericksburg retreat along with the Federal ambulance train remained possible. So Lee took the precaution of ordering Richard Anderson's First Corps to march to Spotsylvania in case that was the Federal destination. Anderson was ordered to move out at three o'clock Sunday morning, in order to prevent Grant from getting his army between Lee and Richmond.

The Federals began shifting toward the southeast out of the Wilderness at twilight, Saturday evening. Generals Grant and Meade left the Wilderness by the Brock Road at 8:30 p.m. Half an hour later, the blue V Corps left their works to march toward Spotsylvania. At 9:30 p.m., Uncle John Sedgwick's VI Corps pulled out of the Wilderness to head south. Regiment by regiment, the weary Yankees carefully studied the dirt roads for the first byway which would take them north or east, and far away from the Army of Northern Virginia. That is the direction they had marched under the commands of Federal Generals McClellan, Pope, Burnside, and Hooker. They did not have to retreat out of Pennsylvania after Gettysburg, since they were already home.

The boys in blue marched through the darkness in stunned silence as they realized that they were not retreating. The Federals cheered as they bypassed the last road northward. Never again would the Federals under Grant's command break contact with Robert E. Lee. Long ago, Old Army regulars had poked fun at the disheveled, cigar-chewing Ulysses Grant by calling him "Useless" S. Grant. As the Army of the Potomac tramped south for the first time ever after doing battle with Robert Lee, the boys in blue knew that this Grant was different from their former commanders.

As the Federals marched in the blackness an hour before midnight, they heard through the Wilderness jungle an eerie sound which made their skin crawl. It was as if the blood-encrusted thickets, where so many dead men lay, were suddenly alive with banshees.

Dick Anderson's Confederate First Corps was preparing to move out from the Rebel right flank to race General Grant to Spotsylvania. Suddenly, the terrifying "Rebel Yell" rose from the former divisions of Old Pete Longstreet. Like a wave, the high-pitched and piercing wail erupted in First

Corps, one regiment at a time. The yell out there in the darkness spread all the way up the Confederate line, from First Corps through Third Corps, all the way up to Baldy Ewell's Second Corps on the north end of the Confederate line. The Rebel Yell traveled up the line for two full miles. Then the Yell was repeated twice more. The marching Federals shivered at the sound.

So, like two old bulls who had already gored each other nearly senseless, the two bloodied armies marched sullenly throughout Saturday night. What awaited them in five days would be the most vicious and the most ferocious hand-to-hand battle of the entire war. More boys in blue and gray had fallen at Antietam and Gettysburg, to be sure, but at least they had exterminated each other almost like gentlemen, in neat and bloody formations, just like they were taught at West Point or at VMI. Spotsylvania would be different. It would be a dogfight—a barroom brawl among 150,000 armed men.

The impoverished, backwoods countryside around Spotsylvania Courthouse was so marshy and poor that the illiterate and toothless locals called their isolated country "the poison fields."

The survivors in gray and blue would remember it that way.

During the first hour of Sunday, May 8, Generals Grant and Meade arrived at Todd's Tavern on the road to Spotsylvania Courthouse. By four in the morning, the gray First Corps dragged itself to Block House Bridge over the Po River, three miles northwest of the courthouse, on Shady Grove Church Road. They had eaten trail dust for five hours during their all-night trek.

By dawn this Sabbath morning, Robert Lee finally made up his mind that the blue divisions were bound for Spotsylvania instead of the more-likely retreat toward Fredericksburg, where their wounded had been sent. Not until sunrise did Confederate scouts confirm that all Federal positions along the Orange Plank Road had been abandoned during the night, with their boot prints pointing toward Todd's Tavern.

General Lee ordered Baldy Ewell's Second Corps to advance along Dick Anderson's trail toward Shady Grove Church. General Ewell was to march down the dirt road, which ran parallel to the Brock Road taken by the Federals. Only three to five miles would separate the two armies, heading southward together.

Toward daybreak, the two mighty armies made serious contact for the third day in a row—the first three continuous days of killing since Gettysburg.

By seven o'clock Sunday morning, Fitz Lee's cavalry division was hotly engaged with Federal horsemen three miles from Spotsylvania. Robert Lee's burly nephew had accompanied Jeb Stuart, whose cavalry corps had screened Anderson's march with his First Corps. Fitz Lee's troopers held off two blue brigades of cavalry along the Brock Road. Horse-drawn light artillery soon pounded both sides as the fighting spilled over onto the sleepy Alsop farmstead.

As the firefight escalated at eight o'clock, Fitz Lee sent word to Dick Anderson that his gray infantry was desperately needed to prevent the cavalry from being overrun. The little skirmish at dawn was quickly becoming a death struggle to capture a strategic hilltop, known locally as Laurel Hill, which overlooked the Brock Road and the Federal route toward Spotsylvania. General Anderson fed two brigades of his footsore infantry from Joe Kershaw's division into the fight at 8:30 a.m.

Fitz Lee and the foot soldiers held back four Yankee divisions from V Corps. The little battle raged only one mile north of Anderson's First Corps. At mid-morning, the blue V Corps plowed five hundred yards toward Fitz Lee's position, while the brass band of the 140th New York Infantry piped the bluecoats into the iron whirlwind. The New Yorkers' Colonel George Ryan was already bleeding to death. When Brigadier General John Robinson of the blue Second Division, V Corps, attacked with six regiments, corps commander Major General Gouverneur Warren shouted, "Never mind cannon! Never mind bullets! Press on and clear this road!" General Robinson lost his leg never-minding the bullets and the cannon.

By 12:30 p.m., the bloodied Federals were backing away from Laurel Hill, where Fitz Lee's boys and the infantry were digging in to secure the commanding hillside. General Robinson's heroic blue division was so badly mauled that it was stricken from the Federal muster rolls within twenty-four hours of its charge against Laurel Hill. The battle continued until dark.

While Fitz Lee's division of Jeb Stuart's cavalry fought all day, General Phil Sheridan begged for and received General Grant's permission to mount an all-out assault to destroy Jeb Stuart. Sheridan would deploy his entire cavalry corps of ten thousand mounted bluecoats in a column thirteen miles long.

Up the long gray line, Richard Ewell's Second Corps was finally marching out of the Wilderness by eight o'clock on Sunday morning. The lead regiments stumbled toward Shady Grove Church by one o'clock, after a choking march in thick dust. Men dropped to the ground in exhaustion seven miles west of Spotsylvania Courthouse. Baldy Ewell prodded his men back to the road for the march toward Laurel Hill.

As Ewell's Second Corps trudged down the road to Spotsylvania, Robert Lee again faced the slow evaporation of his once-invincible command. At eight o'clock Sunday morning, exactly one day after replacing James Longstreet, General Lee had to replace Lieutenant General A. P. Hill. Little Powell was spent. Hill was too sick to mount Champ. Before leaving the Wilderness, Lee had to relieve Hill of command. Division commander Jubal Early was elevated to command of Third Corps, and the hard-fighting John Gordon, wounded five times at Sharpsburg, was given command of Early's division.

But Little Powell was not about to abandon his men so easily. He had not saved the Army of Northern Virginia on the banks of Antietam Creek only to be carted off the field. So as Third Corps started down Orange Plank Road for Spotsylvania, Little Powell insisted upon riding along with it, to be close to his beloved corps. General Hill rode flat on his back in an ambulance toward the courthouse. His barefoot boys would know that he was with them.

Although beaten back once, the Federal assault upon Laurel Hill did not stop until dark. Fighting raged from noon on May 8 until three in the morning on May 9.

At noon on Sunday, Dick Anderson's gray First Corps arrived at Spotsylvania, led by Jeb Stuart's cavalry. Though Grant left the Wilderness first, the Army of Northern Virginia had beaten him to stand between the blue divisions and precious Richmond down the road.

An hour later, Federal V Corps commander, General Gouverneur Warren, asked Major General Meade for help. "Old Snapping Turtle" Meade sent Uncle John Sedgwick's VI Corps into the battle swirling around Laurel Hill. At 1:45 p.m., both Generals Grant and Meade moved their field headquarters to a position one mile north of the Alsop farm battlefield, where Fitz Lee had begun the battle for Laurel Hill. By 2:30 p.m., Robert Lee was finally at the Spotsylvania front as both armies fed new troops into the meat grinder.

Bluecoats from VI Corps deployed all afternoon, aligning by 4:30 p.m. for a final assault. The Federal push rumbled forward at six o'clock in the failing daylight. The massed, blue V and VI Corps attacked along the Brock Road, one and a half miles northwest of Spotsylvania Courthouse. They advanced down both sides of the road about half a mile south of the bloodied Alsop farm. General Lee's weary First Corps deployed west of the road, and Second Corps aligned east, one-quarter mile south of the Federals.

Three Yankee divisions slammed into the Confederates. Vicious charge and countercharge continued for nine bloody hours. Darkness was lighted by musketry and rows of red-hot cannon. The shelling continued until three in the morning.

When the bloodshed stopped for the fourth day of Grant's spring offensive, the Rebels still held Laurel Hill, and the two opposing armies dropped on their rifles to sleep only three-quarters of a mile from their blood enemies.

After dark, Edward "Allegheny" Johnson's gray division of Second Corps filed onto the field at the courthouse.

The lost race against Marse Robert to Spotsylvania was costly to Generals Grant and Meade. From six in the evening on Sunday until three in the morning on Monday, May 9, the Federals lost 1,740 men, and John Robinson's Second Division of the blue V Corps simply ceased to exist at Yankee roll call. The Federal V Corps of General Warren took 1,400 of the Union losses.

At three in the morning, General Lee drew upon the experience of his old days as an army engineer to supervise in the dark the construction of massive fieldworks. His line was now deeply curved, with the bow jutting due north toward the Federals. The bulge marked the center of the Confederates' whole line, which spanned a three-mile front.

The hump, or "salient," in the middle of the gray line was "anchored" on the left flank in the west on the Po River. The right end in the east was fixed just south of the little town of Spotsylvania Courthouse. The gray First Corps held the left and Baldy Ewell's Second Corps manned the center salient. Third Corps, now under Old Jube Early's command, would anchor the right flank toward town once it was brought up later in the day.

The salient bulge was held primarily by Allegheny Johnson's division of the Rebel Second Corps. Their perimeter inside the bulge was half a mile wide and one mile deep. Most of the interior of the salient was dense woods. The infantrymen looked around at first light, saw their upside-down, "U"-shaped line (with the point aimed northward at the Yankees), and did what they did second-best: They gave it a name. The men called the salient "the Mule Shoe." Along with The Sunken Road at Fredericksburg, Bloody Lane at Antietam, and Gettysburg's Bloody Run and The Slaughter Pen, the Second Corps' "Mule Shoe" name would stick forever in the annals of organized massacre.

Five

With dawn on Monday, May 9, General Lee ordered Old Jube's Third Corps to march from Shady Grove Church toward Spotsylvania. They were on the road by six in the morning and arrived east of town on the far right of the line by noon. Confederate artillery was also placed behind the Mule Shoe salient.

Opposite the Mule Shoe, the first light of day found the Federal II Corps of General Hancock filing into the long, blue line to support the V and VI Corps already in position. General Burnside's detached and independent command of IX Corps was on the march to join them. General Grant envisioned bottling up Lee's army well south of the Rapidan River so that Federal General Ben Butler could take 25,000 men up the James River to Richmond without Lee breaking out of Spotsylvania to stop him. Phil Sheridan's blue cavalry also sported three mounted divisions.

As Lieutenant General Grant laid out his plans to take Richmond and align his legions to assault General Lee in the miserable "poison fields" of the little courthouse, the Federal general-in-chief had personal problems of his own: his three-star bottom. This Monday morning, Ulysses Grant had to ride a ragged little pony along his new lines, rather than his warhorse, Cincinnati. General Grant suffered from saddle sores after four days on horseback. Since Cincinnati had a hard trot where the saddle met his blisters, Grant trotted along on a small pony liberated as war booty from a Confederate plantation down in Mississippi. The estate was owned by Jefferson Davis.

Throughout May 9, General Lee's 50,000 infantry and General Grant's 90,000 men spent most of the day digging in and piling dirt upon breastworks of fallen timber. Only each side's snipers and sharpshooters popped off across the lines through the tree stands, with the exception of a skirmish on the Confederate left flank.

In the early morning, General Grant talked war with his VI Corps commander, Major General John Sedgwick—"Uncle John" to his men, who truly loved him. Sedgwick was an old friend of Robert Lee, going back twenty-two years to Lee's work in the Old Army's Corps of Engineers at the New York City harbor. Never afraid to go where he sent his boys—Sedgwick was wounded three times at Antietam Creek—Uncle John (West Point, '37) went up the line to supervise the VI Corps entrenchments near the bloodstained Alsop farm.

Toward nine that morning, General Sedgwick personally directed cannon placements along Brock Road, half a mile south of the farm. When his staff was sent scurrying for cover by the random sniper shots, Uncle John laughed, saying, "They couldn't hit an elephant at that distance!" He repeated the remark twice. Before he could laugh out loud the second time, the old soldier from Cornwall Hollow, Connecticut, had his brains blown out. General Grant was grief-stricken by Uncle John's death, and likened his loss to losing a whole division. By ten o'clock, Grant named Brigadier General Horatio Wright (West Point, '41) to replace Sedgwick.

Only three months earlier, General Lee had written to Mother Lee about "our old friend, Sedgwick," now commanding a Federal corps. After Gettysburg, Lee had mourned for another friend from the Old Army, General John Reynolds, who had also died in Union blue while fighting Robert Lee.

Except for the sporadic sniper fire which had killed Uncle John, the lines went quietly about their digging except on the far left of the Rebel line. There, this May 9, General Anderson's First Corps fought a running skirmish with Federals all day. Blue advance units also attempted to outflank the Confederates by getting behind General Lee's new entrenchments. The Federal force slipped toward the south side of the Po River toward the Southerners' supply wagons parked on the dirt road to Louisa Courthouse. General Lee countered by sending General Early orders to release one division from Third Corps on the right flank to bolster Anderson on the left of the line, and to detail General Heth's division to the south side of the creek toward Shady Grove to guard the wagons. Henry Heth moved out the next morning.

While hungry men felled trees and threw dirt to build General Lee's next stand on the long road to Richmond, the red-eyed god of war set his insatiable evil eye upon Jeb Stuart, the dashing and laughing hero of every female Southern heart. Phil Sheridan led 15,000 blue cavalrymen out of Fredericksburg at daybreak on May 9. Jeb led his paltry corps of 4,500 troopers to intercept Sheridan's thirteen-mile-long column of horsemen.

The two mounted cavalries skirmished at four p.m. on the afternoon of May 9 at Mitchell's Shop on the road to Beaver Dam, Virginia. Jeb had a special interest in Beaver Dam: Jeb's wife, Flora, and their children were there. Major General Stuart rode hard toward the North Anna River and Davenport's Bridge, only five miles north of the dam. Jeb's cavalry rode hard all night. But Yankee cavalry under the command of vain and brash George Armstrong Custer beat him to the dam, where Custer spent this Monday night burning one million bacon rations and half a million bread rations for Lee's famished army. General Custer also ripped up ten miles of the vital Virginia Central Railroad and destroyed one hundred railroad cars and two engines.

Major General Stuart and his horsemen pounded into Beaver Dam at breakfast time, May 10. General Custer's bluecoats had pulled out only moments before. The Federals had thoroughly sacked the Confederate supplies stashed there.

About eight o'clock on Tuesday morning, Jeb paid a visit to Flora, at the dam. After a few private moments in the early Virginia daylight, Jeb kissed his wife good-bye before he continued his pursuit of General Sheridan and the Yankee cavalry.

Trotting away from the burning Rebel supplies and from his wife, Jeb remarked softly to an aide that he did not expect to survive the war.

With Fitzhugh Lee at his side, Stuart's not quite five thousand troopers in two brigades rode southeast toward Hanover Junction. They wanted to get on the eastern flank of the Federal cavalry to beat them to Richmond. Another brigade of Stuart's cavalry rode due south to torment Sheridan's rear guard. Jeb would arrive near Hanover after dark.

In the morning as Jeb Stuart rode toward Hanover Junction, the two great armies dug in at Spotsylvania and drew a bead on each other through the trees and earthworks. To liven up the Rebel line, the Federals brought up two new mortars to the Alsop farm area where General Sedgwick had been killed. The mortars lobbed twenty-four-pound shells high into the springtime air to crash into the Confederate trenches, which were dug behind the Mule Shoe earthworks. Spotsylvania marked the first use of such siege weapons in the open field.

At ten on Tuesday morning, Major General Meade ordered a full Federal attack to take place by five o'clock that evening. The blue V Corps of General Warren would smash into Dick Anderson's gray First Corps at Laurel Hill, on General Lee's left flank. The Federal VI Corps—formerly Uncle John Sedgwick's boys—would also strike Baldy Ewell in the Mule Shoe salient. And General Burnside's independent IX Corps would remain in reserve, ready to plunge into any break in the Rebel lines on Lee's right, eastern flank. This would prevent General Lee from moving reinforcements from the east to the west to shore up Dick Anderson.

As Jeb's cavalry rode hard after Phil Sheridan and George Meade jockeyed his troops to prepare for their evening offensive, three blue divisions from Hancock's II Corps shifted positions along Shady Grove Road. The Federals moved south and west of the Po River in an effort to get behind the gray entrenchments. General Early, standing in for Powell Hill in Third Corps, dispatched the divisions of Billy Mahone and Henry Heth to the Rebel left to stop the Federal movement. Billy Mahone's Confederate brigades took up position at the Block House Bridge on the Po to extend General Lee's left along Shady Grove Church Road, one and a half miles west of Spotsylvania.

At four in the afternoon of May 10, General Warren of the blue V Corps requested and received Major General Meade's permission to attack the graybacks an hour earlier than originally planned. Warren sent in V Corps against the Confederate position at Laurel Hill, but he kept one full division out of the action in reserve. The result was an undermanned and ill-planned offensive. New York City lawyer and Yale alumnus, Brigadier General James Rice, thirty-four, of Second Brigade, Fourth Division, V Corps, was mortally wounded, to die later on May 10.

When Warren's two divisions were finally repulsed with heavy casualties, General Meade ordered Winfield Hancock to withhold his II Corps reinforcements rather than risk further destruction to the blue army.

The early Yankee attack was driven back by Confederate cannon firing the miserable canister rounds. Sheets of flame and iron marbles tore the Federals to pieces. A second blue charge at five p.m. was also driven back after vicious hand-to-hand fighting.

The main Union drive came after two hours of fighting in the "poison fields." Colonel Emory Upton of First Division, VI Corps, now commanded by Horatio Wright (West Point, '41), led the five o'clock assault. Colonel Upton set his sights on the western side of the sturdy Mule Shoe salient.

Twenty-four-year-old Emory Upton (Oberlin College, Ohio, and West Point, '61) had an idea: He felt that his bluecoats were too often slaughtered during charges when they paused to reload their heavy single-shot rifles. If the men rushed the Rebels but did not carry loaded rifles, there would be no temptation to stop for feeding and capping their muskets in the complicated "Load in Nine Times" drill.

The nine steps between an empty rifle and shooting at the enemy were: (1) Take out a paper cartridge with its 120 grains of powder behind one, thimble-size .58 caliber bullet; (2) rip open the paper cartridge with the teeth—hence, the blackened lips on all the swollen corpses; (3) pour the black powder down the long rifle barrel; (4) drop the lead Minié ball and its glued-on paper cartridge into the barrel (undersized for the rifle barrel's "lands and grooves" so it could be forced down a powder-fouled barrel); (5) drive the bullet down with the rifle's iron ramrod, with the torn paper serving as a "patch" to seal the bullet atop the black-powder charge; (6) reseat the ramrod into its sockets, called thimbles, along the barrel; (7) with the thumb, "ear back" the hammer above the iron "nipple" at the breech; (8) press a tiny percussion cap onto the hollow nipple; and, (9) fire!

So, Upton decided to send four waves of infantry against the Confederate entrenchments. Only the first wave would have loaded rifles. The next three waves would have rifles primed with powder and ball, but the ignition percussion caps would not be inserted onto the hammer's iron nipple until the men were on top of the Rebels.

By the time everything was ready, the clock had ticked past the appointed five o'clock attack. A Federal cannonade before the assault did not begin until nine minutes before six. At 6:10 p.m., Colonel Upton's Second Brigade of First Division went forward. Twelve blue regiments from New York, Pennsylvania, Wisconsin, Maine, and Vermont marched calmly toward the northwest corner of the Mule Shoe. Four neat blue lines marched into the breech with ten feet between each wave. Upton's brave boys were to be supported by General Gershom Mott's seventeen regiments. Upton had to cross 250 yards to get to the Confederates, while General Mott had to cross a mile.

Colonel Upton's dangerous plan worked. Without having to pause to reload, his first wave struck the Georgia troops of Brigadier General George Doles, thirty-three, in Baldy Ewell's Second Corps. Yankees broke the Rebel line and poured into the salient with bayonets and hand-to-hand fighting. Upton's bloodied men drove eighty yards through the collapsing Confederate line. The Rebel line was so confused in the hail-storm of lead and cannon that Confederates accidentally fired into their own retreating regiments.

When General Mott's men went in to support Colonel Upton, he only advanced to within one-third of a mile of the Mule Shoe, at the northern point of the salient. He had aimed for a point one quarter-mile east of Colonel Upton's assault. Mott's regiments were finally driven back by Confederate cannon.

Including General Warren's assault earlier by the Federal V Corps, the Yankees punched at Robert Lee's line three times. Their third assault came in the failing daylight, at seven p.m. The Yankee II and V Corps suffered five thousand casualties within three hours. But they took many Confederates with them out of action, some forever.

In the Mule Shoe melee, the rocklike Stonewall Brigade collapsed under the weight of Colonel Upton's blue waves. When the brigade broke, General Lee tried to rally his failing defenders. The Old Man's staff had to restrain General Lee from riding into the fight, just as he had to be held back in the Wilderness when the sweating Texans had cried, "General Lee to the rear!" John Gordon led Lee's countercharge of three brigades against Upton's success.

In darkness, Colonel Upton finally had to fall back, but only after his heroic men had endured enemy cannon spewing triple loads of canister fired into their faces from only thirty yards away. The 86th New York regiment was blown away by the molten lead wind. The New Yorkers lost 115 of 200 men. Colonel Upton left 1,000 men bleeding or dead in the Spotsylvania poison fields. The retreating Federals took 950 Rebel prisoners back with them.

The dreadful slaughter ended toward eight p.m. As in the Wilderness, the dry ground under the riddled trees caught fire and burned the wounded alive. Cartridge boxes on the belts of the wounded exploded in the darkness. Confederate cartridge boxes were usually appropriated from dead Yankees. Each could carry forty paper cartridges of black powder and Minié ball bullet.

Robert Lee's Mule Shoe had held, and his boys still clung desperately to Laurel Hill. Emory Upton may have had to pull back, but he had accomplished the unimaginable: He had broken and penetrated the line drawn in the bloody soil by Robert Lee. Ulysses S. Grant promoted Upton to brigadier general on the spot.

Under the sulfur clouds which obscured the dark sky, a Confederate band struck up "Nearer My God to Thee" in dirge tempo as Rebel burial parties groped for their dead and wounded. When the gray-clad band blew "Home, Sweet Home," both armies cheered. Both sides had cheered that music at Fredericksburg and along the Rappahannock a lifetime ago.

While the wounded burned and the burial details dragged their human wreckage and the band played in the darkness, down the road, Jeb Stuart's cavalry pursued Phil Sheridan.

During the evening of Tuesday, May 10, Jeb Stuart and Fitz Lee rode into Hanover Junction, the vital railroad hub. Scouts confirmed that Sheridan's blue cavalry was only twenty miles north of Richmond. Resolved to stand between Sheridan and the Confederate capital, General Stuart and his weary horsemen pressed on into the night. Past nine o'clock, they rode down the road two and a half miles to Taylorsville, where they dismounted long enough for a quick catnap. The men slept fitfully on the ground as they held their reins in their sleeping hands, hardly eighteen miles from Richmond.

After a four-hour rest, Jeb was back in the saddle by one a.m. on Wednesday morning. The cavalry column snaked down the Telegraph Road in darkness. They arrived with daybreak at Ashland, five miles south of Taylorsville. By seven a.m., they heard gunfire to the southwest along the South Anna River. Within an hour, Jeb Stuart arrived at a dirt cross-roads called Yellow Tavern, Virginia. They had beaten Sheridan by their all-night ride. Stuart deployed along Telegraph Road, just south of where it joined Mountain Road, which came in from the northwest.

The Confederate cavalry waited for Phil Sheridan to ride down Mountain Road. The tavern was an abandoned inn barely six desperate miles north of Richmond. If Jeb could not hold the larger force of Yankee cavalry at the intersection, the capital would hear the sound of Federal horses before dinner.

While Jeb Stuart waited at Yellow Tavern for the Federal cavalry, Lieutenant General Ulysses Grant chatted with Elihu Washburne this Wednesday morning, May 11. Congressman Washburne was a Mainer by birth, but had resettled in Illinois, where he had nominated an ex-soldier for an Illinois appointment to the rank of brigadier general. That soldier was Grant, who leaned heavily upon Washburne's Washington savvy. Congressman Washburne's big brother, Israel Washburn, was one year retired from two terms as governor of Maine, and his little brother, Cadwallader Washburn, was a Federal major general. (Representative Washburne added the "e" to the family name; his brothers did not.)

Congressman Washburne asked General Grant for a note to take back to Washington City for delivery to President Lincoln. Addressed to Major General Henry Halleck, "Chief of Staff" of the US Army, on May 11 Grant penned what would become his most famous assessment of the spring 1864 campaign: "I . . . propose to fight it out on this line if it takes all summer."

Six

AFTER HIS BREAKFAST VISIT FROM HIS POLITICAL MENTOR, GENERAL Grant's troops at Spotsylvania were issued two days' rations: the certain signal to veterans who had "seen the elephant" that fresh blood would flow soon. All available Federal wagons were also hitched up and sent to Belle Plain landing on the James River for more supplies. The landing was a principal Union supply depot seven miles east of Fredericksburg, on a tributary of the Potomac River.

At Yellow Tavern, Jeb Stuart's force of 4,500 troopers awaited Sheridan's 10,000 men in a mounted column thirteen miles long. Waiting at the Telegraph Road and Mountain Road intersection, the ground was familiar to Stuart: He had ridden the Mountain Road hard during his daring, June '62 "Ride Around McClellan." The sweet taste of that day still lingered.

June 10, 1862, General Lee had been in command of the Army of Northern Virginia for exactly nine days. Lee informed Stuart of his desire to attack the Yankees north of the Chickahominy River in eastern Virginia, and he stressed the need to locate Major General George McClellan. Stuart chose for his scouting mission the cavalry brigades of Rooney Lee, Fitzhugh Lee, and John Mosby—1,200 troopers in all. They departed two days later.

Jeb Stuart and his exhausted horse returned to Richmond at dawn on June 15 to report to Lee the location of McClellan's horde of bluecoats. In addition to riding the full, hundred-mile course around the Federal divisions while Yankees nipped at his heels, Stuart had also whipped a unit of Yankee cavalry on June 13. The Federal cavalry was commanded by Jeb's own father-in-law, Union General Philip Cooke.

By morning on June 14, the exhausted Rebels reached the Chicka-hominy River at Forge Bridge near Sycamore Spring. The river was high from spring rains. Rooney Lee nearly drowned when he swam out to test the current before construction of a pontoon bridge. After the adventure, a fellow Southerner asked Jeb what he would have done had the Federals attacked the Rebels when their backs were at the river. Would Jeb have surrendered? the trooper inquired. There was an alternative to surrender, Stuart smiled: "To die game."

The mounted Federals arrived toward noon. Phil Sheridan's men carefully deployed for three hours in mid-morning, Wednesday, May 11, 1864. Bagging the famous Jeb with his more-famous, plumed hat would take a great deal of care. George Armstrong Custer led the blue-clad charge. Custer had crossed swords with Jeb on the third day at Gettys-burg. The youngest general in the Union Army, twenty-four-year-old General Custer, attacked thirty-one-year-old Major General Stuart. The Federals dismounted and plunged into the outnumbered Rebels. Jeb worked to calm his men during the second Federal charge.

"Steady, men. Give it to them!" Stuart called above the rattle of carbines and pistols. Near the Telegraph Road, Private John Huff of the 5th Michigan Cavalry on the ground aimed his revolver at the red-bearded Confederate with the plume in his slouch hat. Huff had already been discharged from Federal service as disabled from a war wound. But he had reenlisted. Private Huff's hammer fell on his .44 caliber Remington, New Army revolver and the cap detonated twenty-five grains of black powder. A lead round ball spun through the spring air toward Jeb Stuart. The bullet slammed into Jeb's right side and he slumped in the saddle. With the air full of lead and curses from fif-teen thousand men, General Stuart turned command over to his close friend, General Fitz Lee.

While the cavalry skirmish continued into late afternoon, Jeb was carried to a wagon for a six-hour ride down the road to Richmond, and the home of his physician brother-in-law, Dr. Charles Brewer, at 206 East Grace Street.

The forty-two-year-old Private Huff had done what whole Yankee divisions had not been able to do. John Huff savored his incredible good fortune back at Yankee camp for seventeen days. As Jeb Stuart was carried from the field, at four o'clock Wednesday afternoon, General Grant at Spotsylvania issued orders for another frontal assault against the Mule Shoe salient with four entire corps at dawn on May 12. The exhausted and lice-infested soldiers of the blue II, V, VI, and IX Corps were ordered to brace for a general advance in twelve hours, at four a.m. on Thursday. Blue-clad divisions of footsore men would deploy all night. And while the Yankees shifted their positions, Robert Lee ordered his graybacks to furiously dig new fieldworks behind the Mule Shoe for a second line of defense at the long base of the salient's southern, open end.

Throughout the afternoon and early evening of May 11 in the poison fields, where the dead still rotted from Tuesday's battle, Lieutenant General A. P. Hill's ambulance stayed close to Little Powell's Confederate boys of Third Corps.

In evening twilight, General Lee held a war council. Among the officers present were division commander Henry Heth and the incapacitated Powell Hill. Lee still doubted that Grant would plow into his lines again. That was simply not the Yankee way. But something about this new man, Grant, ate at Robert Lee, and the work continued on the new defensive line at the base of the salient—just in case. Although confident that Grant would soon retreat back toward his base at Fredericksburg, as every Union commander before him had done, General Lee had to admit to General Heth: "I think General Grant has managed his affairs remarkably well up to the present time."

In the gathering darkness, General Lee was uncomfortable behind breastworks all around him. To the old mountain fighter of the glory days in Mexico, something about digging-in gnawed at him. He ever longed for the open field where his confidence in the maneuvering skill of his Army of Northern Virginia was unshakable. When he could thrust and parry, he could either prevail as he had done at Chancellorsville, or he could at least survive, as he had done beside Antietam Creek, where gray divisions from his battered left rushed to shore up the failing right.

But laying low against superior Federal numbers could be disaster, and Lee knew it. "This army cannot stand a siege," he gravely warned Powell Hill and Henry Heth. "We must end this business on the battlefield, not in a fortified position." The unspoken "position" in the back of General Lee's weary mind was Richmond.

By nightfall, a steady rain began to drench the war-wary men in the salient trenches. General Lee and Baldy Ewell still believed—or hoped—that Grant would use the darkness and the rain to cover an all-night withdrawal to Fredericksburg. To make ready to pursue the Federal retreat for the desired fight in open country, Lee put Henry Heth's division on alert at the courthouse to pitch into the retreating Federals when Grant evacuated Spotsylvania. The Federals had always retreated after a beating by the Army of Northern Virginia. To speed the likely pursuit and attack, Lee ordered Confederate cannon to be pulled out of the muddy Mule Shoe salient during the night.

No one from Confederate headquarters thought to inform Major General Allegheny Johnson, who held the Mule Shoe, that his artillery support was pulling out to chase the certain retreat of Grant and Meade. General Johnson did not know that his heavy guns were leaving the salient until he heard the caisson wheels creaking in the rainy darkness.

Throughout Wednesday night, the wet air was full of that certain unspeakable something that the veterans could smell. Allegheny Johnson sniffed it. In the darkness, the Army of the Potomac was certainly rustling and clanking. The bluecoats were not sleeping in the rain. After midnight, General Johnson sent a written protest to Baldy Ewell about the removal of his salient cannon. The message arrived at Richard Ewell's tent at three in the morning. Perhaps the one-legged general also took a whiff of the chilly night air. He sent the cannon back into the Mule Shoe to arrive at first light. When the artillery rumbled back into the salient held by Johnson's division, it was almost too late for Second Corps and for the Army of Northern Virginia.

During the last seven days, Grant had lost twenty thousand men and eleven generals to his "On to Richmond" spring offensive. Grant simply had to retreat during the night of May 11. Every previous Union commanding general had retreated from Robert Lee. An hour before midnight, Yankee brass bands began blaring in the darkness—surely to drown out the sound of an evacuation.

When the Federal bands began at eleven o'clock Wednesday night, the wounded Jeb Stuart was arriving in Richmond at Dr. Brewer's home. The physician's wife, Maria, was there, but her sister, Flora Stuart, was still at Beaver Dam. As Jeb was carried, gut-shot, into the home on the north side of Grace Street, between Jefferson and Madison Streets, the springtime air was unusually heavy with the overwhelming scent of yellow roses in the Brewer garden. The Brewers and Flora would remember the moist smell forever.

Private Huff's pistol ball had slammed through Jeb's side with excruciating pain. On his bed in the Brewer house, the thirty-one-year-old major general leaked blood and bile onto the sheets. The 180-grain, .44 caliber ball had torn through his bowels, which permitted fecal contamination to ooze into Jeb's belly. Rapid infection caused his intense pain. Shock from blood loss through a probably nicked stomach and right kidney weakened the colorful cavalier.

The midnight darkness at Spotsylvania was broken by a dismal rain and the clatter from the Federal camp north of the Mule Shoe salient. Between midnight and three o'clock Thursday morning, the blue II Corps fell in for its dawn assault. The Yankees mustered so close to Allegheny Johnson's line behind their log breastworks that Federals could see the Confederate camp fires. The boys in blue thought that the fires must be the nearby Federal VI Corps, also forming up. Nineteen thousand bluecoats shuffled through the mud and blood.

At three-thirty in the morning, General Armistead L. Long (West Point, '50), the gray Second Corps artillery chief, finally received Baldy Ewell's hasty orders to return the cannon to Allegheny Johnson's Mule Shoe salient. When the guns creaked back into battery at four o'clock, the Federal assault was thirty-five minutes away.

As the Rebel artillery was unhitched from the horse-drawn caissons, the Confederates within the Mule Shoe huddled in their muddy trenches where they could feel the electricity in the wet night. They dozed and prayed behind their three-mile front of earthworks six feet high on the far side of their trenches. Their network of crisscrossing traverses and trenches inside the Mule Shoe salient were the strongest breastworks ever built in the history of European and North American warfare.

Somewhere in the darkness as the cannon rumbled into position and the Yankees loaded nineteen thousand rifles, Little Powell Hill tossed, anxiously bedridden, in his ambulance parked close to his Rebel Third Corps.

Thirty-five minutes after four, Thursday morning, May 12, General Winfield Hancock sent his blue II Corps toward the Mule Shoe at first light. It had been Hancock who had held Cemetery Ridge at Gettysburg until General Meade could rally the shattered Federal army from the brink of extermination.

The grand charge by Old Jack at Chancellorsville had begun with a stampede of wildlife driven from the Wilderness forest by Stonewall's gray Second Corps. Now, one year and ten days later, the blurry-eyed troops inside the Mule Shoe squinted into the dawn as birds, fox, and deer suddenly burst from the trees toward the Confederate salient.

The 26th Michigan Infantry braved a hail of Confederate fire and reached the Rebel earthen fortress first. Brigadier General Francis Barlow's blue division slammed into Allegheny Johnson so hard that the hungry gray line quickly collapsed under the weight of overwhelming Federal numbers. The twenty-nine-year-old Union general had graduated first in his class from Harvard Law School. It had been Yankee Barlow who was left for dead on the Gettysburg battlefield before he was carried to safety by Confederate John B. Gordon. Allegheny Johnson was crushed by ferocious hand-to-hand fighting. He beat the Yankees over the head with the cane he carried since being wounded under the command of Stonewall Jackson. But it was no use.

Old Blue Light's first command, the Stonewall Brigade, was washed away by the blue tide in the morning twilight. The dead Lieutenant General Jackson was also called "Old Blue Light" by the Second Corps boys, who loved him because of his haunting blue eyes which seemed to glow when the acrid smoke of black powder was in the wind. The Federals penetrated three-quarters of a mile into the Mule Shoe.

For half an hour, the brawl at the northern point of the Mule Shoe raged. But by five o'clock, the Stonewall Brigade at the heart of Allegheny Johnson's division gave way. They were overrun along with as many as twenty of the Confederate cannon which General Johnson had begged to be returned two hours earlier. Confederate Generals Johnson and George Steuart were captured, along with the Stonewall Brigade's exhausted and dazed survivors. Johnson was escorted to the headquarters tent of Winfield Hancock, who warmly greeted Johnson and offered him his first breakfast as a prisoner of war. The breakfast was managed by Seth Williams, Robert Lee's old assistant at West Point. As two thousand men from the Stonewall Brigade were marched off to become prisoners by 5:30 a.m., the fabled brigade ceased to exist on Confederate muster rolls.

When the sullen Stonewall Brigade walked quietly unarmed into history, at least their feet were warm: They wore the 392 pairs of socks knitted by the crippled hands of Mother Lee and her daughters—less the socks soaked with the blood of the brigade's men, who would never leave the trenches.

As Confederate General Johnson sat down to his Union breakfast, John B. Gordon worked to rally the failing gray line inside the Mule Shoe. Toward 5:30, General Gordon had positioned three stunned brigades for a countercharge into the cauldron of the bloody salient. When the first of his brigades lunged toward the northern point of the Mule Shoe, the brigade was driven back and its commander was wounded. A regimental colonel was killed pounding against the wall of blue infantry. Through the dawn ground fog and swirling smoke, a familiar figure rode slowly toward the Yankee wedge, which pierced the Rebel line. General Lee and Traveller again turned their faces toward the enemy.

John Gordon, newly in command of Jubal Early's division, had his troops ready to advance. Robert Lee calmly reined Traveller to their front. As he had done only one week earlier in the Wilderness when the Confederate line had broken, General Lee prepared to die on the field with his Army of Northern Virginia.

General Gordon reached for Traveller's reins to jerk the Old Man out of the line of fire before the countercharge. But Gordon missed. Near the Harrison home at the southwest base of the Mule Shoe, Sergeant William Compton of the 49th Virginia managed to take Traveller's leathers. General Lee held his gray slouch hat in his hand and his weary, windburned face glared toward the broken line where Allegheny

Johnson's division had been overwhelmed. Brave and terrified foot soldiers from Gordon's 52nd Virginia and 13th Georgia regiments shouted wildly, "Lee to the rear!" The same cry had echoed through the Wilderness before James Longstreet's corps had finally stumbled up the road to turn the Federal tide.

Sergeant Compton pulled Traveller back from the line, and General Gordon led his division into the hailstorm of lead.

Before six o'clock, the determined Federals had driven one mile into the Mule Shoe bulge in General Lee's Spotsylvania line. John Gordon led four thousand Confederates across the eastern side of the salient into a firestorm of hand-to-hand killing. Survivors would remember two dead men, one in blue and one in gray, who had bayoneted each other inside the salient. The two wide-eyed cadavers remained standing, propped upright by the other's rifled spear. Gordon managed to drive the weary Yankees backward, out of the center of the salient.

Meanwhile, Brigadier Generals Stephen Ramseur (West Point, '60) and Junius Daniel (West Point, '51) of Robert Rodes's gray division countercharged the Federals, who were overrunning the northwest face of the Mule Shoe. Daniel was mortally wounded as the North Carolina regiments pushed these Federals back. By 6:30 a.m., the Confederate line rallied and the Federals were being held in check by ferocious fighting. Much of the inside Mule Shoe was back in Rebel hands, although Federals still poured over the breastworks into the salient.

The Federal II Corps was now digging in just outside the Mule Shoe's earthen walls from the salient's northwest corner, half a mile eastward toward the salient's northernmost point. General Hancock sent word to George Gordon Meade that the blue VI Corps should now be sent in to support Hancock's bloodied right flank. A single Federal brigade from VI Corps attacked the northwestern corner of the Mule Shoe, three hundred yards west of the salient's apex. By 6:30 a.m., two more blue brigades were fed into this corner.

This battle zone at the northwest face of the Mule Shoe soon became a meat grinder only fifty yards wide. The battle would rage without letup for twenty hours. This muddy corner became "Bloody Angle" in the Mule Shoe perimeter.

At seven o'clock, South Carolina lawyer Brigadier General Abner Perrin, thirty-seven, led his Alabama brigade in another Confederate countercharge on the Rebel left flank. The air was so full of bullets that he was hit by seven Minié balls by the time he fell dead.

Only two hours after he had to be forcibly dragged from the battle line, General Lee again rode toward the musketry at 7:30.

General Gordon was driving the Federals out of the inside center of the salient. But the gray line on the left flank was weakening. General Lee rode to find reinforcements himself. He found Nathaniel Harris's brigade of Billy Mahone's division, which Lee ordered to rush to Robert Rodes's assistance. The Old Man was now in the middle of a Federal artillery barrage. A Federal cannon shell exploded nearby, so close that Traveller reared violently. General Lee kept his seat in the saddle as Traveller's forelegs flayed at the sulfureous air. The instant that Traveller reared, a solid cannon ball bounced under Traveller's airborne belly. Had the horse not reared, the twelve-pound iron ball would have cut Robert Lee in half at the waist. It was the old soldier's closest call since Vera Cruz, Mexico, seventeen years earlier.

Again, the Mississippi infantry shouted, "Lee to the rear!," and again, their Uncle Robert resisted leaving the front. The Old Man only agreed to move back from the line if the barefoot boys promised to retake the Mule Shoe. The soldiers shouted their pledge of blood and ran off into the smoke and fire to die for their Marse Robert. Four Mississippi regiments drove into the salient just east of Bloody Angle. One-third of them died there. But their survivors held their position for nineteen continuous hours of hellfire. They had no choice . . . They had given their word to Marse Robert.

At nine a.m., after four and a half hours of killing, a steady rain began, as if to wash away the first layer of fresh blood. At the Bloody Angle, 1,600 Confederates in three decimated brigades doggedly held back two Federal divisions. All but a two-hundred-yard front of the Mule Shoe had been recovered by the Confederates, at a fearful price. The Yankees now sent cannon to the Mule Shoe to fire over the lip of the earthworks at point-blank range. The blue-clad cannoneers were annihilated by sheets of musket fire. One Federal artillery battery had twenty-two of twenty-four men cut to bloody shreds after getting off only fourteen rounds.

Although most of the Federal assault had been checked or broken by mid-morning, the brave boys in blue only fell back to the outside of the salient. From the far side of the Mule Shoe, they did battle in driving rain for the rest of the day and most of the night. Pinned down for twenty hours, they heaved their bayoneted rifles like twelve-pound spears over the Mule Shoe breastworks and through cracks in the log earthworks. They aimed and fired their rifles through the logs, and men bayoneted each other through the timbers. The Union infantry fired three hundred rounds per man until nearly daybreak the next day, Friday. Many rifles simply exploded from becoming packed with black-powder sludge and mud. Other rifles glowed red-hot and could not be touched because a man's fingers would fry and stick to the barrels.

Neither the Army of the Potomac nor the Army of Northern Virginia had ever seen, smelled, heard, or tasted anything like the Bloody Angle. At least the veterans on both sides who remembered Stonewall's Valley Campaign or Manassas, The Seven Days, Chancellorsville, Antietam, or Gettysburg could recollect orderly lines of soldiers attacking and dying in tidy formations. Spotsylvania was a slugfest. The Bloody Angle this May 12 was not war; it was frenzied murder—the longest hand-to-hand battle of the entire war. The northeast side of the inverted, horseshoe-shaped salient was the bloodiest, two-acre slaughter pen in the recorded history of human warfare.

At ten in the morning, the game, brevet Brigadier General Emory Upton (Colonel, only forty-eight hours earlier) led his brigade from the blue VI Corps to a little hill overlooking Bloody Angle. He sent five regiments into the angle and lost 200 men on the way down the hill. One regiment lost 150 men in thirty minutes. Upton's brigade was pinned down at Bloody Angle for seven hours. James Mangan of Upton's 15th New Jersey Infantry was wounded twice. He lay there bleeding against the Mule Shoe walls for a day until he was hauled into Confederate lines. After Rebel surgeons amputated Mangan's arm, he laid on the ground another ten days. Then he dug a little hole in the bloody earth and buried his own right arm.

Seven

THE YANKEE CANNON WERE HEARD AS FAR AWAY AS RICHMOND—forty-two miles—until one o'clock in the afternoon of May 12. One Federal artillery battery (usually six cannon) from Rhode Island fired 873 rounds into the Mule Shoe. The musket fire was intense. The corpse of an artilleryman in blue lay slumped across a cannon. A steady hailstorm of lead Minié balls thudded one at a time into some mother's son until they sliced the dead Federal in half.

The brawl by dirty-faced men fighting hand to hand with other men exactly like themselves never slackened. After nine hours of it, toward three in the afternoon, the Federals brought up six-inch mortars which lobbed seventeen-pound shells over the crest of the Mule Shoe embankment into the salient. The torn bodies were piled into heaps which were slowly whittled down into bloody puddles by the steady pecking of the musketry.

By late afternoon, General Lee decided to fall back, evacuate the Mule Shoe, and take up position in the new line of earthworks being finished at the wide, southern base of the salient. The new line was 1,200 yards behind the northern point of the Mule Shoe and Bloody Angle just west of that. Orders went into the salient to hold the outer works until the new position was completed. The fighting continued into evening twilight and into the darkness of Thursday night—sixteen hours. The new line would not be ready until after midnight.

While the gray Second Corps held the line, Stonewall's presence was felt in the person of his right-hand man, young Sandie Pendleton, who did his job as Baldy Ewell's chief of staff throughout the battle. Sandie had two horses shot out from under him, but the lieutenant colonel was unhurt.

While the battle swirled in puddles of ankle-deep blood in the Bloody Angle all Thursday, Flora Stuart had bounced in a special train provided to take her and the two children from Beaver Dam to Richmond. The wounded general's wife had left the country for the city at one o'clock, Thursday afternoon. She rode all day to her husband's bedside. But going was slow while Jeb bled to death in her sister Maria's bed. When she reached Ashland, Virginia, at three in the afternoon, the train had to stop where the Federals had ripped up the railroad track. The Stuarts transferred to a wagon for the seven-hour ride through the same rain which fell upon the heaps of dead and wounded up the road at the Mule Shoe.

In the Brewer home, the vigil continued through Wednesday night and into May 12 as the Battle of Spotsylvania raged forty miles north of Richmond. Before Flora could get to the Brewer home where Jeb lay dying, President Davis dropped by to pay his respects to the daring horse soldier. In a lucid moment, Jeb felt his colorful life ebbing away, and he quietly bequeathed his sword to his young son, little Jeb. Then the small circle of friends and relatives sang "Rock of Ages" at the bedside. "I am going fast now," Major General Stuart sighed. "I am resigned. God's will be done."

The thirty-one-year-old major general with the massive beard had seemed born for the mounted cavalry. He trained his troopers on how real cavalrymen sit their warhorses (in their McClellan saddles designed by Little Mac): "A good man on a good horse can never be caught. Cavalry can trot away from anything and a gallop is a gait unbecoming a soldier, unless he is going toward the enemy. We gallop toward the enemy and trot away. Always."

"All I ask of fate is that I may be killed leading a cavalry charge," Jeb Stuart had once proudly proclaimed. Instead of a cavalryman's death at Brandy Station or Gettysburg, under thundering hooves and slashing sabers, James Ewell Brown Stuart died slowly and in agony as his torn bowels rotted from within.

At 7:38 in the evening, Thursday, Jeb Stuart went down the road which Old Jack had gone down, to cross that river and to go into those trees. He died three hours before Flora and their children reached his side. When the grieving widow went through her dead husband's gray pockets, she found a faded newspaper clipping about dying children. Flora and Jeb had buried five-year-old little Flora eighteen months earlier. Also in the dead father's pocket was a tiny lock of hair from his new daughter, seven-month-old Virginia.

When Jeb had served in the Old Army nine years ago in 1855, then-Lieutenant Stuart served in the 1st US Cavalry on the wild frontier of St. Louis, Missouri. The commanding colonel was Edwin Sumner, who would lead the Yankee II Corps beside Antietam Creek and at Fredericksburg. The lieutenant colonel of the old 1st was Joe Johnston, and John Sedgwick was a major. Only three days dead himself, Major General John Sedgwick once called Jeb Stuart "the greatest cavalryman ever foaled in America."

When Jeb stopped breathing Thursday night, the gunfire in the Bloody Angle continued into the darkness of May 12. After sixteen hours of unspeakable carnage, men in blue and gray fought like wild animals with their eyes closed. Exhausted men slept soundly while bullets kicked up the bloody mud around them. In the dark, officers shouted orders to men whom they could not see were dead.

Men fired through the cracks in the breastwork logs past midnight. At one o'clock on Friday morning, May 13, an oak tree just east of Bloody Angle absorbed all the lead it could hold. The tree shattered and fell to the ground as if sawed in half by crazed lumberjacks using Minié balls and cannon shrapnel instead of axes. A boy in gray was knocked senseless when the tree fell on his head. The felled tree was inside the Mule Shoe salient, three hundred yards west of the northern apex of the works. The tree was twenty-two inches around, and bullets had sheared it in two.

Finally, at two in the morning, the new Confederate defensive line was finished at the base of the Mule Shoe. General Lee ordered a slow withdrawal from the salient, back to the new line of fieldworks. The weary gray infantry pulled back, firing as they went.

An hour later, as the careful pullback continued, couriers brought to Spotsylvania word too painful for Robert Lee to imagine: Jeb Stuart was dead in Richmond. The sad Old Man had regarded young Jeb as another son, and now, in the rain and mud of the Mule Shoe, General Lee had lost him. "I can scarcely think of him without weeping," the commanding general sighed. Then he paid Jeb the highest compliment he could give his chief cavalryman and scout: "He never brought me a piece of false information." In seven days, General Lee will issue General Orders Number 44 announcing General Stuart's death and consigning his memory to history: "His achievements form a conspicuous part of the history of this army with which his name and services will be forever associated."

But the Old Man had other things on his mind as daylight approached on Friday, May 13. The Mule Shoe evacuation continued under fire at four in the morning. By 4:30 a.m., most of the Army of Northern Virginia in the Mule Shoe sector had withdrawn into the new line of trenches. They left behind piles of dead in the Bloody Angle, where two Rebel brigades had lost half their men and four regimental commanders. One of the dead Confederate colonels also had a son killed in the Mule Shoe. Slowly, twenty-three hours of bloodshed came to an end.

There had never been fighting like it. The casualty lists for Sharpsburg and Gettysburg were longer than Spotsylvania, but the Bloody Angle fighting was more ferocious, with whole regiments clubbing one another with empty rifles. In twenty-three vicious hours of continuous fire, the Federals lost seven thousand men.

General Lee lost six thousand troops and twenty precious cannon, captured when Allegheny Johnson's division had been swept away. Among the Confederate losses were three thousand prisoners, most of them captured with Allegheny Johnson and the vanished Stonewall Brigade. Two gray-clad generals were captured, two generals killed or mortally wounded, and four generals wounded.

During the last ten days of General Grant's spring offensive, General Lee had given up 7,078 Confederates to Yankee prison camps; another 8,000 men killed or wounded; 5 generals killed; 9 generals wounded, including the irascible Lieutenant General James Longstreet; and 2 generals captured. The last week was General Lee's worst destruction of his general staff since Pickett's Charge.

The Confederates who were captured soon began the seventeen-mile march up the road to the Federal beachhead at Belle Plain landing, six miles southeast of Grant's Virginia supply depot at Aquia Creek on the

Potomac. The disarmed Southerners were herded into a rugged ravine soon dubbed the Punch Bowl. They would mingle there, awaiting the prison trains to POW camps in Maryland.

In Friday's daylight, the exhausted soldiers who were not dead dropped where they stood and slept where they fell. The wounded would be gathered for the terrible trains of pain to Richmond or Washington hospitals. In the Confederate capital, the overburdened surgeons would be sewing wounds and stumps with sutures made from horsehair; they were out of silk thread.

Even Ulysses S. Grant, who fought like no Union general before him, could not imagine the dreadful sights of May 13, Spotsylvania. On that day, he wrote a note home to his Julia. "The world has never seen so bloody or so protracted a battle as the one being fought, and I hope never will again."

This rainy Friday, General Lee heard the story about the oak tree cut in half by musket fire. He asked a member of Baldy Ewell's staff to direct him to the site. When Robert Lee rode over to the west side of the Mule Shoe, where wounded boys still moaned for water, he found not one but two oak trees had been hewn down by bullets. One tree was twenty-two inches in diameter and the other, twenty inches.

Back home in Richmond, the city awoke to the ugly rumor and then the terrible truth that Jeb Stuart lay dead in Dr. Brewer's bed. A few blocks away on Franklin Street, Lee daughter Mary Custis—Jeb's "Marielle" from West Point days—quietly clipped Jeb's obituary from the newspaper. She pasted the sad report in the old scrapbook which Jeb and cousin Fitz Lee had once rescued and returned to her. When Jeb was a West Point cadet, Mary Custis Lee was the superintendent's teenage daughter. Mary Custis went off to Pelham Priory, a girls' school in Westchester County, New York. It was there that the worldly Mary began using the appellation "Marielle" for her signature. She still used it for personal correspondence. To Jeb Stuart, who was Jimmy when he first met Mary Custis, the smartest and most headstrong Lee daughter was Marielle for the nine years when he was not yet dead.

From Friday, May 13, through Tuesday, May 17, General Grant's spring campaign bogged down in continuous rain.

Richmond was draped in black on May 13 for the state funeral of Major General Stuart. Services were held at five p.m. at St. James Church. The rites were attended by President Davis, his entire Cabinet, and both houses of the Confederate Congress. Cannon booming up the James River at the Mule Shoe could be heard in the church. Four white horses slowly pulled Jeb's body to his open grave at Hollywood Cemetery.

Three hours after Jeb Stuart's body was lowered into the Virginia earth he loved, the battle-numbed thousands at Spotsylvania Courthouse went to work again. At eight o'clock Friday evening, Major General Meade reorganized four Federal corps of infantry along his front. With many bluecoats still in shock from forty-eight hours of deployments and killing, the blue V and VI Corps shifted in the rainy darkness from the Federal right flank, southeastward to their left. They took up their new position just east of Spotsylvania. Grant planned an all-night march by divisions which were beyond exhaustion. His plan called for another frontal assault against the Mule Shoe killing fields to begin Saturday at dawn. The four a.m. morning attack would be against General Lee's right flank.

The Federals were too wet, too tired, and too stunned to execute one more midnight mud-march. In heavy rain showers, they did not set off down the soggy roads until 9:30 p.m. on Friday. With his army too shocked and too dazed to fight, Lieutenant General Grant canceled the May 14 advance and postponed it until Sunday, May 15.

May 14 passed quietly as the collection of the dead and wounded continued. Confederate scouts reported to General Lee that during the night the Federal right flank had abandoned their works opposite the Rebel left. The white-haired chieftain took the relative quiet to begin again the work which followed each of his campaigns: the reorganization of shattered commands. From the survivors of General Edward "Allegheny" Johnson's four destroyed brigades, General Lee formed one small brigade which was added to the brigade commanded by the hard-fighting General John B. Gordon, who always seemed to be wherever Lee most needed him. These two brigades became a new but small division to be led by Gordon.

Combining the remnants of decimated commands was easy compared to replacing frontline officers who were dead, wounded, or milling around Belle Plain landing, awaiting assignment to Federal prison camps. In only nine bloody days, Robert Lee's battered army had lost fully seventy colonels and lieutenant colonels, thirty of whom were gone forever in shallow graves usually marked UNKNOWN beside the muddy road and bloody puddles. At least Lieutenant General Grant had to contend with his own casualty lists and empty chairs at his war councils. During the same nine days ending on Saturday, May 14, the blue Army of the Potomac had lost 36,872 men and boys, of whom nearly 11,000 were missing in action in the Wilderness thickets or the poison fields of Spotsylvania.

General Grant's proposed attack did not come on Sunday either. May 15 was another day of rain and muddy marches. General Lee used the day to move Dick Anderson's First Corps from the southern left flank to the far right. This deployment would put First Corps opposite the new position of the shift in Federal divisions southeastward toward the Snell Bridge, across the swollen Po River.

Sometime during the Sunday rain, General Lee shared a private moment with Lieutenant General A. P. Hill. They must have seen and surely smelled the blood and death in the spring gloom. Lee and Little Powell knew that the men and officers of the Army of Northern Virginia had fought gallantly beyond the limits of human endurance, as had the brave Yankees. But on both sides of the Mule Shoe, mistakes were made. "These men are not an army, they are citizens defending their country. I cannot do things that I could do with a trained army," General Lee said. "The soldiers know their duties better than the general officers do, and they have fought magnificently. When a man makes a mistake, I call him to my tent, talk to him, and use the authority of my position to make him do the right thing next time." Little Powell probably nodded, knowing all too well why this citizens' army called the Old Man their Uncle Robert.

Sunday and Monday were quiet as the rain dripped softly upon festering wounds, bloating cadavers, and famished survivors.

Tuesday, May 17, the rain stopped. Sunshine on drying roads inspired General Grant to renew his planned attack against the Mule Shoe and its new line of fieldworks at the salient's southern base. Orders were issued for the Federal II and VI Corps to attack the salient at daybreak on Wednesday. General Burnside's IX Corps would support the assault, with V Corps held in reserve.

At dawn on May 18, the blue II and VI Corps slammed headlong into the salient. The dogged boys in blue ran straight into a line of twenty-three Confederate cannon. The Federals were blown to pieces. By ten o'clock in the morning, Major General Meade had enough of the senseless slaughter of Mr. Lincoln's best. Old Snapping Turtle called the blue divisions back.

A disappointed but undaunted Lieutenant General Grant cut orders for the evacuation of the grim line at Spotsylvania. His II Corps would march after dark on May 19 to move around the Army of Northern Virginia. General Hancock's corps would then march southeast toward General Lee's right flank as bait. Grant hoped that Lee would go after the prize of an isolated Yankee corps. Grant would then slam into Lee from behind. For General Grant's plan to work, Robert Lee had only to do something truly foolish. For the first time.

After the ghastliest fighting of the war, the Battle of Spotsylvania was over when the first sunshine in a week warmed the freshly dug graves and oozing wounds of the 28,000 Americans who fell in the poison fields and in the Bloody Angle.

Perhaps the weary men in blue and gray thought that they had seen all the horror which brave men could inflict upon their fellow men who speak the same language, cherish the same virtues, and, as Mr. Lincoln will say on March 4, 1865, "Both read the same Bible and pray to the same God, and each invokes His aid against the other." But on this day-break, Friday, May 20, 1864, these survivors had not yet been to Cold Harbor.

There, in fourteen days, Lieutenant General Ulysses S. Grant would earn the nickname which would haunt him to his grave: "Butcher Grant."

Eight

When General Grant abandoned any hope of dislodging the Confederates from their breastworks at Spotsylvania, General Lee faced the same reality. On Wednesday, May 18, Robert Lee wired Jefferson Davis to advise that the Federal position "is strongly entrenched and we cannot attack it with any prospect of success without great loss of men. Neither the strength of our army nor the condition of our animals will admit of any extensive movement with a view to drawing the enemy from his position."

While Robert Lee assessed the odds of locking sabers with Grant again, the Federals began to put miles between themselves and the Courthouse. During the night of Wednesday, May 18, into the morning of May 19, the blue II and VI Corps pulled out of Spotsylvania. Sixth Corps left sadly without their beloved Uncle John Sedgwick. The Federal II Corps marched with a fresh division of reinforcements sent up from Washington City's home guard. These new men were from the Federal heavy artillery, which protected the Union capital. The last sight they ever expected to see was an all-night march by infantry. The new cannoneers who were pressed into walking the back roads of Virginia were laughed at by the veterans, who marveled at the artillerymen's clean uniforms and new boots.

As the Federals slid sideways, southeastward to outflank the Confederates, General Lee needed to confirm if the bluecoats were marching from the Rebel left toward the right flank. Such a maneuver would continue Grant's efforts to get around General Lee on the long road which ended outside the Rebel capitol building in Richmond.

Grant and Meade had successfully pulled their II Corps off the Spotsylvania front, with their VI and IX Corps marching to the Federal left flank, toward Richmond. To feel out the Federal position, General Lee detached Baldy Ewell's entire Second Corps, with six thousand hardy souls, for a reconnoiter-in-force. Ewell's Second Corps of the Army of Northern Virginia had mustered twice that number at roll call only three weeks earlier.

Ewell's two divisions, commanded by John Gordon and Robert Rodes, marched toward the northeast on Thursday, May 19. At noon, Ewell's survivors held their six thousand noses and breathed through their mouths when they marched over half-buried and rotting Yankee corpses. The week of rain at Spotsylvania had washed away the shallow graves along the Ny River. When Ewell crossed the Ny, he decided to leave behind his six cannon, which would have slowed their march.

By 4:00 p.m., Ewell's advance skirmish line bumped into the marching Federals. By 5:30 p.m. on Thursday, the weakened and one-legged Ewell was heavily engaged at the Harris Farm. Yankees from the Federal II Corps fought vigorously with the Confederates. The newly posted Federal artillerymen from Washington saw their first battle after hardly two days on the line. Ewell was so heavily assaulted that the brigade of Stephen Ramseur had to be sent out to keep Ewell from being overwhelmed. The battle raged until darkness.

Not until eight p.m. that night could Ewell disengage and withdraw back to the main gray line. He had been sent to find Grant's army—and Grant had nearly destroyed Old Jack's Second Corps. When Ewell finally made good his escape, he left 900 dead and wounded Confederates behind among 1,535 Federal casualties. At least the skirmish had delayed Grant's advance toward Richmond by one full day.

The Battle of Harris Farm was the last gunfire heard at Spotsylvania Courthouse. As the firing in the distance died away in the May 19 darkness, General Lee accepted that the intrepid little corps commander, Baldy Ewell, was seriously weakened in body and judgment from the grievous wound which had cost him his leg. Lee pondered the stark reality that First Corps commander James Longstreet was gravely wounded and perhaps out of action permanently, that Richard Ewell of Second Corps was growing more fragile by the day, and that Third Corps' fiery A. P. Hill remained incapacitated in his horse-drawn ambulance, which followed his divisions. The command structure of the once-invincible Army of Northern Virginia slowly eroded away, like the thin soil washing away from thousands of new graves where stinking holes marked the course of two mighty armies aiming for Richmond.

After dark on May 19, Grant and Meade continued their routine of all-night marching as the blue II Corps took the dirt road from Spotsylvania one hour before midnight. The weary Federals covered eight miles in the Virginia darkness, and arrived early Friday morning at Guinea Station. The same morning, the Federal V, VI, and IX Corps took the trail south from Spotsylvania. Generals Grant and Meade did not leave the poison fields of the Mule Shoe until ten in the morning on May 21. Grant could only hope that Lee would take the bait of the isolated Federal II Corps, which dangled deliciously exposed, and that it would draw Lee away from the main force of the Army of the Potomac.

The additions from the Harris Farm to Confederate casualty lists hanging upon the South's newspaper-office doorways were a tactical necessity. General Lee had confirmation of the Federal evacuation of Spotsylvania. By the evening of May 20, Robert Lee was satisfied that he had again read Grant's mind, and that he understood the blue army would continue its effort to move around Lee toward Richmond. The Confederate commander then issued orders to Baldy Ewell for a Second Corps shift to the Rebel right the next morning. Every step Grant took would be shadowed by General Lee, awaiting the next open ground where the Federals could be attacked. To bolster the flagging Confederate strength, President Davis agreed this Thursday to detach the division of General George Pickett back to Lee in the field. This force would give Robert Lee five fresh brigades of infantry for the next encounter with Grant, somewhere further south.

At noon on May 21, General Lee ordered the entire gray army to march south from Spotsylvania toward the vital railroad hub at Hanover Junction. Lee completely ignored Grant's II Corps trap. By early evening, the gray Second Corps marched southward, and by nine o'clock that night, Powell Hill's Third Corps left Spotsylvania. The gray Third Corps took a road parallel to the path followed by Dick Anderson's First Corps, which led Ewell's Second Corps. Lee watched his troops leave the

Bloody Angle behind. Pulling Traveller's reins southward, General Lee said to his staff, "Come, gentlemen." The Old Man did not look back.

General Lee correctly judged that Grant would move his principal supply base to Port Royal on the Rappahannock River. Confederate scouts knew the Federals were on the move within six hours of their march. When Lee decided to advance toward the North Anna River to keep his army between Grant and Richmond, Lee knew that he would have to allow the sprawling Federal army to come within twenty-three miles of Richmond if Lee were to aim for Hanover Junction on the Richmond-Fredericksburg-Potomac Railroad. But he had no choice until Grant could be caught and destroyed somewhere toward the south. The Federals were already one day ahead.

Before leaving Spotsylvania, A. P. Hill requested that he be returned to the command of his Third Corps. The frail Little Powell could not bear to miss another race against Grant. Lee consented, and posted Hill back with his divisions, which had been temporarily led by Jubal Early. Third Corps marched all night on May 21, bound for Hanover, which they reached at noon on May 22 after covering thirty miles on foot.

With a one-day advantage on Lee, Grant and Meade reached Massaponax Baptist Church by noon on May 21. After a brief rest, they continued on to Guinea Station (sometimes spelled "Guiney's"), ten miles south of Spotsylvania. While his army raced the Confederates, Grant paused to rest the night of May 21 at Guinea, on the road to Hanover Junction.

Lieutenant General Grant stopped at the home of Tom and Mary Chandler at Guinea Station. The tiny barren plot of Virginia had entered history one year and eleven days earlier, when Stonewall Jackson had been carried to their home to die. When Grant removed his dusty hat to bid a courtly "Good evening" to Mrs. Chandler, the woman wept softly when she firmly advised her blue-coated enemy that sad history had been made under her very roof. General Grant was uncomfortable on the front porch, which was already something of a Confederate shrine to the fallen Old Blue Light.

General Grant was moved by the woman's tears when she spoke of Old Jack as if remembering family. "He and I were at West Point together," the Yankee general-in-chief said gravely. "Jackson was a gallant soldier and a Christian gentleman," the general added. Then he bowed to the woman and walked into the night, after first promising that the miles of Federal soldiers would cause no harm to her precious little farm. General Grant kept his word.

There had been enough destruction without despoiling one old lady's plot of sterile farmland. During the last thirteen days, General Grant had suffered 16,141 men killed or wounded, with another 2,258 captured. The price of inflicting those terrible losses by General Lee had been 6,519 Southerners killed or wounded, and 5,543 taken prisoner.

Throughout the night of May 21, the two armies tramped the wet Virginia earth. At two o'clock on the morning of Sunday, May 22, General Ambrose Burnside and his blue IX Corps followed Grant into Guinea Station, where he pitched camp for an eight-hour rest. By three a.m. on Sunday, General Lee had ridden Traveller seventeen miles during seven grueling hours in the saddle. Lee had ridden all night with General Ewell's Second Corps to continue his habit of keeping close to his most unreliable officers. Baldy Ewell had a great heart, and he enjoyed the devotion of Stonewall Jackson's Second Corps, but his body was failing fast. General Lee personally prodded the weary men onward, and the divisions cheered their Uncle Robert as he passed in the moist darkness.

After riding down the Telegraph Road all night, General Lee arrived at 5:30 a.m. on Sunday at his new field headquarters, at Mount Carmel Church near Dickinson's Mill. He was now two miles north of the North Anna River, and only five miles from his objective of Hanover. General Grant marched south along a parallel road only six miles to the east. After a short rest, Lee was on the road again, arriving at Hanover at 9:30 a.m. that morning. George Pickett's fresh division was approaching from the northeast.

When Robert Lee rode into Hanover Junction Sunday morning, only one thing mattered: He had beaten Grant, who enjoyed a one-day head start. Lee quickly deployed Dick Anderson's First Corps on the south bank of the North Anna River. Although Lee had won the race, his staff was alarmed when they saw their chief in daylight. After his all-night ride, the Old Man looked exhausted, even sickly. The weary general wired Richmond that his First and Second Corps were in position, with

Third Corps falling in on their right flank. Lee wanted desperately to attack General Grant in the open country. But there were no Yankees in sight.

Anxious to get at Grant, Little Powell at six o'clock Sunday evening sent the divisions of Henry Heth and Cadmus Wilcox out to trap the Federal V Corps south of the North Anna, at the ford called Jericho Mills. Hill's attack collapsed due to poor coordination in darkness and new rain.

While Little Powell stumbled back into commanding his corps, General Grant was busy completing his change of base, from Belle Plain landing to Port Royal, thirty miles north of Hanover and seventeen miles southeast of Fredericksburg. The Port Royal depot would be used only four days.

Monday, May 23, disaster struck the Confederates. As had haunted them at Gettysburg, General Lee suddenly took sick again. The strain and the filthy water were just too much for his war-weary body. Weak as he was, Robert Lee could still put dip pen to paper to express his passion for stopping that man Grant: "I begrudge every step he takes towards Richmond."

The two great armies snaked down the dirt roads as they raced for the North Anna River on the road to Richmond. The boys in gray and butternut-brown beat the long blue line to the prize.

Both bloodied armies aimed for Hanover Junction, where the railroads came together, just as they had raced for Gettysburg where all the roads converged eleven months earlier.

Four mighty corps of blue infantry marched toward the North Anna on Monday morning, May 23. The Federal II Corps walked southward along the Telegraph Road to the left of their IX Corps. And V Corps closed in on IX Corps' right. Three corps of Yankees pushed toward the river in parallel files. The blue VI Corps brought up the rear.

By noon, a weakening General Lee paused briefly at the home of W. E. Fox. Lee sat on the front porch, where he drank a glass of buttermilk. He could see Federals massing in the distance when a solid Yankee cannonball slammed into the porch close to the general. His army's "Marse Robert" calmly finished his drink, thanked his host, and then rode off. The Yankees were concentrating on the North Anna upriver at Ox Ford, only two miles away.

The Old Man was showing signs of approaching illness. When he inspected his new defensive position along the river, he had to ride in a carriage instead of weathering Traveller's rough trot. By nightfall, General Lee was down.

General Lee had deployed his three corps by noon in an inverted "V" formation, with the point aiming north at Ox Ford on the North Anna. This impromptu and brilliant formation meant that Generals Grant and Meade could only attack one side or the other, but not both, without cutting their own army in half.

By one o'clock in the afternoon, General Warren's blue V Corps on the Federal right flank crossed the North Anna at Jericho Mill, three miles upriver and northwest of Ox Ford. General Wright's VI Corps marched behind Warren's divisions. The Federal II Corps on the Federal far left headed down toward Chesterfield Bridge, one mile downriver and east of Ox Ford, with Ambrose Burnside's IX Corps also bound for the bridgehead.

When the blue V Corps waded the North Anna at Jericho Mill, they could not get their cannon across in deep water. By 3:20 p.m., Federal engineers begin building a pontoon bridge at the mill. Two blue divisions of Generals Griffin and Crawford were already across the river at the mill.

By 4:30 p.m., Yankee artillery were creaking across 160 feet of river over the pontoon bridge. A third V Corps division crossed, along with twenty-four Union cannon. As the cannon crossed into Confederate country, Little Powell Hill, back in command of Third Corps, was anxious for a fight. He detached Cadmus Wilcox's battle-hardened division toward Noel's Station to attack the two blue divisions of Crawford and Griffin, which were now south of the river at the mill, and isolated from the rest of the Yankee force.

At six o'clock Monday evening, Cadmus Wilcox attacked the blue-coats along the Central Railroad line, four and a half miles northwest of Hanover Junction. A furious little fight raged for two hours. Federal cannon firing the vicious canister stopped Wilcox. The battered men of

Hill's Third Corps had to withdraw under cover of darkness. They left behind 642 dead and wounded Confederates who bled or begged for water beside 350 dead or wounded Federals.

General Lee resolved to permit the Yankees to continue their crossing of the North Anna in the darkness, since things were no better downriver on the Rebel right flank. There, Chesterfield Bridge had fallen to the Federals while Powell Hill was being driven back upriver at Jericho Mill. The blue II Corps had deployed off the Telegraph Road one mile north of Chesterfield Bridge. At six o'clock Monday evening, two blue brigades attacked Joe Kershaw's gray division on the north bank of the river. Kershaw was driven into the water toward the south side. In the darkness, Confederate rangers tried but failed to burn the bridge to slow the Federal advance.

At least General Lee had the satisfaction of a perfect, defensive position. The northern apex of his inverted, north-facing "V" line extended on his right flank down to Hanover Junction, and the left flank stretched to the Little River. George Pickett had arrived with his fresh troops, now numbering close to 8,500 reinforcements. If Grant attacked either flank, Lee would enjoy the superior "interior line" just as the Federals had exploited their similar line atop Cemetery Ridge at Gettysburg.

In the darkness, the weary Old Man still longed for open fields where his army could outmaneuver any blue-clad host. In quiet desperation, Robert Lee wired President Davis that "General Grant's army will be in the field, strengthened by all available troops from the north. It seems to me our best policy to unite upon it and endeavor to crush it."

On the night of Monday, May 23, beside the North Anna River on the road to Richmond, Robert Lee took violently sick again. The tired old soldier was dropped in his tracks by paralyzing dysentery—soldiers' diarrhea—which kept him practically a prisoner in his tent and ambulance for the next ten days. With Uncle Robert too ill to move, Generals Grant and Meade built fieldworks, and the blue and gray armies became stuck on the riverbank.

With General Lee bedridden on Tuesday, May 24, the blue II Corps crossed Chesterfield Bridge in the morning. The Federal VI Corps continued crossing the pontoon bridgehead at the mill upriver. At 3:30 p.m.,

Generals Grant and Meade crossed the river at the mill. During the last hours of daylight, the luck of the generals in blue nearly ran out with a sudden annihilation of the Federal offensive.

At four in the afternoon, the blue II Corps was successfully across the North Anna on the south side. But the Confederate lines completely cut off Hancock's brave Federals from the rest of their army. With the river behind him, Hancock looked squarely down the muzzles of the Confederate First and Second Corps on his front and on his right flank. Lee had fully one-fourth of the Yankee army trapped between the river and two corps of gray infantry. Although weak and dehydrated, Lee did not trust either Baldy Ewell or Dick Anderson to lead the attack to destroy Hancock. The Old Man would coordinate the assault himself. The result was no attack at all. Uncle Robert was just too sick.

Meanwhile, Ambrose Burnside's IX Corps stumbled into a skirmish with A. P. Hill's Third Corps near Ox Ford on the south side of the river. Burnside lost two hundred men. Upriver, a division of Hancock's corps engaged Baldy Ewell in a fierce firefight which only an all-night thunderstorm could end in the darkness.

The result of Lee's sickly Tuesday beside the river was more dead men and an entire Yankee corps which got away from certain entrapment. At least the musketry inspired General Grant to stop his march toward Richmond for a while and to dig in at the river. General Burnside was ordered to hold the south side of the river beachhead and to fill the gap in Grant's line between the blue II and V Corps. Grant also officially terminated Burnside's authority to act as an independent command. His corps became part of George Gordon Meade's Army of the Potomac, with whom Lieutenant General Grant pitched his general-in-chief tent. In the darkness, the two weary armies were only seven hundred yards apart.

Wednesday, May 25, found Robert Lee on his back and praying that the Federals would slam into his impregnable line just as they had done at Fredericksburg in December, 1862.

But Hanover Junction was not Marye's Heights, where the Rebels held the Fredericksburg high ground because Lieutenant General Grant was not the Federal Major General Ambrose Burnside.

Nine

ROBERT LEE REMAINED BEDRIDDEN AND HIS ILL TEMPER WORSENED with his stormy bowels. The "blue mass" remedy for field diarrhea and dysentery prescribed by the regimental surgeons did not help. Blue mass was a mixture of mercurous chloride (calomel), strychnine (strychnia), lead acetate, and a pinch of opium.

Lee's trusted aide, Colonel Charles Venable, braved the Old Man's tent long enough to suggest to General Lee that he was too sick to continue in command. Another man should lead the assault to cut Grant's army in half at the river. Venable proposed General Pierre Beauregard (West Point, '38, number two in his class)—Old Bory—to take the helm of the Army of Northern Virginia. Marse Robert exploded, "We must never let them pass us again! We must strike them a blow!" Then General Lee collapsed on his field cot.

The Federals still had their II Corps trapped on one side of Lee's inverted "V" line with the blue V Corps cornered and isolated on the other side. The "interior" Rebel wings were only four miles apart for rapid troop movements from one flank to the other. The two blue corps on the "exterior" line were fifteen to twenty miles from each other.

But Grant was too wise to attack Lee. So the Federals were content to do little more than destroy seventeen precious miles of railroad on the Richmond-Fredericksburg-Potomac line.

Mustering all of his frail strength, General Lee moved his field headquarters three miles south to Taylorsville, where he collapsed again.

By two o'clock Wednesday afternoon, Union Generals Grant and Meade broke camp at Jericho Mill and rode north across the river to pitch camp at Quarles' Mill, one mile downriver from Jericho on the north bank of the North Anna. Grant also ordered up General Ben Butler's two full corps of reinforcements, X and XVIII Corps, from the south via White House Landing—Rooney Lee's old homestead. Butler's men would come up under General William Smith's command to camp at Hanovertown.

Wednesday night, Grant decided to back away from Lee's perfect defensive line. The Federals would do what they had done so well since crossing the Rapidan only three weeks ago: They would simply slide sideways toward the southeast to get around Robert Lee's army. The bluecoats would keep to the east bank of the Pamunkey River, where Sheridan's cavalry could protect them from the Confederates. The day ended with another violent thunderstorm, which lasted until four o'clock Thursday morning.

Although picket fire was heard across the riverfront lines, the Federal army declined to risk being sliced in half by the Confederates' wedge-shaped formation on May 26. Through his stupor, General Lee pondered whether Grant would continue his march toward Richmond by going around the Rebel left or right flank. During Thursday night, May 26, into early Friday morning, May 27, the Yankee legions withdrew to the north side of the North Anna River.

The North Anna front from Jericho Mill downriver to Chesterfield Bridge between May 23 and 26 cost 1,973 Federals killed and wounded, with another 165 captured. The Confederates with their superior, defensive position lost 690 killed or wounded, and 561 lost to Federal prison camps.

When the Federals slid sideways again past the Army of Northern Virginia on May 26, Grant abandoned his new base of operations at Port Royal. His new supply depot would be White House Landing on the Pamunkey, fifteen miles downriver from Hanovertown. Fourteen miles to the west was a nowhere village called Cold Harbor.

White House was full of both American and Lee family history. There, in 1759, George and Martha Washington had been married in the great white home which gave the plantation its name. The white mansion had been burned during the Peninsula campaign of George McClellan in June of '62. In his will, Parke Custis—Mother Lee's father—had bequeathed the farm to Rooney and Rob Lee Jr. upon his death, six and a half years before Lieutenant General Grant seized the estate. The new supply base would be fully stocked with food, cannon, and bullets, all stamped "USA" by June 5.

With Robert Lee still deathly sick on Friday, May 27, the Federal divisions were completely gone from the North Anna line, on the march toward the southeast and to Hanovertown southeast of Hanover Junction. Phil Sheridan's blue cavalry with two mounted divisions was on the south side of the North Anna by nine o'clock Friday morning. The North Anna flows into the Pamunkey River.

The race to Richmond was desperate.

When the Army of the Potomac reached Hanovertown, well over one hundred thousand bluecoats would be only fifteen miles northeast of the Confederate capital. Four blue corps made the march toward Richmond, with two corps on the east bank of the Pamunkey River and two corps a bit to their east, all southbound.

The weak and ill General Lee sent Baldy Ewell's Second Corps southward along the Richmond-Fredericksburg-Potomac Railroad, with First Corps bringing up the rear. Little Powell Hill's Third Corps was ordered to evacuate the North Anna front at nightfall for the race against Grant. Though too sick to die, Robert Lee again rode beside the corps commander who troubled him the most, Lieutenant General Richard Ewell, whose physical energy was nearly gone.

Friday marked the continuing deterioration of the high command of the Army of Northern Virginia. With Lee still under siege from dysentery, with Old Pete Longstreet laid up in a field hospital, and with Powell Hill struggling to stay in his saddle, Baldy Ewell's great heart finally gave out. As the gray army headed south, the crippling camp diarrhea which tormented General Lee got the best of Richard Ewell.

Friday night, the Yankees were marching into Haw's Shop, fifteen miles northeast of Richmond on the dirt road which passed through Mechanicsville of the June '62, "Seven Days" campaign. Robert Lee had taken command of the Virginia Militia on June 1, after his old friend Joe Johnston was severely wounded on May 31. The first thing Lee did was rename his divisions the Army of Northern Virginia. With George

McClellan's mighty Federal army of one hundred thousand well-trained men poised at the gates of Richmond, General Lee attacked on June 26. For the next seven days, Lee pushed the Federals back to Washington in a stunning but costly victory. Lee lost twenty thousand Confederates, and "Little Mac" lost sixteen thousand.

But Richmond would now last another three years.

The Confederate divisions pitched camp at Atlee's Station, ten miles west of the Federal camp at Haw's, and only nine miles due north of Richmond on the vital Virginia Central Railroad. General Lee erected his tent at Hughes' Shop.

Baldy Ewell was so ill this night that he asked to be relieved of command of Second Corps, which had been bequeathed to him upon Old Jack's death at Chancellorsville in May of '63. General Jubal Early—Old Jube—was again elevated from division command to corps command in Ewell's place. The grand old army was slowly becoming a shadow of what it had been during its glory days. With Richard Ewell relieved of command, the army had lost two of three corps commanders within three weeks, and was now functioning with three new division commanders, fourteen new brigade commanders, and no one yet named to replace Jeb Stuart as cavalry commander.

Saturday, May 28, General Lee was still bedridden. He abandoned his tent for a room at the Clarke home at Atlee's. The exact location of the Federals was unknown. So the commanding general sent his nephew, General Fitz Lee, and 1,100 cavalrymen off to scout the Federal position. The Yankees had been crossing the Pamunkey all day, with three blue corps crossing at Hanovertown, and two other corps crossing four miles upriver at Nelson's Crossing. Fitz Lee's cavalry ran into the blue horsemen at Haw's Shop at ten o'clock on Saturday morning. The mounted skirmish lasted until dark.

Among the Federal dead was Private John Huff from Michigan—the trooper whose one lucky shot had killed Jeb Stuart.

As Lieutenant General Ewell made his way toward a weekend of much-needed rest down the road in Richmond, the long wagon trains of Federal misery moved off in the opposite direction. A steady stream of ambulance wagons drifted back along General Grant's trail all the way to Fredericksburg, the principal field hospital for his army on the road to permanent hospitals throughout Washington City.

Three weeks earlier, on May 7, 320 wagons and 488 horse-drawn ambulances had carried the Federal wounded from the Wilderness battlefield toward Fredericksburg. The wagon train of wounded which left Spotsylvania one week later was four miles long, to bring the number of Federal wounded in Fredericksburg to 6,000. By May 18, Washington City overflowed with 14,878 casualties, most of whom were from Grant's Virginia campaign. And by Friday, May 27, over 26,000 wounded boys in blue had followed the trail of pain and amputations through Fredericksburg.

The main Union hospital at Fredericksburg was the 134-year-old home of Confederate Colonel John Marye, called Brompton Plantation. The estate is now part of Washington College, and the great tree where the Federal wounded were laid in its shade still stands, more than 150 years later.

Sunday, May 29, General Lee positioned his lines running southwest to northeast, with the upper end on Totopotomoy Creek. Still bedridden, Marse Robert wrote home to Mother Lee: "Everybody is so kind that I am overwhelmed by it." In his sickbed, the weary and sick general had to entertain President Davis, who came the short distance up the road from Richmond.

Jefferson Davis and Robert Lee might have discussed the ever-waning strength of the Confederates and Grant's growing strength from inexhaustible supplies of Union soldier boys. Union General William "Baldy" Smith left Ben Butler's Federal line near Richmond late this Sunday night to join Grant. General Smith marched toward White House Landing with sixteen thousand men in the blue X and XVIII Corps, and they dragged sixteen cannon for Grant's artillery reserves. They had boarded transport barges for a boat ride along the James River, which flows to downtown Richmond. The boats were aimed for White House and for the Cold Harbor area. The force would reach White House Landing the next day, Monday morning.

On Monday, May 30, the race for the hamlet of Cold Harbor began on the road to Richmond.

When General Smith's reinforcements reached White House Landing at eleven o'clock Monday morning, his two corps were sixteen miles from Cold Harbor. Grant's four infantry corps again were slipping around Robert Lee's right flank, toward the southwest and Richmond. While Grant's numbers were still increasing, General Lee had not yet replaced half of his spring losses.

As Federal Baldy Smith unloaded at White House Landing in time for lunch, General Lee wired Richmond to confirm the southern shift of the blue army. Two blue corps were crossing to the south side of Totopotomoy Creek on the path toward the Chickahominy River, which saw so much bloodshed during The Seven Days. The Yankees were marching to Old Cold Harbor, close to its sister hamlet of Cold Harbor. Although the Confederates had now gone two full days without food, Robert Lee ordered Old Jube to take his Second Corps to pitch into the parts of Grant's army, which were temporarily isolated on the south side of the Totopotomoy.

Robert Rodes's gray division slammed into the Federals at two o'clock on Monday afternoon along the Old Church Road near Bethesda Church, five miles northeast of Mechanicsville, practically Richmond's outskirts. At first, the Federals gave ground. But when Jubal Early delayed his counterpunch, the blue V Corps had time to regroup. Their countercharge came at six o'clock, Monday evening. Yankee cannon fired at point-blank range and exterminated the 49th Virginia regiment of Stephen Ramseur's division. After the slaughter, the gray divisions of Early's Second Corps had to pull back in the darkness. The Battle of Bethesda Church left 1,159 Rebels bleeding on the darkened field beside 731 mangled Federals.

Monday night after Major General Early's debacle, General Lee could smell trouble in the wind. He detached Fitz Lee's cavalry troop southward to Cold Harbor, three miles southeast of Bethesda Church, where the left flank of Grant's mighty army rested. At 7:30 p.m., Lee wired President Davis to immediately send up reinforcements from General Beauregard's command at the Bermuda Hundred position along the James River, twenty-one miles downriver from Richmond. With Ben Butler's Yankee command weakened there by Baldy Smith's pullout, the troops could be spared to shore up Lee's lines at Bethesda, some twelve miles northeast of the capital. Robert Lee pleaded with Richmond that "delay will be disaster." Lee had never used that word before. By 8:30 p.m., orders were issued for Major General Robert Hoke's (Kentucky Military Institute, Class of '54) Confederate division to leave Beauregard's line the next day with seven thousand men.

On Tuesday, May 31, General Lee was still too weak and too sick to ride Traveller. So he rode in a carriage like a white-haired dandy to his new field headquarters at Shady Grove. This position put the weary general in the center of the Confederate battle line, which stretched for nine miles from Atlee's Station southeastward to Old Cold Harbor. At three o'clock on Tuesday afternoon, Richard Anderson's gray First Corps was sent down to within one mile of Old Cold Harbor. General Hoke's reinforcements coming up from Richmond and Fitz Lee's cavalry were also ordered to the Old Cold Harbor front, to place fifteen thousand Confederates there by first light on Wednesday.

The advance units of both armies raced for the Cold Harbor sector during Tuesday evening and through the night.

By seven o'clock on Tuesday night, Fitz Lee reported Yankee infantry falling in at Old Cold Harbor. In a nasty little skirmish, Phil Sheridan's cavalry of 6,500 troopers pushed Fitz Lee out of the hamlet and Old Cold Harbor fell to the Federals. General Grant then planned to have his main force join Baldy Smith's XVIII Corps coming up from Bermuda Hundred. The Federal VI Corps was ordered to march all night to the Cold Harbor front.

Even in his weakened condition, the aggression in Robert Lee's soul longed for the offensive. He sent Joe Kershaw's division to join Hoke's division for a dawn attack against Sheridan's blue cavalry the next day, June 1.

By the first day of June, the Army of Northern Virginia was hungry to the bone. For the last week of fighting along the North Anna and marching down to Cold Harbor, the men in tattered gray lived on hard crackers and rotten bacon. The army was showing signs of an epidemic of scurvy due to their wretched diet. General Lee ordered his weary men to dig and eat sassafras roots to cure the disease.

Seventy-two hours of on-and-off fighting began with General Lee's dawn assault on Wednesday morning, June 1.

Although the combative Robert Lee ordered an assault upon the Federal line at Old Cold Harbor for dawn on Wednesday, the Old Man was still too frail to take the field as he had done in the Wilderness campaign and in the near disaster of the Mule Shoe salient. The June 1 attempt to crack the long blue line had to be coordinated by General Lee's junior officers on the battlefield.

When the Wednesday sun climbed above the treetops at five o'clock in the morning, there was relative quiet between the lines. The Confederate thrust did not come until eight that morning. Former US congressman Colonel Lawrence Keitt led Joe Kershaw's gray First Corps brigade when it pitched into Phil Sheridan's blue cavalry. Federal horsemen on foot opened up with Sharps or Spencer, repeating rifles, the machine guns of the War Between the States. Within five minutes, Colonel Keitt was dead and his grand old brigade was destroyed. Two hours later, a second Rebel assault against the blue VI Corps was also repulsed.

With his army taking a beating, General Lee dragged himself to the field at four p.m. on Wednesday afternoon. The Old Man was behind his gray line one and a half miles west of Old Cold Harbor. When General Lee took the field, Baldy Smith's XVIII Corps of ten thousand Federals was deploying to reinforce General Grant's position. Within an hour, General Smith's bluecoats slammed into the gray First Corps after charging across a quarter-mile of certain death. The brave Yankees overran Dick Anderson's first line of defense but were pinned down by ferocious fire at the second Rebel line, well entrenched in a clearing beyond a large forest.

The Confederate right flank was crumbling as it struggled to extend toward the knoll called Turkey Hill, one mile south of Old Cold Harbor. By six o'clock in evening shadows, the Federals had pushed forward half a mile over the bodies of two thousand dead and wounded boys in bloody blue. Two divisions from the Federal VI Corps deployed in three lines of battle and the brave, battle-hardened Federals plowed heads-down into the Confederate line. Not until eight o'clock did the firefight slacken in the gathering darkness. The determined Federal assaults had cost Generals Grant and Meade 2,200 blue-clad casualties during five hours of fighting.

Neither side had scored a victory this bloody Wednesday. General Grant resolved to concentrate all five of his infantry corps at Cold Harbor for another, full frontal onslaught scheduled for the next day. Exhausted Federals tramped through the darkness all night to align the Army of the Potomac into a huge battering ram spread out between the trees. The blue line from the Yankee left to right flanks posted the I, VI, XVIII, V, and IX Corps, ready for battle.

But the Federal assault did not come on Thursday, June 2. Both armies spent the day digging. Fieldworks were hastily dug while the snipers blew the brains out of any soldier who looked above the breastworks to watch the digging in the opposite, enemy line. While the armies dug, General Grant set up housekeeping in field headquarters one and three-quarter miles northeast of Cold Harbor on the Burnett farm. He would stay there until June 12.

Still sick, General Lee managed to take the field this Thursday to oversee the digging of entrenchments. The gray line was now six miles long. The Rebel right flank was the strongest near Cold Harbor where Little Powell Hill's divisions of Major Generals Mahone and Wilcox were posted. While his army worked, General Lee rode from New Cold Harbor to Mechanicsville to find Major General John Breckinridge.

General Breckinridge brought two fresh brigades from the Shenandoah Valley to join Robert Lee's army. Young Breckinridge had been elected vice president of the United States to president James Buchanan in 1856. The youngest vice president in history, he ran for president in '60 as a Democrat, and so split the Democrat vote with Stephen Douglas that the rail-splitter from Springfield, Illinois, was elected president. General Breckinridge's brigades were sent to the Confederate right flank to assault the commanding Turkey Hill with Cadmus Wilcox's division. Skirmishing increased all day between the lines.

Breckinridge and Wilcox attacked and captured Turkey Hill, Thursday afternoon. Old Jube Early commanding Second Corps in Lee's army blasted into the Federal line on the Yankee right flank at three in the afternoon. The Confederates were beaten back.

At four o'clock, a steady rain began which would continue to drench the two armies all night. By nightfall, the Confederate line, with Turkey Hill added, extended further to the right all the way to the Chickahominy. Now thirteen miles long, the Rebel line was held by A. P. Hill's Third Corps on the left, Early's Second Corps in the center, and Dick Anderson's First Corps on the right.

Although Grant and Meade had planned a June 2 advance, the marching, digging, and rain required a postponement until 4:30 a.m. on Friday.

As the rain Thursday night pounded the war-weary armies, the veterans in the Federal breastworks felt the old familiar uneasiness when that certain something made the nighttime air difficult to breathe. New men swallowed hard when they watched the veterans spend the wet night with their sewing kits. The men who had already "seen the elephant" of mortal combat knew what the terrible stillness meant. So, they spent the night sewing makeshift name tags onto their sweat-stained shirts. No one wanted the wooden marker erected over a new hole in the ground to read UNKNOWN.

Ten

Before daylight Friday morning, three Federal corps of sixty thousand men loaded their single-shot, black-powder rifles and fell into line in the mud. At half past four, the Federals began a cannonade of the Confederate line. The barrage was loud enough to be heard in Richmond twelve miles away. Ten minutes later, John Gibbon's blue division ran cheering into the Confederate line. The Federals charged to within one hundred yards of the graybacks' breastworks.

At 4:50 a.m., in dawn shadows, two divisions of the Yankee VI Corps attacked in one huge battle line supported by Baldy Smith's XVIII Corps. The blue line was one and a half miles long. The Federals took double loads of canister, lead marbles square in the face from Confederate cannon only thirty yards away. The 12th New Hampshire Infantry simply blew away within ten minutes, leaving only torn, bloody shreds of men in the wet mud.

Ten minutes later, the entire Federal II Corps charged the Confederate rifle pits and artillery. The solid line of blue was twenty-eight feet deep. It held formation for only two minutes. Then the line melted into a puddle of blue and streams of red.

Within eight minutes, the Federal assault ground to a bloody and disastrous halt. Stunned bluecoats piled up their own dead in front of them and used the ripped bodies of their friends as cover against the molten wall of Rebel fire. Blood flowed in red rivulets through the rain-soaked muck until eight in the morning. In less than one hour, Lieutenant General Grant lost seven thousand men who were ground up in Robert Lee's meat grinder as the manful Federals launched fourteen assaults against Dick Anderson's gray First Corps.

Firing continued in pockets of pain until 1:30 in the afternoon. When Major General Meade ordered Baldy Smith to attack one more time, General Smith refused to massacre his XVIII Corps. General Grant then suspended his grand assault. The Army of the Potomac had been cut to ribbons.

Within an hour, Robert Lee had lost 1,500 men killed, wounded, or missing at Cold Harbor. But General Grant lost nearly 1,100 men killed, with over 4,500 more wounded.

For the next twenty-one years of his life, General and then President Grant never spoke of the Battle of Cold Harbor, but he did write about it in his deathbed memoirs. "I have always regretted that the last assault at Cold Harbor was ever made," he remembered. "At Cold Harbor, no advantage whatever was gained to compensate for the heavy loss we sustained."

The terrible May 1864 slaughter was also a milestone of sorts for Robert E. Lee: Never again would he have another decisive victory in the field.

This Friday holocaust came one day shy of a full month since General Grant had crossed the Rapidan River for his spring "Overland Campaign" offensive. During that month, the two great armies had never been out of contact with each other. In the bloodletting, General Lee had lost 33,600 men of whom some 16,000 were now marching northward to Yankee prison camps. The Federals suffered 55,000 casualties of whom 38,000 would soon be starving to death in Confederate prison camps.

Since crossing the Rapidan on May 4, Lieutenant General Grant had lost an average of two thousand Federals every day. But there were plenty more pink-faced teenagers where these dead and wounded had come from.

Robert Lee's loss of men was only surpassed by his sacrifice of general officers. The leadership of the Army of Northern Virginia had been nearly destroyed by this man Grant in only thirty days. Of fifty-eight generals present for duty on May 4, by June 3 General Lee had lost twenty-two general officers. Eight were dead, twelve were laid up in ghastly hospitals, and two were in Yankee prison camps. Among Lee's three infantry corps and one cavalry corps, Jeb Stuart was dead, Old Pete

Longstreet was grievously wounded, Richard Ewell was on sick leave in Richmond, and Powell Hill was weakening daily. One month of fighting Grant had cost Lee 37 percent of his generals.

But the real battle toll would be read in the anguished faces of the mothers who went daily to the newspapers, North and South, to see the newly posted casualty lists. Seven thousand Northern mothers and wives would soon see familiar names on the rolls of honor and grief. Perhaps none of them had ever heard of a widening on a Virginia dirt road named Cold Harbor. Now, they would remember it for the rest of their lonesome days.

During the all-night rain of Thursday, June 2, one boy in blue had scribbled in his pocket diary illuminated by campfire. Perhaps he had already printed his name on a slip of paper which he would soon sew to his blue tunic. By the time his bloated and rotting corpse was retrieved by the Federal stretcher bearers, the little slip of paper had worn off or washed away. His name is lost forever, and he lies in an unknown grave far from home. Only his diary survived. Anticipating the battle of Friday, the doomed boy who no longer had a name had scrawled his diary's last entry:

"June 3. Cold Harbor. I was killed."

He was.

Friday afternoon, June 3, passed with only pockets of picket and sniper fire under an early summer sun. The occasional Minie balls whirling through the humid air whistled over more than four thousand wounded Federals who continued to bleed, cry, and pray for water between the lines. Boy by boy, they lay and slowly shriveled from hemorrhage and the excruciating thirst it caused.

Friday marked two years and two days since the still-sickly Robert Lee had taken command of Joe Johnston's ragtag army and had turned its sagging morale into the stuff of legend. For twenty-four months of glory and gore, lightning marches, and bloody bare footprints in the snow, General Lee had nursed one overriding strategic objective: to keep the Federal host from getting their boots wet in the James River. General Lee never lost sight of one tactical certainty: When the Army of the Potomac crossed the James River to get south of Richmond, the war for Virginia was over. The James flowed through downtown Richmond.

Both exhausted armies spent one more day digging deeper into the Virginia soil, which oozed a putrid soup of old mud and fresh blood.

Perhaps Robert Lee felt something new in his weary bones this Saturday, June 4. He knew that he had to stop Grant at Cold Harbor and that he had failed. So in a quiet moment between paroxysms of diarrhea and the *pop, pop, pop* of the snipers, General Lee wrote a quick note to Mother Lee. The letter was dated Gaines Mill, Virginia, a battlefield of his momentous, first victories during the Battle of The Seven Days. This letter home was not about winning. Instead, he urged his crippled wife and his three daughters to leave Richmond before time ran out.

"I think you had better go as soon as you can," the dehydrating and worried father wrote. "Great danger is impending over us and, therefore, those not required to meet it or who might be overwhelmed by it, should it fall upon us, should get out of harm's way in time."

When he was not thinking of his family or of his fast walk to the camp latrine trench, General Lee contended with the never-ending chore of administering his hungry army. Part of Saturday was consumed issuing temporary field promotions. Major Generals Jubal Early and Dick Anderson were brevetted to the temporary rank of lieutenant general, befitting their new commands of Second Corps and First Corps. Brigadier General Billy Mahone was elevated to major general for his new posting to command Richard Anderson's old division. Stephen Ramseur's promotion to major general to take over Old Jube's division was Ramseur's twenty-seventh birthday present from his Uncle Robert. Young Ramseur, only four years out of West Point, became the youngest West Point graduate appointed to such high rank in the entire Rebel army.

By Sunday morning, the thousands of unburied dead and soon to be dead Federals putrefied until the living were vomiting between their knees with each breath. Yankee Major General Winfield Hancock, twenty years out of West Point and the Union general who destroyed Pickett's Charge at Gettysburg, begged George Gordon Meade to arrange a burial truce before Hancock's II Corps came unglued from the unspeakable stench of the corpses, which were quickly swelling until they turned black and exploded from internal, gaseous rot. Hundreds of the bloated and blackened corpses had lain in the Virginia summer sun since the first engagement on Wednesday, three full days ago.

At four o'clock, Sunday afternoon, General Grant sent a message through the lines to Robert Lee, his old comrade from the war in Mexico almost twenty years earlier. Grant suggested that unarmed men from both sides could gather their own casualties during lulls in the picket fire. Deliberately, Lieutenant General Grant did not ask for a formal truce. While dead boys in blue rotted and the wounded whimpered to go home, Generals Lee and Grant engaged in a nasty squabble over nineteenth-century military etiquette.

General Lee rejected Grant's proposal, since an informal truce could lead to dangerous and deadly "misunderstanding." Grant declined to ask for a truce since, traditionally, the officer who first asked for a truce was admitting defeat. So the bodies continued to stink General Hancock out of his breastworks.

After midnight on Sunday, General Grant repeated his request for unarmed burial parties to move between the lines between noon and three p.m., Monday afternoon, June 6. And again, Robert Lee refused unless the proud Federal asked for an official truce under the rules of warfare between gentlemen.

The Monday gathering of the dead and wounded never happened. The dead rotted and the dying bled for another day under the Virginia summer sun.

Late Monday afternoon, General Grant swallowed his pride when he could no longer take a breath without gagging. He sent a message requesting a formal truce which did not reach General Lee until seven o'clock in the evening, June 6. Some wounded men had now lain in the sun for a week.

Lee's acceptance of a Monday-night truce did not reach Grant until midnight, Monday. So the blackened corpses rotted one more night and one more day.

At last, the stretcher bearers went out under white flags at six o'clock Tuesday evening, June 7. Only two hours were allowed to gather the dead and wounded. The Federals needed five grisly days to bury their dead, who were blackened and bloated beyond any resemblance to once-heroic soldiers. When there were the misunderstandings that Lee had feared,

Lieutenant General Grant did not fail to behave like a warrior gentleman. That Tuesday, General Lee received a longhand note passed through the lines from General Grant, who confirmed that,

> *Two officers and six men of the 8th and 25th North Carolina Regts [sic], who were out in search of the bodies of officers of their respective regiments, were captured and brought into our lines, owing to this want of understanding. I regret this, but will state that as soon as I learned the fact, I directed that they should not be held as prisoners, but must be returned to their commands.*

While the bodies rotted and the notes passed between the lines, General Lee on June 4 had ordered a nightly cannonade to harass the Yankees and to prevent their quiet withdrawal southward during the night, which was Grant's usual plan. The nightly bombardment began every night at promptly nine o'clock and continued through June 10. During these six days of digging, waiting, and stinking, the trenches of each army were five miles long, and the opposing armies were no more than thirty yards apart in some places.

Before the diplomacy of the June 7 truce was finalized, Robert Lee wrote another letter home to his wife and daughters in Richmond. He repeated his warning of June 4: "You had better leave Richmond as soon as you can. I hope you will do so."

Also on June 7, General Lee had to take part in more troop shifts to guard all corners of the Virginia front against approaching Federals. General Breckinridge on June 7 was detached with 2,100 men from Lee's force back to the Shenandoah Valley, the back door to Richmond. Lee's army in the field and the Richmond home guard only mustered 73,000 troops to face Grant's 125,000. The graybacks at Cold Harbor only numbered 49,000, with another 9,000 Confederates in the Valley. General Grant's Cold Harbor line was only nine miles from Richmond.

The armies remained behind their fieldworks at Cold Harbor for two weeks.

News from elsewhere in Virginia did little to improve Robert Lee's disposition, although his dysentery attacks had improved. Federal raiders under General David Hunter's command had captured Staunton in the Shenandoah Valley on June 6. By June 7, as the Cold Harbor burial parties went to work, Phil Sheridan's blue cavalry was on the road to join Hunter at the vital hub on the important Virginia Central Railroad. By June 9, General Beauregard reported Federals on the horizon at Petersburg, twenty miles south of Richmond.

Located due south of the Confederate capital city, Petersburg sat astride the Appomattox River, which flowed to the James. Five different, Rebel railroad lines converged on Petersburg. Most of Richmond's food and stores traveled those rails.

To lose Petersburg would be to lose Richmond, and then Virginia, and then the War for Southern Independence.

During the week of June 6, General Lee spoke passionately about the certain result of General Grant crossing the James River. "We must destroy this army of Grant's before he gets to the James River. If he gets there," the Old Man sighed, "it will become a siege. And then, it will be a mere question of time."

Never before during Robert Lee's thirty-five years in uniform, blue or gray, had he spoken of defeat.

Between his casualties, his bad news from the western theater, and his ailing bowels, Robert Lee was beset with continuing trouble feeding his weary army. June 10, he wrote War Secretary James Seddon to beg for vegetables for his scurvy-ridden divisions.

On June 11, Federal Major General David Hunter (West Point, '22) captured the village of Lexington in the Valley. Old Jack's bones rested there. General Hunter rewarded Lexington for her contributions to the Confederate cause: He set fire to the Virginia Military Academy, and he desecrated the town's tiny academy called Washington College. Hunter would aim next for Lynchburg to cut Richmond off from the west. To stop Hunter, on June 13, General Lee detached Jubal Early and all of Second Corps to the Shenandoah Valley. Lee now had only 28,000 men on the Cold Harbor line to face Grant's four-to-one manpower advantage.

With the stroke of his dip pen, General Lee lost one-fourth of his army with General Grant's entire juggernaut in his front.

At least by Sunday, June 12, Robert Lee was finally feeling much better after his twenty-day siege of dysentery. "I am well again, thank God," he wrote to Mother Lee and the girls.

While Old Jube packed for the Valley and General Lee recovered his bodily vigor, Lieutenant General Grant finally had enough of the Cold Harbor field with its 1,100 fresh Federal graves and the piles of amputated arms and legs outside his surgeons' tents. Grant spent Sunday afternoon breaking camp at the Burnett farm. He planned another all-night march around Robert Lee's right flank. Neither the Wilderness nor Bloody Angle nor Cold Harbor could make Grant turn his blue back upon Virginia as had all of his predecessors in command of the Army of the Potomac. Finally, Mr. Lincoln had found his bloody hammer who would never turn northward.

Federal brass bands began playing on the night of Sunday, June 12. They had played merrily before the slaughter at Bloody Angle in the Mule Shoe. Now they played again in the darkness. The concert meant one thing: The Yankees were on the march under a full moon. They could have but one objective—the James River and Petersburg—where, as Lee knew all too well, it would then become only a question of time.

During Sunday night and before daybreak Monday, the blue II, VI, and IX Corps slipped out of their Cold Harbor breastworks and marched southeast toward Charles City Courthouse, twenty miles away. Baldy Smith's XVIII Corps, so badly mauled at Cold Harbor on June 3, marched back to White House Landing to board transport barges for the Bermuda Hundred line. The Federal V Corps marched westward in the opposite direction toward the Confederate right flank as a decoy. This time, the decoy worked: General Lee concentrated on General Warren's blue divisions for a wasted day. During the night of Monday, June 13, the Federals concentrated at Charles City. General Lee would not know the position of Grant's full force for three critical days. Without Jeb Stuart and his cavalry, Robert Lee was blind.

Before first light on Monday, Jubal Early led the gray Second Corps out of the Cold Harbor line. As the long gray line of Stonewall Jackson's foot cavalry turned their backs on their Uncle Robert, they could not know that they were leaving the Army of Northern Virginia forever. Old Jack's man, Sandie Pendleton, rode with them. Only the day before, Sandie had visited with his Kate in Richmond. She was four months pregnant.

As Second Corps pulled out of line, scouts Monday morning advised General Lee that the Federal lines were empty—abandoned to the last man during the night. Lee had no idea whether Grant was marching south to the James or southeast toward the Chickahominy. The Confederate cavalry divisions of Fitz Lee and Wade Hampton had been off since June 7, protecting the Virginia Central Railroad from Phil Sheridan's raids. Only Rooney Lee's little cavalry detachment was present. No long-range reconnaissance was possible.

Lee quickly put his army in motion. By nightfall, Confederates converged on White Oak Swamp. Powell Hill's Third Corps marched to Riddell's Shop, twelve miles east of Chaffin's and Drewry's Bluffs on the James. Dick Anderson's First Corps marched to Malvern Hill, the scene of Lee's first disaster two years earlier during The Seven Days. On the last of The Seven Days, when Lee pushed McClellan's blue army away from Richmond, Lee attacked the bluecoats atop Malvern Hill. More than five thousand Confederates were slaughtered, and Little Mac made good his army's escape to the James River to fight another three years. Robert Lee hoped to attack Grant the next day, June 14—if he could find him.

The two armies marched through Monday, June 13, leaving behind them human carnage never before imagined. During the past two weeks, Lee had given up 4,847 casualties to Grant's 14,931. Of that total, 16,240 men in blue or gray had been killed or wounded in fourteen days. Since Grant's crossing of the Rapidan into the Wilderness, some 84,000 men had been killed, wounded, or captured in both armies. During those five bitter weeks, Grant had suffered 45,551 men killed or wounded to Lee's 20,734.

The next two days were hours of agonizing darkness for Robert Lee. For the first time since May 3, he had no sight of the legions in blue. General Grant could be anywhere.

Lee did not know that by Monday night, June 13, the blue II Corps was already at Wilcox Landing on the north bank of the James River. General Lee had hoped to plow into the Federals with Hill's corps leading the charge on June 14 on Long Bridge Road, just west of the Chickahominy. But that Tuesday morning, Little Powell found no Yankees. Instead, the

Federal II Corps was boarding ferryboats at Wilcox Landing to cross the James. By four o'clock Tuesday afternoon, Federal engineers were busy building a massive pontoon bridge seven hundred yards long across the James at Weyanoke, three miles downriver from Wilcox Landing. The bridge was supported by 101 pontoons, with an opening in the middle to allow Federal gunboats to pass up the James toward Richmond. The pontoon bridge was finished by eleven p.m. Tuesday night.

Robert Lee spent June 14 and 15 resting his First and Third Corps at Riddell's Shop. Lee paced anxiously, waiting for reports from his scouts.

Federal supply wagons formed a train of overwhelming superiority at least fifty miles long, ready to cross the new pontoon bridge at Weyanoke.

On Wednesday morning before dawn, June 15, the Federal IX Corps crossed the pontoons over the James River, bound for Petersburg. The blue V Corps crossed at Wilcox Landing over the bobbing bridge at two in the morning, Thursday, June 16, and continued crossing until late afternoon. Sixty thousand men in blue walked across the James River. To feed themselves, they drove 3,500 beef cattle, and thirty-five miles of supply wagons across the river. Yankee mounted cavalry crossed on June 17. The next day, the pontoon bridge was dismantled.

Ulysses Grant's bridges only operated in one direction.

By midday June 15, Grant already had 45,000 men on the south side of the James River. The Army of Northern Virginia had been depleted to a force of only 28,500 men to defend the Petersburg front since General Early and Second Corps were gone, along with two-thirds of the cavalry and Breckinridge's division. Also detached now was Major General Robert Hoke's division. The thirty-seven-year-old North Carolina officer was sent to defend Drewry's Bluff between Petersburg and Richmond on the James.

While Robert Lee paced and struggled to read Lieutenant General Grant's mind to guess his whereabouts on June 15, Lee received a wire from General Beauregard. The cable arrived at Riddell's Shop at noon and was already four hours old. Beauregard telegraphed dire pleas for reinforcements from Lee since Grant was believed to be at Harrison's Landing about to cross the James and Baldy Smith's XVIII Corps of Federals was scouted back at Bermuda Hundred. Old Bory warned Robert Lee of a likely Federal assault against the vital Petersburg railroad junction.

Well up the Confederate line, Powell Hill skirmished with Federals early Wednesday morning. The little fight occurred near the old battleground at Malvern Hill, on the north side of the James, eighteen miles southeast of Richmond. By nine o'clock in the morning, June 15, Little Powell could report that the Yankees he fought seemed to be only mounted cavalry, but not infantry. This suggested that the real Federal objective was most likely not the north side of the James but the south side—in the direction of Petersburg. Finally, between Hill and Beauregard's intelligence reports, Robert Lee was beginning to see Lieutenant General Grant's plans after three days in the dark. But there still was no hard confirmation that Grant had crossed the James, southbound.

If Grant were driving for Petersburg, then Beauregard was right to panic. The Petersburg front was a fortified line ten miles long with fifty-five artillery pits. The line of works two miles east of town was called the Dimmock Line—a nineteenth-century Maginot Line of breastworks and cannon. Old Bory had only 15,000 men to stave off Grant's 100,000 bluecoats. By dawn on June 15 while Grant was crossing the James, General Smith's blue XVIII Corps from the Bermuda Hundred position was marching hard for Petersburg to assault the town from the northeast. Smith would come in across the Appomattox River at Broadway Landing while the blue II Corps advanced down from Wilcox Landing east of town. The Federal II Corps was fourteen miles east of Smith's corps.

Wednesday night, Lee's doubts ended at seven o'clock when General Smith slammed hard into the Dimmock Line east of Petersburg. By nine p.m., the Federals had captured a mile of the northern end of the north-south, fortified Confederate line. Sixteen Rebel cannon had been captured. The blue II Corps hesitated to continue the attack in the darkness. This fortuitous delay saved Petersburg from being completely overrun on the night of June 15. The town should have fallen then and there.

Old Bory spent all night Wednesday retreating. The Federals were pushing him back from the Bermuda Hundred toward Petersburg. General Lee received Beauregard's panicked wire after two o'clock, Thursday morning. But the cable was dated Wednesday night, 11:15 p.m. General

Beauregard pleaded with Lee for six thousand men to hold the Petersburg front. General Lee ordered George Pickett's famous division to Drewry's Bluff from Frayser's Farm, another battlefield of The Seven Days. Dick Anderson's First Corps was ordered to the collapsing Bermuda Hundred line. This detachment left Robert Lee with only 24,000 men north of the James River. Pickett crossed the James for the bluff by eight a.m. on Thursday morning, June 16. Two hours later, General Lee left Riddell's Shop for the bluff, seven miles north of the Bermuda Hundred. Beside the dirt road, Robert Lee knelt and prayed for divine deliverance.

When General Lee received word from Beauregard at ten o'clock Thursday morning that an advance infantry probe of Federals was laying siege to Petersburg, Lee still had no confirmation that Grant's whole force was moving either south to Petersburg or north to attack Richmond directly. By one p.m. Thursday afternoon, Anderson's First Corps skirmished with Federals west of the Bermuda Hundred, where the bluecoats blocked the Petersburg Pike halfway between Drewry's Bluff and Petersburg. George Pickett's division was blocked from marching south from the bluff to Petersburg.

General Lee had no choice but to send another division to Drewry's Bluff, twelve miles north of Petersburg. The bluff overlooked the river on the west side of the James, which runs north and south between Petersburg and Richmond. By Thursday, General Lee had two divisions south of the James, one division north of the river, with Powell Hill's three divisions east of the river near Malvern Hill. The Confederates then had 23,000 men north of the James and 23,000 south—with no real confirmation of where Grant had his main body of troops.

Desperate for military intelligence, at four p.m. on Thursday afternoon, Lee wired General Beauregard at Petersburg for confirmation that Grant had crossed the James. Three hours later, Old Bory wired back that he did not know if Grant had crossed the James for Petersburg, or remained north of the river for an assault against Richmond.

Old Bory had his hands full defending Petersburg. The second Federal assault against the town came Thursday when General Burnside's IX Corps, Hancock's II Corps, and Baldy Smith's XVIII Corps all pushed hard against Beauregard's thin lines. Working in concert, unlike yesterday, the Federals captured another four miles of the Dimmock Line. Late Thursday, the blue V Corps arrived on the field and deployed all night while George Gordon Meade took command of the Petersburg offensive.

After falling in all night Thursday, the third Federal assault came with first light, Friday, June 17. A general advance was led by Burnside's IX Corps, and the bluecoats captured the southern end of the beleaguered Dimmock Line. This position had been Beauregard's right flank, anchored on the Shand farm. The Yankees pushed one and a half miles closer to town on the northern end of the Confederates' inner line of fieldworks. The outer line was gone. With his lines collapsing at nine in the morning, Old Bory had to wire Lee again that he still could not confirm Grant's position, although Petersburg was under siege from the east.

But the news was not all bad. George Pickett brilliantly attacked the Yankee position and drove them from the Bermuda Hundred line abandoned by Beauregard. Two divisions from Anderson's gray First Corps pushed the Yankees back by four o'clock, Friday afternoon. Meanwhile, downriver the Yankee cavalry was crossing the James with five thousand beef cattle at Weyanoke.

Finally, at 4:30 p.m. on Friday afternoon, Beauregard wired General Lee confirmation that the Army of the Potomac had indeed crossed the James River, and that no less than thirty thousand Federals were marching toward Petersburg. Confirmation had come for the first time from Federal prisoners. General Lee ordered Powell Hill to take Third Corps to Chaffin's Bluff, on the east bank of the James opposite Drewry's Bluff. Joe Kershaw's gray division was detached from Chaffin's to the Bermuda Hundred. By dusk this Friday, Robert Lee was on the Petersburg field with his headquarters established at the Clay house, three miles southeast of Chester, east of the Petersburg Pike. The glory days of outmaneuvering poorly generaled Federals by lightning strikes were gone forever.

Eleven

By ten o'clock Friday night, June 17, General Lee had received a 6:40 p.m. wire from General Beauregard warning that Old Bory would soon have to evacuate Petersburg. Such a disaster would expose Richmond to frontal assault up the James River. Lee immediately ordered Joe Kershaw to head downriver to Petersburg at daybreak and Powell Hill to cross the James from Chaffin's. Once on the Petersburg Pike north of town, Hill was to wait for further orders on Saturday.

While General Lee labored on Friday to save Petersburg, Lieutenant General Grant prepared for siege warfare.

Grant ordered expansion of the new Federal supply base at City Point on the James, seven miles northeast of Petersburg. From this new supply depot, he would besiege Richmond if it took forever. Before the sun had set on Friday, General Grant issued orders to renovate the old railroad between City Point and Petersburg. The rails were operational by July 5, and an entirely new, railroad complex would be finished by August 1.

Friday night and Saturday morning, June 18, intelligence reports to Robert Lee were confirming the Federal invasion of the Virginia heartland. Forty minutes after midnight, Friday, General Beauregard wired Lee a simple report: "Grant on the field with his whole army." Lee had already dispatched General Charles Field's division to follow Kershaw's division on the road to Petersburg. By 3:30 Saturday morning, Rooney Lee's cavalry had reached Wilcox Landing on the north bank of the James, only to find it empty. The Yankee crossing must have been complete. This was the first, ironclad confirmation of Grant's course since the Federals had left the Cold Harbor line five days earlier. General Lee

94

ordered Powell Hill to leave one division on the north side of the Appomattox River and to continue with his other two divisions, south to the Petersburg line. Anderson's First Corps would complete the deployment of gray divisions.

Saturday, June 18, marked the fourth day of death. At dawn, the Federals made their fourth assault to take Petersburg. Three blue corps of infantry were aligned along a three-mile-wide front for the attack. They found the Confederate defenses empty. Behind Petersburg, the graybacks were coming in at a run to bolster Old Bory's fragile line. By 7:30 Saturday morning, Joe Kershaw's division was jogging through Blandford Cemetery southeast of town across the Jerusalem Plank Road. General Field's division followed two hours later as General Lee fed troops into the line. By eleven a.m., Robert Lee stood at Beauregard's side. Petersburg held.

As always, Powell Hill's boys arrived Saturday afternoon at the last possible moment. The gray Third Corps had been on the march since three o'clock in the morning. By the time the Army of Northern Virginia dug in along Old Bory's front, John B. Hood's embattled and ferocious Texas Brigade had been decimated, mustering only 435 men.

Saturday marked the fourth day of massive troop shifts. After the Federals spent June 15 crossing the James River, there were 45,000 Yankees south of the river, with less than 19,000 Confederates to stop them. By the next day, Grant had 63,000 men across the James, without any apparent increase in the gray troop strength. By the third day, June 17, Grant mustered 94,000 men marching toward Petersburg, where Lee's concentration of troops had increased Southern arms to a mere 27,000 men. By Friday night, the final troop disposition was nearly in place, with 111,000 Federals facing only 31,000 Confederates. This Saturday, the fourth day of the Petersburg offensive, only 50,000 Confederates held in check 113,000 Yankees, now that the better part of Lee's two remaining corps were on the field.

The four days of fighting east of Petersburg, June 15 through June 18, had cost Grant and Meade 8,000 casualties. Since crossing the Rapidan River on May 4, the Federals had lost 65,000 men to death, wounds, and Rebel prison camps. Union Generals Grant and Meade had suffered more casualties in six weeks than Robert Lee had infantry troops in his entire army on the day that the Federal Overland Campaign began.

The mass killings abated for the next three days. Sunday, June 19, Robert Lee enjoyed church services in Petersburg after living six weeks under canvas. By this Sabbath morning under summer Virginia sunshine, the gray Petersburg front was twenty-six miles long, from White Oak Swamp twelve miles east of Richmond all the way around to the Jerusalem Plank Road south of Petersburg. The Confederate line of rifle pits and field fortifications crossed the James River twice.

That momentarily quiet Sunday, General Lee sent a longhand note to Mother Lee. "Never forget me or our suffering country," wrote the weary old soldier.

Between Richmond and Petersburg was the bulge in the James River called the Bermuda Hundred—an eastward-pointing peninsula filled with Federals. On June 21, Grant ordered General Ben Butler in the Bermuda Hundred bottleneck to lay another pontoon bridge across the James on the peninsula's northernmost point, east of the Petersburg-Richmond line.

The next day, Wednesday, Billy Mahone's gray division of three brigades skirmished with two Yankee divisions. In the action south of Petersburg along the Jerusalem Plank Road, the fiery Mahone captured 1,600 Federal prisoners and four cannon.

That same Wednesday, June 22, Lieutenant General Grant had a visitor from Washington City. Abraham Lincoln had come to call at Grant's base at City Point, only eight miles from Petersburg. The haggard president had visited George McClellan beside Antietam Creek after that horrific battle. Today, Mr. Lincoln was much more at ease with his first, fighting general. However long it might take, the president had no doubt that the end of the war was within the grasp of Ulysses Grant.

While General Grant and President Lincoln visited at City Point, the Federal VI Corps tried to maneuver around General Lee's far right flank—as they had labored to do since the Wilderness. The goal was the strategic Weldon Railroad running southward out of Petersburg. The vital tracks linked the Petersburg-Richmond front with supplies from the Deep South. The assaults of June 22 and 23 failed to cut the railroad, but did cut the Jerusalem Plank Road, which ran north and south from Petersburg. This movement lengthened Grant's line into a semicircle running from east of Petersburg down toward the southwest.

June 24, the Federals brought up their terrifying mortars. The squat cannon could lob shells up and into the Confederate trench line around Petersburg until the bitter end, no matter how long it took.

As if Robert Lee had nothing else to haunt his weary mind and weakening heart, Mother Lee and daughter Mary Custis battled deadly typhoid fever in Richmond during the last week of June. Summer heat and the pestilence of Richmond's military hospitals overflowing with festering wounds had turned Richmond into a swamp of death and disease. Mother Lee was especially ill. When the Yankee mortars arrived June 24, General Lee wrote to his sick and crippled wife about leaving Richmond. Finally, Mrs. Lee had agreed to leave for healthier climates. "I am glad to hear that you have appointed a time for leaving Richmond," the worried husband wrote. "As sorry as I shall be to be farther separated from you, I shall take great comfort in your safer and more pleasant situation. Do not delay your departure."

By late June, Little Powell Hill's Third Corps was the only whole corps left in the Army of Northern Virginia. Although Hill was rapidly wasting away from his chronic pelvic disease, he exhibited superhuman endurance. Along the Petersburg line, Little Powell was everywhere. He rode up and down the line on Champ to personally inspect the growing network of trenches.

With James Longstreet still hospitalized from his Wilderness wound and Baldy Ewell still recovering in Richmond from his recent collapse, A. P. Hill was the last of Lee's original corps command structure. The Old Man came to rely heavily upon Lieutenant General Hill and to have great affection for the red-bearded, green-eyed general, who wore his red "battle shirt" when the air was white with gunpowder smoke.

The gray, legendary Second Corps continued its isolated trek through the Shenandoah Valley under the command of Jubal Early. On Saturday, June 25, Second Corps marched through Lexington, where General Hunter's Yankees had burned Virginia Military Institute. At Lexington, the corps paid its respects to Stonewall Jackson, the corps' great captain.

Second Corps marched past Old Blue Light's lonesome grave. Brigade after brigade passed with heads bare and rifles reversed in silent tribute to their own Old Jack, now one year in the sacred Valley soil.

The next day, Sunday, Robert Lee sweated in the Petersburg heat. He described the misery of siege warfare in a letter to Mother Lee. "It is perfectly stifling and then the dust is so dense that the atmosphere is distressing," he wrote. "The men suffer a great deal in the trenches and this condition of things with the extreme heat of the sun nearly puts an end to military operations."

Four days later, General Lee wrote to daughter Mildred, his Precious Life, to plead for the speedy departure of Mother Lee from Richmond. "The sooner she leaves Richmond, in my opinion, the better."

Thursday, June 30, General Lee's thoughts again turned to home. He had taken up residence in field headquarters at Petersburg on the Shippen family estate, called Violet Bank, beside the Appomattox River.

When he stood amid the carnage at Fredericksburg in December of '62, Robert Lee had looked for the old tree in whose shade he had courted Mary Custis. Now, on this June 30, the husband reflected upon his marriage to Mother Lee thirty-three years ago, on this day. Under the withering sun and among vermin-infested trenches, the old soldier thought of kinder times. "Do you recollect what a happy day thirty-three years ago this was?" he wrote to his crippled wife only twenty miles up the road. "How many hopes and pleasures it gave birth to. God has been very merciful and kind to us."

The Army of Northern Virginia had refused to die in the sea of boys' blood which ran in black puddles during The Seven Days' bloodbath at Malvern Hill, at Second Manassas, in the stupefying slaughter beside Antietam Creek, on the heights of Fredericksburg, in the screaming charge through the briars at Chancellorsville where Stonewall fell, on the bloody mile and a half of open ground beneath Cemetery Ridge where George Pickett had failed to do the impossible at Gettysburg, and during the six weeks of daily carnage from the Wilderness through Bloody Angle, Cold Harbor, and the race to Petersburg.

Now, instead of dying soldiers' deaths on an open field of glory, the gray army of Robert Lee dug deeply into the Petersburg trenches to await a slow grinding down. The harried shifts of a division from the left to prop up the sagging right would be replaced by a daily war against starvation and disease. Never again would the cloud of dust on the horizon be Little Powell's Light Division rushing the field to save the day when the gray army's life hung in the balance. The sound of two hundred cannon shaking the earth like God's own tread would be replaced by that sound made when rail-thin bellies go hungry for days on end. Courage hard as flint cannot defeat hunger, thirst, and pustulating infection.

For two years, the Army of Northern Virginia had run on glory and on the single-minded leadership of Robert Lee, who was to his men and boys their Uncle Robert, or Marse Robert. By Petersburg, the army was running only on memories.

More than ever, the wasting gray army endured simply because their Uncle Robert endured.

In the white-bearded shadow of Robert E. Lee, the Army of Northern Virginia down to the last teenage drummer boy saw the kind of man each boy hoped to become. For this legion under siege to keep from turning into dust and softly blowing away, Robert Lee only had to keep on being. Lawyer, former Virginia governor, and brigadier general in the Confederate Army, Henry Wise understood the Army of Northern Virginia's devotion to their Marse Robert. The son of Henry Wise was killed in February of 1862. "You are the country to these men," General Wise would say. "They fought for you." Yankee Major General George Gordon Meade was married to the sister of the second wife of Virginia governor and general, Henry Wise.

Twelve

WHEN THE LONG BLUE LINE HAD MARCHED OUT OF THE WILDERNESS, they had cheered when they realized that they were not marching north. And they kept cheering from lonely bivouacs and along miles of shallow graves beside the road, which led ever closer to Richmond. Their horrendous casualties paled before the simple fact that, under Ulysses S. Grant, they had continued to put one boot ahead of the other, and always toward Richmond. After the defeats these boys in blue had suffered under the leadership of Generals McClellan, Pope, Hooker, and Burnside, the cigar-chewing Grant had turned the survivors into winners. They could taste it, even while they roasted under the same searing sun which burned the Confederates inside their trench line.

And Lieutenant General Grant listened to his military engineers.

Beyond the thirty miles of Petersburg trenches and rifle pits, the massive Army of the Potomac tightened the noose throughout the summer of '64. With engineering precision, Generals Grant and Meade laid siege to the town. During the two months since crossing the Rapidan, General Grant had done what no Federal commander in the East had done before him: He had never turned back; he had never retreated. Grant kept his eye on Richmond with the will of a freight train going down the track. His bloodied divisions knew it, and cheered him for it.

By the first day of July after only two weeks entrenched at Petersburg, the Confederates imagined that they heard the strange sound of digging underneath their trench lines and breastworks. General Lee, the old civil engineer, ordered listening shafts to be dug along his front. But the holes produced only more sweat and thirst.

On July 9, Lieutenant General Grant ordered the building of permanent siege works for starving out the Rebels beside the Appomattox River. Two days later, General Lee's muster rolls counted 55,000 men. The suffering in both armies was aggravated by a Virginia drought. When rain finally fell mercifully on July 19, it was the first rain in six weeks.

As heat, filth, and thirst reduced both armies to dust-caked specters, General Lee began to view his worthy enemy as a sledgehammer. "Where are we to get sufficient troops to oppose Grant?" an impatient Robert Lee complained in a July 24 letter to son Custis. "His talent and strategy consists in accumulating overwhelming numbers."

Wednesday, July 27, the Yankee II Corps crossed the James River bound for Richmond. Robert Lee sent Henry Heth's Third Corps division up to Chaffin's Bluff to deflect the new threat to the capital. Blood flowed on Thursday. Friday, Charles Field's Confederate division was sent north to support Heth. By Friday night, General Lee had concluded that the push by the blue II Corps was only a feint, a diversion to mask something on the main line at Petersburg. At two o'clock Saturday morning, July 30, General Lee put his entire line on alert in the trenches. Perhaps after six weeks of sitting under the cruel sun, General Grant was planning some kind of demonstration.

Saturday morning, at sixteen minutes before five a.m., the Confederate line exploded in an earthquake on Baxter Road, one mile southeast of Petersburg, just east of the Jerusalem Plank Road.

The ground convulsed. Hungry sleeping soldiers who had burrowed into their trenches like grayback moles awoke flying into the Virginia sky. Some must have died while still airborne, imagining that they had opened their eyes already halfway to Heaven.

The strange digging sounds heard beneath the Rebel lines for a month had been coal miners in the 48th Pennsylvania Infantry hacking a 510-foot tunnel from the Federal trenches into the earth beneath the Confederate fieldworks.

With first light, the Federals detonated four tons of black powder under the Petersburg works. At least 278 Confederates were instantly killed or buried alive, to suffocate. Nine South Carolina infantry companies and four cannon evaporated into thin air.

General Lee heard the horrendous explosion and received the first reports of a massive breech in his defenses by 6:10 a.m. The explosion created a crater 30 feet deep, 135 feet long, and 90 feet wide. When eleven Federal regiments poured shouting into the broken Rebel line, the Battle of the Crater began.

By the time Robert Lee and General Beauregard stood side by side only five hundred yards from the bedlam, one of the war's most ferocious and pitiful brawls was under way.

By 8:00 a.m., fourteen Federal regiments had stormed the opening in General Lee's fortifications. To stem the tide, four Confederate cannon near the crater fired six hundred shells at point-blank range into the Federals' faces. Between 8:00 and 10:30 a.m., two Confederate countercharges stopped the bluecoats. Two and a half hours of hand-to-hand combat followed.

The crater quickly became a muddy cauldron of blood, bowels, and brains as wild-eyed men shot and clubbed each other with the abandon of the Bloody Angle at Spotsylvania.

Not until 3:30 p.m. on Saturday did the Confederates push the exhausted and brutalized Federals out of their shattered line. The crater was a slaughter of trapped Federals. When an entire division of proud black troops climbed into the pit, the 29th US Colored Infantry regiment went into the hole with 450 men and lost 322. Of the 4,000 Federals killed, wounded, or captured, the black infantrymen accounted for 40 percent of the dead Union troops. Repulsing the assault cost General Lee 1,500 men. Some 1,500 bluecoats were rounded up as prisoners. Looking back, Lieutenant General Grant would remember the Battle of the Crater at Petersburg as a "stupendous failure."

The next day as the burial details dragged gray- and blue-clad limbs and bodies out of the crater, Robert Lee's thoughts turned to his ailing wife and to his underwear.

Mother Lee was recovering from her summer bout of typhoid and a serious bruise from a fall. She had finally left Richmond for the Bremo Plantation of Dr. Cary Charles Cocke, eighty miles west of Richmond on the James. Her anxious husband in the Petersburg trenches remained concerned that she would tax her crippled legs while her crippled fingers made the old soldier a set of long woolies for the coming winter.

"How came you to be walking about on polished floors and making me drawers?" the general demanded with mock gravity. "My Agnes considers herself a great cutter and fitter. Why did you not let her try her hand upon some masculine garments?" And with a gently paternal wink to his twenty-three-year-old unmarried daughter, the weary father added, "It is time she was learning, for my hopes in a certain quarter are not yet relinquished."

After three quiet days of worrying about feeding his army and marrying off his three daughters, General Lee had to deal with another troop shift by General Grant. On Thursday, August 4, scouts confirmed that Grant was sending a force downriver on the James, probably bound for the Shenandoah Valley, where Jubal Early camped with Second Corps. Two days later, Lee rode the twenty miles up to Richmond with Dick Anderson. A capital council of war agreed to detach Joe Kershaw's division and Fitz Lee's cavalry division from the Petersburg front. They would march to Culpeper, seventy miles northwest of Richmond, to harass the Federals' left flank on the eastern side of the Shenandoah Valley. Dick Anderson would leave First Corps to command the detachment. The force set out the same day.

On August 9, while Lieutenant General Anderson headed west, Confederate sappers blew up an ammunition dump at General Grant's City Point base. The blast nearly blew Grant out of his chair where he was sitting only 150 yards from the explosion. The exploding magazine killed forty-three Federals.

The day Rebel rangers were blowing up City Point, General Lee continued his constant vigil over his starving and filthy army in the trenches. "The soap ration for this army has become a serious question," Robert Lee wrote to President Davis. "The great want of cleanliness which is a necessary consequence of these very limited issues is now producing sickness among the men in the trenches, and must [a]ffect their self-respect and morale."

Two days later, Lee finally appointed a successor to Jeb Stuart, whose death the Old Man still grieved. General Wade Hampton was made overall commander of the cavalry of the Army of Northern Virginia. Two of Hampton's sons served in their father's cavalry.

Under blistering sunshine on Sunday, August 14, the stagnant Sabbath heat was shattered by a Federal attack on the north side of the James, above the Bermuda Hundred bottleneck. The Yankees captured Confederate positions seven miles east of Chaffin's Bluff. The bluecoats had to retreat when Charles Field's division counterattacked. Marse Robert looked around him and penned a note to Mother Lee borne of Sunday reflection: "We must suffer patiently to the end when all things will be made right." General Lee was on the cliff line the next day as Rooney Lee's cavalry division deployed northwest of the dismal White Oak Swamp.

Monday, August 15, young Rob Lee, twenty, was wounded in the arm during action on the James River front.

Tuesday, the Federals attacked and drove Rooney Lee's cavalry along the Charles City Road in the vulnerable rear of his father's Petersburg lines. Again, General Lee called upon Charles Field's trusty division, which engaged the Federals east of New Market Heights on the Darbytown Road. These two days of action took place on the north side of the James, east of where the river flows north-south between Richmond and Petersburg. Field's line was broken by the determined bluecoats. The resolute Federals were not pushed out of the Rebel works until Wade Hampton's cavalry division rushed to the aid of hard-pressed Rooney Lee and General Field. The determined boys in blue were driven into the stinking morass of White Oak Swamp.

Federal harassment continued three days later on August 19, when three full Federal divisions plowed into the far right flank of Lee's Petersburg line. The Federals attacked Powell Hill's hungry line two and a half miles south of Petersburg at Globe Tavern. The Yankees captured 2,700 Confederate prisoners and the vital north-south Weldon Railroad. The tracks were the besieged town's lifeline to fertile North Carolina. The railroad loss was a desperate setback for Petersburg's filthy defenders.

When the railroad fell into Federal hands and cut off supplies to Petersburg from the Deep South, the food situation in the Petersburg trenches became even more critical. Thinking of Grant's apparent strategy of destroying rail links while poking at the Confederate line along its whole length, General Lee on August 22 again begged Richmond for food. Lee wrote directly to President Davis this Monday that "It behooves us to do everything in our power to thwart his new plan of reducing us by starvation."

Not until Grant had stood poised to cross the James nine weeks earlier did Robert Lee finally speak of possible defeat for the Confederate cause. Now the commanding general was writing wearily about starvation and disaster. The day after writing to the president about hunger, Lee wrote to Jefferson Davis about the desperate shortage of troops. "Unless some measures can be devised to replace our losses," Lee wrote August 23, "the consequences may be disastrous."

But the unspeakable filth and unbearable August heat also oppressed the Federals, who lived underground in trenches of their own. Sufficient food was the only comfort enjoyed by the Yankees, which was denied to their adversaries in the parallel trench lines twenty miles long. From the heat, the dirt and lice, and the dreadful waiting, the huge Federal army suffered eight thousand desertions and surrenders to the Rebels during the two terrible months, which ended August 24.

On August 25, Lee broke the boredom with a desperate attack by seven gray brigades against the Federals holding the Weldon Railroad. The assault by Confederates who were more scarecrows than soldiers came seven miles south of Petersburg, at Reams Station. They drove into the blue II Corps and were supported by the cavalry of Rooney Lee and Wade Hampton. The emaciated Confederates retook the station along with 2,000 Yankee prisoners. Another 742 Federals were killed or wounded. But the actual railroad tracks to the vital South remained in General Grant's control.

While the battle for Reams Station raged along his front, the brave Little Powell Hill was fading fast. General Hill was now so wasted from excruciating groin pain and kidney failure that he had to lay down to rest on the battlefield close to the Federal fieldworks. His twenty-year fight against a teenage West Point cadet's brush with venereal disease would soon kill him—unless the enemy put him out of his daily misery first.

On August 28, General Lee wrote to Mother Lee and spoke sadly of Lieutenant General Grant's basic strategy: "His attempt is now to starve us out."

The Federal stranglehold on the waning Confederacy was hardly limited to the Petersburg front. The South was slowly shrinking inside the multifront pressure. On September 2, 1864, the vital railroad hub of Atlanta, Georgia, fell to a Federal siege which had dragged on for six weeks. The day Atlanta fell and cracked the Confederacy in half, Robert Lee penned yet another plea to his president for more troops for Petersburg. And again, Lee spoke of the long sunset of his new country: "I beg leave to call to your attention the importance of immediate and vigorous measures to increase the strength of our armies," General Lee wrote with unusual resignation. "Our ranks are constantly diminishing by battle and disease, and few recruits are received. The consequences are inevitable." The general's desperation was clear: "No man should be excused from service for any reason not deemed sufficient to entitle one already in service to his discharge . . . [N]o man capable of bearing arms should be excused unless it be for some controlling reason of public necessity." The South was running out of blood, unlike the North, in which Lieutenant General Grant and Mr. Lincoln had an inexhaustible supply.

The inevitable defeat bore heavily on the sickly A. P. Hill. Most of the Federal harassment was aimed at the southwestern end of the Petersburg front, which was manned by Hill's Third Corps. The fragile Lieutenant General Hill had his spirits lifted in late September when his wife, Dolly, and their two daughters arrived on the Petersburg line. Dolly set up housekeeping on the west side of the city, and her weary husband finally had a home after three years in the field. Though in constant pain and wasting away from prostatitis, Little Powell still had what it took to render his beloved Dolly pregnant amid the hunger and the daily shelling.

The chronic starvation inspired the hearty Wade Hampton to demonstrate his ability to fill the dead Jeb Stuart's boots. On September 14, Hampton's cavalry division executed a raid near Grant's own headquarters at the City Point supply base. Hampton's troopers became rustlers and rounded up 2,486 head of beef cattle whose rumps were branded "USA."

Three days later, General Lee's shortage of manpower in the trenches forced him to make a demand upon War Secretary James Seddon which better times would have made impossible. "There is immediate necessity for the services of five thousand Negroes for thirty days to labor on the fortifications at this place."

The next day, September 18, General Lee invited Mother Lee and his daughters to set to work making socks for Rebel bare feet. "Shall want for the army all the socks we can get, so you need not fear having too many. Put the girls to knitting." Mrs. Lee and two daughters remained at Bremo Plantation until October.

On September 19, the beginning of the end came to the Valley campaign of the Second Corps of Lee's army. Twelve thousand men from Stonewall's mighty corps engaged Phil Sheridan in the Valley. Jubal Early sent the divisions of John Gordon and Robert Rodes against 40,000 Federals at Winchester, the Valley hamlet which now saw its third major battle on its doorsteps. Major General Rodes (VMI, '48), thirty-five, had seen action at First Manassas (Bull Run); The Seven Days, where he was wounded; Antietam, where he held the Bloody Lane; Chancellorsville, where he led Old Jack's famed assault; Gettysburg; and Spotsylvania, where he had led the last-ditch countercharge which saved the Bloody Angle in the Mule Shoe.

At the Third Battle of Winchester this day, General Rodes was killed in action northeast of town. Second Corps was almost crushed, and suffered 4,600 casualties, which included two generals killed. The Old Man's favorite nephew, General Fitzhugh Lee ("Chuddy" to the Lee girls), was gravely wounded. Second Corps fell back to Fisher's Hill.

On Thursday, September 22, the bloodied remnant of Stonewall Jackson's shock troops slammed into Phil Sheridan at Fisher's Hill near Massanutten Mountain in the Shenandoah. Sheridan's 32,600 troops wrecked Old Jube's 15,000 survivors of Winchester. After suffering 235 killed or wounded and 1,000 lost as prisoners, the shattered Second Corps limped into the Blue Ridge Mountains and left the fertile Valley of Virginia open to be sacked and burned by Phil Sheridan. Virginia's breadbasket was gone in an afternoon.

As with all great battles, the deaths of hundreds of mothers' sons is harder to imagine than the death of one son.

Among the Second Corps wounded who lay bleeding on Fisher's Hill was Lieutenant Colonel Sandie Pendleton.

Five months earlier, Sandie had refused a promotion to brigadier general so he could remain on Jubal Early's staff, where he had faithfully served Baldy Ewell before Old Jube, and Old Jack before that. Dr. Hunter McGuire, who had amputated Stonewall's arm, lingered to dress Sandie's wounds. Then Sandie was left behind when the Yankees overran the field. Although surgeons in blue faithfully ministered to Sandie Pendleton, the young adjutant loved by all as "Stonewall's man" died on September 23—five days short of his twenty-fourth birthday. "To the war shall my powers be devoted," Sandie had written to his beloved Kate two weeks after Gettysburg, "until it or I am finished by the act of God."

The death of Sandie Pendleton hit Baldy Ewell hard. Recovering in Richmond from his battle fatigue, the greathearted little man wrote a condolence letter to Sandie's father, General William Pendleton. "I know the men of my old corps said it is not Ewell but Sandie who commands the Second Corps," Richard Ewell wrote graciously, "but I never felt a pang of jealousy."

Another devastating blow to the Army of Northern Virginia came on September 29. Two blue divisions of the Federal XVIII Corps crossed the James River at Aiken's Landing by pontoon bridge. The Yankees captured Fort Harrison on the outer defensive perimeter of Richmond. Located on the east side of the river just one mile east of the Chaffin's Bluff outpost, the fort was critical to holding a unified front between Richmond and Petersburg. The fort fell, with sixteen Rebel cannon dragged off to join the Federal arsenal. The importance of the fort forced General Lee to detach two divisions and four brigades from George Pickett's famous division to retake the position. Rooney Lee's cavalry and six artillery batteries completed the task force. Robert Lee went along to personally oversee the desperate action.

The day after Fort Harrison fell, the Confederates tried to pry it loose. General Lee stood on the field of fire to watch the action. General Hoke's gray division was repulsed. Although the powder-blackened faces wildly cheered their Uncle Robert, two more Confederate assaults also failed. The fort was lost, leaving only Fort Gilmore now commanded by Baldy Ewell to protect the gates of Richmond.

When Fort Harrison fell, only one mile separated the pitiful trenches of the two mighty armies.

Thirteen

By the fall of 1864, the Petersburg line was withering away to a skeleton force of starving and wretched men. Only fifty thousand men held the entire Confederate front along the James River flowing straight to Richmond. The Petersburg trenches were losing ten men every day to desertion. As always, the officer corps dwindled, too. Between July 30 and October 1, General Lee had lost four generals in the Shenandoah Valley and at Petersburg.

By October, the Petersburg line on the right flank south and southwest of town was desperately weak where Grant was hitting the most often. Only Bushrod Johnson's starving division held Powell Hill's six-mile front from the Appomattox River west of Petersburg around to the Boydton Plank Road south of town. Originally, two and a half divisions had manned that segment of front.

Desperate for reinforcements for the Petersburg front, General Lee wrote to President Davis with Lee's first explicit warning about the impending fall of Richmond: "The men at home on various pretexts must be brought out and be put in the army at once." If not, the worried general warned, "The discouragement of our people and the great material loss that would follow the fall of Richmond, to say nothing of the great encouragement our enemies would derive from it, outweigh, in my judgment, any sacrifice and hardship that would result from bringing out all our arms-bearing men."

Without waiting for the needed men, Robert Lee resolved to try again to retake Fort Harrison on Richmond's outer line of defenses.

The second attempt to recover Fort Harrison was launched on Friday, October 7. As before, Robert Lee was on the field to supervise the vital operation. The gray divisions of generals Field and Hoke were deployed to assail the position from the northwest and from the northeast. Their target was the Yankee line running northeastward from the fort. General Field was repulsed and General Hoke never engaged at all. Among the Confederate dead lay Texas judge, Brigadier General John Gregg, ten days past his thirty-sixth birthday. With this second failure, all hope of retaking the strategic position was abandoned.

Wednesday, October 19, was a day of joy for General Lee in the trenches and of disaster in the Valley of Virginia.

Old Pete was back.

Half-recovered from his May wound in the Wilderness and with his right arm still paralyzed from the gunshot, Lieutenant General James Longstreet limped to the command of his old First Corps of the Army of Northern Virginia. Starving boys threw what was left of their caps into the air to welcome their rough-and-ready chief home. Robert Lee gladly returned First Corps to Old Pete. General Anderson stepped down from the corps' command. His reward for faithful service was assignment to a new, small Fourth Corps in the army. The broken divisions of Major Generals Hoke and Bushrod Johnson composed his new command. General Lee dispatched Longstreet and First Corps to the north side of the James River, still on the Petersburg line.

While First Corps was welcoming back Old Pete on October 19, the Battle of Cedar Creek finally removed the fabled Second Corps from contention in the Shenandoah Valley. Jubal Early had been concentrating Stonewall's old corps in the Valley between Strasburg and Middletown on October 12 and 13. On October 19, Old Jube sent his entire corps after Phil Sheridan. Five gray divisions attacked the Federals at daybreak. Two Yankee corps collapsed by ten a.m., leaving Early with 1,300 blue-clad prisoners and eighteen captured cannon.

At 4:30 p.m., Sheridan caught his breath and countercharged. The grand old Second Corps crumbled. Old Jube lost 3,000 men and a stagger-ing twenty-three cannon. He took 5,665 Federal killed and wounded out of action before retreating with his survivors to the village of New Market.

Among the Confederate wounded was General Stephen Dodson Ramseur, who had to be abandoned on the field. When the bluecoats discovered the bleeding general, Phil Sheridan assigned his personal surgeon to save the prisoner's life. General Ramseur died of his wounds the next day, three days after word had reached him that his child had been born. The Shenandoah now belonged to the Federals. General Early at least escaped with twelve thousand troops, but the Second Corps was gone as a corps-size, fighting unit.

A week of quiet in the Petersburg trenches followed Early's defeat at Cedar Creek.

While Stephen Ramseur's family grieved for their twenty-seven-year-old son, mourning continued in the Sandie Pendleton house. Although Sandie fell on September 23, word of his death did not reach his wife, Kate, until October 17. She had gone back to Lexington in the Valley on July 11. Sandie's body did not reach Lexington from Yankee embalmers until October 24. He was laid to rest the next day in the shadow of Stonewall's grave.

The numbing boredom in the Petersburg trenches was shattered on Thursday, October 27, when Lieutenant General Grant launched a massive assault against both ends of Robert Lee's thinning line.

On the Confederate left flank north of the James River, two Federal corps pounded General Longstreet's First Corps. Twenty thousand bluecoats advanced through White Oak Swamp toward the Seven Pines battlefield, where Robert Lee had taken command in June of '62. Old Pete was attacked along a three-mile front north of the lost Fort Harrison. Longstreet and his boys fought desperately, repulsed the Yankees in the rain, and captured six hundred prisoners.

That same day, southwest of Petersburg along the vital Southside Railroad, two blue corps and one Federal cavalry division drove into Little Powell Hill's Third Corps south of the James on Lee's far right flank at Burgess Mill on Hatcher's Run creek. Two blue corps and one Federal cavalry division drove into the gray line at Burgess Mill on Hatcher's Run creek. Thirty-five thousand Yankees were repulsed with the assistance of Wade Hampton's gray cavalry. Hampton lived up to Jeb Stuart's command which he had inherited. Hampton attacked the Federals along Boydton Plank Road with the support of Powell Hill's three divisions, driving the Federals from the field.

When the burial parties went out after the firing stopped, they found Wade Hampton's trooper son, Frank, among the dead. Another Hampton son was wounded.

Two days later, Robert Lee poured out his breaking heart to Wade Hampton. Two years earlier the Old Man had lost his precious Annie, always "Sweet Annie" in the father's letters two years and one week earlier, and he knew the pain. "I grieve with you," General Lee wrote, "at the death of your gallant son. So young, so brave, so true."

The Petersburg lines on the Confederate side became even more miserable as the fall air grew chilly and barefoot men awaited winter. The starving Rebels dug holes into the sides of the trench walls to keep warm. They named their burrows "rat holes." With the wry humor of condemned men, the Army of Northern Virginia began calling themselves "Lee's Miserables" as a play on words of *Les Misérables*, published two years earlier by Victor Hugo.

As the ground hardened and his divisions became ever more ragged, General Lee continued to plead for more troops. On November 2, he wrote President Davis that "Grant will get every man he can, and 150,000 men is the number generally assumed by Northern newspapers and reports. Unless we can obtain a reasonable approximation to his force," Lee warned, regarding Grant's three-to-one superiority, "I fear a great calamity will befall us." The Old Man no longer hesitated in private correspondence to acknowledge the obvious.

Two days after Robert Lee's desperate letter to Richmond, Kate Corbin Pendleton gave birth to her dead husband's only child. The infant boy was named Alexander Swift Pendleton Jr. In ten months, the infant will die of diphtheria and Kate will have nothing left of Sandie Pendleton.

For more than thirty years, Robert Lee had sent letters to his children. From western and far western bivouacs, the long-absent father had sent his maxims for growing up. Such was the best he could do when Mother Lee was raising their seven children with an absent, soldier father. Returning to that lifelong habit, the general wrote to daughter Mildred, his "Precious Life," on November 6, "Never neglect the means of making yourself useful in the world."

On November 25, General Lee moved his Petersburg siege headquarters to the Turnbull Plantation called Edge Hill, two miles west of town.

By the last day of November, Lee had nearly 61,000 men in the Petersburg trenches as the Second Corps survivors began to come in from the Shenandoah. With Jubal Early's threat in the Valley all but gone, Ulysses Grant could afford to recall his blue VI Corps from the Valley to Petersburg. These Federal reinforcements arrived December 5.

Though the Army of Northern Virginia was now shivering in their rags at Petersburg, Robert Lee never ceased to be the cheerful father his children remembered from his homecomings from the prairie so long ago. Lee son Custis, thirty-two, was to have sent his father some photographs of the white-haired, white-bearded general to be given by Robert Lee to the many Southern ladies who begged for them. The Old Man teased Custis that family honor was at stake if General Lee could not honor the requests. On December 13, the second anniversary of the Battle of Fredericksburg, General Lee must have smiled when he sat in his tent and wrote to his unmarried son in Richmond: "I am afraid you will ruin my character with the young ladies, and may cause that of the family for fidelity to be suspected. Several of them wishing, I suppose, to see how they would like me as a father-in-law, have requested my photograph, which I have promised and have relied on those you were to have sent me. Not one has reached me," the father wrote warmly, "and I am taxed with breach of promise. See what a strait you have placed me in."

The next day, Lee continued to patch his army together as winter tightened its grip on the Petersburg front. He recalled his Second Corps division of the dead Major General Robert Rodes (VMI, '48), thirty-five, back from the Valley where it camped. The division arrived in Petersburg on December 18 under the command of Brigadier General Bryan Grimes (University of North Carolina, '48). Some 8,600 Second Corps survivors had returned to the Petersburg front in the persons of John Gordon's old division, now led by Georgia lawyer and judge Brigadier General Clement Evans and Grimes's division. These two divisions remained Second Corps under the new command of John B. Gordon, who never knew when to give up. Old Jube remained in the Valley with the remnant of his old division, commanded by John Pegram.

On December 19, General John Bell Hood (West Point, '53) lost Nashville while General William T. Sherman's blue divisions pounded at the gates of Savannah, Georgia. The vital Georgia city fell December 21, while eighty-five Yankee gunboats laid siege to Wilmington, North Carolina, the South's last seaport. General Lee sent Hoke's division down to Wilmington for a final defense on December 22.

The sailors in gray this December had sent the boys in the Petersburg trenches their naval ration of salt pork when Petersburg ran out of stale meat.

Christmas 1864 on the Confederate side of the Petersburg front was far from merry. Good tidings meant a meager ration of meat once every three days. The normal, daily ration was one pint of cornmeal with one ounce of fatty bacon.

On New Year's Day, 1865, General Lee commanded 62,088 starving and freezing men of whom only 51,776 were fit to fight. Facing them were 134,278 well-fed Yankees.

Daily sniper fire caused casualties along the lines, which were now thirty-five miles long. General Lee had to detach a brigade of infantry and one cavalry division to Charleston, South Carolina, to fend off General Sherman in mid-January 1865. The graybacks in the Petersburg trenches were starving and their horses were shuffling skeletons. "We have but two days' supplies," a desperate Robert Lee wrote to War Secretary Seddon on January 11. Supplies from Europe, such as they were, ended abruptly on January 15, when the Confederacy's last seaport, Wilmington, fell after a two-day Federal bombardment.

While struggling against overwhelming odds to save Richmond, the capital city of his country, Robert Lee reflected upon the central contested issue of the War Between the States: slavery. On January 11, 1865, he penned a letter to Virginia State Senator Andrew Hunter:

Considering the relation of master and slave, controlled by humane laws and influenced by Christianity and an enlightened public sentiment, as the best that can exist between the white and black races while intermingled as at present in this country, I would deprecate any sudden disturbance of that relation unless it be necessary to avert a greater calamity to both.

General Lee's letter to Hunter was written eight years after he had expressed his revulsion at the "peculiar institution" of Southern, African-American slavery: "In this enlightened age, there are few, I believe, but what will acknowledge that slavery as an institution is a moral and political evil in any country." And yet, defending his "country" was defending the slavery which Robert Lee abhorred.

Four days after Wilmington, North Carolina, was captured, Robert Lee celebrated his fifty-eighth birthday, probably with his daily fare of cabbage boiled in salt water. His birthday present from Richmond was an invitation from the president to shoulder even more administrative burdens. On January 19, Jefferson Davis proposed to General Lee that he become the South's first general-in-chief, commanding all troops who still wore the gray.

An exhausted Lee answered in writing from the Petersburg trenches: "If I had the ability, I would not have the time." But, the dutiful soldier continued, "I am willing to undertake any service to which you think proper to assign me, but I do not wish you to be misled as to the extent of my capacity."

The same day that Robert Lee reluctantly accepted the president's proposal, the general lost the services of his able cavalry commander, Major General Wade Hampton. Hampton was dispatched to his native South Carolina to rally public morale and to raise reinforcements.

Within the week, another plea arrived in Richmond from General Lee. "There is suffering for want of food," the candidate for the new position of general-in-chief wrote to Secretary of War James Seddon. "The ration is too small for men who have to undergo so much exposure and labor as ours."

The frozen boredom was broken on February 5 when the Federals conducted a protracted skirmish for three full days along the Hatcher's Run line of Powell Hill's front. Third Corps held out against 35,000 Yankees for seventy-two hours without meat, living only on light rations. Grant lost 1,512 men getting a foothold on Lee's western flank.

Among the Federal honored dead at Hatcher's Run was a Union dog, Sallie, the mascot of the 11th Pennsylvania Infantry. Sallie followed the regiment for nearly four years. On the Gettysburg battlefield, she sat loyally beside the bodies of her dead friends without food or water for three full days. At Hatcher's Run, the regiment buried her under fire with full honors. In twenty-four years, her bronze likeness would sleep forever at the base of the 11th Pennsylvania's Gettysburg memorial.

When Stephen Ramseur was killed in the Valley, Brigadier General John Pegram (West Point '54) took Ramseur's place with Jubal Early. On January 19, Pegram enjoyed the spotlight of Richmond high society when he married Hetty Cary, a red-haired belle who was driven to her wedding in the Confederate president's carriage. On February 2, Hetty reviewed her husband's emaciated but proud division on the Petersburg front. General Lee stood at Hetty's side when the regiments passed in review. Four days later, John Pegram was killed on the Hatcher's Run front, thirteen days after his thirty-third birthday.

Fourteen

THE DAY YOUNG GENERAL PEGRAM DIED, FEBRUARY 6, 1865, THE AIL-
ing James Seddon resigned as Confederate secretary of war. Eighteen
months earlier, Seddon's own War Department clerk, John B. Jones,
wrote in his diary that Seddon looked like a "galvanized corpse which
had been buried two months." He was replaced by Kentucky's General
John C. Breckinridge, a distant cousin of the stepmother of another Kentucky native: Mary Todd Lincoln of Lexington. Breckinridge would be
the Confederacy's sixth secretary of war.

As Secretary Seddon was packing to leave and John Pegram was
bleeding to death, Robert Lee was officially appointed the Confederacy's
general-in-chief, a position formally created January 23.

Two days after assuming this new command, General Lee on
February 8 sent another plea to Richmond for food. "Some of the men
have been without meat for three days and all were suffering from
reduced rations and scant clothing, exposed to battle, cold, hail, and
sleet," he begged departing Secretary Seddon. "The physical strength
of the men, if their courage survives, must fail under this treatment . . .
[Y]ou must not be surprised if calamity befalls us." Never before had
the Old Man breathed a word of doubt about his army's unflagging
courage.

Jefferson Davis conceded the desperation of the Confederate States
of America on February 10 when he introduced a bill in the Confederate
Congress which defied Southern history. The legislation called for the
arming of black slaves to defend their own servitude by fighting Federals.
The South was out of draftable white men.

On February 17, General Sherman's bluecoats burned Columbia to the ground, the capital of South Carolina. Only North Carolina separated Sherman's army from linking arms with General Grant.

On February 19, General Lee wrote candidly to new Secretary of War Breckinridge: "I fear it may be necessary to abandon all our cities and preparations should be made for that contingency."

President Davis's daring plan to arm the slaves passed the lower house of Congress by a narrow forty to thirty-seven head count on February 20. The measure then went up to the Confederate Senate.

The same day on the Petersburg front, Lieutenant Colonel Walter Taylor, the Old Man's chief of staff, spent some quiet minutes with his wartime diary. Taylor looked into the cruel trenches filled with the starving remnant of what had been the continent's most feared army only two years earlier. Then he looked across half a mile toward the Federal lines, in place now for eight bitter months. "They are trying to corner this old army like a brave old lion brought to bay at last," the twenty-six-year-old banker wrote sadly. "It is determined to resist to the death, and if die it must, to die game."

To die game. Had not Jeb Stuart, dead now, said exactly the same thing when he was nearly caught on the flooded banks of the Chickahominy, where Rooney Lee almost drowned during Jeb's Ride Around McClellan in June of '62?

By February 21, General Lee thought of his crippled wife, who stubbornly refused to leave the tottering Richmond. He wrote anxiously to Mother Lee: "Should it be necessary to abandon our position to prevent being surrounded, what will you do? Will you remain or leave the city?" His despair rang like the boom of the cannon along the Petersburg front. "You must consider the question and make up your mind. You will be able to retain nothing in the house and I do not see how you can live or where to go. It is a fearful condition."

On February 24, General Lee had to worry about the crumbling of his lines from within. In just twelve days, four hundred men had quietly laid down their guns in Third Corps to go home. Desertions were now epidemic in the freezing, filthy, lice-ridden trenches. Lee wrote bitterly to the new war secretary, former general John Breckinridge: "It seems that the men are influenced very much by the representations of their friends at home who appear to have become very despondent as to our success. They think the cause desperate and write to the soldiers, advising them to take care of themselves."

The desertion problem was probably discussed when Robert Lee left the Petersburg line February 26 for a two-day war council in Richmond. Lee returned to the trenches with only 50,000 men defending the entire Richmond-Petersburg line. Only 36,000 of them were infantry, which Lee most needed. Between Generals Grant and Meade at Petersburg and William Tecumseh Sherman moving northward through the Carolinas, General Lee faced 160,000 Yankees.

On March 2, Jubal Early's Valley contingent of the mighty Second Corps ceased to be. At Waynesboro in the Shenandoah Valley, Old Jube and a paltry one thousand survivors were overwhelmed by Phil Sheridan's command of ten thousand in the Blue Ridge Mountains. In a searing flash of musketry, Confederate presence in the Shenandoah ended. Major General Early barely escaped with his life to straggle into Petersburg fourteen days later. The desolate Valley of Virginia would now be Phil Sheridan's road to Robert Lee's far right flank west of Petersburg.

On March 4, General Lee was summoned to Richmond for another council of war with the president. Before leaving Petersburg, Robert Lee paced his indoor headquarters all night, from March 3 to early March 4 at Petersburg. Finally, at two o'clock this Saturday morning, the Old Man needed the company of his general staff. But Old Pete Longstreet and Powell Hill were at the front line. So he called for General John Gordon, who commanded what was left of Stonewall's Second Corps, which had escaped in September from Jubal Early's first catastrophe in the Valley.

Needing to think out loud, Lee showed General Gordon the army's field reports, which showed 65,000 Confederates on all fronts in the South facing combined Federal armies of 280,000 men. The Old Man asked Gordon for his frank assessment of the options left. Lee's line was down to 35,000 effectives facing Grant's 150,000, with Sheridan's blue-clad reinforcements already on the road to Petersburg from the Valley.

Major General Gordon outlined three choices: attempt to negotiate a settlement with Grant; attack Grant here and now; or, retreat westward and abandon Richmond altogether with the hope of joining General Joe Johnston's Rebel army down in North Carolina. Robert Lee nodded his agreement with his young subordinate's view of the situation. Then the Confederate general-in-chief dismissed General Gordon at dawn and headed to an early-morning train for the ride twenty miles up the line to Richmond. At noon, Abraham Lincoln would take his second oath of office as President of the United States, and he would speak of "malice toward none."

Lee spent March 4 and 5 in the capital. He urged the president to accept the unacceptable: evacuate Richmond so Lee could escape with the army to join General Johnston further south. Jefferson Davis reluctantly agreed with Lee's assessment. On Sunday, March 5, Robert Lee went to St. Paul's Episcopal Church in Richmond for the last time as a soldier. After a Sabbath visit with Mother Lee and the girls, General Lee left Richmond for the last time as a Confederate.

Upon his return from Richmond, General Lee wrote bitterly to son Custis: "I have been up to see the Congress and they do not seem to be able to do anything except to eat peanuts and chew tobacco while my army is starving."

On March 8, the Confederate Senate passed the statute allowing the conscription of an army of slaves, if their owners and home states agreed.

The next day from Petersburg, Lee wrote to War Secretary Breckinridge a final, desperate plea for food for his starving army in the thawing trenches. "Unless the men and animals can be subsisted, the army cannot be kept together and our present lines must be abandoned."

Friday, March 10, General Lee sent a dispatch to President Jefferson Davis, endorsing the plan to arm slaves. "Those owners," Lee wrote, "who are willing to furnish some of their slaves for the purpose can do a great deal to inspire them with the right feeling to prepare them to become soldiers."

The slave army bill became Confederate law with the president's signature on March 13. General Lee objected that the slave-arming legislation did not assure slaves of their freedom upon completion of their Confederate military service.

For the two weeks between March 11 and 23, General Lee had been considering a last desperate assault by his wasted army against the center of Grant's line at Petersburg. Such a bold attack might force the Federals to shorten their line so Lee could maneuver around it to make good an escape from the dreadful trenches to join Joe Johnston. The Old Man could not shake either his ultimate faith in his starving troops or his aggressive blood, which still longed for a fair fight on open ground. He approved the daring plan on March 23. Robert Lee had become the old lion that Lieutenant Colonel Taylor had imagined.

March 19, Federal General Sheridan completed his march to Petersburg from the Valley. He arrived at Rooney Lee's old estate, White House Landing, with 13,000 mounted reinforcements for Grant. Sheridan's cavalry faced the remnant of Lee's cavalry of 5,500 hungry men riding wasted horses. Lee men led two of the three Confederate cavalry divisions: Rooney Lee and his first cousin, Fitzhugh Lee.

Robert Lee's army continued to melt away even as he planned one final charge on the field of glory. Between February 15 and March 18, the army had lost 2,934 men who left the ranks to go home to burned-out farms and homeless children. Eight percent of Lee's army had deserted. The once mighty Second Corps had dissolved into the army's smallest corps, with 8,600 hungry men.

As his army vaporized into the warming spring nights and as his last offensive plans were being made, Robert Lee's command family also began to unravel. The brave Lieutenant General A. P. Hill was quickly winding down. Little Powell's prostatitis had matured into kidney failure. He had been laid up for most of February, with his Dolly nursing him as best a pregnant wife could. Finally, Little Powell's strength cracked. On March 20, he had to take sick leave for the next eleven days. He could hardly walk, let alone lead Third Corps in Marse Robert's last desperate gamble.

As he planned his breakout maneuver, General Lee on March 22 took hold of his new job as overall general-in-chief of the Confederate war machine. He sent orders to General Joe Johnston to take command of the remaining gray forces in North and South Carolina, the last two states outside Virginia which were still strongly in rebellion. But Johnston could muster only 15,000 die-hards.

A day or two later, Lee again sought the counsel of General Gordon. Lee asked Gordon for his recommendation for the assault planned to force Grant to shorten his long lines on the western front at Petersburg. John Gordon proposed an attack against Fort Stedman, three-quarters of a mile from the Appomattox River east of town. Attacking the eastern end of the Federal line would make Grant call in his western troops to the battle zone. On this front, the trenches of the opposing armies were only 150 yards apart. The Old Man nodded and gave to Gordon Old Blue Light's Second Corps of eight thousand survivors, plus six other brigades. The grand offensive was set for Saturday, March 25.

General Gordon planned a clandestine ranger operation. Confederate sappers, no more than fifty handpicked veterans, would lead the way in darkness across the haunted space between the opposing armies. They would cut through the Yankees' outer perimeter so three hundred more graybacks could steal in behind the rangers to penetrate the blue position. Once these brave souls had sliced through the Federal line, four and a half divisions of gray infantry and Rooney Lee's cavalry would rush into the breach to cut the Federal army in half.

It was a daring and desperate plan. Rooney Lee's emaciated horses and hungry troopers had to ride hard for forty miles to reach Fort Stedman. Gordon's attack force represented fully half of the effective strength of the Army of Northern Virginia. When the Federal lines were pierced at the fort, Longstreet's gray First Corps would then attack the bluecoats on the north side of the James River. Grant would have to pull in his outer flanks from the left to defend Fort Stedman on the Federal right flank. Then Lee could escape with the army around Grant's contracted left (western) end.

At four in the morning on March 25, John Gordon's rangers crawled through the Federal defenses in the darkness. Their backups quickly captured Fort Stedman and fanned out within the Federal line. But the Confederates became disoriented in the dawn twilight. The surprised Yankees regrouped and fought vigorously under the support of a heavy

Federal artillery barrage. The fighting raged four bloody hours inside the fieldworks of the Army of the Potomac.

But by eight o'clock Saturday morning, John Gordon had to send word to Robert Lee that his bloody assault was stalled. General Lee recalled Second Corps from the offensive.

Rather than go back to their starving trenches, 1,900 Confederates threw down their weapons and surrendered inside the blue works. During the afternoon, General Meade's boys counterattacked along the Fort Stedman front.

By day's end, Lee had lost 5,000 men to the Federals' 2,080 casualties. The haul of Rebel prisoners for the Yankees was the worst Confederate mass surrender since the bloodbath in the Mule Shoe at Spotsylvania ten months earlier.

Robert Lee's desperate breakout had failed.

Sunday, General Lee wrote to Jefferson Davis to confirm that the end of the Petersburg front was at hand after nine months of siege and starvation. Lee wired that his shattered army had to evacuate quickly to prevent being encircled and trapped by General Grant and the approaching General Sherman. Sheridan's Yankee cavalry was expected to join Grant within forty-eight hours. The muster rolls this March 27 showed only 36,000 Rebel infantry on the Petersburg-Richmond front, including the capital's home guard of walking wounded commanded by the sickly Baldy Ewell.

On top of his awful loss at Fort Stedman, Lee resolved to deal once and for all with the desertion wave which threatened to leave his trenches empty. March 27, Lee issued General Orders Number 8 requiring that Confederate Army regulations on desertion—and the death penalty for desertion—would be read to each infantry company daily for three days, and to each regiment weekly, for one month.

The same day, Monday, Confederate scouts reported that the Federals were planning to drive against General Lee's weak right flank at Hatcher's Run, seven miles southwest of Petersburg. Only three miles north of the creek, on the Confederate side, was the Southside Railroad: Lee's last rail link to the west. By now, the gray line of trenches was twenty-seven miles long. The infantry force along the line had evaporated down to 1,140 soldiers per mile. At Gettysburg, Lee mustered 12,000 men per mile along his Seminary Ridge front.

North of the James River, Longstreet's First Corps was down to 9,700 infantry and 1,800 horsemen. John Gordon's Second Corps east of Petersburg covered four miles of front, with 5,500 wasted men. The gray Third Corps on Gordon's right along the western side of Lee's line counted 9,200 men hanging on to an eight-mile front. And Dick Anderson's new Fourth Corps held the westernmost end of the Confederate line, with 4,800 troops over a three-mile front.

Within twenty-four hours, the mighty blue legions were on the march toward Lee's far right flank west of town. General Lee had to bring George Pickett's division of five thousand men from First Corps north of the river on the left, down to the Confederate right, to strengthen the line there.

That same day, Tuesday, March 28, President Davis was clearly getting the message. His wife sent their household goods and personal clothing to auction before the fall of Richmond. They earned $28,400 in worthless, Confederate paper money and $500 in real gold. Secretary of State Judah Benjamin sent Confederate State Department documents down to Charlotte, North Carolina, for safekeeping.

While the Davis family was pawning their clothes, Robert Lee was packing. During the winter doldrums, he had finally had time to read the autobiography of his lifelong mentor, General of the Army Winfield Scott—"Old Fuss and Feathers." When General Lee had resigned from the Old Army four years and one week earlier, to General Scott he had written: "To no one, General, have I been as much indebted as to yourself for uniform kindness." Now, with his career and his army in ruins, Lee gently packed the treasured book to send home to Mother Lee. In a cover letter to Mary Lee dated March 28, the old soldier wrote of General Scott's book: "He appears the bold, sagacious, truthful man as he is."

Wednesday morning, Federals began their push by sending blue infantry and cavalry across Hatcher's Run creek west of Petersburg. Lee detached General Pickett's legendary division to the train depot to get to Sutherland Station, ten miles west of town, to defend the Southside Railroad. The line was vital to Lee's escape westward before turning south to reach Joe Johnston. The gray cavalry divisions of Rooney Lee and cousin Fitz Lee rode hard to the Confederate right flank. The mounted Lees and twenty-eight-year-old Major General Tom Rosser, leading the third cavalry division, were sent to attack Phil Sheridan at Dinwiddie Courthouse. Fitz Lee was elevated to overall command of the cavalry. By nightfall, the new Federal position extended six miles west of Petersburg to Dinwiddie. Rain drenched the two armies all night.

As vital Confederate documents were being shipped out of the line of Federal fire, Jefferson Davis sent his family with them. His wife, Varina, and their surviving four children abandoned Richmond on Wednesday for North Carolina. The Davis children ranged from Maggie, the oldest at nine years, to baby Varina Anne, nine months, still breastfed by the First Lady. The harried president called his baby daughter "Piecake."

By daylight on Thursday, March 30, the rain continued to turn the evacuation roads into swamp. John Gordon's Second Corps shifted two miles further west to face the sudden concentration of Federals. This further weakened the center of the Confederate line. Lee ordered Pickett to rendezvous with Fitz Lee at the hamlet of Five Forks for a combined assault against Sheridan, to protect the Southside tracks. George Pickett commanded a division of 6,400 men and six cannon as he headed to Five Forks, which he reached at 4:30 p.m. Major General Pickett decided to delay the attack until Friday, since his weary and starving men had walked for eighteen hours. Rooney Lee and Tom Rosser's cavalry divisions arrived after dark.

By first light on Friday, 10,600 Confederates faced not less than 53,700 Yankees at Five Forks, fifteen miles southeast of Petersburg on the south side of the Appomattox River.

Early this March 31, General Lee rode down the line westward to Hatcher's Run. There, he could see for himself that Grant's left flank was dangerously exposed—"in the air," like Joe Hooker had been before the Yankee disaster at Chancellorsville. Lee longed to throw four gray brigades into the Federal line, which dangled there for the taking. An hour before noon in rain which had begun at three a.m. on Friday morning, Confederate infantry plowed into the careless Federals. Half a Rebel division stormed the entire Federal V Corps along White Oak Road.

The blue line was perfectly "rolled up" for a mile, where it was unanchored along the Boydton Plank Road. But just like Fort Stedman, Lee had to break off the assault when Federal resistance was stiffened by two divisions of blue reinforcements. These bluecoats, winners at long last, could feel victory in the air and they continued to fight hard.

When Robert Lee was down on his right flank drawing Federal blood, his daughter Agnes rode in from Richmond to see her exhausted father. But General Lee did not see her, and she went home disappointed. The Old Man was busy elsewhere, massing his troops for the Five Forks attack by Pickett. His mind was full of numbers: The pullout by Pickett left only 27,000 Confederates to hold a twenty-seven-mile line.

While Confederates fought their last battle at Petersburg, George Pickett spent all day March 31 on the muddy road from Five Forks to Dinwiddie Courthouse. He skirmished with Yankees the entire way until he stopped for the night within a half-mile of the village. Although dusk fighting at the courthouse was heavy, Pickett's infantry and Fitz Lee's cavalry held on as darkness closed in upon them.

March, 1865, ended for Robert Lee as the Petersburg campaign had begun the preceding June: with hasty troop movements and an all-consuming worry about food. What was left of his army was on the march to break out around Grant for the dash to North Carolina. From the Deep South, Lee and Joe Johnston could continue the War for Southern Independence. For the army in gray to enjoy the required seven days of rations on the bloody, muddy road, General Lee had to collect five hundred tons of supplies. The only commissary wagons stuffed with that kind of manna had "USA" inked on their canvas sides.

Fifteen

THE FIRST DAY OF APRIL, GENERAL LEE HAD TO ADMIT THE OBVIOUS. He wired to his president confirmation that the successful extension of the Federal left flank westward to Dinwiddie Courthouse had cut off Lee's access to forage for cavalry horses. Phil Sheridan had cut off the way westward from White Oak Road. Robert Lee's options were all closed but one. "This, in my opinion," General Lee lamented, "obliged us to prepare for the necessity of evacuating our position on the James River at once." The critical Southside Railroad line westward was also in serious jeopardy.

On the morning of April 1 after Lee's day of shifting troops, Henry Heth's single gray division held a three-and-a-half-mile front northeast of Burgess Mill on the far right flank, southeast of Petersburg. East of Heth, the lone division of Cadmus Wilcox secured a two-and-a-quarter-mile front. Between Wilcox and the Appomattox River, the six-mile line was held by John Gordon's weary Second Corps. On the north side of the James, only the divisions of Charles Field and Joe Kershaw held First Corps' old position.

After Lee sent his hopeless dispatch to President Davis, Major General Pickett reported that he had been pushed back from Dinwiddie by the Federals. The village was only seven and a half miles from the Southside Railroad. The desperate situation made General Lee send Pickett unmistakable orders: "Hold Five Forks at all hazards . . . Prevent Union forces from striking the Southside Railroad."

The only bright spot this Saturday was the return of Powell Hill from his sick leave. His Third Corps was depleted to only eleven thousand men holding an eleven-mile front along Hatcher's Run, southeast of Petersburg. At least Third Corps would be led by its beloved and fiery Little Powell, who would not have it any other way. Hill left his pregnant wife and babies to lead his corps.

Well down the Confederate line southwest of Petersburg, General Pickett withdrew his division to the superior position at Five Forks. The division had been on the march since four o'clock Saturday morning. Five exhausted gray brigades stumbled into Five Forks in late morning. By one o'clock in the afternoon, the position was quiet enough along the two-mile line for Major Generals Pickett and Fitz Lee to make the worst decision of their lives. They accepted an invitation to ride two miles to the Nottoway River for a shad bake, a southern delicacy. After so many weeks of starvation, they could not resist. The kind invitation had come up the line from General Tom Rosser.

Major General George Pickett was the absolute bottom man at West Point, class of '46. The Virginian only won appointment to the academy because his uncle, Andrew Johnston of Quincy, Illinois, was close friends with a prominent Springfield, Illinois, lawyer named Abe Lincoln. With Mr. Lincoln's influence, Richmond-born Pickett went to West Point on an Illinois nomination.

While Pickett, Fitz Lee, and General Rosser grilled fish beside the creek, the Federals swept down upon Five Forks at three o'clock. They attacked the left flank of Pickett's division. Six thousand Confederates were overwhelmed by Phil Sheridan's 30,000 Yankees, which included 17,000 infantry from the blue V Corps. Rooney Lee's cavalry countercharged, but Pickett's grand division was shattered. The brigades dissolved. Pickett's division was gone. Their proud banners had snapped defiantly in the stifling July breeze along the slopes of Cemetery Ridge at Gettysburg on the third day. Now at Five Forks, 3,244 Confederates surrendered after taking 1,000 Federals out of action.

Among the Rebel wounded was Colonel Willie Pegram, the brother of newly dead General John Pegram. Bleeding to death, Willie, a boy colonel at twenty-three, gasped to his friend, "Give my love to my mother." He died the next day.

By 5:45 p.m. on Saturday, General Lee had received the report of the Five Forks disaster. He then ordered General Bushrod Johnson to take his division out of the Hatcher's Run line toward Church Crossing. This left the Hatcher's Run front manned by one Confederate every twenty feet of trench. Lee ordered Longstreet to bring First Corps south of the James, with Field's infantry division falling in at the almost-deserted Hatcher's Run position. The area north of the James evacuated by Old Pete would be manned by Baldy Ewell's ragtag command of home guard from Richmond.

South of the James along a twenty-mile front at Petersburg, the Confederate Army was down to 16,000 men, not quite the strength of two divisions during the glory days. The far right of Lee's shrinking line was held by 23,000 men, from Petersburg westward. Lee maintained his headquarters one and a half miles west of town at the Turnbull House.

As the bloody Saturday sun faded south of the Appomattox River and the evaporating Petersburg front, Little Powell Hill rode along his Third Corps line. He had been in the saddle for sixteen hours. Between his inflamed groin, destroyed kidneys, and general weakness, Lieutenant General A. P. Hill could hardly move or speak when he finally dismounted.

In the first minutes of Sunday morning, April 2, just after midnight, the Federals began an all-night cannonade against the entire Confederate line at Petersburg. What Grant hoped would be the last frontal assault by the Army of the Potomac was scheduled for 4:40 a.m., Sunday morning.

Lieutenant General James Longstreet had arrived at the Turnbull House, General Lee's field headquarters, by four a.m. The desperately sick A. P. Hill had been there for an hour. The Federals attacked on schedule forty minutes later. They drove the weary gray line of Powell Hill's front west of Petersburg along the Southside Railroad bed. Third Corps held together and executed an orderly withdrawal under fire.

When Robert Lee looked out his window after the musketry started, he saw morning twilight and shadowy figures running eastward on Cox Road, past the Turnbull House and the Edge Hill estate where Lee camped. Lee, Longstreet, and Hill quickly conferred. When General Lee, still in his nightclothes, realized that the indistinct men on the road were the cracking Third Corps, he dressed.

Robert Lee soon returned, decked out in full dress uniform with his saber on his hip.

In the half-light, Lieutenant Colonel Venable of Lee's staff and Powell Hill mounted. The fragile Hill rode his gray Champ to assess the damage. Yankees had broken through the Confederate line and were now only half a mile from overrunning General Lee's own headquarters. Lee knew his impetuous and brave Little Powell. The Old Man yelled after Colonel Venable to tell General Hill to be careful. Venable and Hill rode toward Henry Heth's collapsing Rebel line.

Hill broke off to ride with only his personal courier, Sergeant Tucker, toward Heth's headquarters.

Ahead of Hill and his aide there were only Yankees.

Corporal John Mauck of the 138th Pennsylvania Infantry drew a bead on approaching mounted men in gray. He fired a single round.

The thimble-size lead Minié ball slammed into Lieutenant General Powell Hill's hand, sheared off his thumb, and continued on into the great heart. Ambrose Powell Hill, thirty-nine, was dead before he hit the Virginia ground under Champ's feet.

The sun was barely up when Sergeant Tucker led Champ with empty saddle back to General Lee's headquarters. The Old Man wept when he was told that Lieutenant General Hill was dead and had been left on the bloody earth. Lee recovered his bearing and ordered Hill's chief of staff, twenty-nine-year-old Colonel William Henry Palmer, to gently break the news to Dolly Hill, seven months pregnant and living close to the sudden warfare. Colonel Palmer had started his military career as a private in the 1st Virginia Infantry.

Mrs. Hill was living with her children in the home of Lee's aide, Colonel Charles Venable. Dolly knew instantly what it meant when Colonel Palmer arrived in the early morning. The colonel was riding Champ.

The Confederate line was broken by seven o'clock, Sunday morning. The gray divisions of Wilcox and Heth west of Petersburg were overwhelmed. John Gordon led a vigorous countercharge which was driven back. By 10:30 a.m., Robert Lee knew that the Petersburg line had dissolved after nearly ten months under siege. The break in Lee's line west of town confirmed the unthinkable: The Federals were already in position to block Lee's flight westward. General Grant was in his front.

At 10:30 a.m., General Lee sent a desperate wire to War Secretary Breckinridge. "I see no prospect of doing more than holding our position here till night. I am not certain that I can do that." Then he added the worst: "I advise that all preparation be made for leaving Richmond tonight." The message was hand-delivered by 10:40 a.m. to Jefferson Davis as the president walked to Sunday-morning services at St. Paul's church. While Davis read the dispatch, Lee was fighting for his military life twenty miles down the road. When Yankee artillerymen were close enough to Lee's headquarters to recognize the Confederates' Uncle Robert, the blue cannoneers deliberately aimed their shells at Robert Lee. The horse of one of Lee's aides was wounded.

Within half an hour, the full extent of the collapse of his Petersburg line became clear to General Lee. At eleven a.m. on Sunday morning, he sent a second wire to Richmond. "I think it absolutely necessary that we should abandon our position tonight or run the risk of being cut off in the morning." This new dispatch was delivered to Jefferson Davis in church during services.

The decision had been made by General Lee to hold the Petersburg line until nightfall, if possible. On the western end of his shattered but holding line, the battered Confederates were eight feet apart from each other. Lee resolved to march his band of survivors westward to Amelia Courthouse, thirty-six miles away on the road to Joe Johnston in North Carolina. The Yankees were being held. On the Rebel right, John Gordon still held the line. He secured Fort Gregg, one and a half miles south of Lee's Turnbull House headquarters. Only hours earlier, John Gordon had become a father.

By noon, Jefferson Davis convened his last Cabinet meeting in Richmond. His ministers agreed to a seven o'clock evacuation of the Executive Branch of the Confederate government, which would escape by train to Danville, Virginia, 140 miles southwest of the capital.

By one o'clock, General Lee abandoned the Turnbull House headquarters as John Gordon held the western sector of the Petersburg line. Federal artillerymen recognized General Lee and they lobbed more shells directly at the white beard and the great gray horse. When a cannonball struck the house, it burst into flames as Robert Lee rode westward.

Six hundred hungry and dazed men from the divisions of Billy Mahone and Cadmus Wilcox held Fort Gregg southwest of Petersburg on the Southside Railroad. General Lee sent orders to hold the position at all costs, to give the rest of the army breathing space to execute the complex withdrawal. Because their Marse Robert had given the order, 600 men held off three Federal divisions at bayonet point. When six blue regiments finally overran Fort Gregg with hand-to-hand fighting, 55 Rebel defenders were dead, 129 wounded, and 30 captured. The rest escaped to a new defensive position secured by Pete Longstreet and First Corps. Over 700 Federals were lost. The desperate fight was the gray army's last stand at Petersburg, and had given General Lee the rest of the day to put the retreat together.

As Sunday afternoon wore on and Fort Gregg's defenders held on, General Lee planned the army's evacuation from the Petersburg trenches. At the home of Captain Robert McIlwaine, Lee laid out the logistics for marching his survivors forty miles westward to Amelia Courthouse, where the army could catch the Danville train to North Carolina. The gray infantry divisions of First, Second, and Third Corps would head north-ward to cross the Appomattox River at Petersburg before marching west. They would have to cross the river again to reach Amelia. James Long-street was given command of both his First Corps and the dead Powell Hill's Third Corps. Dick Anderson's tiny Fourth Corps would remain south of the river on the westward march. Bridges would be burned as the Confederates crossed to slow the pursuing bluecoats. Meanwhile, Baldy Ewell would organize the Richmond home guard and march them southwest from Richmond to join the fleeing Army of Northern Virginia.

Under cover of Sunday-night darkness, the army pulled out of Petersburg. The cannon were dragged off the trench line by eight o'clock.

While the evacuation began, Lieutenant Colonel Walter Taylor, Robert Lee's essential aide, received the Old Man's permission to leave his post for the night on personal business. Young Taylor snaked through the lines up to Richmond on an important errand: He wanted to get married. He promised to rejoin the army's retreat the next day.

As Walter Taylor arrived in Richmond during the capital's last hours as a Confederate city, President Davis's wife and children reached Charlotte, North Carolina.

In the darkness, the evacuation of Petersburg and the abandonment of Richmond continued. General Lee crossed to the north bank of the Appomattox with 12,500 troops. He commanded less men than were in any one of the five Federal corps which chased him. The three gray corps north of the river and the single Fourth Corps south of the creek numbered a total of 29,000 men and two hundred cannon. A supply train of one thousand wagons pulled by skin-and-bone horses and mules stretched into the night for thirty miles.

While Robert Lee rode slowly northward, Jefferson Davis made ready to leave Richmond later Sunday night. While packing what was left of his personal belongings, the president took the time to send his most comfortable chair over to Franklin Street to Mother Lee for her old arthritic bones.

After sending his favorite chair to Mrs. Lee, Jefferson Davis finally reached the Richmond train depot at eleven p.m. on Sunday, four hours after his Cabinet had assembled there. When the train left Richmond with the Confederate government on board, the old locomotive also pulled a boxcar filled with horses in case the officials had to make a hasty escape from the train.

Three hours after the government disappeared into the darkness on the southbound railroad, Lieutenant General Richard Ewell began his evacuation of the capital city along with the home guard. After midnight Monday morning, April 3, Baldy Ewell burned the city's cotton and tobacco warehouses to deny the invading Federals anything of value. To lessen the civilian chaos certain to follow, General Ewell also had his troops dump barrels of liquor into Richmond streets. Mobs quickly filled the nighttime streets as the warehouses burned.

Rampaging civilians were kneeling in the streets to lap the rivulets of liquor out of the gutters. At two in the morning, the fires swept to the main arsenal and 750,000 artillery shells exploded. The fire approached Franklin Street and burned to the ground the church directly across the dirt street from the home of Mother Lee and her daughters. The roof burned on the house next to the Lee women, but the rented Lee home was spared.

Twenty miles down the road from the burning warehouse riverfront of Richmond, the Army of the Potomac pursued the bare footprints in the rain-soaked ground. The tracks were all that was left of the Army of Northern Virginia. Both armies left behind them ten thousand boys in blue and gray who had died or were wounded during the past four days.

General Lee was marching toward Burkeville, Virginia, by way of Amelia Courthouse. At Amelia, the Southside Railroad junctioned with the Danville line, where the tracks led to Joe Johnston in North Carolina. Most of Lee's command walked on the north side of the Appomattox. The Confederates had to travel 55 miles. The Federals marched westward on the south bank of the river. Grant and Meade's bluecoats had the shorter march of only 36 miles to the Burkeville rail hub. The rendezvous with Johnston on the Roanoke River was 107 miles away for Lee, but only 88 miles for Grant's pursuit.

Early Monday morning, April 3, Walter Taylor returned as a newly-wed of twelve hours. By seven o'clock in the morning, Baldy Ewell and the Richmond home guard had evacuated the capital to rendezvous with Lee at Amelia Courthouse. The Federal army of occupation was right behind them. When the blue divisions marched into Richmond this day, they captured a town which had not been occupied by "enemy" forces since British troops had occupied the city in 1781 during the American Revolution.

When Richmond fell, Mother Lee and the girls refused to abandon the capital of their new country, which had survived for exactly four years. Fires still burned, mainly along the riverfront. Agnes Lee swallowed her fierce pride and went to see the Yankee occupiers. She bravely introduced herself as the daughter of Robert E. Lee to German-born general Godfrey Weitzel, commander of the army of occupation. Fearful of fire and of rioting mobs, Agnes asked for the protection of her enemies—the men who still struggled to destroy her father.

The war was over for twenty-nine-year-old Major General Weitzel (West Point, '55, when Lieutenant Colonel Robert Lee, USA, was superintendent). He promptly sent three men in blue from the 9th Vermont Infantry to stand guard at the Franklin Street home of Mother Lee. A Federal ambulance waited outside in case the fires necessitated a rescue of the crippled Mrs. Robert E. Lee.

Sixteen

While Federal sentries paced off in front of the Lee home in Richmond on Monday, April 3, 1865, General Longstreet's First Corps and General Gordon's Second Corps marched toward Bevill's Bridge over the Appomattox, twenty-five miles northwest of Petersburg. They found the bridge flooded by the constant rains. The weary Confederates had to divert to Goode's Bridge, five miles further north. They reached the new bridge by evening. After First and Second Corps crossed, Dick Anderson's Fourth Corps with George Pickett's survivors from the Five Forks disaster continued along the south side of the Appomattox.

Between four and five o'clock Monday afternoon, Jefferson Davis and his Cabinet pulled into Danville, Virginia. The train had managed to cover only 140 miles during eighteen uncomfortable hours. The government in exile was warmly welcomed by the little hotbed of secession. The president boarded in the home of William T. Sutherlin. The Cabinet ministers set up their mobile departments at the Benedict House, formerly a school for Southern girls.

All Monday night, the regiments in gray rags marched westward. General Lee crossed Goode's Bridge early Tuesday morning by 7:30 after Longstreet's First Corps had crossed. Lee was desperate to reach Amelia Courthouse where he expected to find food. At seven p.m. on Sunday night, Lee had wired Richmond to send the rations to Amelia.

When General Lee led his starving divisions into Amelia, he did find Confederate supplies waiting for him—tons of artillery ammunition. But there was no food for thirty thousand men who had not eaten for days. Powell Hill's old Third Corps followed First Corps into Amelia by midday. John Gordon and Second Corps were five miles behind them. Billy

Mahone's division guarded Goode's Bridge until General Ewell could get there with the home guard fleeing Richmond. When Baldy Ewell finally crossed, Custis Lee was with him. George Washington Custis Lee had graduated first in his West Point class of 1854. His father, Robert, had been only graduate Number Two at the Point in 1829. The younger Lee, thirty-two, was now a major general in his father's army, and he led a regiment of non-soldier mechanics.

General Lee set up camp for Tuesday evening, April 4, at the Francis Smith home at Amelia Courthouse. Desperate for provisions, the weary chief issued a proclamation to Amelia County farmers, dated April 4. He pleaded for them to fill commissary wagons which would scour the countryside. "I must therefore appeal to your generosity and charity to supply as far as each one is able," General Lee begged, "the wants of the brave soldiers who have battled for your liberty for four years."

The army which had stood beside Antietam Creek and had glared up at the Federal cannon on the high ground at Gettysburg was reduced to asking for charity from farmers as hungry as themselves. Lee wanted to telegraph another prayer for 200,000 rations back to Richmond. He wanted the message telegraphed from Jetersville, seven miles south of Amelia, since the Amelia wires had been cut by Yankees. But the Jetersville message was never sent for fear that the Federals were tapping the wires which survived.

While Lee pitched camp this Tuesday at Amelia's empty pantry, Jefferson Davis in Danville convened his first Cabinet meeting on the road. The result was the Wednesday issuing of a Presidential Proclamation. As he usually did when the words had to be perfectly chosen, President Davis delegated the writing of the decree to Judah Benjamin. The proclamation called for continuing the struggle for Southern independence. "Let us but will it," Secretary of State Benjamin wrote in the name of his president, "and we are free."

As General Lee spent Tuesday pacing his quarters and the displaced president labored to rally his countrymen, occupied Richmond had a visitor.

Abraham Lincoln stepped off a barge at Rockett's Landing on the James River and walked into Richmond to see at last the prize for which he had struggled so long. President Lincoln had been a hanger-on at Grant's City Point base since March 24.

Mr. Lincoln looked remarkably old and worn as he ambled on too-long legs through the Confederate capitol grounds. When he visited the office of Jefferson Davis in the old US Customs building, his face darkened with a distant sadness as if the desk still somehow radiated the long struggle and war-weariness of his fellow Kentuckian, President Davis. When he sat in Jefferson Davis's chair, perhaps Lincoln sensed that no one except "President" Davis could understand the dreadful burden which Lincoln had borne. The strange light in Abraham Lincoln's gray eyes would forever haunt the men in Union blue who accompanied him on his triumphant but saddening tour.

Wednesday morning, April 5, at Amelia Courthouse marked another day of rain. Even the gray skies seemed to conspire against Robert Lee by reducing the road south to rivers of mud. The foraging parties were slowly returning from the Virginia countryside. The wagons were empty. The country had been bled dry long ago by the passing armies in blue and gray. Lee's last hope against starvation by the side of the muddy road was Danville, Virginia, where 1,500,000 rations waited 105 miles and four days of forced march down the road. The army spent the rest of the morning destroying the tons of useless artillery ammunition so the Yankees could not capture it and fire it at the retreating army.

Baldy Ewell finally arrived at Amelia by noon. The rain became harder and would continue through the day. At one o'clock Wednesday afternoon, the long gray line stumbled back to the dirt road for the march south to the Virginia border at Danville. Their objective for the day was Jetersville on the Richmond-Danville Railroad. Rooney Lee's cavalry led the way ahead of the exhausted and starving First Corps and the depleted divisions of Charles Field, Billy Mahone, George Pickett, Henry Heth, Cadmus Wilcox, and the division of Dick Anderson doubling as Fourth Corps. Baldy Ewell's home guard and Joe Kershaw's division straggled along with them.

On the road between Amelia and Jetersville, Robert Lee understood the desperation of his situation. By early afternoon, Rooney Lee's cavalry found that the pursuing Federals had beaten them down the road. The Yankees blocked the road to Jetersville southwest of Amelia. Jetersville was a vital railroad hub: a four-way intersection of tracks running west to Lynchburg and south to Joe Johnston. After a seven-mile march, the elder Lee found his cavalryman son fighting off three whole Federal corps: II, V, and VI Corps. There was no other rail line to Johnston in North Carolina.

With his southwest path blocked by overwhelming numbers, General Lee decided to head further west to Lynchburg for supplies. This required an exhausting backtrack, seven miles northeastward back to Amelia. From the dry hole of the courthouse, they would march west to Farmville, which had a spur of the Southside Railroad leading off to Lynchburg. Baldy Ewell brought up the rear. The one-legged general did not know that the Yankee cavalry of Phil Sheridan had already captured his rearguard supply wagons loaded with twenty thousand rations: one meal for only two-thirds of the retreating Rebel army.

The fourth day of the retreat began with another all-night march on Wednesday, April 5. The ragged gray line walked along wretched roads from Amelia Springs (between Jetersville and Amelia Courthouse) to the hamlet of Rice in the direction of Farmville. Confederate wagons took another, roundabout route. Wednesday evening, General Lee stopped for dinner at the home of Fourth Corps commander General Dick Anderson, near Amelia Springs.

After midnight, scouts reported that Lieutenant General Grant himself had ridden into Jetersville and planned an assault against the Rebel line at daybreak, April 6. Sheridan's blue cavalry massed on the Confederate left flank for the morning push. The retreating army made a good target: The whole force had to crowd a single road for five miles out of Amelia Springs.

General Lee was up and working all night, April 5 into April 6. He personally supervised engineers who worked under torches to repair the bridge across Flat Creek near Amelia Springs. Lee hoped to find provisions at Rice along the railroad which ran up to Lynchburg.

With Longstreet's First Corps leading, the gray infantry trudged through the night along muddy roads. Dick Anderson's Fourth Corps followed, with Ewell's home guard and John Gordon's Second Corps bringing up the rear. Troops straggled off in the darkness and dropped by the side of the road from chronic starvation. Emaciated boys who could catch stray farm animals ate their catches raw along the westward road beside the Southside Railroad. General Lee had wired Richmond during the capital's last hours, requesting that eighty thousand rations be sent to Farmville, nineteen miles from Amelia Springs.

Thursday, April 6, began for Robert Lee at four a.m. Lee had already been up all night. The Old Man ordered his nephew Fitz Lee to move out with his cavalry division to guard the long column's left flank against Phil Sheridan's cavalry harassment. Rooney Lee's division of gray cavalry was sent to guard John Gordon's Second Corps survivors in the rear of the westward-marching formation. What was left of the army was disintegrating hourly. Baldy Ewell's Richmond home guard of walking wounded had lost three thousand stragglers out of six thousand men within the last seventy-two hours.

By ten o'clock Thursday morning, Robert Lee had ridden twelve miles from Amelia to Rice Station on the Southside Railroad line. Old Pete's First Corps milled around the station, too. Seven hundred Yankee cavalry were spotted shortly after the Confederates' arrival, and General Longstreet sent his cavalry to chase them off. The gray divisions of Generals Wilcox, Heth, and Mahone arrived before noon. George Pickett's division—what was left of it after Five Forks—did not arrive. Pickett was well east of Rice at Sayler's Creek.

The long retreat through Rice was strung out along the wet dirt roads. Dick Anderson's Fourth Corps followed the First Corps wagons westward. Baldy Ewell was behind Anderson. Ewell's supply train followed Ewell's infantry, with John Gordon well behind everyone else. The supply wagons had been continuously harassed by Federal cavalry.

At eleven o'clock Thursday morning, Dick Anderson stopped on the road. No one advised the rear guard of First Corps ahead of Anderson. The First Corps continued to file into Rice Station without knowing that a gap had opened between Longstreet and Anderson.

Federals filled the gap west of Dick Anderson's command. At two o'clock, Baldy Ewell ordered his supply wagons to take a detour to the northwest of the main road. No one informed John Gordon, bringing up the rear. So, when General Gordon saw Ewell's wagon train divert to the right, Gordon followed the wagons. He assumed that Ewell's infantry was ahead of the supply train.

There was now a gap between Dick Anderson and Ewell, and a second gap between Ewell and Gordon.

Federals surrounded Dick Anderson west of Ewell's division and then surrounded the separated Baldy Ewell. The two gray forces fought Yankees back-to-back on the dirt road: Anderson faced the enemy to his west, and Ewell faced the blue-clad enemy to his east.

General Grant's Federals destroyed the exhausted commands of Dick Anderson and Baldy Ewell, one at a time.

Anderson and Ewell's boys fought ferociously hand to hand, but to no avail. Fourth Corps lost 2,800 men, and Ewell lost 1,500. When Old Bald Head surrendered, he gave up the brave division of Joe Kershaw and the hapless engineer division commanded by Custis Lee. The young Lee had to surrender his first command after his first battle, after only four days of real soldiering. Pickett's division was shattered.

At five p.m., the Federals tracked down John Gordon's isolated corps northwest of the main road. Gordon's command collapsed and broke for the rear. Although they manfully regrouped to fight another day, John Gordon lost 1,700 men.

In a single afternoon of miscommunication, the Army of Northern Virginia lost some eight thousand men—half of the army. The last of the division of George Pickett was destroyed after barely surviving Five Forks five days earlier.

By late Thursday afternoon, General Lee understood the magnitude of his calamity. He rode Traveller to the point where the Appomattox joins Sayler's Creek northwest of Rice Station. He paused to look down into a valley where his anguished black eyes saw the unbelievable: hundreds, perhaps thousands, of running men and boys in gray and butternut-brown rags. Many had thrown down their heavy rifled muskets to better flee the debacle up the road, where their divisions of Dick Anderson and Richard Ewell had disintegrated.

General Billy Mahone sat his horse at Robert Lee's side. The Old Man glared hard at the broken men and he fumed at Mahone, "My God! Has this army dissolved?"

Then, in a moment which old, old men would remember with tears in their faded eyes, Robert Lee grabbed a Rebel flag and held it high. The dazed, starving, and unarmed boys were frozen in their tracks like Lot's wife turned to salt.

Billy Mahone waved the survivors over and he quickly and expertly formed a new battle line of armed and unarmed men to fend off the next wave of Yankees if they should come down the road. The men took a deep breath and rushed to form a cordon with their emaciated bodies around General Lee, their Marse Robert. One dirty-faced survivor cried out from the bottom of his full heart and empty belly, "Where's the man who won't follow Uncle Robert!" None could be found, and the brave line formed up and held. Their Marse Robert raised the tattered flag as their guide-on.

The scene beside Sayler's Creek late on April 6, 1865, was more than the stuff of old soldiers' fading memories. It was the last rally of the Army of Northern Virginia.

At dusk after a bitter, bitter day, Billy Mahone and Robert Lee reviewed the day beside Sayler's Creek. The army had given up 8,000 men to the enemy. Lee's force had now dwindled to six divisions and a cavalry whose horses were too run-out to fight another battle. The old army was down to 12,000 infantry and 3,000 useless cavalry with which to do battle against 80,000 Federals, in hot pursuit with full bellies. Longstreet's mighty First Corps was down to the shrinking divisions of Heth, Wilcox, and Field. John Gordon's battered Second Corps was down to the division of Billy Mahone and a few stragglers and survivors from Anderson and Pickett's commands. Richard Ewell hobbled on his one leg to prison camp along with Custis Lee, who was missing in action as far as his father knew.

Thursday night, Robert Lee decided to send Longstreet's First Corps to Farmville, two miles south of the Appomattox. Gordon would march to Farmville by High Bridge north of Longstreet's route. For the third night in a row, the army would march all night on empty stomachs.

General Lee rode on to Farmville and a quick nap at the Patrick Jackson home. War Secretary John Breckinridge arrived there for a personal briefing to take to Jefferson Davis at Danville. Lee was bleak and not hopeful of reaching Joe Johnston. Too much of the army had been destroyed. Robert Lee enjoyed no more than three hours of rest before moving on.

General Lee left the Jackson house after enjoying a rare cup of hot tea before first light on Friday morning, April 7. He stopped briefly in Farmville to pay his respects to the widow of a cavalry officer killed at Sharpsburg. Then he supervised the dispersal of eighty thousand rations which had arrived the preceding day. Many of the ravenous troops had not eaten in five full days.

James Longstreet's weary corps shuffled into Farmville after another all-night march up from Rice Station. John Gordon's remnant of Second Corps followed with Fitz Lee's dilapidated cavalry behind them. The men wolfed down their tooth-breaking hardtack ("worm castles," they called it) until nine o'clock, when breakfast was interrupted by Federals.

After drawing two days' rations, Gordon's Second Corps marched off to burn High Bridge across the Appomattox to slow the Yankees approaching from north of Farmville. But the Federals arrived in time to extinguish the fires and to cross on the charred bridge. Billy Mahone fought off the blue-clad advance units.

Three miles north of town, Porter Alexander's artillery batteries were aligned to stop the massed Federal advance. It had been young Alexander's guns which covered Pickett's Charge so long ago. With the entire blue II Corps coming hard down the road, General Lee detached Billy Mahone's veteran fighters to Cumberland Church as rear guard for the fleeing Confederates. Lee rode toward Cumberland Church ahead of Old Pete's First Corps, which chewed their hard crackers as they marched upon bloody bare feet. Barefoot or not, Old Pete's hearty troops cheered their Marse Robert when he and Traveller rode past.

By the time Lee arrived at Cumberland in early afternoon, General Mahone's bloodied and depleted division was hotly engaged with an entire blue corps. By 4:30 p.m. on Friday, he had managed to repulse the bluecoats. Sunset stalemated the contest, to resume on Saturday. Yankees were closing the noose from all sides. The blue VI Corps was just south of Farmville, where Fitz Lee's horsemen had held them off.

Rooney Lee's cavalry was on hand in the twilight. With a father's voice, the Old Man took his son aside and firmly told him not to permit his men to speak among themselves of surrendering. Robert Lee had never before used the word.

The harried army lay down to sleep after making only four miles from Farmville. It was a rare night without marching under the stars. The men dropped to the soft ground. Most had been marching for eighteen hours; some had not slept for forty hours.

In the spring darkness, a Confederate courier approached General Lee. He carried a note passed between the enemy armies for his commanding general. The longhand message was signed, "U. S. Grant."

Seventeen

Friday night, April 7, Federal Major General Seth Williams (West Point, '42), forty-three, assistant adjutant general of the Army of the Potomac, delivered a note from Lieutenant General Grant. Williams had served on Robert Lee's faculty during Lieutenant Colonel Lee's superintendency at West Point. The note was passed through the lines to Billy Mahone's post. From General Mahone, the note dated 5:00 p.m. was relayed to General Lee in conference with James Longstreet at 9:30 p.m.

"The results of the last week must convince you of the hopelessness of further resistance," Lieutenant General Grant wrote. "I regard it as my duty to shift from myself the responsibility of any effusion of blood by asking of you the surrender of that portion of the C. S. Army known as the Army of Northern Virginia."

General Lee grimly handed the note to "Old Pete" Longstreet, who carefully read the message from his kinsman by marriage, U. S. Grant.

"Well?" the commanding general asked his "old warhorse" of so many great and bitter campaigns.

"Not yet" was all that Lieutenant General James Longstreet said.

So began the exchange of nine notes between the War Between the States' greatest captains, and the last forty-six hours of the Army of Northern Virginia. Both Ulysses S. Grant and Robert E. Lee would spend the next two days laboring mightily to demonstrate that the true test of manhood is the extent to which one can remain a gentleman under unbearable stress.

Unknown to James Longstreet, General Lee sent a written answer to Grant's note. "I have read your note of this date," the white-bearded Virginian wrote. "Though not entertaining the opinion you express of the hopelessness of further resistance on the part of the Army of N. Va., I reciprocate your desire to avoid useless effusion of blood and, therefore, before considering your proposition, ask the terms you will offer on the condition of its surrender." The Old Man used the dreadful word *surrender*, which he had forbidden his son Rooney Lee to use only two hours earlier.

In the literary convention of the day, General-in-Chief Lee signed his longhand notes with the affectation "Very respectfully, your obedient servant." And Lieutenant General Grant signed his notes to Robert Lee, "Very respectfully."

After sending off his note through the lines to Grant, General Lee ordered his troops awakened after their momentary nap in the evening twilight. The march must resume, or the old army would perish in the mud.

With Lee at Cumberland Church four miles north of Farmville, the wagon train was well ahead at New Store, twenty miles from Farmville. The army was only two wings: Old Pete still at the helm of First Corps, along with the remains of A. P. Hill's Third Corps, and John Gordon's Second Corps, combined with Dick Anderson's stragglers from Fourth Corps. An hour before midnight, Friday night, Gordon's command resumed the mud march westward to Lynchburg and its prayed-for food at the railroad hub. During the first minutes of Saturday, April 8, Lieutenant General Longstreet followed, with the exhausted cavalry bringing up the rear. They moved out for Appomattox Station on the Southside Railroad, along the Lynchburg Road. The Lynchburg rations were to be sent to the station.

Marching all Friday night and into Saturday, General Lee had to beat Grant to Appomattox Station, where the supply train from Lynchburg was anticipated. At the station, the Appomattox River was shallow and narrow toward the west where it joined the James River. The James flowed past Lynchburg and the Appomattox ended at Appomattox Courthouse. Once Lee's army passed the end of the Appomattox, there would be no other water barrier to slow the pursuing Federals, who could then march further west, cross in front of Lee, and block the road to Lynchburg. The winner of the race to the headwaters of the Appomattox would win the endgame of the retreat from Petersburg.

Before dawn on Saturday, General Lee was unaware that the blue II and VI Corps were closing in on him only four miles away on the north bank of the Appomattox River, where Lee marched. Yankee cavalry along with the blue V, XXV, and XXIV Corps of infantry chased Lee along the south side of the narrowing river. Phil Sheridan's blue cavalry was twenty miles away. By the time the sun was up, General William Pendleton—Sandie's grieving father—informed Robert Lee that several of his generals were recommending surrender. The Old Man's neck reddened as it always did when he had to bridle his fierce temper. General Lee proclaimed that the orderly retreat would continue down to Joe Johnston, who waited for Lee in North Carolina.

Saturday required General Lee to attend to administrative details. He relieved George Pickett, Dick Anderson, and Bushrod Johnson of their commands. With their divisions destroyed at Sayler's Creek, there were no troops left for these generals to lead. George Pickett sullenly walked off into the mists of history, forever convinced that Robert Lee had exterminated his grand division at Gettysburg. Colonel John Mosby, expelled from the University of Virginia, and commander of Mosby's Rangers, quoted General Pickett as saying of Robert Lee in 1870: "That old man had my division massacred," referring to Pickett's Charge at Gettysburg. Whether or not General Pickett really made that statement is still disputed after more than a century and a half.

The march all night and into Saturday, April 8, 1865, was more a race than war. There was little gunplay as the troops in blue dogged their starving prey. John Gordon's command arrived within one mile of Appomattox Courthouse by three in the afternoon. First Corps dragged into camp by twilight with its wasted divisions strung out for six miles. By nightfall, the Confederates, who collapsed from hunger and exhaustion, were stunned by what the darkness revealed of their future: These last Rebels saw Yankee campfires dotting the horizon to their south, east, and west. The fires to the west confirmed the worst—that the Federals had beaten them, and were in front of them to block with walls of molten lead the last road to Lynchburg.

While the Union fires flickered all around the hungry Confederates, Lieutenant John Wise (son of former Virginia Governor Henry Wise) reported to Jefferson Davis in Danville. The younger Wise had returned from private consultations with General Lee. To the sickly President Davis, Lieutenant Wise confirmed that the Army of Northern Virginia was in the most dire straits, and that its surrender was likely. In disbelief, the president told his youthful emissary to return to General Lee the next day, Sunday, April 9, for further updates.

In the Saturday-night darkness, couriers brought to Robert Lee a second dispatch from General Grant out there among his encircling campfires. Grant was replying to Lee's note inquiring about the surrender terms being demanded. Ulysses Grant began his careful reply by affirming "Peace being my great desire." Then he stated that his only demand of General Lee was that his army should surrender, never to take up arms again in opposition to the national government. Ever the gentleman, Grant then added a delicate touch. "I will meet you, or will designate officers to meet any officers you may name for the same purpose, at any point agreeable to you." The courtly Federal was giving Robert Lee the chance to be spared the humiliation of surrendering his gallant army in person. In effect, Grant's seconds would deal with Lee's seconds if the grief-stricken Virginian could not abide personally handing over his heroic survivors.

Although Robert Lee's note to Grant on Friday, April 7, had clearly asked for Grant's surrender conditions, Lee was overwhelmed by the sudden and terrible reality of speaking about surrender. General Lee drew back from that awful brink. He penned a reply to Grant and declined to speak further about surrender. "To be frank," the Confederate general-in-chief wrote, "I do not think the emergency has arisen to call for the surrender of this army." Declining to surrender, Lee asked for a Sunday conference with Grant between the lines to review Grant's overall agenda for restoring peace to the shattered and grief-stricken United States. Lee proposed meeting Grant at ten o'clock Sunday morning between the two armies' lines.

The nighttime sky was now lit by Federal artillery, which had begun at nine p.m.

After sending his note off to Grant, General Lee conferred with his lieutenants at ten p.m. on Saturday: Lieutenant General Longstreet, and Major Generals John Gordon and Fitzhugh Lee. Also present was General Pendleton of the artillery corps. The group decided to attempt one final breakout westward to Lynchburg. The old army would attack the Yankees at dawn, Sunday morning. There was only one real purpose for this last assault: to determine if the Federals blocking the Lynchburg Road were cavalry or infantry.

If the road west was blocked only by cavalry, the gray army might be able to break free. But if they were Federal infantry, that would be the end.

Fitz Lee would command the shell of the cavalry, now only 2,000 troopers. John Gordon would attack with Second Corps, only 2,000 infantry. Only two weeks earlier, Second Corps counted 7,500 men. And Longstreet's First Corps of 6,000 would protect the rear of the army if they could break out. The gray artillery of General Pendleton numbered sixty-one cannon and 2,000 cannoneers. These 12,000 men were all that was left of an army which had mustered nearly 80,000 men two years earlier. What was left of George Pickett's division numbered sixty hungry and barefoot stragglers. The required deployment would begin one hour after midnight, Sunday morning.

Fitz Lee with his massive black beard nearly touching his saber belt took his uncle aside for a private petition. He asked General Lee for permission to be given enough time to pull his cavalry division out of Appomattox Courthouse to ride for North Carolina should any surrender be declared. General Lee granted his nephew's request not to be present if the army laid down its weapons.

When the iron-willed John Gordon asked General Lee in the campfire's glow where Gordon should plan to camp Sunday night if the breakout worked, Robert Lee looked him square in the eye and said softly, "Tennessee."

April 9 was Palm Sunday, 1865.

An hour after midnight Saturday night, Old Pete's First Corps deployed in the rear of Lee's thin line to protect the last push from pursuit by Federals should the breakout work in four hours. At two o'clock Sunday morning, Robert Lee changed uniforms.

In the middle of the night, General Lee removed the gray waistcoat he had worn since Petersburg, April 2. Then he donned a new gray dress uniform with shining brass "CSA" buttons. He carefully adjusted his red-silk saber sash. The Old Man looked like he was going to dress parade when he mounted Traveller in the darkness. General Pendleton commented on his chief's new clothes. General Lee replied grimly that he wanted to be at his best if he were to become Grant's prisoner by day's end. At three o'clock in the morning, Lee turned Traveller's gray head toward Appomattox Courthouse.

At dawn, about five a.m., the Confederates attacked the surrounding Federals half a mile west of Appomattox Courthouse. General Lee was in the rear of General Gordon's Second Corps. Fighting raged for three hours as Gordon pushed back the Federals and captured two Yankee cannon. But by that time, John Gordon had discovered the truth: He was not fighting blue cavalry, but infantry. He sent word back that he could not hang on without help from Old Pete's First Corps. Gordon's two thousand men were fighting three blue divisions of infantry. Federal cavalry was now pushing Fitz Lee's cavalry out of their way.

At eight o'clock, Robert Lee had fought his last battle for his real country, Virginia.

James Longstreet approached General Lee in his new uniform as word came in of Gordon's situation. Lee was surrounded. Two Federal corps were doing battle with the gray ghost of an army. The blue V Corps was in Lee's front and the blue II Corps harassed Longstreet's rear guard.

By 8:30 in the morning, April 9, 1865, it was all over.

Robert Edward Lee (West Point, '29) spoke softly to his aide, Charles Venable. The air was filled with Minié balls and shrapnel. "How easily I could be rid of this and be at rest," the army's Uncle Robert sighed, listening to the cannon fire. "I have only to ride along the line and all will be over."

General Lee ordered Lieutenant General Longstreet to have John Gordon cease fire.

Lee needed the company of Old Pete. Sometimes slow to engage, James Longstreet had always been like a rock once he was on the field: an immovable object which neither bullet nor shell could chip away. The fighting was certain to be ferocious wherever Old Pete made his stand, if his heart were in it. Robert Lee asked Longstreet for his opinion. Longstreet candidly stated in his gruff and direct tone that the army should fight it out beside the Appomattox River if the old army's annihilation would somehow help the Confederate cause on other fronts. When General Lee shook his white and thinning head and said that his army's destruction would not serve a higher strategic purpose, Old Pete replied that the facts then spoke for themselves.

"There is nothing left for me," Robert Lee said to Lieutenant Colonel Venable, "but to go and see General Grant. I would rather die a thousand deaths."

Eighteen

LIEUTENANT GENERAL ULYSSES S. GRANT SPENT SATURDAY NIGHT soaking his feet in hot water laced with mustard. Suffering from one of his "sick headaches," he also applied mustard poultices to his wrists and to the back of his neck. Only Robert Lee could cure his pain, and he did.

The Army of Northern Virginia since Petersburg had endured by sheer heart. It ran not on food or sleep, but on the strength of its collective memories. "That army," said its old blue enemy, General "Fighting Joe" Hooker—whom Stonewall had shattered at Chancellorsville—"has, by discipline alone, acquired a character for steadiness and efficiency unsurpassed, in my judgment, in ancient or modern times."

General Lee in his dress grays mounted Traveller and set off slowly to rendezvous with General Grant for the ten a.m. meeting on April 9, 1865, which Lee had requested in his muddled note the previous night.

When Robert Lee rode out from his line in search of General Grant, Lee rode with aides Colonel Charles Marshall, the Baltimore lawyer, and Lieutenant Colonel Walter Taylor, the bridegroom of seven days. They rode under a white truce flag for the first time in Robert E. Lee's thirty-six years of military life, boy and man, blue or gray.

Federal Lieutenant Colonel Charles Whittier, assistant adjutant general of Hancock's II Corps, intercepted Lee's party. Grant had not come to meet Lee. The AAG delivered to General Lee a disappointing third note signed by General Grant. The Federal general-in-chief rejected Lee's proposal for a between-the-lines chat about ceasefires without unconditional surrender. "I have no authority to treat on the subject of peace," wrote Grant. With physical pain in his voice, Robert Lee dictated to his aide Lieutenant Colonel Marshall another message for Lieutenant General Grant.

US Supreme Court Chief Justice John Marshall's great-grand-nephew wrote out Lee's response for relay to Grant: "I received your note of this morning on the picket line," Lee dictated, "with respect to the surrender of this army. I now request an interview in accordance with the offer contained in your letter of yesterday." The new note was handed to Lieutenant Colonel Whittier for his chief.

Taking no chances of more unnecessary killing, General Lee sent a second message to Grant from between the lines. "It would probably expedite matters to send a duplicate through some other part of your lines," Lee wrote to Grant. "I therefore request an interview, at such time and place as you may designate to discuss the terms of the surrender of this army in accordance with your offer to have such an interview, contained in your letter of yesterday."

General Lee dictated a third message as Federal forces continued to mass around him for the final thrust to crush the gray army. "I ask a suspension of hostilities pending the adjustment of the terms of the surrender of this army."

Notes were passed between the lines through mid-morning. Evidently, the Federals on the Appomattox field did not know that their most feared enemy was done fighting. As the blue divisions continued to deploy for a Palm Sunday attack, a solicitous Federal officer under a white flag approached General Lee's little party. He respectfully advised the Confederates that a Union assault was moments away, and that General Lee should withdraw to a position of safety. The Yankee saluted Robert Lee as the Army of the Potomac closed to within one hundred yards of the devastated hulk of Lee's army. General Lee sullenly rode back to Longstreet's lines.

At the last possible moment, an hour before noon, Lieutenant Colonel Whittier returned under a white flag with a message from Major General George Gordon Meade. Old Snapping Turtle had agreed to a one-hour delay of the Federal attack. Lee used the reprieve to send his fifth note through the lines to ask for a surrender interview with Grant.

Upon Grant's receipt of General Lee's concession to surrender, Grant's headache was suddenly cured.

Elsewhere on the Appomattox front, General Phil Sheridan rode over to John Gordon's last battlefield. Sheridan agreed to cease fire in his sector of the line until Grant and Lee could have their meeting.

By noon, an uneasy ceasefire was in effect west of Appomattox Courthouse along the route of Lee's retreat. In the company of James Longstreet, Robert Lee expressed his private fear of harsh terms at the hands of the Yankee, known as U. S. "Unconditional Surrender" Grant. Old Pete assured General Lee that Grant would dictate only fair and honorable terms of surrender. While Lee paced and awaited word from Grant, General George Meade extended the afternoon truce from one to two p.m. A breathless silence prevailed between the lines of the two armies, which had been in almost daily contact in a death struggle since the Federal crossing of the Rapidan eleven months earlier.

Robert Lee waited with First Corps inside Longstreet's perimeter. The Old Man rested quietly beneath an apple tree. Just after noon, Lieutenant Colonel Orville Babcock of Grant's staff rode between the lines. He delivered to Lee a message from Grant. The Federal general-in-chief stated that he had not received Lee's 9:00 a.m. note until 11:50 a.m. Grant was now four miles from Lee's position. The courteous Federal invited Lee to choose the place of their meeting: within Confederate or Union lines. Grant would come to Lee's post if requested. General Lee, Colonel Marshall, and Sergeant Tucker (the dead Powell Hill's trusted aide) set off on horseback with Lieutenant Colonel Babcock. Colonel Marshall went on ahead to find a suitable place for the historic meeting.

Marshall found the home of Wilmer McLean. Lee and his party rode on until the old soldier in his new gray uniform paused at a creek to allow his faithful Traveller a quick drink. Lee's principal aide Walter Taylor excused himself from the meeting with Grant. Taylor could not bring himself to attend his army's undoing. His general released him from going further.

General Lee arrived at the little brick house between 12:30 and 1:00 p.m. Due to the distance Grant had to travel, he did not arrive for half an hour.

Lieutenant General Grant arrived about 1:30, accompanied by General Phil Sheridan and General Edward O. Ord. Grant and Lee stiffly shook hands. Eight officers in blue filed in.

Laboring in the awkward moment, Grant struggled to make small talk. He recalled meeting a Captain Robert Lee in Mexico during that war of their collective youth, eighteen years earlier. Equally uncomfortable, General Lee confessed that he could not remember Grant from those old days under the same flag.

General Lee directed the conversation to the task at hand: the surrender of his army. Grant presented a draft instrument of surrender.

Robert Lee took his spectacles from his gray pocket, slowly wiped the lenses, and read carefully the document. Lee was pleased when he read that officers could keep their sidearms.

By this simple act, Grant declined the nineteenth-century ceremony of accepting a defeated general's sword. Old Pete had been right about his cousin.

Lee broke the brittle silence by stating that Confederates had brought their own horses to their war for independence. The mounts, emaciated as they were, would be needed for spring plowing when the army dispersed and went home. Grant indicated his ignorance of that practice but agreed instantly to issue orders that Confederates would keep their private animals. Again, Lee was relieved.

When General Lee agreed to the terms of the document, Grant handed the pencil edition to an aide to reproduce the surrender in ink. While they waited, Grant introduced his generals. Robert Lee was quite reserved as he shook hands with his captors. Only when Grant introduced Seth Williams was Lee animated and cheerful as he greeted his old aide from West Point days. So much blood had passed between them since the happier days on the Hudson River.

Robert Lee reread the surrender terms when presented in ink and found them in compliance with Grant's letter of yesterday. All that was required for the hungry Confederates was that they not take up arms against the United States, and that they observe the terms of their paroles when the gray army disbanded. General Lee dictated his formal capitulation. Of the terms of surrender he wrote, "As they are substantially the same as those expressed in your letter of the 8th instant, they are accepted." The old soldier then signed, "R. E. Lee, General."

In another gesture of goodwill for the afternoon, General Grant offered to immediately send twenty-five thousand rations over to the starving Confederates. General Lee was genuinely moved and expressed his profound appreciation.

On paper, the Army of Northern Virginia was surrendered Sunday afternoon at 3:30 p.m.

At West Point more than thirty-five years earlier, Cadet R. E. Lee was so reserved, dignified, and austere in his courtly bearing that fellow cadets dubbed him "the marble model." Over the decades of victory and painful defeat, that severe dignity had not changed. Of the surrender ceremony at the McLean house, Grant would remember: "What General Lee's feelings were I do not know. As he was a man of much dignity, with an impassible face, it was impossible to say whether he felt inwardly glad that the end had finally come, or felt sad over the result, and was too manly to show it. Whatever his feelings, they were entirely concealed."

Robert Lee saluted General Grant and walked heavily down the front steps of the McLean porch. Observers would remember that the back of the general's neck was remarkably red as he stood awkwardly on the porch and waited for Sergeant Tucker to fetch Traveller. For the lifetime of his military career, aides and comrades had noted that the only way to truly confirm the Marble Model was under grave stress or anger was the sudden redness of his neck, which happened whenever Robert Lee was struggling to control his emotions.

Traveller's bridle had been removed and the gray warhorse had grazed peacefully during his master's supreme ordeal. Tucker slipped the bridle over Traveller's head and General Lee mounted. When the somber Virginian gathered his reins, General Grant stepped onto the porch.

Without a single word, the shabbily dressed Ulysses Grant lifted his dusty blue hat in silent salute to the man he had drowned in Federal blood. A dozen Federal officers doffed their hats in unison. Robert Lee lifted his gray slouch hat, paused, and rode off to his troops—now prisoners of war.

General Grant attributed to Robert Lee's defeated army the same "last full measure of devotion" which Lieutenant General Grant had bestowed upon his mighty host in blue, acknowledging twenty years afterward that "the men . . . had fought so bravely, so gallantly and so long for the cause which they believed in—and as earnestly, I take it, as our men believed in the cause for which they were fighting."

At four o'clock, General Lee rode into James Longstreet's lines. Barefoot men and boys pressed close to their Uncle Robert. The weary general removed his hat and spoke uncovered in a voice choked with tears. "Men, we have fought the war together and I have done the best I could for you. You will all be paroled and go to your homes." Their Uncle Robert was too overcome to continue. He went back to the apple tree where he had awaited word from Grant. He paced there alone for a while as his staff kept the troops at a distance.

Toward evening, Lee mounted Traveller and rode one mile back toward his field headquarters in the rear of First Corps. The remnant of his defeated army stood reverently on both sides of the dirt road.

For a full mile, the survivors of the Army of Northern Virginia cheered the old man as he rode past. They cheered and wept as their chief and his gray charger advanced slowly. These men with their sunken faces pinched by starvation would remember to their last breath how Robert Lee rode with his head uncovered, his chin bowed, and his wind-burned face streaked with tears.

When General Lee finally arrived at his headquarters tent, he dismounted, said nothing, and went into his last bivouac to be alone. He would remain in command of his army for three more days.

This Palm Sunday, the mighty Army of Northern Virginia was reduced to 7,892 survivors. Over the next two days before the formal April 12 surrender ceremony, another 10,000 stragglers would stagger into the lines by ones and twos. They would number 28,231 men when they stacked arms for the last time on Wednesday. Of Jeb Stuart's 9,700 cavalrymen, only 676 were left to surrender, excluding Fitz Lee's cavalry, which had made good their escape as Robert Lee had promised his nephew.

Before Palm Sunday ended, General Lee had one more administrative task to complete. What could he say to these survivors who had stood by him since the first day of June, 1862? What could he say to these men who had suffered for him at The Seven Days massacre of Malvern Hill, had held back the blue tide at Burnside Bridge across Antietam Creek and had refused to yield the Bloody Lane, had stood shoulder to shoulder at Fredericksburg, had routed Joe Hooker at Chancellorsville, had marched up that hillside into the hailstorm of bullets and cannon at Gettysburg, had turned the mud to puddles of Confederate blood at Bloody Angle in the Spotsylvania Mule Shoe, and had starved nearly to death in the Petersburg trenches? The Old Man paced his lonesome tent and grasped for the right words.

Monday morning, April 10, Robert Lee asked Colonel Charles Marshall to begin a first draft of an appropriate Farewell Address to men such as these.

Toward mid-morning, while Marshall worked on his assignment, aides informed General Lee that Ulysses Grant had come calling. Lee mounted Traveller and rode to meet the Federal who had fought him so furiously, as if there were no end to Yankee blood, yet had demanded surrender terms more lenient than Lee had dared to imagine. No other day in Grant's later life would be as great as his April 9 moment with Robert Lee, gentleman to gentleman, in the McLean house. Now, Grant wanted to visit Lee again.

Sitting atop their warhorses, Traveller and Cincinnati, the two generals-in-chief spoke quietly for half an hour, out of earshot of their nearby aides. General Grant would remember their meeting on horseback as "a very pleasant conversation of over half an hour." They spoke of peace among what Robert Lee still regarded as two separate peoples. When Grant wanted Lee to exert his influence to end the war still raging elsewhere in the crumbling Confederacy, Lee respectfully declined, just as Grant had refused to negotiate a truce yesterday. Ever the democrat, Lee deferred to the civilian governments on matters of statecraft. Before parting, General Lee gave Grant permission to allow his generals to come through Confederate lines if they wished to visit with their former Old Army friends who wore the gray—for two more days.

Among the Federals who came into Confederate lines to pay their respects was Seth Williams, who wanted to see his old friend, former Lieutenant Colonel Lee, again. With Williams was George Gordon Meade, who had challenged Lee at Gettysburg. Major General Meade took pride in introducing Lee to Meade's captain son, George Junior. Regaining a semblance of his cheer, the exhausted Lee asked General Meade where he had acquired so much gray hair since their last peace-time meeting? "You have to answer for most of it," Old Snapping Turtle said, smiling gently. With that, Robert Lee and George Meade enjoyed a quiet and private meeting inside Lee's tent. They were countrymen again.

Sometime Monday, word finally reached Danville and Jefferson Davis that Robert Lee had surrendered the Confederacy's greatest army. The government would have to move on.

After dinner Monday evening, Lieutenant Colonel Marshall presented to Lee a draft of a farewell to the troops. After penciling in a few changes, General Lee issued the statement as his last battlefield orders, General Orders Number 9. The Farewell Address remained in Colonel Marshall's handwriting. Although Robert Lee autographed hundreds of copies of G. O. 9, there are no copies of the actual address in his own hand.

For generations, Yankee schoolchildren would stand trembling before their fourth-grade classmates to recite Abraham Lincoln's Gettysburg Address.

And for generations, children of the long-gone Old South would stand and recite Robert E. Lee's Farewell Address:

After four years of arduous service, marked by unsurpassed courage and fortitude, the Army of Northern Virginia has been compelled to yield to overwhelming numbers and resources. I need not tell the brave survivors of so many hard-fought battles, who have remained steadfast to the last, that I have consented to the result from no distrust of them. But feeling that valor and devotion could accomplish nothing that would compensate for the loss that must have attended the continuance of the contest, I determined to avoid the useless sacrifice of those whose past services have endeared them to their countrymen. By the terms of the agreement, officers and men can return to their homes and remain until exchanged. You will take with you the satisfaction that proceeds from the consciousness of duty faithfully performed. I earnestly pray that a Merciful God will extend to you His blessing and protection. With an increasing admiration of your constancy and devotion to your country, and a grateful remembrance of your kind and generous considerations for myself, I bid you all an affectionate farewell.

As always, the manuscript was signed "R. E. Lee." Never in his life did he ever sign as "Robert E. Lee."

The Farewell Address was Robert Lee to the core: Nowhere was the word *surrender* used; nowhere was there reference to the United States; and twice did he refer to the Confederacy (not by name) as his country. And the ultimate hallmark of manhood was noted as duty faithfully performed.

As G. O. 9 was read from regiment to regiment, to men who wore gray or butternut-brown rags and ate Federal rations, courtesy of U. S. Grant's well of goodwill, Jefferson Davis was packing again down the road at Danville. President Davis wired Joe Johnston to meet the government train at Greensboro, North Carolina. Johnston now commanded the only significant Confederate force still alive to fight another day. The Cabinet and the president boarded the train at ten o'clock, Monday night. At midnight, they pulled out to continue the war.

By Tuesday, April 11, Robert Lee was finally able to use the dreadful word. The dutiful general, he wrote a detailed dispatch to Jefferson Davis: "It is with pain that I announce to your Excellency the surrender of the Army of Northern Virginia."

By noon Tuesday, the government train had reached Greensboro. The train had traveled from Danville, making only four miles per hour. The Confederate First Lady and her children left Charlotte the same day to head further south. Compared to the Confederate hotbed of Danville, the government's reception in Greensboro was quite cool. There were no loyal crowds of citizens to cheer the fugitives. No townsfolk offered their homes to the president or his Cabinet. Jefferson Davis had to board in an aide's tiny apartment. No city facilities were offered as government ministries, and the Cabinet secretaries had to set up shop inside their miserable train cars. Greensboro was fed up with the war, and fearful of Federal reprisals if they sheltered the Davis government.

Wednesday, April 12, 1865, the Army of Northern Virginia ceased to be.

Neither Robert Lee nor Ulysses Grant attended the formal dissolution of the gray army. General Grant was on his way to Washington City, and Robert Lee paced alone in his canvas tent.

Federal Brigadier General Joshua Chamberlain of Maine conducted the last stacking of arms of the Rebel army. To the gentleman from Downeast Maine who had held Little Round Top at Gettysburg at bayonet point, the marching barefoot Confederates were like the passing of the honored dead. General Chamberlain knew what this war had been about. He had been wounded four times, and he would be awarded the Congressional Medal of Honor for Gettysburg.

When John Gordon led his Second Corps to stack arms and lay down riddled battle flags for the last time, Joshua Chamberlain barked an order. The massed blue line instantly snapped their muskets into the order-arms parade-ground salute to their enemies. Years later, ancient men, blue and gray, would cry as they recalled the moment of that salute, forever frozen in their memories.

As the Army of Northern Virginia surrendered one division at a time, laying rifles, cartridge belts, and shredded battle flags into piles at Yankee feet, Jefferson Davis conducted government business at Greensboro, North Carolina. In his rolling railcar office, Davis conferred with Generals Joe Johnston and Pierre Beauregard. The tension between Davis and General Johnston was intense. They may have hated each other for thirty-five years. Rumor was that they fought over the same girl when they were West Point cadets.

General Johnston reported that his army camped eighty miles east of Greensboro, but he objected to continuing the war. The general, whose wounding three years earlier had sent Robert Lee into the field, wanted to negotiate a surrender with General Sherman. The president was adamant: He would fight on. Jefferson Davis hoped to muster deserters, stragglers, and the walking wounded into another army to fight Federals in the Deep South. All of the Cabinet except one agreed with Johnston.

Only Secretary of State Judah Benjamin wanted to continue the war to the death like his president.

After the surrender Wednesday afternoon, Robert Lee broke camp at Appomattox Courthouse. He had spent his last day as a soldier since leaving West Point thirty-five years earlier. He began the slow ride to Richmond that afternoon.

Lee left camp with James Longstreet, Walter Taylor, and Charles Marshall. The victorious Army of the Potomac sent over an honor guard of twenty-five cavalry troopers to escort General Lee back to Richmond, a horseback ride of one hundred miles and three grueling days. Lee gently declined, saying that he knew the way. But the blue escort followed him a respectful distance behind for a few miles.

In the warm spring weather of Wednesday, April 12, Robert Edward Lee on Traveller's gray back left soldiering behind forever. He still wore his new dress grays.

During the thirty-four months that Robert Lee had commanded this army, he had suffered 121,000 killed and wounded Confederates. He knew few of their faces.

As Robert Lee rode slowly home to his burned and occupied Richmond, perhaps his weary mind walked again those ghastly and silent fields where his army had been ground away. Perhaps he lingered upon the faces he did know: Stonewall, Jeb Stuart, Sandie Pendleton, John Pelham, John and Willie Pegram, Dorsey Pender, Lewis Armistead, William Barksdale, and Little Powell Hill. The honor roll had two things in common: They had fought for Robert Lee.

And they were all dead.

Nineteen

THE ARMY OF NORTHERN VIRGINIA HAD DISSOLVED EARLIER WEDNES-
day afternoon, April 12. On the long ride home to Richmond, General
Lee and Lieutenant General Longstreet camped Wednesday night at
Buckingham Courthouse.

Thursday morning, Robert Lee and James Longstreet began their
first full day as civilian, paroled prisoners of war, and as men without a
country. Neither old soldier was a lawful citizen of anywhere. Their country was evaporating and Virginians were now an occupied people. The
Confederacy was quickly becoming the first English-speaking country
to be conquered on the battlefield since 1066 at the Battle of Hastings.

Breaking camp, the once wounded and still powerful Old Pete shook
hands with his exhausted, white-haired chief.

Lee and Longstreet parted company as friends beside the dirt road to
Richmond. Not even their painful disagreement over tactics on the third
day at Gettysburg could obscure the reality that Old Pete had stood by
Robert Lee from beginning to end.

The eccentric and dazzling Stonewall Jackson surely impressed General Lee. But Lee and Jackson had never been friends. Old Jack had no
friends. Only Jeb Stuart and Sandie Pendleton ever became close to Old
Blue Light. Yet, *friends* was still too heavy a word to attach to Jackson's
relationships with others. With Lee and Longstreet, it had been different.
Old Pete had ever been Lee's Old Warhorse, as Lee had called Longstreet beside Antietam Creek.

Their parting Thursday morning was sad for both weary men when
Robert Lee, civilian, warmly shook hands with James Longstreet, civilian.
Neither old warrior would look upon the other's face again.

General Lee and his handful of aides continued down the road eastward toward Richmond, where the smoke still rose from the burned-out warehouse district.

Leaving Longstreet, who headed for his home in Georgia, Robert Lee may have permitted his numbed mind to contemplate his crop of generals. The general staff of the Army of Northern Virginia had been pulverized during three years of unspeakable violence. Many men rose to generalships only to be dismissed for incompetence. Many lay wounded or dead throughout Virginia, Maryland, and Pennsylvania. Some of their graves would become shrines to The Lost Cause; some would repose in unmarked, mass graves where barefoot privates lay beside their shredded officers.

During Robert Lee's thirty-four months in command of his disbanded army, 6 men had become lieutenant generals. One day after the surrender, only 1 remained: James Longstreet. Two had been killed outright, and the rest wounded, captured, or relieved of command as the army disintegrated. Forty-seven men had become major generals; 7 remained by Appomattox, and of the rest, 7 were dead. And of 146 brigadier generals commissioned, 22 remained at their posts. Thirty-five brigadiers had been slain in the bloodbath between The Seven Days and Appomattox. The army which straggled in to stack arms only the day before had but 85 surviving colonels; the 28,231 men who surrendered should have had 200 colonels.

Robert Lee could be proud of his officer corps. The Army of Northern Virginia had more officers with college or military academy training than any other Southern army. During the first six months of Lee's command in 1862, all of his major generals were from West Point. By 1863, 8 of 9 were from the Point. During the war's last full year, 1864, 8 of 11 had trained at the Point. Among Lee's junior- and middle-grade officers, some 1,965 men achieved the rank of major, lieutenant colonel, and full colonel. Of these, Virginia Military Institute had graduated 156, West Point had trained 73, the Citadel in South Carolina produced 37, the Georgia Military Institute had turned out 14, and the US Naval Academy had graduated 4 officers who found their way to Virginia. The army which was no more had demonstrated the value of educated, professional officers commanding disciplined fighting men.

Thursday night, after all day on horseback, Robert Lee camped in Cumberland County, where the loyal Traveller had to have his sore feet reshod by the local smithy.

While Traveller was getting new shoes on April 13, the exiled Confederate government continued to function at Greensboro, North Carolina. Jefferson Davis remained defiant when his Cabinet convened in the president's tiny apartment. Generals Johnston and Beauregard both advocated a negotiated truce with the surrounding Federals. Again, all of the Cabinet agreed, with the one exception of Judah Benjamin.

Generals Johnston and Beauregard estimated that they could still muster 25,000 graybacks to do battle with fully 300,000 Yankees. Even the new secretary of war, John Breckinridge, argued that further fighting was hopeless. The mutiny of generals and Cabinet ministers forced President Davis to reluctantly propose truce terms to the Federals commanded by General Sherman.

The Greensboro truce terms were drawn to the president's satisfaction—terms which the Federals could not possibly accept: The Confederacy would revert to the state governments which had existed before the war; civilians would negotiate the restoration of the Union; Southern state governments would be recognized by Washington as if there had never been a rebellion; Southern private property would be respected; and there must be a general amnesty for all Confederates with the exception of President Davis and his Cabinet. The proposal was perfectly silent on the seminal question of the generation: the continuation or abolition of slavery in the Old South.

While the Confederate government-on-the-run convened to propose an impossible peace, President Davis received a visitor from the collapsed Appomattox front. Captain Robert E. Lee Jr. arrived at Greensboro. The young Lee brought official confirmation of the unthinkable: His father had surrendered four days earlier. Captain Lee had escaped just prior to the capitulation.

The president made plans to evacuate his government within two days to push farther south.

During April 13 and 14, General Lee's little caravan of bedraggled survivors continued eastward, back to Richmond and home. Good Friday,

April 14, Robert Lee camped for the night at the home of his older brother, Charles Carter Lee, in Powhatan County. Rather than accept a bedroom, the old soldier in gray pitched his battered tent in his brother's yard to sleep in bivouac. It would be his last night under canvas in a lifetime of soldiering.

Down the road in Greensboro, Jefferson Davis and his Cabinet spent Good Friday packing in preparation for a Saturday evacuation of the town. Among the townsfolk who watched the comings and goings of their government was a three-year-old boy, Billy Porter, whose uncle was the town druggist. The little boy would grow up to be a writer, signing his stories as "O. Henry."

Further east in Washington City, Abraham Lincoln enjoyed a light day which began with a good laugh by his son at his breakfast in the Executive Mansion. The president's son, Robert, had given his weary but relieved father a gift over breakfast: a framed portrait of Robert E. Lee, paroled prisoner of war.

Mr. Lincoln was overcome with the same strange sadness which had afflicted him when he sat in Jeff Davis's chair in captured Richmond. Looking at the white-bearded Rebel, the president's gray eyes radiated an overwhelming melancholy. He said to young Robert of the older, defeated Robert: "It is a good face. It is the face of a noble, brave man."

As Robert Lee pitched his tent for the last time Friday night, Abraham and Mary Lincoln took their carriage to Ford's Theatre. Abraham Lincoln would be carried from the theater to die across the street in a bed too short for his long legs.

Saturday morning, while President Lincoln faded away to become something even larger, Jefferson Davis and his government left on horseback with a mounted escort of 1,300 cavalrymen. From Greensboro, they covered only fifteen miles over muddy dirt roads. They camped for the night at Jamestown, North Carolina. The presidential party left Greensboro in a state of shock. One or two days before Jefferson Davis moved on, starving Confederate stragglers had shuffled into town where they stormed government warehouses to search for food. Civilians joined the crush. The survivors of the 45th North Carolina Infantry had to fire into their own kind to stop the looting. Four people in the mob were shot dead.

Any chance for postwar reconstruction "with malice toward none" expired with President Lincoln at 7:22, Saturday morning. Rooney Lee joined his father's little group of horsemen for the last miles before Richmond. At midday, Robert Lee and his major general son rode into the smoking capital city. Pacing their thin horses at a slow walk, they passed through dirt streets where Southerners kept their distance from massed formations of blue-clad infantry. But when the gentleman on his great gray warhorse rode by, even the Yankees removed their dusty hats in silent salute to Robert Lee, just as Ulysses Grant had done six days earlier on the front porch steps at Appomattox.

The two riders, father and son parolees, stopped at 707 East Franklin Street, known throughout Richmond as The Mess, since so many boys in gray had taken food and cheer from Mother Lee's table and meager pantry. At least the Lees did not have to worry about being evicted for failure to pay the rent. The home's owner, John Stewart, refused to accept any rent at all from his famous tenants—unless they paid exclusively with worthless Confederate money.

Robert Lee sullenly walked up the path, past the Federal guards dispatched to protect the house at the request of Agnes Lee two weeks earlier. Mother Lee sent a breakfast tray outside to the Yankee sentries every morning. The food for her family was provided generously by the blue invaders.

General Lee, former colonel in the US cavalry and the Corps of Engineers, closed the door behind him, took off his gray slouch hat, and hung up his saber forever. General Grant had graciously declined to demand that sword as war tribute. One side of the sword bore a gift inscription etched into the polished steel: "General Robert E. Lee, from a Marylander, 1863." And the reverse side carried the perfect motto for the old soldier's career: *Aide-toi, et Dieu t'aidera.* "Help yourself, and God will help you."

While Robert Lee spent his first night of peacetime at home with his family, the First Family of his shattered country remained on the lam. When Jefferson Davis camped Saturday night, April 15, at Jamestown, North Carolina, First Lady Varina and her children bounced in wagons bound for Abbeville, South Carolina. When the wagons bogged down in muddy roads Saturday evening, Mrs. Davis carried nine-month-old Varina Anne in her arms for five miles on foot. Mother and children slept Saturday night on the floor of a country church, Woodward Baptist.

Sunday, the northern half of the bloodied nation reeled in shock at the death of their belabored president. On the back porch on East Franklin Street, Richmond, cameraman Matthew Brady coaxed former general Robert E. Lee to pose stiffly beside his son Custis and his aide, Walter Taylor. All three prisoners still wore their gray uniforms in proud defeat. The photographed face of the Old Man was stony and haggard, but the fire of Chancellorsville and Sharpsburg still burned in the weary black eyes.

Far down the road from occupied Richmond, Jefferson Davis had reached High Point, North Carolina, where he dispatched War Secretary John Breckinridge at General Joe Johnston's request. Johnston had asked for Breckinridge to be present for a planned truce talk with General Sherman, scheduled for Monday, April 17.

During daylight on April 17, Joe Johnston finally came face-to-face with William Tecumseh Sherman between Durham and Hillsboro, North Carolina. They had never met. General Sherman rejected the Davis truce platform as anticipated. The Federal demanded that Davis surrender upon Grant's Appomattox terms, with Davis and the Rebel Cabinet excluded from an otherwise general parole of Confederate veterans. To prevent a bloodbath of vengeance, for two days Sherman had deliberately withheld from his blue divisions word of Abraham Lincoln's death. The talks broke up so General Johnston could confer with Secretary Breckinridge, who arrived at Hillsboro on Monday evening.

The Johnston-Sherman negotiations resumed at two o'clock on the afternoon of Tuesday, April 18. Joe Johnston was joined by Robert Lee's last cavalry chief, Lieutenant General Wade Hampton. Generals Johnston, Hampton, and Sherman, together with former general Breckinridge, enjoyed a very cordial meeting loosened by good Yankee whiskey all around. With the good cheer and good drink perhaps overly warming Major General Sherman to his Confederate guests, the Federal suddenly accepted President Davis's peace proposal which he had rejected the previous night. Sherman excused himself to return to Yankee-controlled

Raleigh, where he could wire a signed truce document off to Washington. Meanwhile, Jefferson Davis and his Cabinet made camp Tuesday night at Concord, North Carolina.

Joe Johnston and the gray-clad secretary of war spent Wednesday waiting for word from Washington on the Davis peace initiative, which would essentially restore the Old South—with slavery intact—to its prewar status of sovereign states. Meanwhile, Jefferson Davis arrived in Charlotte. The president learned that his old nemesis, Abraham Lincoln, was dead. "It is sad news," Jeff Davis lamented. "I am sorry. We have lost our best friend in the court of the enemy. I fear it will be disastrous for our people and I regret it deeply." Perhaps Davis truly mourned for his fellow Kentuckian, who lay dead with a Confederate bullet in his brain. Davis and Lincoln were born eight months and 102 miles apart.

The Confederate government remained in Charlotte for a week.

Jefferson Davis convened a Cabinet meeting on Saturday, April 22. The Executive Branch met in a Charlotte bank building. Everyone agreed that the truce terms unexpectedly accepted by General Sherman were highly favorable, although Davis remained convinced that Washington would reject the terms. Certain of such rejection, President Davis restated his determination to fight for Southern independence to the last drop of Confederate blood.

Next day, Sunday, Jefferson Davis enjoyed a quiet Sabbath in church at Charlotte. To the north in his captured capital, Mother Lee was less moved by Sunday-morning charity. "The cruel policy of the enemy has accomplished its work too well," Mary Lee wrote to a cousin. "They have achieved by starvation what they never could win by their valor." Nevertheless, General Lee's wife probably began her day in her wheelchair by sending a hot tray outside to the Yankees who guarded her rented home on Franklin Street.

Monday, April 24, was a day of disappointment for Jefferson Davis. He held a discouraged meeting of the Confederate Cabinet, where Attorney General George Davis submitted his resignation. Later, General Sherman reported that Washington had rejected the Davis peace proposal. The Federal ceasefire would end in forty-eight hours and the bloodletting would begin anew. At dinnertime, Joe Johnston at Hillsboro wired Davis confirmation of the collapse of negotiations. General Johnston resolved to surrender his army to Sherman even without his president's approval, to prevent more rivers of needless bloodshed before the fighting resumed Wednesday.

So it had come full circle: Robert Lee had succeeded a gravely wounded Joe Johnston to take command in Virginia on the first day of June, 1862. Almost three bloody years later, Johnston would surrender the South's last great army with or without the consent of Jefferson Davis.

Tuesday, General Johnston wired Davis in Charlotte of his determination to surrender. War Secretary Breckinridge ordered Lieutenant General Wade Hampton to leave Johnston with Hampton's cavalry division rather than lose the cavalry, too. Hampton's six hundred hungry troopers would leave Johnston the next day to fight on.

Wednesday, April 26, Joseph Johnston surrendered his army to William T. Sherman at Hillsboro, North Carolina, despite his president's objection and formal order to continue the retreat southward. Jefferson Davis would never forgive Johnston for handing over the South's last major force.

While Johnston's remnant of graybacks stacked arms for the last time, President Davis held his last full Cabinet meeting in Charlotte. Sickly adjutant general Samuel Cooper resigned at the meeting. Johnston was surrendering his army at noon as President Davis and the remainder of his Cabinet abandoned Charlotte. The chief executive left on horseback, escorted by three thousand cavalrymen commanded by War Secretary John Breckinridge. The presidential party camped for the night at Fort Mill, South Carolina, with Davis taking a room in the A. B. Springs home.

Wednesday night, Jefferson Davis down on his knees played marbles with his host's small boys. Thursday, the Cabinet met on the Springs family lawn. Scouts reported Federals were closing in. The outdoor Cabinet session was the last day in the government for Treasury Secretary George Trenholm of Charleston, South Carolina. He resigned due to serious illness. Postmaster John Reagan of Tennessee, a former US congressman, assumed the Treasury.

The exiled Executive Branch returned to the dusty trail southward through South Carolina after the meeting. They rode south four days, crossing the Catawba River and camping in succession at Yorkville, Love's Ford, and Unionville. By Monday, May 1, they pitched camp at Cokesbury and pressed on the next day toward Abbeville. The next day, Jefferson Davis became a wanted man: The new Federal president, Andrew Johnson, issued a proclamation putting a $100,000 bounty on the head of President Davis. Johnson accused Davis of complicity in the murder of Abraham Lincoln.

President Davis arrived at Abbeville early May 2, Tuesday, and rested for the day at the Armistead Burt home. Varina Davis and the children had stayed at the Burt home on their flight south. By eleven o'clock Tuesday night, Davis and the Cabinet were back on the wearisome road for an all-night ride toward Georgia. Their cavalry escort had now evaporated to only one thousand troopers.

Wednesday morning, the presidential party entered Georgia, bound for Florida. The president's staunchest defender and his closest friend in the government, Judah Benjamin, finally had to fend for himself. The only man to hold three Cabinet posts—attorney general, secretary of war, and secretary of state—left Davis to make his own escape to Cuba.

Benjamin had vowed the previous week that he wanted to get as far away from the newly United States as he could, "if it takes me to the middle of China." Now beside the South Carolina–Georgia border along the Savannah River, Judah Benjamin made good on his pledge to leave America forever. Only treasurer and postmaster Reagan remained of the Rebel Cabinet.

By noon Wednesday, Jefferson Davis and John Reagan, along with their cavalry, arrived in Washington, Georgia, fifty miles northwest of Augusta. The exhausted president with a price on his head was only four hours behind his wife and children, who had spent the night at Washington. This May 3 marked the last day of the national government of the Confederate States of America. Jefferson Davis disbanded the government so he could ride on into Alabama accompanied now by only ten cavalrymen. Davis spent the rest of the day at Washington.

Jefferson Davis and his ten horsemen left Washington on Thursday morning. John Reagan rode south with him. Later this May 4, the president's brother-in-law, General Richard Taylor (President Zachary Taylor's son), surrendered his Rebel army fighting in Alabama and Mississippi. Another Confederate army had left the field. Only one real gray army was left, under General Kirby Smith's (West Point, '45) command, on the west side of the Mississippi River.

But Jeff Davis pressed on to fight again—without any army east of the Mississippi River and without a capital city.

Twenty

PRESIDENT DAVIS RODE ALL NIGHT ON HIS WEARY HORSE, KENTUCKY. The magnetic compass built into the pommel of his McClellan saddle was of little help to his primary mission: find his Varina and his children, whose wagons were not far ahead.

As the dispossessed Davis rode hard after his family, Robert Lee had company in occupied Richmond this Friday, May 5.

General Lee received George Gordon Meade as a guest in the Lee house. Major General Meade was on his way to Washington City to attend the scheduled Grand Review of the victorious Federal armies in the capital. Meade and Lee enjoyed a reserved but cordial meeting in the Lee parlor much as they had done just after the surrender. Their family connection went back a generation. In 1791, General Meade's father had ridden at the side of Robert Lee's father, General Henry "Light Horse Harry" Lee, to help President Washington put down the "Whiskey Rebellion" when Pennsylvania distillers protested a federal tax on whiskey to pay down the debt of the Revolution.

Major General Meade gently urged Lee to take the new loyalty oath required to regain his citizenship in the re-United States. Meade also expressed his hope that Robert Lee would one day run for governor of Virginia. After all, Robert Lee's ancestors did include three Virginia governors, including his father, along with three members of the Continental Congress almost ninety years earlier, three US congressmen, and five of Virginia's seven signers of the Declaration of Independence.

But this Lee respectfully declined to take the loyalty oath until he learned more about the Reconstruction policy of the new Andrew Johnson administration. The Virginian could not swear allegiance to his captors if the southland were to be subjugated and oppressed. Parting with genuine civility among old soldiers, Robert Lee and George Meade never saw each other again.

Although his father had served as Virginia's governor from 1791 through 1794, Robert Lee knew that he would never enter politics. He was old at fifty-eight, and his weary heart hurt from his angina seizures and from having been broken. All he wanted was quiet in the loving company of his wife and grown children. Only a few days before General Meade's kind visit, Robert Lee had told his friend General Armistead Long what he needed most. "I am looking for some little quiet house in the woods," General Lee had sighed.

In addition to George "Old Snapping Turtle" Meade, Robert Lee had other friends in Yankee blue. On the day Meade visited Lee, Ulysses Grant wrote to Federal army chief-of-staff, Major General Henry Halleck, that President Johnson should grant Lee a general amnesty. "It would have the best possible effect toward restoring good feelings and peace in the South," General Grant wrote. But Andrew Johnson would not hear of it.

After Lee bid farewell to his old Gettysburg adversary on Friday, Jeff Davis camped far from Richmond at Sandersville, Georgia. In her own camp elsewhere in the wilderness, Varina and the Davis children were attacked in the dark by a band of marauding, Confederate troops. The renegade Rebel soldiers were searching the countryside for the Rebel treasury wagons rumored to carry Richmond's gold. The plunderers only withdrew when they recognized their terrified victim as the former First Lady of the Confederacy.

Jefferson Davis rode southward all day Saturday, May 6. An hour before midnight, his little party stumbled in the dark into another camp of fugitive wagons near Dublin, Georgia. Varina Davis tearfully recognized the thin, gaunt figure who dismounted Kentucky in the darkness. The Davis household was united at last beside a dirt road. They embraced, parents and children, for the first time since March 29 when Varina had fled Richmond ahead of her husband.

After their brief night together, the Davis family rode south all day Sunday. They camped Sunday night thirty miles southwest of Dublin.

Monday morning, May 8, President Davis rode on ahead of his family to make better time on his flight to Florida. But heavy rains slowed his progress over muddy Georgia roads, and Varina's wagon caught up with him by nightfall. The family continued on all night in a blinding thunderstorm with Yankees closing in on them. After thirty-six continuous hours on the run, they arrived Tuesday evening at Irwinville, Georgia, where they made camp one mile north of the hamlet. The Florida line was still sixty-five miles farther south.

As the First Family of the Confederacy slept on the night of May 9, the 4th Michigan Cavalry hot on their trail rode into Irwinville at one o'clock in the morning of May 10, Wednesday. At dawn, 150 mounted Federals swooped out of the morning fog to attack the Davis wagons and the 60 Confederate troops still protecting their chief. In the dim light, the 1st Wisconsin Cavalry fired into the 4th Michigan. As the Federals shot at each other in the confusion, two boys in blue were killed and four were wounded by Yankee bullets.

After Jefferson Davis surrendered, Federal Lieutenant Colonel Ben Pritchard allowed his frenzied troopers to go on a rampage. Although the Davis family was neither touched nor harmed, the Federals ransacked the Davis wagons, broke open Varina's trunk to scatter her clothing and underwear across the ground, and even stole infant Varina Anne's baby clothes. Finally, Colonel Pritchard halted the looting.

As the Georgia sun rose and burned off the ground fog, the blue cavalry herded the last of the Executive Branch of the Confederate government into wagons as prisoners of war after six weeks on the run.

Under close arrest, the First Family of the Confederacy spent three more hard days on Georgia dirt roads. On Saturday, May 13, the prisoners and their escort of blue-clad cavalry arrived at military headquarters, Macon, Georgia. The Yankee garrison was commanded by twenty-seven-year-old Major General James Wilson (West Point, '60).

In the first and last salute Jefferson Davis would receive from his enemies, the teenagers in Union blue snapped to attention and presented arms as the Davis family was led into the Lanier Hotel. Davis knew his young captor: When Federal Secretary of War Jeff Davis had visited West Point before the war, he had met cadet James H. Wilson. Now that cadet wore stars upon his blue shoulders and Jefferson Davis was his prisoner. General Wilson cordially greeted his old chief and provided a comfortable lunch. After their brief rest, the Davis family left Macon at seven p.m. for the coast.

Sunday evening, the Davises and their guards arrived by train at Augusta, Georgia. They were joined by the captured Alexander Stephens, Davis's vice president. As the Executive Branch of the Confederate government was led through town, they were silently watched by nine-year-old Tommy Wilson. The boy would be known to another generation of Americans as Thomas Woodrow Wilson, President of the United States. A ferryboat took the prisoners to Savannah where they arrived at one in the morning, Tuesday, May 16. Another Federal boat waited offshore to take Jefferson Davis north to stand trial for high treason—a hanging offense.

The prison steamboat docked at Hampton Roads, Virginia, on Friday, May 19. The next day, Varina Davis and her children were removed from the steamer, but her husband was held behind. The former president spent two more days pacing his floating jail. Not until May 22 was he taken off the boat and escorted to Fortress Monroe—young Second Lieutenant Robert Lee's first post with the Corps of Engineers thirty-four years earlier. Varina was shipped back down to Savannah.

The day of his arrival at the old fort, Davis was jailed in a cell behind walls thirty feet high and fifty feet thick. He was placed in solitary confinement. A lantern was lighted to burn around the clock to deprive him of sleep. His guards were forbidden to speak with him and all of his actions were to be carefully observed, even his visits to the chamber pot in his cell. His jailer was twenty-six-year-old Brigadier General Nelson Miles. The day after his imprisonment, the former president of the Confederate States of America was clapped in leg irons at the order of Secretary of War Edwin Stanton. It was Secretary Stanton who said, "Now he belongs to the ages," at the bedside of the dead Abraham Lincoln. When Davis demanded to be treated with the dignity due prisoners of war, four Yankee guards held the old man down while a blacksmith applied hot iron to his ankles.

Three days after Davis was manacled, General Edward Kirby Smith (West Point, '45) surrendered the last Rebel army in the field on May 26.

At last the War Between the States was over, six weeks to the day after Abraham Lincoln went to Ford's Theatre to celebrate Appomattox.

In May of '65, the sudden peace meant maimed and crippled men hobbling south in time for spring planting or north to big-city sweatshops. For more than 620,000 households, North and South, spring would be remembered forever as an empty chair in front of the fireplace.

In 1861 when Abraham Lincoln took the train from Springfield for the last time, the states which would become the North counted twenty-two million people and the South numbered only nine million, of whom less than six million were white. There were more white adults in New York and Pennsylvania than in the entire Confederacy. Over three-quarters of the military-age men in the prewar country were Yankees. The draft-age men in New York were equal to three-quarters of the draftable white men available to the entire Confederacy. The Federals enjoyed five factories for every one factory in the South. Ninety percent of the money in the country before the war was deposited in Northern banks. And it was no wonder that the Army of Northern Virginia marched barefoot: The whole South had 1,365 shoe manufacturers, while New York alone had 2,277.

It was no accident that Robert Lee's Virginians haunted Mr. Lincoln's nightmares. The Old Dominion state produced 79 generals over four years. Georgia was second in the Confederacy, with 42. Of Virginia's 79 generals, 67 men had military experience before Fort Sumter. Of the Army of Northern Virginia's 169 men who were commissioned general, 27 were killed and 13 were captured. But, of General Lee's 1,763 men who rose to the rank of colonel, only 72 were "professional soldiers" by career. Of his colonels, 78 had graduated from the US Military Academy at West Point, New York, 4 were graduates of the US Naval Academy, 157 had graduated from the Virginia Military Institute, 40 were from the South Carolina Military Academy, and 16 were from the Georgia Military Academy.

Death on a distant field or from disease touched 360,222 Northern homes. And Johnny would never come marching home to at least 258,000 Southern families. Many of the dead had starved or frozen or festered to death in prison camps. Of 408,000 men on both sides who made the march to prison camp, fully 56,000 died in captivity. Thirty thousand Federals died while prisoners of war, and 26,000 Confederates died in Yankee prison camps. The Southern camp at Andersonville, Georgia, would become infamous when the records confirmed 13,000 Federal deaths there during one year ending in February, 1865. But during that same year, nearly 3,000 Confederates died at the rate of ten every day in the prison camp at Elmira, New York.

And, forty-seven years before *Titanic's* loss of 1,512 lives in the freezing North Atlantic, there was *Sultana*, a severely overloaded steamboat transporting more than 2,100 Federals up the Mississippi River. They were newly released Federal prisoners of war, sick and emaciated from their time in Confederate prison camps. On April 27, 1865, *Sultana's* overworked steam boilers exploded at two o'clock in the morning, seven miles north of Memphis, Tennessee. Some 1,800 skin-and-bone Federals burned to death or drowned. *Sultana* remains the worst US maritime disaster in history.

The reunited nation's grief and mourning were reflected in the one out of every three homes of Southern white men where a soldier would never be coming back. In the North, one of every ten homes of military-age men had suffered a death.

The race consciousness of the South was clearly reflected in the May 1863 statute by the Confederate Congress which declared that any white Yankee captured while in command of black Federal troops would be executed, and his black Union soldiers would be sold into Southern slavery. An outraged President Lincoln countered by ordering the execution of one Rebel prisoner of war for every Federal executed under this statute. Of the 180,000 black men who proudly wore Union blue, at least 68,000 died to ensure his country's new birth of freedom.

And then there were the casualties who neither voted nor volunteered nor had monuments erected to their heroism: 1,500,000 horses and mules were killed as their masters slaughtered one another. These, and the 11th Pennsylvania's beloved dog, Sallie, who would be honored by her own Gettysburg monument.

After five days in leg irons, Jefferson Davis was freed from his shackles on May 28 when his treatment raised cries of outrage even among

THE LAST YEARS OF ROBERT E. LEE

his Yankee enemies. But former US senator and Federal Secretary of War Davis still had to bear his real physical pain from multiple ailments without benefit of Yankee medicine. The former Confederate president's blind left eye and occasional facial tic caused him immense pain, as did his chronic migraine, peptic ulcer, and nausea. Davis always thought himself a warrior by birth: His father had fought in the Revolution, and his three older brothers had fought under Andrew Jackson at the Battle of New Orleans during the War of 1812. So severe was the sickly president's insomnia before his capture and imprisonment that his Confederate physicians had forced him to sniff chloroform anesthesia to induce sleep. For his manic restlessness and the intense pain of his facial spasms, they had convinced former First Lady Varina Davis to administer twice daily to her reluctant husband a nauseating potion of castor oil and quinine, with two grains of opium. Such medicinals were not available to a prisoner of war, with or without leg irons.

The next day, Andrew Johnson issued a proclamation of general amnesty covering all but fourteen classes of former Confederate politicians and soldiers. Southerners in the excluded categories were forced to request individual pardons from the new President Johnson. Robert Lee fell into three of the unforgiven exclusions: He had been a Confederate general, he had graduated from West Point, and he had resigned from the Old Army with the coming of war. The presidential pardon required the signing of a loyalty oath to the federal government.

With amnesty in the air, clamor continued to indict Robert E. Lee for high treason. True to his generous chivalry at Appomattox, Lieutenant General Grant wrote to President Johnson to urge that no indictments be issued against Confederates who had been paroled at Appomattox. Grant also threatened to resign his commission as lieutenant general in protest if General Lee were indicted.

But no amnesty or pardon for Robert Lee was forthcoming in a climate so hostile that on Memorial Day, May, 1865, Federal armed guards prevented Southerners from laying flowers on the graves of their war dead. Confederate corpses were denied burial on the bloodied battlefield beside Antietam Creek unless burial was necessary to prevent an outbreak of disease from their rotten meat.

The postwar and post–Lincoln assassination bitterness touched Robert Lee in Richmond on Wednesday, June 7, 1865, when a federal grand jury at Norfolk, Virginia, indicted him for treason. The worn-out old man on Franklin Street might hang after all.

Six days later, Robert Lee made a decision almost as difficult as the one which had kept him up all night pacing in April of 1861, after Mr. Lincoln's envoy had offered Lee command of the Union Army. Lee decided to submit his request for a presidential pardon. He did so to set an example for reconciliation between what he still believed were two separate cultures and two distinct countries: one vanquished, and the other victorious. But he carefully phrased his request to be conditional upon confirmation that his Appomattox "parole" did not prevent any trial for treason. "I do not wish to avoid trial," he wrote to the Federal authorities. Ulysses Grant countersigned Lee's request with a recommendation of acceptance to President Andrew Johnson. The new president never answered Lee's petition. The pardon request may have been waylaid in transit after it left Grant's desk and may never have reached President Johnson.

While his most trusted general agonized over his duty to reconcile with his enemies and his former friends, Jefferson Davis languished at Fort Monroe. On June 17, he protested that the all-night lantern was destroying his one good eye, and that the round-the-clock pacing of the guards was preventing sleep. At last, General Miles relented and ordered the guards to let Davis sleep in peace—but the lantern light around the clock would continue.

Three days later, Robert Lee poured out his heart where he always had, and as he did for twenty-six years: to his "Markie." He wrote to his cousin by marriage, Martha Williams, thirty-eight, Mother Lee's cousin, who had left Richmond for her home in New York: "I shall avoid no prosecution the government thinks proper to institute. I am aware of having done nothing wrong." The weary old soldier added that "There is nothing that I want except to see you and nothing that you can do for me except to think of me and love me."

Martha "Markie" Custis Williams was the great-granddaughter of Martha Washington, George Washington's wife, and the orphaned daughter of Mother Lee's first cousin. Martha had spent her life as part of the Lee clan. When visiting Arlington House as a young girl, she had lived in Lee daughter Mary's room. Her younger brother Orton had courted Agnes before the war. Agnes had loved her cousin Orton and he, her. Then, the Yankees hanged Orton as a Rebel spy. In 1859, Orton Williams was a civilian member of the Army Corps of Engineers surveying Minnesota. The project was led by then-Captain George Gordon Meade.

Ulysses Grant also had a personal connection to Martha Williams. During the Mexican War, in September, 1846, Martha's father was mortally wounded while he served like Robert Lee in General Zachary Taylor's Corps of Engineers. When Martha's father lay dying in Mexico, young Lieutenant Grant sat by his bedside to comfort the wounded soldier. Through her war-dead father, Markie somehow bonded together future enemies, Generals Grant and Lee. After her father's death in Mexico, Captain (brevet Major) Robert Lee retrieved her father's sword belt and sent it north to Cousin Markie.

For two months, Robert Lee had tended his crippled wife and his three daughters who all lived in someone else's house, provided as charity. Depending upon the kindness of others gnawed like a boil at the retired general. He had been defeated, but living in the vanquished capital city of the Confederacy was a daily reminder of the depths to which he had sunk so soon after his stunning victory at Chancellorsville. There, he and Stonewall had wrecked the enemy's army; now, his enemies brought him the food he ate. He had to leave or pace himself to death.

Robert Lee's great-great-great-grandfather, Richard Lee, had arrived in Virginia from England in 1639. By 1642, he owned sixteen thousand acres of rich Virginia soil. But never in his life did General Lee own one square inch of Virginia land. Arlington House belonged to Mother Lee through her father's estate. Her husband owned little more than his warhorse Traveller and the saddle he threw over his back.

Relief for the paroled soldier arrived in late June in the form of an invitation to settle fifty miles west of Richmond—again, on someone else's land. But at least he could await the result of his pardon request, or his indictment, away from ranks of Federal soldiers.

June 29, Robert Lee accepted an invitation to move his family to a four-room cottage in the country on the Oakland plantation. The little house in Cumberland County, Virginia, was called Derwent, and was donated by Mrs. Elizabeth Cocke. Her grandfather, Edmund Randolph, had been Virginia governor after the Revolution, had been a Virginia delegate to the 1787 Constitutional Convention, and had refused to sign the new Constitution out of protest. More recent memories were painful: Mrs. Cocke's son had died in Pickett's Charge at Gettysburg.

The Lees were soon packed and out of the Franklin Street home. Lee accompanied his crippled wife and daughters Mildred and Agnes on a canal boat up the James River to the cottage. Custis went overland so he could ride Traveller to his new country home.

Robert Lee's summer of '65 at the Derwent cottage marked the first peace he had known as a family man in over thirty years. He had been home on leave for extended periods over the years, but now, for the first time, there would be no sudden call to go west to fight Indians, east to build harbors with the Army Corps of Engineers, or south to fight Yankees. At last, he lived in the little house in the woods for which he had longed.

The pastoral summer at Derwent was interrupted by a deadly attack of typhoid which struck daughter Agnes. She was nursed slowly back to health by sister Mildred, her father's Precious Life.

As the weakened Agnes slowly recovered, Robert Lee turned again to those ghastly battlefields, at least in his mind. To leave something of value behind, he determined to write a history of his beloved Army of Northern Virginia. On July 31, he sent a circular letter to his former generals, asking them for copies of battle reports and documents. From these records, he would fashion a suitable monument of words to his legion. "I want that the world shall know," the old soldier wrote, "what my poor boys, with their small numbers and scant resources, succeeded in accomplishing."

After his family, he loved that army the most. As General Lee had written to the now-dead Jeb Stuart on December 9, 1863, "My heart and thoughts will always be with this army."

If the weary and defeated general still held dear his faith in his old gray divisions, his confidence in his own life of soldiering had evaporated with the morning fog beside Appomattox Creek. Within a year of soliciting records for his projected book, he would remark that "the great mistake of my life was taking a military education."

Restless, suddenly impoverished, and under federal indictment for a hanging offense, Robert Lee took his only solace at his Derwent cottage on old Traveller's gray back, taking solitary rides through Cumberland County, Virginia.

As he contemplated ending his career dangling from a Federal scaffold, how could he have known that the repose he sought would come for him in a borrowed suit of clothes, and that he would cross paths one more time with the ghost of Stonewall Jackson in the Valley of Virginia?

Twenty-One

IN THE WAR-RAVAGED SHENANDOAH VALLEY, A DILAPIDATED AND nearly bankrupt college gave an element of culture to the tiny hamlet of Lexington, Virginia.

To stave off bankruptcy, the trustees of Washington College voted on August 4, 1865, to offer Robert Lee the presidency of their little school. It was an audacious gesture to the most famous man in all of the Old South. The trustees hoped that having General Lee's name associated with their college might increase enrollment, and that the annual salary of $1,500 might give some financial relief to the fifty-eight-year-old general, now unemployed and pensionless. The outlandish proposal was hand-delivered to Derwent by Judge John Brockenbrough. In the postwar poverty of the summer after the war, the judge had to wear a borrowed business suit to look presentable.

Washington College began in 1749 as Augusta Academy, not located in Lexington. Between 1776 and 1812, the school was called Liberty Hall Academy. During the War of 1812, the place took on its new name of Washington College, to honor the new nation's first president who had given money to the academy, now relocated to Lexington in the Valley. The endowment of the academy by George Washington had been suggested by Henry Lee, Robert Lee's father. The year Robert was born, 1807, his half brother Henry "Dark Horse Harry" attended the school for one year. Since Stonewall Jackson had lived in Lexington and was buried there after Chancellorsville, the Yankees punished the town in 1864 by looting Washington College and burning Virginia Military Institute nearby, because Stonewall had taught there. Robert Lee's life and family certainly had ties of blood and passion with Lexington and its run-down college.

Robert Lee pondered the college offer for three weeks. He had spent all of his adult life in the company of young men. Presiding over the all-boys' school in the Valley would be easier than managing an army of 75,000. Likewise, his stint as superintendent at West Point would serve him well. But more than anything, it was honorable employment by which he could feed his family. On August 24, he accepted the offer with reservations.

To the Washington College trustees, Lee sent a carefully drafted letter in which he gave the trustees one last chance to withdraw their offer if, upon reflection, they thought that his selection might do damage to the reputation of the little school. After all, he was still excluded from the May general amnesty, and he remained indicted for high treason. He also expressly declined to teach any classes, but would agree to function only as an administrator. In his chest, his heart was too sore from heart disease and scar tissue from his battlefield coronaries to take on a teaching load.

The job offer was not withdrawn. Robert Lee would become a college president in the same backwater country village where the bones of Stonewall Jackson and Sandie Pendleton reposed. Lee would become president of the same college at which Stonewall's first father-in-law had been president before the war.

One week after Lee's acceptance letter, another letter was written and addressed to the still-bleeding heart of the Old South. Judah Benjamin had reached England on August 30. The next day, he wrote to his close friend and confidant Varina Davis, whose husband languished in prison. Benjamin informed Mrs. Davis that Confederate businessmen in England had deposited the enormous sum of $12,500 into an account for the benefit of the Confederacy's deposed and homeless First Family. The money represented Jefferson Davis's unpaid wages as president. Varina would have access to the funds while she waited in Savannah to learn the fate of her husband. The Davis children had already been shuffled off to exile in Canada. The stipend represented nearly eight years of General Lee's salary at Washington College.

Friday, September 15, Robert Lee mounted Traveller and rode alone from the Derwent cottage toward Lexington in the Valley. He wore his Rebel-gray uniform, but all Confederate buttons and the gold stars on the collar had been removed. It was now illegal to wear any badge of Confederate service. Daughter Mary Custis carefully preserved her father's collar stars in an envelope. The old man's trunk went to Lexington by canal boat. Three days later, Robert Lee rode into the sleepy college town. His wife and daughters would not follow for three more months.

As General Lee packed for his solitary ride toward the Shenandoah, Jefferson Davis down at Fortress Monroe moved to new quarters. The prison physician had pleaded with General Miles to move the weakening Davis to a drier cell. His cell had been so damp that mold was growing on the ex-president's shoes. Nelson Miles finally relented and Davis was locked in a warmer, drier cell.

October 2, Robert Lee took the oath to become president of Washington College. He was quietly inaugurated in the physics classroom. The white-haired warrior would now preside over fifty students, all who could afford college at the time. The poor school could hire only four professors. The old soldier lived at the Lexington Hotel like a transient brush salesman. Three years earlier, the muster roll of the Army of Northern Virginia had reached its maximum of 91,000 men, commanded by the new college president who now had only 50 young men to inspire.

Robert Lee's pleasure at becoming gainfully employed did not stop the anguish of justifying in his own mind his 1861 decision to abandon his Old Army career to defend his real country, Virginia. The day after assuming the college presidency, he wrote to former Confederate general Pierre Beauregard that "True patriotism sometimes requires of men to act exactly contrary, at one period, to that which it does at another. The motive which impels them—the desire to do right—is precisely the same. The circumstances which govern their actions change. Their conduct must conform to the new order of things."

College president Lee quickly fell into a routine as regimented as his lifetime of soldiering. He left the hotel in time to be in his office by eight o'clock in the morning, where he worked until two p.m. Then, it was midday dinner and a nap for his ailing heart. At four o'clock, he enjoyed a quiet ride through the hills on Traveller, his friend. A light, evening meal was taken at seven-thirty, and he was in bed back at the Lexington Hotel by ten p.m.

To the students at the college, Robert Lee was the living legend in their midst. A stolen moment with General Lee would instantly become a memory fit for a lifetime of retelling. Old, old men who could not remember their wedding anniversaries would recall like yesterday a chat in Marse Robert's college office. The new president called the students "yearlings," as he had done with the cadets at West Point when he was superintendent, though many of the students were young and crusty veterans of Chancellorsville or Shiloh, or dreadful fields which had no name, only casualties.

Each new student began his first year with a private audience with former general Lee. The old man prided himself on never forgetting a boy's name, addressing each student as "Mr." so-and-so. With Robert Lee, there were no first names. Behind their backs, the college president simply called his students "my boys."

The rules under Robert Lee's presidency of Washington College were simple—painfully simple to some of his yearlings. "We have but one rule here," he counseled his boys, "and it is that every student must be a gentleman."

When a student failed to measure up to Lee's standard for proper gentlemen, he would summon the offender to his office. When all else failed to inspire some incorrigible student, Robert Lee would level his deadly weapon which cracked the hardest heart. "I have a way of estimating young men which does not often fail me," the college president said gravely. "I cannot note the conduct of anyone, for even a brief period, without finding out what sort of mother he had."

When he was not reducing some wayward boy to mush, General Lee would pen a longhand letter of praise to the parents of boys who had done well.

After one month of bachelor living at the Lexington Hotel, General Lee received welcome company. While twenty-two-year-old Rob Jr., suffering from malaria, remained with Mother Lee and the girls in Richmond, Custis Lee made the journey to Lexington to start his postwar life as a paroled prisoner of war. The oldest Lee son at thirty-three, former Major General Custis Lee had been surrendered at Sayler's Creek during the last days of his father's army. (Brother Rooney was also commissioned major general.) Custis had accepted an appointment to join the faculty at Virginia Military Institute. Up the road from Washington College, VMI had been gutted by the Federals. Custis would teach mathematics and civil engineering, and would join his father on his afternoon horseback rides through the Valley hills. The two bachelors lived at the Lexington Hotel, enjoying country life as they awaited the arrival of the Lee women in early December.

By November, Lieutenant General James Longstreet followed his chief's lead and petitioned President Johnson for a presidential pardon for his part in what Congress called "the rebellion." As had been the case with Robert Lee, Old Pete's request for restored citizenship carried the personal endorsement of General Grant. Grant penned for his cousin by marriage a testimonial borne of family ties and battlefield respect. "I have known him well over twenty-six years," Lieutenant General Grant wrote to his president. "I have no hesitation, therefore, in recommending General Longstreet to your Excellency for pardon. I will further state that my opinion of him is such that I shall feel it as a personal favor to myself if this pardon is granted." Grant's November 7 letter failed to move President Johnson, who refused to pardon the man whom Grant's troops had nearly killed in the Wilderness eighteen months earlier.

At long last, Mother Lee, daughters Mildred and Mary Custis, and son Rob left Derwent for Lexington on November 30. They arrived at the little college town on December 2. Daughter Agnes stayed behind in Richmond to attend a friend's wedding. With his womenfolk at his side, General Lee finally moved from the hotel to the president's old house at the college. Robert Lee and his children now lived in the same house where Stonewall Jackson had lived with his first wife, Elinor Junkin, when her father was president of the college. To make the ratty old residence more like home to Mother Lee, Lexington ladies put in carpet and curtains, which had been rescued from Mother Lee's Arlington estate, now a federal military cemetery.

The Lee household soon acquired the people and things which made it home. Continuing the daily connection with Stonewall's ghost, which slept just down the hill beside Sandie Pendleton, the Lee family quickly became fast friends with Margaret Junkin Preston, Stonewall's sister-in-law by his first wife. Margaret's daughter was soon Mildred's first close friend in Lexington. In his bedroom next to Mother Lee's bedroom, General Lee set up his old camp cot where he had slept fitfully on all the battlefields between The Seven Days and Appomattox.

General Lee now took his afternoon rides with nineteen-year-old Mildred, his Precious Life. The father rode Traveller and Mildred rode her father's favorite mare, Lucy Long.

Down the Valley in Washington, in mid-December the new Congress created a Joint Committee on Reconstruction to inquire into the conditions throughout the conquered Southland. The Committee quickly lunged for the postwar spotlight by serving a subpoena on the South's favorite son, Robert Lee. The old soldier was summoned to testify in early 1866.

Federal subpoena in hand, Robert Lee confided to his Markie on December 20: "In looking back upon the calamities that have befallen us, I cannot trust my hand to write the feelings of my heart."

Robert Lee returned to Richmond in mid-January. On January 11, 1866, he testified before the Virginia state legislature about money needed to resuscitate Virginia schools. He went home to Lexington after one week. The legislature regarded itself as the governing body for the Old Dominion state, just as it had before the war.

College president Lee inspired grants for his tiny school. Early in 1866, inventor and financier Cyrus McCormick made a gift to Washington College of $10,000 to endow a McCormick Chair in Natural Philosophy for a professorship to teach mechanical engineering.

Just having General Lee's name associated with Washington College brought in grants. Within four years, Cyrus McCormick would donate the astounding sum of $350,000. Another $60,000 came from Thomas Scott, president of the Pennsylvania Railroad—and Abraham Lincoln's assistant secretary of war. Money would also come in from New York politician Samuel Tilden, who would win the Democratic presidential nomination in 1876.

While her husband worked to manage his college, Mother Lee returned to her wartime talent for sewing. She became president of the Grace Episcopal Church Sewing Society. The Lexington ladies sold favors they had sewn to raise money to refurbish the little church down the hill from Washington College. Sewing Society meetings were held in Mother Lee's bedroom so the crippled woman would not have to ride in her wheelchair down the hillside. Lee daughters Mary Custis and Agnes participated in church affairs by teaching Sunday school.

As the Lee ladies sewed, General Lee renewed contact in January, 1866, with his "old warhorse," General Longstreet. "My interest and affection for you," Lee wrote Old Pete on January 19, "will never cease, and my prayers are always offered for your prosperity." One week later, General Lee wrote to Longstreet's new business partner in New Orleans, "I do not consider my partnership with him yet dissolved, and shall not let him go during life."

The congressional subpoena to General Lee took him to Washington in mid-February. It was his first return to the reunited nation's capital since he had resigned from the Old Army on April 18, 1861, a lifetime earlier. On February 17, he was asked by the Congressional Committee to defend his decision to side with his native Virginia during the war. The Virginian's decision was as clear now as it had been then. With no grant of immunity from prosecution for his testimony, the witness spoke with resolution. "The act of Virginia in withdrawing herself from the United States," he testified firmly, "carried me along as a citizen of Virginia. Her laws and her acts were binding on me." Now as always, Lee's country remained Virginia. Staying in the capital at the Metropolitan Hotel, he did not visit his lost home, Arlington. General Lee returned to Lexington on February 20.

It was just as well that he did not stop at the old homestead overlooking the Potomac. Mother Lee's famous rose garden already had 16,000 dead Federals buried where her flowers had once bloomed.

General Lee's solitary trip to Washington City tired him. He returned to Lexington to a crippled wife and three city-bred daughters who missed the bustle of Richmond even with its ruins and its bluecoat invaders. The press of spring term at the college and the approach of the new president's first commencement taxed his waning energies. "I am easily wearied now," he wrote wistfully to the cousin he loved, Martha Williams, in April, "and look forward with joy to the time which is fast approaching that I will lay down and rest." In the same letter of April 7, he felt obliged to apologize to Markie for his failure to visit old friends in Washington—friends cultivated over a lifetime. "I am considered now such a monster that I hesitate to darken with my shadow the doors of those I love lest I should bring upon them misfortune."

As the old man struggled to control his depression and to grow into his new civilian role, the imprisonment of Jeff Davis brightened if only for an afternoon. On May 3, Varina Davis was permitted a visit with her husband for the first time during the year of his detention at Fort Monroe. Varina brought baby Varina Anne to her father's cell.

During the spring and summer, General Lee nurtured the same faith in the power of religion that had inspired the revival which had swept his divisions beside the frozen Rapidan, thirty months earlier. In June, the grateful trustees of the college doubled Lee's salary to $3,000. But more important to the retired general, they also approved construction of a campus chapel. To help the project, Robert Lee donated $6,000 to the building fund.

Washington College continued to rise from the ashes. Along with planning the new chapel, the trustees created a new school of law in July. But it was the chapel project that captivated the president. With his battlefield eye for terrain, the former civil engineer personally chose just the right spot to build the new house of worship. And when the site was carefully selected, the old engineer then designed the building itself. From the foundation to the rafters, the chapel would be Robert Lee's.

But no matter how he labored to set his sights on celestial matters, his country life was encumbered with stark realities. In August, Mother Lee bruised her face in a painful fall. Her crippled legs were not up to supporting her.

Tired but cheerful to his yearlings and to his family, Robert Lee shared his true feelings only with the distant Markie Williams and with his faithful Traveller, whom he rode almost daily. The tall gray mount grazed freely in the front yard of the Old President's House. Often, the general would ride his warhorse for twenty miles of solitude and reflection.

Late in 1866, Robert Lee reminded Cousin Markie of his wish that she paint Traveller's portrait. He wrote from the heart:

> *If I were an artist like you, I would draw a true picture of Traveller—representing his fine proportions . . . Such a picture would inspire a poet whose genius could then depict his worth and describe his endurance of toil, hunger, thirst, heat, cold, and the dangers and sufferings through which he passed . . . He might even imagine his thoughts through the long night marches and days of battle through which he has passed. But, I am no artist. I can only say he is Confederate gray.*

By September, 1866, enrollment at the college had exploded from the previous year's 50 to fully 345. By June 1867, attendance was up to 399. The Lee name brought students from throughout the South.

January, 1867, brought new excitement to the Lee table. Virginia's political leaders had invited Robert Lee to seek nomination for the Old Dominion's governorship—a post held by his father. Mother Lee urged her husband to take the plunge. The general declined, believing that his entry into politics would do harm to Virginia's relationship with the North.

On March 13, Virginia was stripped naked of her political sovereignty. The First Reconstruction Act passed by a hostile federal Congress completely disenfranchised the state. Virginia as a state ceased to be, and it became Military District Number One. Congress had finally made up its collective mind on Reconstruction. Retribution had replaced "with malice toward none and charity for all." Virginia and the rest of the old Confederacy were now conquered provinces with neither state nor civil rights.

Robert Lee quietly went about his business of planning his chapel and greeting his students, always by name. On Virginia's sudden slide into government by martial law, Mother Lee was less stoic. "The country that allows such scum to rule them must fast be going to destruction," she wrote to a friend. "My indignation cannot be controlled, and I wonder how our people, helpless and disarmed as they are, can bear it. Oh God, how long?"

Some consolation came to the Lees on May 13, when Jefferson Davis finally saw the light of day. After two years in prison without benefit of trial, he was released on a massive $100,000 bond. The bond was posted by Northerners. The federal treason charges still hung over his head and the head of General Lee. But for now, the former president would not have to wear moldy shoes.

Shortly after Jeff Davis left his damp home of prison bars, plans were afoot for a new home for the Lees. The college trustees in June appropriated funds to build a new presidential house.

In the heat of July, Mother Lee's arthritis continued to torture her. To find relief for his crippled wife, Robert Lee took his family west just over the mountains to the White Sulphur Springs health spa in Greenbrier County, West Virginia. The general, Mother Lee, Custis, and Agnes journeyed to "The Old White," renamed The Greenbrier in 1913. Although his family went by carriage and train, General Lee rode Traveller. For the horse, it was a homecoming. Traveller had been born nearby, and was first named Greenbrier before Robert Lee renamed him Traveller.

When the Lees entered the resort's main dining room on their first night, five hundred guests rose in absolute silence until General Lee had taken his seat. Even the few Yankees stood in silent salute, just as the congregation had done so long ago at the church in Richmond before Christmas, 1863. The Lee clan ate in the main building but lived in Harrison Cottage on Baltimore Row. They "took the waters" of the sulfur springs for three weeks.

Twenty-Two

ON THE WAY HOME FROM THE OLD WHITE, GENERAL LEE SUDDENLY took sick. He was bedridden for the first time since his attack on the North Anna River three years earlier, when Grant was hot on his heels. The severe respiratory condition forced the old soldier to remain in bed for two weeks at the Old Sweet spa. The family did not return to Lexington until September 18. Robert Lee, only sixty, came home exhausted and frail. School would begin with General Lee feeling very old.

The day before Robert Lee's return to Lexington, the federal government dedicated a national cemetery at Sharpsburg to give honored repose to the blue-clad dead killed beside Antietam Creek exactly five years earlier. Conspicuously absent from the ceremonies was Major General George McClellan, who had built the Army of the Potomac. Little Mac was not invited.

With the beginning of the new 1867–1868 school year that September, the college had grown to four hundred students and twenty-two professors. The old general's tireless efforts to administer the growing institution were again rewarded when his salary for the year was increased to $4,756.

The pains of old age and old memories were both eased and stressed in November. Rooney Lee, a lonesome widower since his Charlotte's death four years earlier, was getting remarried. The burly son was to wed Mary Tabb Bolling of Petersburg. During the dreadful siege there, General Lee had known her, and he heartily approved of his son's selection. But when Rooney invited his father to the wedding, General Lee declined. Returning to Petersburg was too emotionally painful to contemplate.

Rooney traveled to Lexington to beg his weak father to change his mind. The father relented and agreed to go, and to stay in Petersburg at the home of former Confederate general, Billy Mahone, who had stood fast at Lee's side during the final retreat from Petersburg to Appomattox. The trip would be full of joy and sad recollections.

Reality again intruded into the general's country retirement and family happiness. Along with a wedding invitation, General Lee received another federal subpoena demanding his return to Richmond. He would stop there en route to Petersburg. The subpoena came from the grand jury investigating Jeff Davis's alleged treason in siding with the Confederacy.

Lee arrived in Richmond on November 25 and testified to the grand jury for two hours on November 27. Davis was there, and the two men had their first meeting since the last days of Confederate Richmond. The grand jury was working on a formal indictment of Davis. The federal prosecutors wanted Lee to confirm that the whole rebellion had been Davis's idea. Lee resisted, and testified that he fully agreed with and had acted in concert with President Davis's military decisions. General Lee insisted upon sharing his former president's fate. Davis boarded in Richmond at the Spotswood Hotel as a prisoner out on bail, the same place he had stayed six years earlier as Confederate president.

November 28, a pensive Robert Lee and his son Custis took the train from Richmond twenty-two miles south to Petersburg. Memories of the grim trenches and of starvation haunted the elder Lee. He anticipated a city in ruins, with citizens still angry at General Lee for abandoning them to their enemies at the last possible moment on April 2, 1865.

Now, two and a half years later, father and son were not confronted with squalor and resentment when they pulled into Petersburg. Instead, they arrived at a town quickly rebuilding its way out of devastation. A large crowd at the train depot vaporized the old man's fears. A brass band joyously played "Dixie" for the former chieftain. The visit and the wedding were warm moments for Robert Lee, who attended Rooney's nuptials in the company of sons Custis and Rob, and daughter Mildred. The general's nephew and former major general, Fitz Lee, also attended.

General Lee returned to Richmond on November 30, and quietly visited old friends until December 5. Two days later, a happy and relieved old soldier returned to Lexington and to Mother Lee, who was too crippled to attend her son's wedding.

The year 1867 ended peacefully with a Lee family Christmas in Lexington, with all of the Lee children (except Rooney) around Mother Lee's table.

During the short gray days of winter, Robert Lee carried on as college president. The Valley snows did little to cheer him, and he worked to master the old depression which tormented him.

On New Year's Day, 1868, Lee thought of his own mortality as his aching heart deteriorated. "My interest in time and its concerns is daily fading away," he confided to Cousin Markie. "I try to keep my eyes and thoughts fixed on those eternal shores to which I am fast hastening." But worldly affairs still made him smile, so he added in his letter to Martha, "How are you progressing with Traveller's portrait? He is getting old like his master, and looks to your pencil to hand him down to posterity."

Few days passed without haunting reflection on the South's failed war for independence. On February 25, Lee wrote to Maryland's US senator, Reverdy Johnson: "[T]hough opposed to secession and deprecating war, I could take no part in an invasion of the Southern States."

When a Lee cousin died in March, General Lee wrote from his wounded heart to the new widower that "death in its silent, sure march is fast gathering those whom I have longest loved so that when he shall knock at my door, I will more willingly follow."

Not even the cheerful company of his "yearlings" at the college could comfort the general for long. "I find too late," he wrote sullenly on March 3 to Richard "Baldy" Ewell, that "I have wasted the best years of my life."

The paroled Confederate prisoner twice broke his daily routine at the college president's office during the spring to testify at the Jefferson Davis grand jury hearings. He traveled to Richmond to give testimony on May 1 and June 3. Both times, he waited impatiently in the hallway only to be sent away when the hearings were canceled.

Ten days after his return to Lexington from the second aborted hearing, Robert Lee's sagging spirits were lifted high. On June 14, 1868, the new chapel at Washington College was dedicated. Among the guest speakers at the convocation was former lieutenant general Wade Hampton, late of the cavalry of the Army of Northern Virginia. The two old soldiers spoke together softly about those bitter, somehow better days.

Between them was a cheerful ghost in yellow gauntlets, proudly plumed slouch hat, and massive beard. Hampton, whose son had died for The Cause, listened while his old chief reflected upon the four-years-dead Jeb Stuart. "General Stuart was my ideal of a soldier," Robert Lee said, sadly nodding. "He was always cheerful under all circumstances, always ready for any work, and always reliable. He was able to stand any amount of fatigue and privation." Jeb's untimely absence from Gettysburg had been left far behind.

Wade Hampton would be twice elected governor of South Carolina, and then to a seat in the US Senate.

Lee's pleasure at the dedication of the chapel he had designed was soon crushed by family anguish. Just after the dedication and the end of the school term, Lee's Precious Life nearly died. Mildred fought a hard fight against typhoid fever for a month.

The general, Mother Lee, young Rob, and Mildred had been on the road toward their second vacation at White Sulphur Springs and The Old White resort. But they only got as far as the Warm Springs spa forty miles from Lexington when Mildred took sick. Her father sat at her bedside and stroked her feverish brow for the four weeks of her illness, until August 14. Robert Lee never left her side. He set up a cot to sleep beside his twenty-three-year-old child, named for his sister. Three years earlier, typhoid had almost claimed daughter Agnes.

When Mildred recovered, the family went to the Hot Springs spa. The general riding Traveller went on alone to The Old White.

While at The Old White, Robert Lee made his only foray into postwar politics when he lent his name to the "White Sulphur Springs Letter."

The resort in mid-August boiled with political foment. Among the guests was former Yankee general, William Rosecrans (West Point, '38). Old Pete Longstreet had nearly destroyed Rosecrans's command at Chickamauga four years earlier. Now, Rosecrans was at The Old White to solicit political support for the Democratic presidential ticket headed by New York governor Horatio Seymour. With General Beauregard and former Confederate vice president Alexander Stephens also at The Old White, Rosecrans wanted a public declaration from the old Rebels that would help the national Democratic Party in the 1868 presidential campaign. They were running, after all, against U. S. Grant.

Rosecrans wanted the former Confederates to sign a public declaration of Southern moderation on matters of Reconstruction and "Negro" rights. He desperately wanted Robert Lee's signature on the document.

A draft statement was circulated by Virginia lawyer, Alexander Stuart. The final document, dated August 26 and known as the "White Sulphur Springs Letter," was aimed at securing Virginia's readmission to the Union. The declaration denied Southern hostility toward their former slaves, but opposed quick grants of voting rights to black men. "The Negroes," they wrote, "have neither the intelligence nor the other qualifications which are necessary to make them safe depositories of political power. They would inevitably become the victims of demagogues." Thirty-two leading men of the South signed the White Sulphur Springs Letter. The first signature was "R. E. Lee."

The Republicans won in November.

General Lee left While Sulphur Springs and The Old White and returned to his family in Lexington by September 14. He had been gone for over two months.

The beginning of the Washington College 1868–1869 school year found Robert Lee at work in his office in his new chapel. As another winter in the Valley approached, the war continued to intrude into the old soldier's peaceful retirement.

Controversy swirled around the new federal Gettysburg Association, which wanted to move Confederate graves on the battlefield as expansion of the military park continued. Robert Lee did not abandon his fundamental faith in the American people. "I have no fears that our dead will receive disrespectful treatment," he wrote to nephew and former major general, Fitz Lee in mid-December. "I know of no fitter resting place for a soldier than the field on which he has nobly laid down his life."

Two weeks later, President Andrew Johnson issued his Christmas Amnesty, which pardoned all Confederates, even Jeff Davis and Robert Lee. Although still not quite a citizen again, General Lee's war was finally over. At least on paper, the war which one veteran elegantly remembered for its "dirt, lice, shit, grease and hard crackers," was finished. The pending indictments for treason against General Lee, his sons Rooney and Custis, and cousin Fitz were all dismissed ten weeks later.

As had been the case last year, the Lee Christmas table was full, with everyone except Rooney and his new wife in attendance.

February, 1869, was twice brightened for Robert Lee. His treason indictment was dismissed and he was a grandfather again. Rooney and Tabb gave birth to Robert E. Lee III. Rooney and the dead Charlotte had buried the first Robert Lee III, their infant son.

Mother Lee busied herself during the winter of 1868–1869 by attempting to reclaim her cherished Custis family and George Washington heirlooms, confiscated by the Yankees when Arlington House had been captured. In February, she wrote to the departing President Johnson and asked for the return of her treasured mementos from George Washington, whom her father regarded as his adopted stepfather. The artifacts had been deposited in the US Patent Office as war booty. In a final act of charity, Andy Johnson and his Cabinet consented. But the war was not quite over for everyone in Washington during the last weeks of the Johnson administration.

On March 1, three days before General Grant took office, Illinois Congressman John Logan introduced a resolution in the US House of Representatives which would block the return to Mary Custis Lee of the Mount Vernon and Arlington relics. The resolution passed during the last twenty-four hours of Johnson's term, calling the return of Mother Lee's property "an insult to the loyal people of the United States."

In April, General Lee left Lexington on railroad business. He traveled to Baltimore with a Virginia delegation seeking funds from Maryland businessmen to build the Valley Railroad. The Virginians wanted to lay a spur on the Baltimore and Ohio line through the Shenandoah. Lexington in 1869 was twenty-three miles from the nearest railroad depot on the Chesapeake and Ohio. A spur to Lexington would stimulate the local economy and end the hamlet's isolation. Lee left Lexington April 20 and attended the Baltimore conference on April 22. A week later, he participated in one of the most remarkable footnotes to American history.

On Saturday, May 1, Robert Lee took the carriage down the dirt road of Pennsylvania Avenue in Washington City for a handshake with new president Ulysses S. Grant.

Before noon, General Lee and President Grant met quietly and privately in the Executive Mansion, which did not officially become "The White House" until 1901. When Robert Lee was ushered in, Grant introduced Lee to the president's aide, Robert Douglas. The aide's father had beaten Abraham Lincoln in the 1858 Illinois US Senate race, only to have the favor returned two years later when Judge Douglas ran for the presidency against Lincoln. Grant and Lee conferred alone for fifteen minutes.

President Grant would remember a strained and sad meeting between two proud men who had caused each other much grief only four years earlier. When they parted before 11:30 a.m., neither old soldier would look upon the other's face again.

Whatever Lee's thoughts might have been, no record survives. But Lee's respect for Grant never wavered from their horseback meeting the day after Appomattox. The year before the two men met at the Executive Mansion, a college professor in Lexington had spoken unkindly of General Grant in Robert Lee's presence. The college president flashed his famous temper and informed his colleague that either Lee or the professor would have to resign if the incident were ever repeated within Lee's earshot.

From Baltimore, Robert Lee went over to Alexandria, Virginia, on May 4. He shared a warm reunion with his close older brother, Sidney Smith Lee, and Smith's son, former general Fitz Lee. Robert and Smith had not seen each other in four years. In Alexandria, General Lee stayed with Mother Lee's aunt, Maria Fitzhugh, who owned the Ravensworth Plantation where Robert's mother had died and was buried. Alexandria had been young Robert's boyhood home. After his father had deserted the family, Anne Carter Lee and her children had lived there from the time Robert was five years old until he left for West Point. Lee left his old home on May 7 and arrived back at school the next day.

Before the end of the month, Lee was back on the road. During the last week of May, the Lexington Episcopal Church sent him as a delegate to a church council in Fredericksburg. The city where he had courted Mother Lee and where he had slaughtered Ambrose Burnside's Federals met him with a brass band. The musicians were from George Pickett's old division. May 29, Lee went down the Potomac to see brother Smith for two happy days.

When Lee returned to Lexington by May 31, his family moved into the new presidential house on a green knoll overlooking his beloved chapel down the hill, on the college green. The college trustees had appropriated $15,000 for the home. The builders had conceded to the old soldier's wishes and had constructed a stable for Traveller, attached to the house. Lee expressed great pleasure at living under the same roof with his trusted warhorse.

July 6, Virginia ratified a new constitution to assure its readmission into the Union. The Old Dominion would rejoin the newly re-United States in January. But any joy at Virginia's return to self-government was shattered during the last week of July. Sidney Smith Lee, "the Navy Lee," was dead.

Robert Lee hurried to Alexandria for his brother's funeral, but he arrived one day too late. The mourning brother and his son, Rob, then made a pilgrimage to Ravensworth, where Anne Hill Carter Lee was buried. Overwhelmed with the death of loved ones, General Lee toured the old mansion with Rob. "Forty years ago, I stood in this room by my mother's deathbed," General Lee sighed to his son. "It seems now but yesterday."

From Alexandria and Ravensworth, the two Robert Lees went down to Rooney and Tabb's farm at White House Landing to see the new baby. The farm had been burned by the Yankees.

August 1, General Lee with his daughters Agnes, twenty-eight, and Mildred, twenty-three, went on to The Old White for Lee's third visit. They mingled with one thousand guests for three weeks.

Lee went without Traveller this time. He was there to rest his sore heart at doctors' orders. Mother Lee did not go to White Sulphur Springs this season, but remained at the Rockbridge Baths spa for her arthritis. She was joined by the happy company of Rooney's wife, Tabb, and the baby, Robert Lee III. By the end of August, the family had returned to Lexington in time for the new term at school.

Back at school, General Lee reluctantly agreed to pose for an oil portrait by Swiss painter, Frank Buchser. The former general refused to wear his gray uniform with Confederate buttons, long since removed by congressional order. He posed wearing a black suit. The young painter became a close and welcomed guest of the Lee household. The face frozen in time by the artist looked vigorous, and the fire of the Chancellor House in May 1863 glowed in the black eyes. The finished portrait was taken to Switzerland where it would hang in the Swiss National Museum for 120 years. The portrait was finally returned to the college at Lexington by way of the Swiss Embassy on Robert Lee's 183rd birthday in January, 1990.

When artist Buchser left Lexington for Europe in October, Robert Lee took to a sickbed the next day. He suffered from a severe cold and chest pain. The sixty-two-year-old heart was failing. He was bedridden for a week, and the congestion and angina lingered for three months.

Christmas found Robert Lee weak and frail. The gray winter brightened on January 26, 1870, when President Grant signed legislation readmitting Virginia into the Union.

Robert Lee struggled through his college duties during the winter of 1869–1870. His chest cold and congestive heart failure continued through February, four months. Privately, he doubted if he would survive until June commencement. When spring came slowly to the mountains of the Valley, General Lee could not walk 150 yards without pain in his chest. He could not walk the 200 yards from his chapel office to the president's home up the hillside without stopping to rest along the way.

On March 22, the college president asked the trustees for a leave of absence. An acting president was appointed. The old general had one more journey to make in this life. He had to visit for the first time the grave of his daughter Anne, "Sweet Annie" he had called her, for the twenty-three years and four months that she lived. He would go to North Carolina with daughter Agnes at his side. "I think," he wrote to Rooney, "if I am to accomplish it, I have no time to lose." Lee wrote to his son the same day that he took temporary leave from the college presidency.

Father and daughter left Lexington for the Deep South on Thursday, March 24. Without the railroad spur into Lexington, they had to travel by canal boat to Lynchburg on the eastern side of the mountains. Lee and Agnes would catch the train there for Richmond.

Robert Lee was weak and in pain. His hair and beard were completely white, and his hair was noticeably thinning. When the general and Agnes arrived in Richmond, March 25, General Lee declined to accept an invitation to address the Virginia State Senate. He was too exhausted to visit friends or to shop for Mother Lee.

Saturday, March 26, was spent with the probing fingers and listening tubes of three Richmond physicians. The doctors listened to the old heart and lungs, which struggled to propel the general on his journey. The doctors shook their heads.

Monday, March 28, General Lee and his daughter left the capital by train and arrived at Warrenton, North Carolina, late Monday night.

Tuesday, General Lee stood beside the grave of his Sweet Annie. He and Agnes laid white hyacinths on the cool ground. The grieving father had chosen the words of a favorite hymn for her marker: "Perfect and true are all His ways, whom heaven adores and earth obeys."

Seventeen years earlier, Lieutenant Colonel Lee, US Army, and superintendent of West Point, had written to then thirteen-year-old Annie, who had stayed behind with her grandparents at Arlington: "I hope you will always appear to me as you are now painted on my heart." Standing beside his daughter's grave, the father saw his child in his heart as the twenty-three-year-old young woman which Annie would stay forever. And that was all he had. When "Sweet Annie" was a toddler, she cut her face with scissors. The accident left a scar which made her self-conscious as a teenager and young woman. She never permitted her face to be photographed.

The old soldier and Agnes left by train the same day. The general left behind in Warrenton the white flowers and a lock of his white hair as a keepsake for the daughters of his North Carolina host.

Twenty-Three

WORD SPREAD QUICKLY OF ROBERT LEE'S TRIP THROUGH THE HEART OF the old Confederacy. His wish for a private farewell to friends and dead family became, against his will, a triumphant but exhausting tour. The train from Warrenton became General Lee's Train, and shouts of "General Lee's coming!" were heard at every whistle stop along the way. From Warrenton, the train was cheered by crowds and brass bands at Raleigh and Charlotte, North Carolina, and at Columbia, South Carolina.

When the train pulled into Columbia, Edward Porter Alexander of Longstreet's old artillery was at the depot to meet the Lees on March 30. Alexander had been a cadet at the Point when Lee was superintendent. Cadet Alexander was assigned to Company D with Lieutenant Colonel Lee's nephew, Fitzhugh. Later that night, Robert Lee and Agnes went on to Augusta, Georgia, to spend the night. At the Augusta depot, the cheering throng contained thirteen-year-old Tommy Wilson, who, five years earlier, had watched Jeff Davis march by his window under Yankee guard.

The same crowd cheered Lee and Agnes on April 1 when they returned to the depot after a day's rest. Another crowd, even larger, met the train in the dark when it arrived at Savannah, Georgia. It was the largest crowd in the city's history. The next day, General Lee enjoyed a reunion with rapidly aging General Joe Johnston, whose wounding eight years earlier had sent Lee into the field. The two frail old soldiers posed stiffly together for a photograph. Their sitting portrait is one of weariness and ineffable sadness. Lee and Agnes remained ten days in Savannah.

Tuesday, April 12, the fifth anniversary of his army's last muster to stack arms, General Lee and Agnes left Savannah by boat for another graveyard.

They sailed to Cumberland Island, Georgia, and the grave of Robert Lee's derelict father. Lee had made the same trip eight years earlier. Now, for the first time, the old man's heart hurt even when he rested. On the island, the grandson of Revolutionary War general Nathaniel Greene escorted the Lees to the grave of Henry "Light Horse Harry" Lee. Grandfather General Greene had given his old Revolutionary War comrade a secluded place to die when Henry ran out of time on the boat home to the family he had deserted. Henry Lee had his ways. In 1781, Lieutenant Colonel Light Horse Harry hanged a North Carolina deserter from his Revolutionary War regiment. Then he sent the severed head with rope attached to George Washington.

April 18, the melancholy son wrote about the grave of his father in a letter to Mother Lee: "I presume it is the last time I shall be able to pay to it my tribute of respect."

Father and daughter took a boat to Jacksonville and Palatka, Florida, April 13 through 15. When a crowd of Confederate veterans stood on the dock for a glimpse of their Uncle Robert on his ferryboat, they did not cheer when they saw the fragile old man. Instead, they stood in silence absolute and removed their hats in a final salute to their Marse Robert. The men who had worn gray or butternut-brown were simply too full to make a sound. It was the same silence which met General Lee three years earlier on his first visit to The Old White.

By April 16, the Lees were back in Savannah for nine days of rest for the weakening general. Back at Lexington in the mountains, the Washington College trustees on April 19 voted to give Mother Lee a lifelong stipend of $3,000 annually, and the right to live out her days in the new presidential house. The trustees understood that Mother Lee would soon be living alone.

April 25, father and daughter left Savannah by train and arrived the same day at Charleston, South Carolina. A small group of old friends met them at the depot. They stayed for three days. A band serenaded the Lees on Wednesday, April 27, and the general labored to endure a two-hour reception in the afternoon. The next day, the Lees boarded the train for Wilmington, North Carolina, where they stayed for two days. On April 30, they were off to Portsmouth, Virginia, on the road home to the Shenandoah Valley. Lee's principal field aide, Walter Taylor, met the train, and a cannon salute boomed the Lees a smoky black-powder welcome. They went on to Norfolk.

The Lees left Norfolk May 5 to take a ferryboat up the James River to visit friends. There, they enjoyed five days of rest and quiet, the first real rest for Robert Lee since leaving Lexington six weeks earlier. In the country, there were neither bands nor crowds and he could conserve his waning strength. May 10, they traveled to the ancient family homestead of Shirley Plantation to visit cousin Hill Carter. In this great house, General Lee's parents had wed. Two days later, the general and Agnes were off to Rooney's White House Landing farm where Mother Lee had been staying for three weeks.

General Lee watched his fifteen-month-old namesake bounce on Rooney's knee. During his ten-day visit with his married son and Mother Lee, the general and Agnes rode over to the Romancoke farm of his bachelor son, Rob.

From May 22 to May 26, the general returned to Richmond. On May 24, he again endured a physical examination from Dr. M. H. Houston, who diagnosed the old man's illness as chronic inflammation of the heart. On Thursday, May 26, Robert Lee left Richmond. Two days later, he arrived wearily back at Lexington.

Robert Lee shuffled into the college president's house. His chest hurt too much to walk. The same day as his return after two months on the road, General Lee wrote a letter to the college trustees. He did not waste a day before refusing to accept the home and the annuity which the trustees had voted for Mother Lee six weeks earlier. Behind his back, the trustees went to the Rockbridge County courthouse and recorded Mother Lee's life estate in the home.

Weakening daily, the general returned to his college duties. Thursday, June 23, he handed out the Washington College diplomas at commencement.

One week later, he journeyed alone to Baltimore for two weeks. Arriving July 1, the seventh anniversary of the first day at Gettysburg, General Lee sat through two more useless examinations by the big-city physicians. On July 14, he crossed the Potomac on the road home. He lingered five days in his boyhood hometown of Alexandria, where he said a tired old man's farewells to the friends who cherished him. He left July 19 for Ravensworth, where he rested until July 25. He stood again in his mother's bedroom, and then he went home to the Valley of Virginia.

With all his might, Robert Lee pressed on through August. On August 9, he went without his family to the Hot Springs resort to rest for three weeks. Only a college aide rode beside him. On August 29, he went to Staunton in the Valley for a shareholders meeting of the Valley Railroad. He returned to Lexington after a day or two.

From the Hot Springs spa, Robert Lee dropped a note to Cousin Markie. On August 27, 1870, he closed his letter to Martha Williams with, "May God help the suffering and avert misery from the poor. Good bye." He signed his farewell to Markie, "Most truly, R. E. Lee."

When the fall term at school began on September 15, General Lee spoke softly to the new boys assembled for opening convocation. As the Valley trees slowly changed color for fall, he still managed to haul himself atop his loyal Traveller for quiet rides through the Lexington hills. He still worked at his office in his chapel and he still shuffled home at two o'clock for his afternoon nap.

Tuesday, September 27, the weary president of Washington College attended a faculty meeting at the school which he had single-handedly resurrected from the ashes of war.

Wednesday, it rained in the mountains all day. Robert Lee sent a letter to friends in Baltimore. "I am much better," he wrote. As always, General Lee went to his chapel office early in the morning. Before noon, he left for lunch and his daily nap. A boy student stopped him in the hallway to request a signed autograph from his Marse Robert for a girl-friend. The old soldier smiled, returned to his office, signed the autograph for one of his "yearlings," and then closed his office door. His signature for a teenage sweetheart was the last time he would scrawl "R. E. Lee."

The rain continued, and the air was crisply miserable. After lunch, Robert Lee enjoyed his nap. At four o'clock, he walked down the rain-swept hillside to Grace Episcopal Church for a vestry meeting. The assembly did not adjourn until after dark. He walked home in more rain at seven o'clock.

As was his way, Robert Lee stood in his place at Mother Lee's table to say grace before dinner. But the words would not come. Confused and silent, he sat down heavily.

Alarmed, Mother Lee sent Custis down the hill for the general's physician. The doctor had a bed set up in the dining room where the silent soldier slept until the next day. The dining room became a hospital room, like the red-splattered surgeons' tents which had marked his path from The Seven Days to Appomattox.

Through October 10, Robert Lee slept fitfully and spoke rarely. When daughter Mildred sat beside his bed, he would kiss her hand and mumble, "Precious baby."

Monday, October 10, the stuporous patient spoke little. The crippled fingers of Mother Lee penned a desperate note to Francis Smith, superintendent down the road at Virginia Military Institute, where Custis taught engineering. "The doctors think it would be well for General Lee to have some beef tea at once. As I cannot get it at market before night," she wrote from her rolling chair, "I send to beg a small piece if it can be found at the Institute, lean and juicy, if possible."

Perhaps the beef was donated, for the next day General Lee was slightly more lucid. In his mind, he walked again those fields where he and his divisions had become legend. Just as Stonewall, buried down the road, had called for the green-eyed Little Powell Hill at the last, so did Robert Lee dream again of Antietam Creek. "Tell Hill he *must* come up," he said, his worn-out chest heaving. The old soldier's voice was clear, at least as the witnesses recalled it.

Then the patient dropped off again to spend a restless night. Mother Lee sat in her rolling chair beside his bed and held his hand through the night. The quiet company thought they heard the old voice croak, "Strike the tent!" Had not Old Blue Light meant the same thing after Chancellorsville when he had sighed, "Let us cross over the river and rest in the shade of the trees."

General Robert E. Lee's framed photograph suddenly fell from its nail in the wall. The frame was broken. Mother Lee remarked that she was glad she was not superstitious.

At nine o'clock Wednesday morning, October 12, 1870, Agnes woke sister Mildred from an exhausted nap. The dying father's Precious Life rushed down to the old man's bedside. She found Mother Lee holding the soldier's cool hand while Custis stood beside her. Soft prayers were uttered by reverend and former Confederate major general William Pendleton, dead Sandie's father. General Lee struggled hard as he had done when watching the shattered remnant of Pickett's division stumble back through the sulfur clouds rolling down from Cemetery Ridge at Gettysburg.

Wife and children held their breath and watched the fall sunshine outside the dining room window. The sun in the eastern sky hung just above the blue mountains of the Valley of Virginia. It was nine-thirty in the morning.

Robert Edward Lee was dead.

Twenty-Four

ANNE HILL CARTER LEE'S YOUNGEST SON HAD CROSSED STONEWALL'S river where Old Blue Light waited, along with Sandie Pendleton, Little Powell Hill, Jeb Stuart, Uncle John Sedgwick, even Mr. Lincoln, and all the best blood of a generation, blue and gray.

Eleanor Agnes Lee dressed the dead soldier's body in civilian clothes. The general wore the same black suit he had bought three years earlier for Rooney's Petersburg wedding.

Because Robert Lee was too tall for the only coffin the family could find, he was buried without shoes on Saturday, October 15. The great gray warhorse, Traveller, was led by hand with saddle empty in the funeral procession to the college library. Confederate battlefield aides Walter Taylor and Charles Venable were present for the rites. The week of rain had so swollen the Valley creeks that other ranking veterans could not make it to Lexington. After the hymns were sung, Robert Lee was laid in the dark of the college library's vault until a crypt could be dug in the basement of his chapel.

Among the dead warrior's personal effects, his family discovered the golden eagles of a US Army colonel. Though he had left the Old Army behind forever after his meeting with General-in-Chief Winfield Scott so long ago, Robert Lee had kept the embroidered eagles which had taken thirty years to earn.

Mother Lee remained in the Washington College president's home when Custis succeeded his father to the college presidency.

Nine months after General Lee died, his faithful Traveller died from tetanus. After surviving the sheets of hot lead which had filled the air at Malvern Hill, Antietam Creek, Chancellorsville, Gettysburg, the Wilderness, and the terrible trenches of Petersburg, the Rebel-gray animal was killed by stepping on a rusty nail.

Three years later in June, 1873, Mother Lee traveled in great discomfort back to her cherished Arlington. The old plantation was now a garden of headstones, and so it would remain. She was devastated by the sight. But she did recognize a few of the ancient trees of her girlhood and trees planted by her husband over a lifetime.

What Mrs. Lee most regretted was the loss of her father's relics and treasures that had belonged to George Washington. Federal troops had seized the Arlington House Plantation during the first month of the war, on May 23, 1861, when Federal General Irvin McDowell invaded the estate. Mother Lee and her daughters fled to the Lee homestead of Ravensworth. From there, Mrs. Lee penned an angry protest to Yankee General-in-Chief Winfield Scott. She had abandoned Arlington only to keep Robert from worrying about her, she wrote. "Were it not that I would not add one feather to his load of care, nothing would induce me to abandon my home." Mother Lee signed her letter to family friend General Scott, "Yours in sorrow and sadness."

Lee daughter Mary Custis inherited her strong will from her mother. One week after Arlington fell to the Yankees, Mother Lee sent another angry letter to Federal Major General Charles Sandford, who occupied her childhood home. Writing on May 30, 1861, she fumed, "It never occurred to me, Gen'l [sic] Sandford, that I could be forced to sue for permission to enter my own house and that such an outrage as its military occupation to the exclusion of me and my children could ever have been perpetrated."

In that time when men could slaughter old friends and even family in civil warfare, West Point graduates did not forget how to be honorable gentlemen. Federal Brigadier General Irvin McDowell (West Point, '38, and classmate of Pierre Beauregard, CSA) responded instantly to Mother Lee's letter, with a reply signed the same day as Mrs. Lee's written protest to General Sandford. General McDowell wrote Mrs. Lee: "When you desire to return, every facility will be given you for doing so. I trust, Madam, you will not consider it an intrusion when I say I have the most sincere sympathy for your distress, and, so far as compatible with my duty, I shall always be ready to do whatever may alleviate it."

While her mother sadly toured the lost Arlington, Lee daughter Mary Custis traveled to New York City where she set sail for England, Scotland, France, Belgium, and Italy. She was abroad when her sister Agnes took sick in the fall. On October 15, 1873, three years to the day after her father's funeral, Eleanor Agnes Lee died.

On her deathbed, Agnes bequeathed her Bible to Cousin Markie. The Bible had been a gift to Agnes long ago from Markie's brother Orton, for whom Agnes had grieved for ten years. Then Agnes whispered to her brother Custis, "You must not forget me when I'm gone." The most beautiful of the Lee daughters, the one among them who always loved to write in her journals and diary, was only thirty-two.

Agnes was Mother Lee's favorite. With Agnes in the cold ground, Mary Lee had nothing left for which to live. The crippled widow, whom her doting husband had called Molly, was laid beside her husband in the temporary vault of the college library, three weeks after Agnes.

Mother Lee and Agnes died when Mildred Lee, her father's Precious Life, was twenty-seven. Within ten years, Mildred was overweight, with her hair completely white. Like all of the Lee daughters, she never married. For the fifteen years following her mother's death, she spent winters living with her brother Rob and summers at the college, keeping house for her bachelor brother Custis. Every June, the aging Mildred happily presided over Washington College commencements.

In Lexington, the Sunday school which Stonewall Jackson had founded for slave children in 1855 continued until 1884.

On Memorial Day, 1885, George McClellan finally returned to Antietam Creek, where he had failed to destroy Robert Lee. Little Mac spoke to the assembly about General Lee, whom he called "that splendid man and soldier." Potbellied veterans of the Army of Northern Virginia marched proudly past General McClellan's reviewing stand.

Former President Ulysses S. Grant died in July, 1885, at Mount McGregor, New York, on the Hudson River, at the age of sixty-three— the same age as Robert E. Lee at his death. His eight years in the White House had been a disappointment. He never again rose to that sterling and fleeting moment of greatness when he had quietly walked across the parlor in the old McLean house to shake hands with Robert Lee, electing not to demand his proud prisoner's sword.

Grant never displayed vanity or pleasure or ill will toward Robert Lee's defeat. As he remembered the McLean parlor twenty-one years earlier, "I felt like anything rather than rejoicing at the downfall of a foe who had fought so long and valiantly, and had suffered so much for a cause, though that cause was, I believe, one of the worst for which a people ever fought, and one for which there was the least excuse."

During his last days of a horrible death from throat cancer, President Grant could no longer speak. His pain could no longer be managed by cocaine injections and morphine to help him sleep. And injections of brandy did nothing. The old soldier who had ground down the Army of Northern Virginia could only scratch out written notes to his doctors and to his hovering family. "The fact is, I think I am a verb instead of a personal pronoun," he wrote at the end. "A verb is anything that signifies to be, to do, or to suffer. I signify all three." At President Grant's New York City funeral on August 8, honorary pallbearers included former Confederate generals Simon Bolivar Buckner and old Joe Johnston.

One year later, Stonewall Jackson's trusted and favorite little yellow horse, Fancy, died of old age in the pasture of the Old Soldiers Home at Richmond.

Mary Custis Lee, who had once called herself Marielle when she made eyes at young Jeb Stuart, continued to gallivant around the world. Between her father's death and World War I, she visited twenty-six countries. Once, she met the Pope.

On May 29, 1890, a massive equestrian statue of Robert E. Lee was unveiled in downtown Richmond, Virginia. A troop of old men slept the night at the foot of Stonewall Jackson's Richmond memorial. "We wanted to sleep with the Old Man just once more," one of the frail veterans said proudly.

Former enemies, Generals Joe Johnston and William Tecumseh Sherman, died in 1891. They had become close friends after the war, corresponded regularly, and enjoyed dinners together when Johnston could visit Sherman in his retirement in Washington. When General Sherman died, Joe Johnston was an honorary pallbearer at Sherman's New York City funeral on February 19. The old and fragile Confederate stood bareheaded in the cold rain to show his respect for the man who had tried to destroy him twenty-seven years earlier. General Johnston's friend begged the eighty-four-year-old Rebel to put on his hat. Johnston replied firmly, "If I were in his place and he were standing here in mine, he would not put on his hat." Joseph Johnston left New York with a cold which became pneumonia. Within a month, he was dead.

On the twenty-first anniversary of Robert E. Lee's funeral, former Confederate major general Rooney Lee died at the Ravensworth Plantation in October, 1891. He was buried beside Anne Hill Carter Lee, his grandmother. In 1922, his body was moved to the college-chapel basement crypt beside his parents. Both Rooney and Agnes had died on October 15.

Lieutenant General Ambrose Powell Hill was buried three times after he fell at the beginning of General Lee's last retreat from the Petersburg front. In 1867, his body was moved to Hollywood Cemetery, Richmond. In 1891, Little Powell was reburied in a monument in a Richmond suburb. Fifteen thousand people attended the memorial's dedication in 1892. His daughter Russie died during World War I. Powell Hill's beloved wife Dolly died in 1920. The Powell Hill line was extinguished in 1931, when daughter Lucy Lee died childless.

Years after the war, General McClellan finally commented on the story of his wife's courtship by A. P. Hill. Little Mac had been reminded of Confederate troops shouting, "Why didn't you marry him, Nelly!" when the boys in gray joked that a Yankee artillery barrage against Hill's corps was retaliation for Little Powell's proposal to Ellen Marcy McClellan. "Fiction no doubt," the chivalrous McClellan smiled. "But surely, no one could have married a more gallant soldier than A. P. Hill." Such were the men and boys, blue and gray, of the American Civil War.

In 1893, the old oak tree cut in half by gunfire at Spotsylvania's Bloody Angle was displayed at the Chicago World's Fair. It reposes now in the Armed Forces History Section at the Smithsonian Institution, Washington.

The years were not kind to Robert Lee's "Old Warhorse," Lieutenant General James Longstreet. To the Old South, Old Pete committed three cardinal sins after the war: He became a Republican; he accepted employment from Republicans; and then he compounded that affront to the Southern shrine of The Lost Cause by publishing criticism of Robert Lee's handling of Gettysburg.

"When the smoke cleared away," he had written, "Pickett's division was gone. Mortal men could not have stood that fire." And he dared to write that he had protested Pickett's Charge to Robert Lee, who ordered it anyway. As Lieutenant General Longstreet would remember, "That day at Gettysburg was one of the saddest of my life." For a century, worshippers at the shrines of The Lost Cause never forgave him.

By March, 1892, the sting of his throat wound in the Wilderness in '64 was far behind Old Pete, as were the enmities of the time. On St. Patrick's Day, he journeyed to Atlanta, where he enjoyed a hearty reunion with Yankee Major General Daniel Sickles, whose division Longstreet had nearly annihilated on the second day at Gettysburg. Sickles had left his leg behind near the Emmitsburg Road.

The two old soldiers got falling-down drunk together as they sang arm in arm through the nighttime streets of Atlanta. Full of Irish whiskey, Dan Sickles generously forgave Old Pete for having blown off his leg. "Forgive me?" Old Pete slurred. "You ought to thank me for leaving you one leg to stand on after the mean way you behaved to me at Gettysburg."

By April, 1893, the seventy-two-year-old Longstreet was feeble and down to 100 pounds of skin and bone. At Gettysburg, Old Pete had carried 240 robust pounds. Now, he returned to the Pennsylvania countryside to see for the last time the Emmitsburg Road where he had nodded to General Pickett to march uphill over open ground for more than mile, into the Federal cannon atop Cemetery Ridge.

Longstreet made his Gettysburg pilgrimage with Southerner Porter Alexander and former Federal Generals Sickles and Oliver O. Howard. In the rain, they sat in a horse-drawn buggy. As the tide of red memories flooded Old Pete's mind, General Howard gently patted General Longstreet's bony leg.

In March, 1901, General Longstreet attended the inauguration of President William McKinley. The Republican president from Canton, Ohio, was the last Civil War veteran elected president. When Old Pete later attended the West Point centennial celebration, he sat next to Teddy Roosevelt. After President McKinley's assassination in 1901, General Longstreet went to Washington for Memorial Day, 1902. He sat beside President Teddy Roosevelt as Federal veterans paraded by. Old Pete also shared the stand with Dan Sickles for the last time.

General Lee's "Old Warhorse" died January 2, 1904. His casket at Gainesville, Georgia, was draped in both the Stars and Stripes and the Stars and Bars of the Confederate States of America. Over the old Rebel's grave, a bugler blew "Taps." The haunting tattoo was composed by Federal Major General Daniel Butterfield, Congressional Medal of Honor recipient, so long ago on George Gordon Meade's staff. But because he had become a Republican—Mr. Lincoln's abolitionist party—James Longstreet's widow enjoyed no outpouring of mourning and tribute. The Georgia and the Wilmington, North Carolina, chapters of the Daughters of the Confederacy refused to pass a condolence resolution.

To this day, there is no statue of Robert E. Lee's close friend Lieutenant General James Longstreet anywhere in the Old South.

In December, 1897, Mildred Lee finally moved out of the president's house at Washington College, now Washington and Lee University.

During the Spanish-American War of 1898, President McKinley signed the commission which made Robert Lee's nephew, Fitzhugh Lee, a Federal general. Affectionately known as The Old Rebel, Fitz Lee became the only Confederate general who became a Federal general later. Three months before his death at age seventy, Fitz Lee made his last public appearance at Canton, Ohio, in January, 1905, for a memorial birthday tribute to the assassinated President William McKinley.

In March, 1905, Mildred Lee fell dead at the home of friends in New Orleans. Precious Life was fifty-nine. Her father's old veterans formed a guard of honor to escort her body back to Lexington to repose in her father's chapel. Her sister Mary Custis stayed in France and missed the funeral.

When Custis died in 1913 at age eighty, he too was buried in the basement of his father's chapel at Washington and Lee College.

Also in 1913, Robert E. Lee's mother's body was brought from Ravensworth to Lexington, along with the bones of Light Horse Harry Lee. Robert Lee's parents were reburied in the college crypt with General Lee, Custis, Agnes, Mildred, and Mother Lee. Rob Lee, the only Lee son never to advance beyond the rank of Confederate captain, died in 1914 at the age of seventy-one, one year after his brother Custis, and he was buried in the chapel's Lee family crypt.

With the First World War imminent, Mary Custis Lee, the last living Lee child, returned to America. She set up housekeeping in Washington, DC, the capital of her father's one-time mortal enemies. She dined at the White House with the same Tommy Wilson who as a boy had seen both her father and Jefferson Davis on the dirt streets of Augusta. Now Woodrow Wilson had a war of his own to wage.

Mary Custis finally returned to Lexington in 1917, at age eighty-two. She had been gone nearly fifty years. She died in November, 1918, and bequeathed $10,000 to her father's Grace Episcopal Church of Lexington. General Lee now reposed in his chapel with his parents, Mother Lee, and all of his children, except Sweet Annie, who was buried in North Carolina.

Jeb Stuart's wife Flora died in 1923 within two days of the fifty-ninth anniversary of her husband's death, in her sister's bed.

On the third day of July, 1938, President Franklin Roosevelt kindled the Eternal Light Peace Memorial on the battlefield at Gettysburg. Nearly two thousand, feeble veterans attended the seventy-fifth reunion of the boys who had become men between the ridges and the red-hot cannon.

Six days before Christmas, 1959, the last Confederate veteran died. Walter Williams was 117 years old, and he had worn the tattered gray in John Bell Hood's Division of the Army of Northern Virginia. One day earlier, the nuclear ballistic missile submarine *Robert E. Lee* (SSBN 601) was launched. The US Navy Band wore gray and played "Dixie."

In 1957, the US Congress declined to pass a special resolution on the eve of the Civil War centennial which would have restored Robert E. Lee to full citizenship in the United States.

General Lee had submitted his postwar oath of allegiance in October, 1865. But it was lost until discovered 105 years later. In 1970, the faded document was found among old records in the National Archives.

US Senator Harry Byrd of West Virginia introduced Joint Resolution 189 in 1974 to restore Robert Lee to full US citizenship. The bill bogged down in debates for a year as the Congress wrestled with attempts to add an amnesty amendment for Vietnam War deserters and draft evaders. Finally, the Resolution passed the US Senate unanimously. But the favorable vote in the House of Representatives was 407 to 10. When the vote was taken, Rooney's grandson, Robert E. Lee IV, was in the congressional gallery.

On August 5, 1975, President Gerald Ford signed the Resolution. Robert E. Lee was an American citizen again, 105 years after his death.

In 1988, excavations at Sharpsburg beside Antietam Creek still produced the bones of unknown Federal soldiers from the Irish Brigade who died taking Bloody Lane from John Gordon's bloodied Confederates.

In June, 1989, the last seven daughters of Confederate veterans were evicted from Richmond's Confederate Home for Women, founded in 1898. The oldest of the real Daughters of the Confederacy was ninety-eight.

On October 13, 1990, the last likely widow of a Confederate veteran died at the age of 105, in Sumter, South Carolina.

Lee daughter Annie remained in a tiny North Carolina cemetery, where her grave was tenderly maintained by the Warrenton chapter of the Daughters of the Confederacy. In 1866, an eleven-foot obelisk was carved by a Confederate veteran and erected over the grave of "Sweet Annie." But in 1993, vandals toppled the monument and her grave was strewn with beer cans. After a little squabble between Virginia and North Carolina historical societies, 132 years after her death, "Sweet Annie" was moved from North Carolina to her father's Lexington chapel on September 29, 1994.

In 2002, two steamer trunks belonging to world traveler Mary Custis were discovered at the Burke and Herbert Bank and Trust in Alexandria, Virginia. Lee daughter Mary had deposited the trunks there in 1917, when World War I ended her forty-three years of exile. She died within a year, at the age of eighty-three. Between 2002 and 2007, the Virginia Historical Society inventoried more than four thousand previously unknown family photographs, documents, postcards, and letters. Included was an envelope in which Mary Custis had carefully placed the cloth gold stars cut from her father's Confederate uniform, fifty-two years earlier.

On July 7, 2015, the "Confederate flag," originally only the battle flag of the Army of Northern Virginia, was removed from the grounds of the capitol building in Columbia, South Carolina. The flag was first flown over the capitol dome in April, 1961, to celebrate the one hundredth anniversary of the beginning of the War Between the States. Later, the flag was demoted to a position on the grounds of the capitol building.

One month later, on August 6, 2015, Confederate Memorial Day and Robert E. Lee's birthday were removed from the calendar of official state holidays in Georgia. The names of these historic dates were changed merely to "State Holiday."

These 2015 events suggest that perhaps the Civil War—or the War Between the States, or the War of the Rebellion (as the Federal Congress called it)—is over at last, with the memories alone remaining. And perhaps not. Yet, the flaking cannon still stand in silent battery as eternal monuments upon those green fields which once ran red with the blood of men and boys wearing blue or gray or butternut-brown, all of whom bled for their countries.

How remarkable that the actual veterans of that bloodbath refused to deny the heroism and the courage and the devotion to "country" which were shared by friend and foe alike.

Monday, May 22, 1905, the State of Ohio dedicated its Civil War monuments on the silent, green battlefield of Vicksburg, Mississippi. Ohio dedicated thirty-nine monuments and twenty historic markers on the battlefield which gave Mr. Lincoln control of the Mississippi River on the same day long ago and far away when Robert E. Lee lost the Battle of Gettysburg on July 4, 1863.

At the 1905 dedication of the Ohio memorials on the Vicksburg battlefield, Brigadier General Charles W. Miner spoke for Ohio and for his country. Remembering the ferocious 1863 Vicksburg siege, he proclaimed to the ancient veterans assembled, both blue and gray:

The sun of the morning was in our faces then, your hearts beat high with hopes of youth, and faith in the cause we fought for. Today, the echoes are silent, and the roar of the mortar and crash of the musket are but memories, and now it is the evening light we see . . . We are stragglers who bring up the rear of those armed millions. We wait our call to join the departed host. . . .

The shadows of these intervening years have taught us charity— charity to believe that those who stood against and those who stood with us were as one in nobleness of faith and creed.

Acknowledgments

WITHOUT HACHETTE BOOK GROUP's KIND PERMISSION TO USE excerpts from *The Wartime Papers of Robert E. Lee*, this project would have been impossible. Excerpts from Robert E. Lee letters and battlefield dispatches in *The Wartime Papers of Robert E. Lee*, edited by Clifford Dowdey and Louis H. Manarin, copyright © 1961 and renewed 1989 by the Commonwealth of Virginia, are reprinted with the permission of Little, Brown and Company. All rights reserved. The author gratefully acknowledges the generous kindness and assistance of the Huntington Library, San Marino, CA, for the author's use of *"To Markie": The Letters of Robert E. Lee to Martha Custis Williams* (Cambridge: Harvard University Press, 1933), the Huntington Library, San Marino, California (HM 8807-8845). The author cannot adequately thank James M. McPherson, PhD, Professor Emeritus, Princeton University, author of the Pulitzer Prize winning, Civil War history, *Battle Cry of Freedom* (2003). Professor McPherson generously reviewed a draft of *The Last Years of Robert E. Lee* and offered wise counsel and historic insight to keep this author from looking foolish. And then, there is Ms. Emily Tyler, assistant editor at Taylor Trade Publishing, whose generous patience, kindness, and encouragement this author repeatedly tried and failed to exhaust for two years. Without Ms. Tyler, Ms. Lauren Szalkiewicz, Ms. Melissa Hayes, and Mr. Rick Rinehart, all at Taylor Trade Publishing and Rowman & Littlefield Publishing Group, *The Last Years of Robert E. Lee* would still be molding in a shoebox where all manuscripts go to die. And, if Dr. Robert Pigeon and Mr. Kenneth Gallagher, formerly of Combined Books, Conshohocken, PA, think that this author might have forgotten their contributions to this project long ago and far away: Thank you, both.

Endnotes

Chapter One

1. Winter camp, Orange County, January, 1864. *The Official Military Atlas*, Plates 87 (4) and 100 (1).

1. At least fifteen thousand Confederates were newly baptized . . . Freeman, *R. E. Lee*, 3:241. Pryor, *Reading the Man*, 236. Robertson, *Soldiers*, 187. Trudeau, *Bloody Roads South*, 17.

1. The religious fervor . . .; General Orders Number 15. Dowdey and Manarin, *The Wartime Papers*, 668–69.

1. "I am sorry to hear . . ." General Lee letter to Mrs. Lee, February 7, 1864. Ibid., 668. Mother Lee and her daughters living at "The Mess" in Richmond by December, 1863: Thomas, *Robert E. Lee*, 317.

1. "The young men . . ." General Lee letter to Mrs. Lee, February 14, 1864. *The Wartime Papers*, 671. Pryor, *Reading the Man*, 407. Thomas, *Robert E. Lee*, 319.

2. From Robert Lee's fifty-seventh birthday . . . Sandy and Kate Pendleton honeymooned in hungry Richmond . . . reference to Moss Neck Plantation. Bean, *Stonewall's Man*, 185–86.

2. "The general remedy . . ." General Lee letter to Jefferson Davis, August 8, 1863. Dowdey and Manarin, *The Wartime Papers*, 589–90. Thomas, *Robert E. Lee*, 307–08.

3. Sam Houston, "One drop of Jeff Davis's blood . . ." Burke Davis, *The Long Surrender*, 8.

3. "Suppose, my dear friend . . ." Jefferson Davis letter to Robert E. Lee, August 12, 1863. Freeman, *R. E. Lee*, 3:157–58. J. William Jones, *Life and Letters*, 282. Thomas, *Robert E. Lee*, 308. This elegant letter was composed by Judah P. Benjamin. Evans, *Judah P. Benjamin*, 239.

3. "The number of desertions . . ." General Lee Letter to Jefferson Davis, August 17, 1863. Dowdey and Manarin, *The Wartime Papers*, 591. Thomas, *Robert E. Lee*, 309.

4. "Nothing prevents my advancing . . ." General Lee letter to Jefferson Davis, August 24, 1863. Dowdey and Manarin, *The Wartime Papers*, 594.

4. "The want of supplies . . ." General Lee letter to General Alexander Lawton, Quartermaster General, October 9, 1863. Ibid., 610.

4. "Thousands were barefooted . . ." General Lee letter to Mrs. Lee, October 19, 1863. Ibid. 611.

4. Robert Lee's failing heart . . . and angina attacks. Clark, *Gettysburg*, 69. Dowdey, *Lee*, 339, 384. Freeman, *R. E. Lee*, 2:502. Katcher, *The Army of Robert E. Lee*, 23. Miers, *Robert E. Lee*, 132. Robertson, *General A. P. Hill*, 220.

4. "An attack of rheumatism in my back . . ." General Lee letter to Mrs. Lee, September 4, 1863. Dowdey and Manarin, *The Wartime Papers*, 595 (punctuation slightly changed).

4. Sixteen days later, angina chest and back pain . . . Dowdey, *Lee*, 406. Freeman, *R. E. Lee*, 3:171, 189. Thomas, *Robert E. Lee*, 310.

4. "I am too old to command . . ." General to aide, Lieutenant Colonel Marshall, probably said December 2, 1863. Freeman, *R. E. Lee*, 3:202.

4. "Summer returns . . ." General Lee letter to Charlotte Lee, June 22, 1862. Dowdey and Manarin, *The Wartime Papers*, 197. J. William Jones, *Life and Letters*, 185.

5. Rooney Lee was wounded June 9, 1863, at Brandy Station, Virginia; Rooney captured while recuperating, June 26, 1863: Thomas, *Robert E. Lee*, 305. Custis Lee offers Federals to take his brother Rooney's place as a POW as Rooney's frail wife, Charlotte, lay dying. Coulling, *The Lee Girls*, 132. Lee Jr., *Recollections and Letters*, 117. Robert E. Lee Jr. puts Rooney's imprisonment during December 1863, at Fort Monroe, Virginia, but Clifford Dowdey has Rooney Lee's prison camp on freezing Lake Erie's Johnson Island, Ohio. Dowdey, *Lee*, 411.

5. General Lee returns to winter camp for Christmas, 1863. Thomas, *Robert E. Lee*, 316.

5. Wasted by grief and tuberculosis, Charlotte died on Christmas Day, 1863 . . . buried Shockoe Cemetery, Richmond. The secondary historical sources disagree on the date of Charlotte Wickham Lee's death. She died either on Christmas Eve or Christmas Day, 1863. Anderson and Anderson, *The Generals*, 354. Coulling, *The Lee Girls*, 132–33. Tuberculosis as cause of death: Nagel, *The Lees of Virginia*, 279.

5. "I feel for her all the love . . ." General Lee letter to Mrs. Lee, December 25, 1863. Dowdey and Manarin, *The Wartime Papers*, 644.

5. "Thus dear Mary is link by link . . ." General Lee letter to Mrs. Lee, December 27, 1863. Ibid., 645. Freeman, *R. E. Lee*, 3:217. J. William Jones, *Life and Letters*, 298. General Lee wrote a very similar letter to his cousin Margaret Stuart two days later: Ibid., 297.

5. On February 15, 1864, General Lee wrote to War Secretary James Seddon . . . Dowdey and Manarin, *The Wartime Papers*, 671–72. Freeman, *R. E. Lee*, 3:256.

5. Sandie Pendleton managed a furlough, and Kate Pendleton pregnant. Bean, *Stonewall's Man*, 188.

5. From February 22 to 29 . . . Freeman, *R. E. Lee*, 3:219.

6. General Lee's daily rides through winter camp; soldiers stand in silent tribute. Ibid., 3:241.

6. General Lee's usual dinner during the winter of 1863–1864 is cabbage soup. Ibid., 3:247, 251–53.

6. Death of Jeb Stuart's banjo player, Sam Sweeney. Burke Davis, *Jeb Stuart*, 369.

6. With James Longstreet's large First Corps . . . Orange Courthouse. Freeman, *R. E. Lee*, 3:253. Trudeau, *Bloody Roads South*, 7.

6. Jeb Stuart's cavalry mustered . . . Burke Davis, *Jeb Stuart*, 376. Thomas, *Bold Dragoon*, 283.

6. The manpower crisis . . . Freeman, *R. E. Lee*, 3:255, 264.

6. And "Little Powell" Hill (West Point, '47) barely had the strength . . . Robertson, *General A. P. Hill*, 250.

7. On March 10, 1864, General Lee returned to Richmond . . . Freeman, *R. E. Lee*, 3:261–63.

7. Hiram Ulysses Grant had arrived in Virginia. Trudeau, *Bloody Roads South*, 8.

7. Now Lieutenant General Grant would command all Federal armies . . . Anderson and Anderson, *The Generals*, 352. Frassanito, *Grant and Lee*, 33–34.

8. General Grant's remarkable, memorable voice. Anderson and Anderson, *The Generals*, 361.

8. General Grant's relationship by marriage to Lieutenant General James Longstreet, CSA. Longstreet, *Lee and Longstreet*, 96, 101.

8. "We must make up our minds . . ." Piston, *Lee's Tarnished Lieutenant*, 87.

Chapter Two

9. Parole of Rooney Lee, March, 1864. Coulling, *The Lee Girls*, 136. Freeman, *R. E. Lee*, 3:262. Thomas, *Robert E. Lee*, 319.

9. Mrs. Lee and daughters knitting socks. MacDonald, *Mrs. Robert E. Lee*, 177. Thomas, *Robert E. Lee*, 318. "Can you not teach Mildred that stitch?" General Lee letter to Mrs. Lee, March 18, 1864. Dowdey and Manarin, *The Wartime Papers*, 679. General Lee's series of spring 1864 letters requesting socks from his family. Ibid., 680–81, 687, 694, 717.

9. On Saturday, March 26, 1864, Lieutenant General Grant . . . Trudeau, *Bloody Roads South*, 12.

10. "All the information I receive . . ." General Lee letter to Jefferson Davis, April 5, 1864. Dowdey and Manarin, *The Wartime Papers*, 690.

10. "A soldier's heart, you know, is divided . . ." General Lee letter to cousin Margaret Stuart. J. William Jones, *Life and Letters*, 302.

10. "I feel a marked change in my strength . . ." General Lee letter to son Custis Lee, April 9, 1864. Dowdey and Manarin, *The Wartime Papers*, 695–96.

10. "I want for nothing . . ." General Lee letter to Mrs. Lee, April 9, 1864. Ibid., 695.

10. On April 11, General Longstreet, camped at Bristol, Tennessee. . . Freeman, *Lee's Lieutenants*, 3:336–37. Freeman, *R. E. Lee*, 3:263. Douglas Southall Freeman seems to give two separate dates for Longstreet's orders to return to Virginia: April 7 (*R. E. Lee*) and April 11 (*Lee's Lieutenants*).

10. "My anxiety on the subject of provisions . . ." General Lee letter to Jefferson Davis, April 12, 1864. Dowdey and Manarin, *The Wartime Papers*, 698. Freeman, *R. E. Lee*, 3:247.

10. Longstreet's First Corps trickled back . . . Ibid., 3:249.

10. By April 16, 1864, General Lee's field intelligence . . . Ibid., 3:265.

10. "I am not yet able to call to me . . ." General Lee letter to Jefferson Davis, April 16, 1864. Dowdey and Manarin, *The Wartime Papers*, 700. Freeman, *R. E. Lee*, 3:266.

11. "We have now but one thing ..." General Lee letter to Jefferson Davis, April 19, 1864. Dowdey and Manarin, *The Wartime Papers*, 704 (punctuation slightly changed).

11. General Lee's 64,000 men confront 119,000 Federals as of April 18, 1864. Thomas, *Robert E. Lee*, 321.

11. On April 23, 1864, Rooney Lee was promoted ... Freeman, *Lee's Lieutenants*, 3:411.

11. "If defeated, nothing will be ..." General Lee letter to son Rooney Lee, April 24, 1864. Horn, *The Man Who Would Not Be Washington*, 209. J. William Jones, *Life and Letters*, 299.

11. "Getting old, am I not?" General Grant letter to Julia Grant. Trudeau, *Bloody Roads South*, 19.

11. "You must sometimes cast your thoughts ..." General Lee letter to cousin Margaret Stuart, April 28, 1864. Freeman, *R. E. Lee*, 3:268. Lee Jr., *Recollections and Letters*, 123.

11. ... as tears streamed down the ruddy cheeks ... Freeman, *Lee's Lieutenants*, 3:342–43. Freeman, *R. E. Lee*, 3:267. Trudeau, *Bloody Roads South*, 24.

11. Death of little Joseph Davis, April 1864. Nevins, *The War for the Union: The Organized War 1863–1864*, 35. Trudeau, *Bloody Roads South*, 24.

12. Baptism of Lucy Lee Hill, daughter of Lieutenant General A. P. Hill. Robertson, *General A. P. Hill*, 249.

12. General Lee on Clark's Mountain, May 2; Grant and Meade about to cross the Rapidan River. Freeman, *R. E. Lee*, 3:268. Trudeau, *Bloody Roads South*, 21, 25–26.

12. A. P. Hill's Third Corps strength, May 1864. Robertson, *General A. P. Hill*, 251.

12. May 2, 1864: General Lee writes home to request new suspenders. Dowdey and Manarin, *The Wartime Papers*, 718.

13. May 3, 1864: General Grant's staff meeting in A. P. Hill's hometown. Anderson and Anderson, *The Generals*, 363. Robertson, *General A. P. Hill*, 35.

13. May 4, 1864: Federals begin crossing the Rapidan River. Frassanito, *Grant and Lee*, 41–46. Trudeau, *Bloody Roads South*, 31.

13. Confederate First, Second, and Third Corps converge to meet Grant. Freeman, *Lee's Lieutenants*, 3:344. Freeman, *R. E. Lee*, 3:269–70.

13. Federals' supply wagon train sixty-five miles long. Dowdey, *Lee*, 421.

13. Brigadier General Micah Jenkins has a troubling dream. Trudeau, *Bloody Roads South*, 34.

14. April, 1864, loss of brigadier generals since May, 1863, in the Army of Northern Virginia. Thomas, *Robert E. Lee*, 320.

14. May 4, 1864, Federals march past eroded graves at Chancellorsville. Trudeau, *Bloody Roads South*, 33.

14. Jeb Stuart's cavalry joins Third Corps. Thomas, *Bold Dragoon*, 284–85.

15. General Lee worries about untested, newly promoted officers. Freeman, *R. E. Lee*, 3:270, 272–73 (Note 21, page 273).

15. May 4, 1864: Confederate Second and Third Corps clog the road. Dowdey, *Lee*, 422. Freeman, *R. E. Lee*, 3:270. Robertson, *General A. P. Hill*, 251. Trudeau, *Bloody Roads South*, 36–39.

15. Robert Lee with Third Corps planned ... Freeman, *R. E. Lee*, 3:273.

16. General Lee at Verdiersville as his troops converge. Ibid., 3:274. Trudeau, *Bloody Roads South*, 37.

16. Federals' II, V, VI, and IX corps converge in Wilderness. Ibid., 39.

16. General Lee orders Ewell to wait for Longstreet before attacking. Freeman, *R. E. Lee*, 3:276. Trudeau, *Bloody Roads South*, 40.

16. By first light on May 5 . . . Dowdey, *Lee*, 425. Thomas, *Bold Dragoon*, 286–87. Trudeau, *Bloody Roads South*, 41–42.

17. By seven-thirty on this Thursday morning . . . Ibid., 42–43, 45.

17. General Ewell confused by conflicting orders. Ibid., 45–46.

17. By ten o'clock in the morning . . . and General Meade buttons General Grant's coat. Anderson and Anderson, *The Generals*, 370. Trudeau, *Bloody Roads South*, 49.

17. General Ewell sends Sandie Pendleton to confer with General Lee. Ibid., 50.

CHAPTER THREE

18. General Ewell is attacked. Freeman, *Lee's Lieutenants*, 3:350 (Note 58).

18. Wilderness fighting; death of General Jones, CSA. Dowdey, *Lee*, 426–27. Freeman, *Lee's Lieutenants*, 3:277.

18, 19, 20. Fierce combat in the Wilderness; Saunders Field; "Remember your name!"; severed head knocks down Federal soldier; Confederate Third Corps attacked five times; no word from General Longstreet on First Corps' position. Freeman, *R. E. Lee*, 3:279, 281–82. Robertson, *General A. P. Hill*, 255–60. Trudeau, *Bloody Roads South*, 53–62, 64–68.

20. Generals Lee, Stuart, and A. P. Hill nearly captured. Dowdey, *Lee*, 429. Freeman, *R. E. Lee*, 3:278. Robertson, *General A. P. Hill*, 254–55. Thomas, *Robert E. Lee*, 324. Trudeau, *Bloody Roads South*, 52.

21. Night of May 5–6, 1864: Longstreet still three miles away. Dowdey, *Lee*, 434–36. Trudeau, *Bloody Roads South*, 71.

21. Lieutenant General A. P. Hill in severe pain and exhausted, night of May 5. Freeman, *Lee's Lieutenants*, 3:353. Robertson, *General A. P. Hill*, 263.

21. Longstreet's First Corps marches all night, May 5–6. Freeman, *R. E. Lee*, 3:283. Trudeau, *Bloody Roads South*, 78.

21. Dawn, May 6: Burnside's IX Corps reinforces Federal position. Ibid., 84.

22. The five a.m. attack was a full frontal assault . . . Dowdey, *Lee*, 437–38. Freeman, *Lee's Lieutenants*, 3:355–56.

22, 23, 24. May 6, 1864: all-day combat; Longstreet finally on the field; "Hurrah for Texas!"; "Lee to the rear!"; five hours of desperate fighting pauses at ten a.m. Ibid., 3:356–60. Freeman, *R. E. Lee*, 3:285–90. Piston, *Lee's Tarnished Lieutenant*, 88. Robertson, *General A. P. Hill*, 263–67. Thomas, *Robert E. Lee*, 325. Trudeau, *Bloody Roads South*, 86–93. Wert, *General James Longstreet*, 387.

24. May 6, 1864, 11:45 a.m.: Longstreet attacks. Freeman, *Lee's Lieutenants*, 3:360, 361 (Notes 115 and 118), 362. Freeman, *R. E. Lee*, 3:291–94. Trudeau, *Bloody Roads South*, 95–100.

25. May 6, 1864, afternoon: fighting resumes; Lieutenant General James Longstreet gravely wounded. Dowdey, *Lee*, 440–41. Freeman, *Lee's Lieutenants*, 3:365–67. Thomas, *Robert E. Lee*, 325. Trudeau, *Bloody Roads South*, 105, 107.

25. May 6, 1864, afternoon: Lee takes field command; fighting until dusk; at least two hundred wounded burned as underbrush burns. Freeman, *Lee's Lieutenants*, 3:372. Freeman, *R. E. Lee*, 3:295–97. Trudeau, *Bloody Roads South*, 109–12.

26. "More desperate fighting . . ." Grant, *Memoirs and Selected Letters*, 534.

CHAPTER FOUR

27. East of the bloodied Federals . . . ; 25,000 casualties, blue and gray, in thirty-eight hours. Anderson and Anderson, *The Generals*, 376–77. Dowdey, *Lee*, 443. Freeman, *R. E. Lee*, 3:428. Robertson, *General A. P. Hill*, 267. Trudeau, *Bloody Roads South*, 119.

28. On Saturday, Lieutenant General Grant issued marching orders . . . Freeman, *R. E. Lee*, 3:298–99. Trudeau, *Bloody Roads South*, 121–23.

28. May 7, 1864: General Lee reorganizes his command personnel; promotion of Major General Richard Anderson, who cried when greeted by Longstreet's First Corps. Dowdey, *Lee*, 444. Freeman, *Lee's Lieutenants*, 3:375. Freeman, *R. E. Lee*, 3:301. Matter, *If It Takes All Summer*, 14.

28. May 7, 1864: Federals withdrawing from Germanna Plank Road position; Federals remove pontoon bridge from Ely's Ford; General Grant: ". . . punctuality and promptitude." Freeman, *Lee's Lieutenants*, 3:376–79. Matter, *If It Takes All Summer*, 14–15, 22–23, 27–28, 30.

29. May 7, 1864: Federal Assistant Secretary of War Charles Dana joins General Grant. Frassanito, *Grant and Lee*, 178.

29, 30. May 7, 1864: Federal ambulance wagons leave the Wilderness; General Lee believes Grant pulling out to advance toward Spotsylvania; as Grant moves around General Lee, the Federals cheer when they realize that, for the first time, they are not retreating after fighting General Lee. Dowdey, *Lee*, 446. Matter, *If It Takes All Summer*, 21, 33. Trudeau, *Bloody Roads South*, 125–26, 128–29.

30. Midnight, May 7–8, 1864: Terrifying and ghostly "Rebel Yell" in the darkness. Freeman, *Lee's Lieutenants*, 3:380. Freeman, *R. E. Lee*, 3:303. Matter, *If It Takes All Summer*, 45–46.

31. The "poison fields" of Spotsylvania. Anderson and Anderson, *The Generals*, 382.

31, 32, 33. Dawn, May 8, 1864: Generals Grant and Meade lead Federals to Spotsylvania; General Lee sends Second Corps toward Spotsylvania; Fitz Lee's cavalry engages Union cavalry; Federal General Warren, "Never mind cannon!"; Battle of Laurel Hill: Federal General Sheridan resolves to attack Jeb Stuart. Freeman, *Lee's Lieutenants*, 3:304, 381–82, 386–87. Matter, *If It Takes All Summer*, 49, 53, 55–63. Thomas, *Bold Dragoon*, 288. Trudeau, *Bloody Roads South*, 130, 135–37.

33–34. General Ewell's gray Second Corps marches for five hours toward Spotsylvania; Lieutenant General A. P. Hill temporarily relieved of command of Third Corps; fighting continues at Laurel Hill for another fifteen hours, until three in the morning, May 9; ferocious fighting with General Lee arriving on the Spotsylvania field with Union and Confederate armies only three-quarters of a mile apart. Dowdey, *Lee*, 446. Freeman, *Lee's Lieutenants*, 3:390–91. Freeman, *R. E. Lee*, 3:304–07. Matter, *If It Takes All*

Summer, 76, 84–87, 89–95, 108. Robertson, *General A. P. Hill*, 268. Thomas, *Robert E. Lee*, 326. Trudeau, *Bloody Roads South*, 131–32, 139–42.

34. May 8–9, 1864: Federals suffer 1,740 casualties, with V Corps destroyed. Matter, *If It Takes All Summer*, 108. Trudeau, *Bloody Roads South*, 108.

35. May 9, 1864: Bulge in the new Confederate line between Po River and Spotsylvania Courthouse is dubbed the "Mule Shoe." Dowdey, *Lee*, 448. Freeman, *R. E. Lee*, 3:309–10, 312.

CHAPTER FIVE

36. May 9, 1864, Spotsylvania: Lieutenant General Grant suffers from saddle sores. Anderson and Anderson, *The Generals*, 382.

36, 37, 38. May 9, 1864: Generals Lee and Grant build breastworks at Spotsylvania; long friendship between General Lee and "Uncle John Sedgwick"; death of Federal Major General John Sedgwick; Confederate forces detached toward Shady Grove. Freeman, *R. E. Lee*, 3:311. Matter, *If It Takes All Summer*, 102–03. Priest, *Antietam: The Soldiers' Battle*, 127. Sears, *Landscape Turned Red: The Battle of Antietam*, 227. Trudeau, *Bloody Roads South*, 144–45. "[O]ur old friend, Sedgwick." General Lee letter to Mrs. Lee, February 7, 1864. Dowdey and Manarin, *The Wartime Papers*, 671.

38, 39. Jeb Stuart's 4,500 cavalry horsemen ride to intercept Federal General Sheridan's 15,000 cavalrymen; skirmish at Mitchell's Shop; Federal General Custer destroys Confederate supplies and railroad tracks; May 10, 1864: cavalry Generals Jeb Stuart and Fitz Lee ride toward Hanover Junction. Burke Davis, *Jeb Stuart*, 385–88, 390–91. Freeman, *Lee's Lieutenants*, 3:413–16. Thomas, *Bold Dragoon*, 288–89.

39, 40, 41, 42. May 10, 1864: Federals use mortars for the first time; Federal Major General Meade orders a late-afternoon assault at Laurel Hill; Confederate Generals Mahone and Heth deploy; Federal Brigadier General James Rice killed; Federal Colonel Emory Upton orders an assault with his men carrying empty rifles; "Load in Nine Times" drill for loading single-shot, black-powder rifles; Federal General Warren assaults Confederate entrenchments three times; Battle of the Mule Shoe at Spotsylvania; "General Lee to the rear!"; ground burns, igniting cartridge boxes on the bodies of the wounded; promotion by Lieutenant General Grant of Colonel Upton to brigadier general. Freeman, *R. E. Lee*, 3:313–14. Katcher, *The Army of Robert E. Lee*, 66 (cartridge boxes carried by Confederate infantry). Matter, *If It Takes All Summer*, 131, 134, 137, 139, 141–52, 155–59, 162–67. McLaughlin, *Gettysburg: The Long Encampment*, 54 ("Load in Nine Times"). Trudeau, *Bloody Roads South*, 148–51, 153–55, 157–62.

42. May 10, 1864, evening: Confederate band plays in the darkness; Jeb Stuart and Fitz Lee lead their cavalries to within six miles of Richmond to take on General Sheridan. Anderson and Anderson, *The Generals*, 384. Burke Davis, *Jeb Stuart*, 391, 393–95; Freeman, *Lee's Lieutenants*, 3:417–19. Trudeau, *Bloody Roads South*, 163–64.

43. Lieutenant General Grant memo to Major General Halleck, May 11, 1864: ". . . if it takes all summer." Freeman, *Lee's Lieutenants*, 3: 396. Grant, *Memoirs and Selected Letters*, 550–51. Matter, *If It Takes All Summer*, 170. Trudeau, *Bloody Roads South*, 165.

CHAPTER SIX

44, 45, 46. May 11, 1864: Federals issued two days of rations; "to die game"; General Jeb Stuart gravely wounded at Yellow Tavern by shot fired by Private John Huff and carried to his sister-in-law's home in Richmond. Burke Davis, *Jeb Stuart*, 398, 400–01. Freeman, *Lee's Lieutenants*, 1:302 (Stuart's "Ride Around McClelland"). Ibid., 3:421–25. Matter, *If It Takes All Summer*, 170–71. Thomas, *Bold Dragoon*, 290–93.

46, 47. Evening of May 11 and night of May 11–12, 1864: Grant plans another assault against the Mule Shoe; A. P. Hill commands Third Corps from an ambulance; General Lee: "I think General Grant has managed . . ."; General Lee: "This army cannot stand a siege . . ."; Grant's casualties after only seven days; Federal brass band. Dowdey, *Lee*, 452. Freeman, *Lee's Lieutenants*, 3:316 (Note 60), 398, 442. Matter, *If It Takes All Summer*, 170, 174–77, 183–85, 187, 189. Trudeau, *Bloody Roads South*, 166–67, 169. These sources disagree as to whether General Lee said "This army cannot stand a siege" to General A. P. Hill or to General Henry Heth.

48. May 11–12, 1864: Jeb Stuart is dying in Richmond at Dr. Brewer's home. Burke Davis, *Jeb Stuart*, 411. Freeman, *Lee's Lieutenants*, 3:427, 762.

49, 50, 51. May 12, 1864 (3:30 a.m.–6:00 a.m.): Ferocious Battle of the Mule Shoe at Spotsylvania begins; Johnson's Confederate division and its famous Stonewall Brigade destroyed; Union infantry penetrate the Mule Shoe salient; General Lee rides to the front to lead counteroffensive; "Lee to the rear!" Anderson and Anderson, *The Generals*, 382–83. Freeman, *Lee's Lieutenants*, 3:402, 404–06. Freeman, *R. E. Lee*, 3:317–18, 326 (Note 104). Matter, *If It Takes All Summer*, 190–91, 194–99, 201–02, 218. Robertson, *General A. P. Hill*, 270. Thomas, *Robert E. Lee*, 328–29. Trudeau, *Bloody Roads South*, 169–73, 176–77.

51, 52, 53. May 12, 1864 (6:00 a.m.–9:00 a.m.): Battle of the Mule Shoe continues; two dead men stand where they had killed each other with bayonets; Federals pushed back by 6:30 a.m.; General Lee's horse Traveller saves Lee from being blown apart by a cannonball; yet again, General Lee rides to the front and Mississippi troops plead, "Lee to the rear!"; in the Mule Shoe's "Bloody Angle," three Confederate brigades hold back two Federal divisions; torrential rains do not stop twenty hours of hand-to-hand combat. Dowdey, *Lee*, 453–55. Freeman, *Lee's Lieutenants*, 3:407. Freeman, *R. E. Lee*, 3:318–22. Matter, *If It Takes All Summer*, 202, 205, 207–09, 211–12, 217–18, 244, 248–49. Trudeau, *Bloody Roads South*, 171, 177–81.

53. May 12, 1864, Bloody Angle: Federal James Mangan wounded; he buries his own amputated arm. Matter, *If It Takes All Summer*, 217, 219–20.

CHAPTER SEVEN

54. May 12, 1864, the Mule Shoe: Cannon heard forty-two miles away; dead Federal artilleryman cut in half; 3:00 p.m., Federals bring up mortars; Confederates furiously dig second defensive line at Mule Shoe after sixteen hours of hand-to-hand slaughter. Freeman, *R. E. Lee*, 3:324–25. John B. Jones, *A Rebel War Clerk's Diary*, 2:206. Matter, *If It Takes All Summer*, 244, 250. Trudeau, *Bloody Roads South*, 183, 185.

54. Lieutenant Colonel Sandie Pendleton has two horses killed. Bean, *Stonewall's Man*, 199.

55. Jeb Stuart: "We gallop toward the enemy and trot away . . ." Thomas, *Bold Dragoon*, 72.

55, 56. May 12, 1864: Death of General Jeb Stuart and his connections to General Joe Johnston, CSA, and General John Sedgwick, USA. Burke Davis, *Jeb Stuart*, 34, 72, 412–19. Freeman, *Lee's Lieutenants*, 3:428–29, 431. Thomas, *Bold Dragoon*, 294–96, 299.

56. May 12–13, 1864, night in the Mule Shoe: Officers give orders to dead men; oak tree falls, severed by rifle fire; Confederates begin falling back to second line of defense within Mule Shoe salient at 2:00 a.m., May 13. Matter, *If It Takes All Summer*, 257, 259. Trudeau, *Bloody Roads South*, 185, 187.

56, 57. General Lee on the death of Jeb Stuart, "I can scarcely think of him . . ."; General Orders Number 44, "His achievements form a conspicuous part . . ." Freeman, *R. E. Lee*, 3:326–27. Lee Jr., *Recollections and Letters*, 124–25. Dowdey and Manarin, *The Wartime Papers*, 736. Trudeau, *Bloody Roads South*, 184–85.

57, 58. May 13, 1864, the Mule Shoe: 13,000 casualties in twenty-three hours; Confederate POW's shuffle toward the Punch Bowl holding pens at Belle Plain. Frassanito, *Grant and Lee*, 49, 51, 54. Freeman, *Lee's Lieutenants*, 3:409. Freeman, *R. E. Lee*, 3:326, 332. Matter, *If It Takes All Summer*, 260, 267. Trudeau, *Bloody Roads South*, 187.

58. May 13, 1864, the Mule Shoe at Spotsylvania: Confederate surgeons; General Grant, letter to wife, May 13, "The world has never seen . . ."; General Lee inspects two oak trees toppled by rifle fire. Anderson and Anderson, *The Generals*, 391. Dowdey, *Lee*, 488. Freeman, *R. E. Lee*, 3:329. Trudeau, *Bloody Roads South*, 186.

58. Lee daughter Mary Custis was "Marielle" to dead Jeb Stuart, who was Jimmy to her at West Point. Coulling, *The Lee Girls*, 137. For Mrs. Coulling's elegant sketch of young Mary Custis: Ibid., 7, 11–12, 15, 35–36.

58, 59. May 13–14, 1864: Heavy rain at Spotsylvania; funeral of Jeb Stuart in Richmond; Federals too exhausted for another all-night march and dawn attack. Burke Davis, *Jeb Stuart*, 420. Frassanito, *Grant and Lee*, 102. Freeman, *R. E. Lee*, 3:329, 334. Matter, *If It Takes All Summer*, 296. Thomas, *Bold Dragoon*, 296. Trudeau, *Bloody Roads South*, 188–90.

59, 60. May 14–15, 1864: General Lee reorganizes his shattered command; CSA and USA losses after nine days of fighting; General Lee moves his First Corps. Freeman, *R. E. Lee*, 3:330. Matter, *If It Takes All Summer*, 275, 298. Trudeau, *Bloody Roads South*, 190–91.

60. "These men are not an army . . ." General Lee to Lieutenant General A. P. Hill, May 15, 1864. Freeman, *Lee's Lieutenants*, 3:449. Freeman, *R. E. Lee*, 3:331. Thomas, *Robert E. Lee*, 332.

61. May 17–20, 1864, Spotsylvania: Generals Grant and Lee pull out of Spotsylvania to continue their running battle. Freeman, *R. E. Lee*, 3:335. Trudeau, *Bloody Roads South*, 193, 195, 197.

CHAPTER EIGHT

62. May 18, 1864: "[Federal position] is strongly entrenched and we cannot attack it . . ." General Lee letter to Jefferson Davis. Freeman, *R. E. Lee*, 3:337. This communication is not published in Dowdey and Manarin, *The Wartime Papers*.

62, 63. May 18–19, 1864: Federals withdrawing from Spotsylvania; Confederates march past shallow graves of rotting corpses uncovered by the rain; Battle of Harris Farm; General Lee has two corps commanders failing in physical strength. Frassanito, *Grant and Lee*, 106–09. Freeman, *R. E. Lee*, 3:338–39. Trudeau, *Bloody Roads South*, 198–208.

64, 65. May 19–21, 1864: Generals Grant and Meade move Federal troops out of Spotsylvania to outflank General Lee; General Lee moves Ewell's corps to keep between Grant and Richmond; General Pickett's division dispatched to General Lee; General Lee moves his force toward Hanover Junction; General Lee, "Come, gentlemen"; sickly Lieutenant General A. P. Hill returned to command of Third Corps. Dowdey, *Lee*, 459. Frassanito, *Grant and Lee*, 116. Freeman, *Lee's Lieutenants*, 3:441 (Note 53). Freeman, *R. E. Lee*, 3:339–44. Robertson, *General A. P. Hill*, 273–74. Trudeau, *Bloody Roads South*, 211–13.

65, 66. May 21, 1864: Nighttime visit by Lieutenant General Grant to home of Tom and Mary Chandler, Guinea Station, Virginia. General Grant says of Stonewall Jackson, "Jackson was a gallant soldier and a Christian gentleman." Frassanito, *Grant and Lee*, 116, 122. Trudeau, *Bloody Roads South*, 220–21.

66. Federal and Confederate casualties after just thirteen days: Trudeau, *Bloody Roads South*, 213.

66, 67. May 21–23, 1864: General Lee is cheered by Second Corps after seven hours in the saddle; General Lee arrives at Hanover Junction; General Lee's staff alarmed by the general's exhaustion; Lieutenant General A. P. Hill's assault at Jericho Mills collapses; General Lee is again sick from dirty water; "I begrudge every step . . ."; General Lee letter of May 23 to Mrs. Lee. Dowdey, *Lee*, 461. Dowdey and Manarin, *The Wartime Papers*, 748. Frassanito, *Grant and Lee*, 122, 151. Freeman, *R. E. Lee*, 3:346–48, 350–51. Robertson, *General A. P. Hill*, 274–75. Trudeau, *Bloody Roads South*, 221–23.

67, 68, 69. May 23, 1864, as both great armies race for Hanover Junction: Three Federal corps converging on road to Hanover; Yankee artillery fire on General Lee, relaxing with a cup of buttermilk; with his sudden illness worsening, General Lee must ride in a carriage instead of on Traveller; Confederate line forms "V" near North Anna River; Federals crossing North Anna at Jericho Mill on pontoon bridge; General Wilcox of A. P. Hill's corps engages Federals near Hanover Junction, losing 642 men; General Pickett's fresh division arrives; General Lee letter to Jefferson Davis, May 23, "General Grant's army will be in the field . . ."; General Lee down with serious dysentery, crippling him for next ten days. Dowdey, *Lee*, 462–63. Dowdey and Manarin, *The Wartime Papers*, 747 (punctuation changed). Frassanito, *Grant and Lee*, 127, 130, 132. Freeman, *Lee's Lieutenants*, 3:496. Freeman, *R. E. Lee*, 3:221, 352–53, 355–58. Trudeau, *Bloody Roads South*, 224–25, 227–34.

69, 70. May 23–24, 1864, Hanover Junction: General Lee is bedridden with dysentery; Confederate "V" formation traps one-quarter of Grant's army, but General Lee is too sick to conduct offensive; skirmish at Ox Ford; by nightfall, blue and gray armies dig in, only seven hundred yards apart. Dowdey, *Lee*, 464. Frassanito, *Grant and Lee*, 130, 138, 140. Trudeau, *Bloody Roads South*, 236–40.

CHAPTER NINE

71. "Blue mass" remedy for field dysentery. Katcher, *The Army of Robert E. Lee*, 164.

71. "We must *never* let them pass us . . ." General Lee to Colonel Charles Venable. Freeman, *R. E. Lee*, 3:359. Thomas, *Robert E. Lee*, 330.

71, 72. May 25–27, 1864: Grant avoids Confederate "trap" on North Anna River; Federals move around the Army of Northern Virginia yet again; three days of casualties. Frassanito, *Grant and Lee*, 138, 142, 146, 155–56. Freeman, *R. E. Lee*, 3:360. Trudeau, *Bloody Roads South*, 241–42, 245–47.

72, 73, 74. May 26–28, 1864: General Lee still sick; General Grant moves his supply base to White House Landing, Rooney Lee's homestead; Federals evacuate North Anna position; four Federal corps within fifteen miles of Richmond; General Ewell's health failing, he asks to be relieved of command of Lee's Second Corps; General Lee has lost two of three corps commanders within three weeks. Coulling, *The Lee Girls*, 67. Dowdey, *Lee*, 465–66. Frassanito, *Grant and Lee*, 148, 151, 165. Freeman, *Lee's Lieutenants*, 3:498–99. Freeman, *R. E. Lee*, 3:360–63. Trudeau, *Bloody Roads South*, 247–48, 250.

74, 75. May 28–29, 1864: General Lee still sick; General Fitzhugh Lee engages Federals at Haw's Shop; Private John Huff, USA, killed in action; Federal ambulance wagons stream toward Fredericksburg; Brompton Plantation, Federal field hospital and its ancient tree at Fredericksburg. Dowdey, *Lee*, 466. Frassanito, *Grant and Lee*, 71, 77, 148. Freeman, *R. E. Lee*, 3:362–68. Trudeau, *Bloody Roads South*, 214–18, 248–49.

75. "Everybody is so kind . . ." General Lee letter to Mrs. Lee, May 29, 1864. Dowdey and Manarin, *The Wartime Papers*, 756.

75, 76, 77. May 29–June 1, 1864: Sixteen thousand Federals march toward White House Landing; Lieutenant General Grant again maneuvers around the Army of Northern Virginia toward Cold Harbor; Confederates go two days without food; annihilation of 49th Virginia Infantry regiment at Bethesda Church; "delay will be disaster", General Lee dispatch to Richmond; sick General Lee must ride in a carriage; Federal and Confederate armies race toward Cold Harbor and Old Cold Harbor; General Lee hopes to attack Federal General Sheridan's cavalry on June 1. Dowdey, *Lee*, 467–69. Frassanito, *Grant and Lee*, 156. Freeman, *Lee's Lieutenants*, 3:502, 504–05. Freeman, *R. E. Lee*, 3:369–71, 374–77. Trudeau, *Bloody Roads South*, 253–63, 265.

77, 78, 79, 80. June 1–2, 1864, Cold Harbor/Old Cold Harbor, Virginia: Confederate hunger and scurvy; death of Colonel Lawrence Keitt, former US congressman; five-hour battle for Turkey Hill; five Federal corps on the field; June 2: Generals Lee and Breckinridge, former vice president of the United States; Confederates capture Turkey Hill; all-night rain, June 2; Federals sew name tags onto their shirts. Anderson and Anderson, *The Generals*, 398. Dowdey, *Lee*, 470–71. Frassanito, *Grant and Lee*, 157, 174. Freeman, *Lee's Lieutenants*, 3:506–07, Freeman, *R. E. Lee*, 3:379–80, 382–83, 385–86, 389. Trudeau, *Bloody Roads South*, 265–70, 275–80.

CHAPTER TEN

81, 82. June 3, 1864, Cold Harbor/Old Cold Harbor: Federals attack with battle line one and a half miles wide; Federals are slaughtered in fourteen assaults between

5:00 a.m. and 1:00 p.m.; nearly 7,000 Union casualties. Anderson and Anderson, *The Generals*, 399–401. Dowdey, *Lee*, 472. Frassanito, *Grant and Lee*, 157–58. Freeman, *Lee's Lieutenants*, 3:508. Freeman, *R. E. Lee*, 3:386–91, 398. Trudeau, *Bloody Roads South*, 281–95.

82. "I have always regretted . . ." Grant, *Memoirs and Selected Letters*, 588.

82, 83. Between May 4 and June 4, 1864, General Lee suffered 33,600 casualties and General Grant lost 55,000 Federals. General Lee lost 37 percent of his generals during that single month. Freeman, *Lee's Lieutenants*, 3:513–14. Freeman, *R. E. Lee*, 4:170. Hogan, Jr., *The Overland Campaign*, 70–1. Thomas, *Robert E. Lee*, 331. Trudeau, *Bloody Roads South*, 300.

83. "June 3. Cold Harbor. I was killed." Ibid., 297.

84. "I think you had better go . . ." General Lee letter to Mrs. Lee, June 4, 1864. Dowdey and Manarin, *The Wartime Papers*, 765.

84. June 4, 1864: Battlefield promotions for Confederate generals Early, Anderson, and Ramseur. Freeman, *Lee's Lieutenants*, 3:510–11. Freeman, *R. E. Lee*, 3:364.

85. June 5–7, 1864: General Lee's surly and petty responses to Lieutenant General Grant's request for ceasefire to gather the dead and wounded at Cold Harbor. Ibid., 3:392. Thomas, *Robert E. Lee*, 334–35. Trudeau, *Bloody Roads South*, 302–07.

86. "Two officers and six men . . ." Lieutenant General Grant's note to General Lee, June 7, 1864: Grant, *Memoirs and Selected Letters*, 588.

86. June 4–10, 1864: Nightly Confederate cannon fire against Federals. Frassanito, *Grant and Lee*, 159. Freeman, *R. E. Lee*, 3:400.

86. "You had better leave Richmond . . ." General Lee letter to Mrs. Lee, June 7, 1864. Dowdey and Manarin, *The Wartime Papers*, 768.

86. June 7, 1864: General Lee's disposition of forces; General Breckinridge ordered back to the Shenandoah Valley. Freeman, *R. E. Lee*, 3:396–97.

87. June 6–9, 1864: Staunton falls in the Valley; Federals near Petersburg; General Lee to Jubal Early, "We must destroy this army . . . a mere question of time." Dowdey, *Lee*, 485. Freeman, *Lee's Lieutenants*, 3:498. Freeman, *R. E. Lee*, 3:398. Horn, *The Man Who Would Not Be Washington*, 213. Thomas, *Robert E. Lee*, 339. Trudeau, *Bloody Roads South*, 321.

87. June 10, 1864: General Lee begs War Secretary Seddon for vegetables. Dowdey and Manarin, *The Wartime Papers*, 773.

87. June 11–13, 1864: Federals capture Lexington in the Valley, burning VMI and sacking Washington College; General Lee detaches Second Corps to the Valley giving Lieutenant Grant a four-to-one manpower advantage in Lee's front. Dowdey, *Lee*, 474–75. Freeman, *R. E. Lee*, 3:401.

88. June 12, 1864: "I am well again . . ." General Lee letter to Mrs. Lee. Dowdey and Manarin, *The Wartime Papers*, 775.

88. June 12–13, 1864, Cold Harbor: General Grant breaks camp to again slide his army around General Lee's right flank; Yankee bands playing during the night signal Federal withdrawal from Cold Harbor front toward James River and Petersburg. Frassanito, *Grant and Lee*, 174, 197–99. Trudeau, *Bloody Roads South*, 315.

88, 89. June 13, 1864: Second Corps leaves Cold Harbor line for the Valley; Sandie Pendleton leaves with Second Corps after visiting his pregnant wife Kate in Richmond. Ibid., 315–16. Bean, *Stonewall's Man*, 197.

89. June 13–14, 1864: Both armies on the move, Grant toward the James River and Lee toward White Oak Swamp; armies leave behind 84,000 dead, wounded, or missing men since May 4. Dowdey, *Lee*, 476. Freeman, *Lee's Lieutenants*, 3:502 (Note 50). Freeman, *R. E. Lee*, 3:402–03. Trudeau, *Bloody Roads South*, 315, 341.

89, 90. June 14–15, 1864: Without Jeb Stuart, General Lee not certain of Grant's course; Federals building 700-yard-long pontoon bridge across the James River; wagon train of Federal supplies is thirty-five miles long as Federals begin crossing the James. Anderson and Anderson, *The Generals*, 406–07. Dowdey, *Lee*, 476. Frassanito, *Grant and Lee*, 205–07. Freeman, *R. E. Lee*, 3:402–03.

90. June 15, 1864: General Lee sends General Hoke's division to Drewry's Bluff on the James; General Beauregard warns Lee of impending Federal concentration toward Petersburg. Ibid., 3:405–08, 439.

91. June 15, 1864: General Lee finally believes that Grant is crossing the James for Petersburg, but no real confirmation yet. Frassanito, *Grant and Lee*, 211, 213.

92, 93. June 16–17, 1864: General Lee again depletes his force by sending Pickett's division to reinforce Drewry's Bluff, leaving Lee with only 24,000 men north of the James. Beauregard defends Petersburg against increasing Federal assaults, but still no confirmation that entire Federal army is crossing the James toward Petersburg. Not until June 17 can General Beauregard assure Lee that the Federals are marching in force to Petersburg. General Lee finally on the Petersburg line by late June 17. Federal siege of Petersburg has begun. Dowdey, *Lee*, 478–79, 481. Frassanito, *Grant and Lee*, 207, 213–14. Freeman, *Lee's Lieutenants*, 3:531, 533. Freeman, *R. E. Lee*, 3:410–20.

CHAPTER ELEVEN

94. June 17–18, 1864, Petersburg front: General Beauregard's defense of Petersburg crumbling; Lee dispatches Joe Kershaw's division and Lieutenant General Hill's Third Corps to Petersburg; Lieutenant General Grant moves supply base to City Point, closer to Petersburg in preparation for a siege; General Beauregard wires Lee on June 18 from Petersburg, "Grant on the field with his whole army." Frassanito, *Grant and Lee*, 272. Freeman, *R. E. Lee*, 3:420–21, 423–24.

95. June 18, 1864, Petersburg: Fourth, heavy Federal assault on Petersburg defensive line; by evening, only 50,000 Confederates face 113,000 Federals; General Lee on the field beside General Beauregard; 8,000 Federal casualties in last three days near Petersburg; 65,000 Federal casualties since May 4, 1864. Anderson and Anderson, *The Generals*, 409. Dowdey, *Lee*, 482–85. Frassanito, *Grant and Lee*, 214–15. Freeman, *Lee's Lieutenants*, 3:537. Freeman, *R. E. Lee*, 3:425, 444. Robertson, *General A. P. Hill*, 283.

96. June 19, 1864. Sudden quiet along Petersburg front allows General Lee to go to church; Confederate line of defense twenty-six miles long. Freeman, *R. E. Lee*, 3:448.

96. "Never forget me . . ." General Lee letter to Mrs. Lee, June 19, 1864. Dowdey and Manarin, *The Wartime Papers*, 793.

96, 97. June 21–22, 1864, Petersburg: the "Bermuda Hundred" Federal position with new pontoon bridge across the James; Confederate General Mahone captures 1,600 Federals; President Lincoln visits Lieutenant General Grant at City Point, eight miles from Petersburg; Federal assault against Weldon Railroad; Grant's lines lengthen opposite Petersburg. Frassanito, *Grant and Lee*, 215, 257, 303. Freeman, *R. E. Lee*, 3:453.

97. June 24, 1864: Federals deploy mortars along their line opposite General Lee. Ibid., 3:463.

97. Typhoid fever strikes Mrs. Lee and daughter Mary Custis in late June, 1864. Coulling, *The Lee Girls*, 138. Dowdey and Manarin, *The Wartime Papers*, 810 (General Lee letter to daughter Mildred, June 28, 1864, noting Mother Lee's illness). MacDonald, *Mrs. Robert E. Lee*, 178.

97. "I am glad to hear . . . Do not delay . . ." General Lee letter to Mrs. Lee, June 24, 1864. Dowdey and Manarin, *The Wartime Papers*, 804.

97. Lieutenant General A. P. Hill's amazing endurance as his strength wanes along the Petersburg front. Dowdey, *Lee*, 495.

97, 98. June 25, 1864, Lexington, VA: Confederate Second Corps parades past sacred grave of Lieutenant General Jackson. Bean, *Stonewall's Man*, 205.

98. "It is perfectly stifling . . . end to military operations." General Lee letter to Mrs. Lee, June 26, 1864. Dowdey and Manarin, *The Wartime Papers*, 808.

98. "The sooner she leaves Richmond . . ." General Lee letter to daughter Mildred, June 28, 1864. Ibid., 810.

98. "Do you recollect . . . kind to us." General Lee letter to Mrs. Lee, June 30, 1864. Ibid., 812. Freeman, *R. E. Lee*, 3:457. Horn, *The Man Who Would Not Be Washington*, 212. Lee Jr., *Recollections and Letters*, 133. MacDonald, *Mrs. Robert E. Lee*, 178. Pryor, *Reading the Man*, 89.

99. "You are the country to these men . . ." General Henry Wise, lawyer, and former Virginia governor in April, 1865. Connelly, *The Marble Man*, 16. Pryor, *Reading the Man*, 421, noting no definitive record of this statement by General Wise.

CHAPTER TWELVE

100. July 1, 1864, Petersburg: Confederates hear digging beneath their trenches. Freeman, *R. E. Lee*, 3:465.

101. July 9, 1864: Grant is building permanent siege works; July 19 marks first rain in six weeks. Frassanito, *Grant and Lee*, 258. Freeman, *R. E. Lee*, 3:459. Robertson, *General A. P. Hill*, 289.

101. "Where are we to get sufficient troops . . ." General Lee letter to son Custis, July 24, 1864. Dowdey and Manarin, *The Wartime Papers*, 825. Thomas, *Robert E. Lee*, 343.

101. July 27–30, 1864: Grant feints raid on Richmond; Confederates on high alert. Freeman, *R. E. Lee*, 3:465–67.

101, 102. July 30, 1864, Petersburg: The Battle of the Crater; eight hours of slaughter; 29th US Colored Infantry regiment decimated; four thousand Federal casualties. Dowdey, *Lee*, 497. Freeman, *Lee's Lieutenants*, 3:542–43. Freeman, *R. E. Lee*, 3:467–77 (Note 68). Glatthaar, *Forged in Battle*, 150. Thomas, *Robert E. Lee*, 341.

102. "[a] stupendous failure." Grant, *Memoirs and Selected Letters*, 613.

102. Mrs. Lee leaves Richmond for Bremo Plantation in July to recover from typhoid, returning to Richmond in October. Coulling, *The Lee Girls*, 139–40.

103. "How came you to be walking . . . my hopes in a certain quarter . . ." General Lee letter to Mrs. Lee, July 31, 1864. Dowdey and Manarin, *The Wartime Papers*, 828.

103. August 4–6, 1864: General Grant sends a detachment toward the Valley; Generals Lee and Dick Anderson attend war council in Richmond; General Anderson to pursue Grant in the Valley. Freeman, *R. E. Lee*, 3:479.

103. August 9, 1864, City Point: Confederates destroy Federal ammunition dump, killing forty-three Federals. Frassanito, *Grant and Lee*, 271.

103. "The soap ration for this army . . ." General Lee letter to Jefferson Davis, August 9, 1864. Dowdey and Manarin, *The Wartime Papers*, 830.

103. General Lee appoints General Wade Hampton to succeed Jeb Stuart. Freeman, *R. E. Lee*, 3:493.

104. "We must suffer patiently . . ." General Lee letter to Mrs. Lee, August 14, 1864. Dowdey and Manarin, *The Wartime Papers*, 837. Lee Jr., *Recollections and Letters*, 137.

104. August 14, 1864: Federal attack along the James River beaten back; Rooney Lee's cavalry division deployed. Freeman, *R. E. Lee*, 3:480–82.

104. August 15, 1864: Rob Lee Jr., wounded. Ibid., 3:492. Lee Jr., *Recollections and Letters*, 137.

104. August 16, 1864: Federal assault against Rooney Lee's cavalry. Freeman, *R. E. Lee*, 3:483–84.

104. August 19, 1864: Federals assault Petersburg line, capturing vital railroad. Ibid., 3:485–87.

105. "It behooves us to do everything . . ." General Lee letter to Jefferson Davis, August 22, 1864. Dowdey and Manarin, *The Wartime Papers*, 842–43.

105. "Unless some measures can be devised . . ." General Lee letter to Jefferson Davis, August 23, 1864. Ibid., 843–44.

105. Federal desertions to the Confederates at Petersburg, August, 1864. Dowdey, *Lee*, 497.

105. August 25, 1864: General Lee assault at Reams Station to recapture the Weldon Railroad line. Freeman, *R. E. Lee*, 3:488–90.

105. Lieutenant General A. P. Hill struggles with disease and exhaustion, late August, 1864. Robertson, *General A. P. Hill*, 299.

106. "His attempt is now to starve us out." General Lee letter to Mrs. Lee, August 28, 1864. Dowdey and Manarin, *The Wartime Papers*, 847.

106. September 2, 1864: Atlanta falls to the Federals; "I beg leave to call to your attention . . . [N]o man capable of bearing arms . . ." General Lee letter to Jefferson Davis, September 2, 1864. Ibid., 847–48. J. William Jones, *Life and Letters*, 338–39.

106. September, 1864, Petersburg: Sickly Lieutenant General A. P. Hill; Dolly Hill and two daughters visit Petersburg front; Dolly leaves pregnant. Robertson, *General A. P. Hill*, 303, 309.

106, 107. September 14, 1864, City Point: General Wade Hampton rustles 2,486 head of Federal cattle to feed the starving Confederate lines at Petersburg. Freeman, *R. E. Lee*, 3:493.

107. "There is immediate necessity for the services of five thousand Negroes . . ." General Lee letter to CSA Secretary of War Seddon, September 17, 1864. Dowdey and Manarin, *The Wartime Papers*, 853.

107. "Shall want for the army . . ." General Lee letter to Mrs. Lee, September 18, 1864. Ibid., 855.

107. September 19, 1864, the Shenandoah Valley ("the Valley of Virginia"): General Lee's Second Corps engages Federal Phil Sheridan's cavalry; Third Battle of Winchester; death of Major General Rodes, CSA; Fitzhugh Lee wounded. Freeman, *Lee's Lieutenants*, 3:578–81. Freeman, *R. E. Lee*, 3:494.

107. September 22, 1864, the Shenandoah Valley: Battle of Fisher's Hill; Stonewall Jackson's Second Corps almost destroyed by Federal Phil Sheridan. Dowdey, *Lee*, 504. Freeman, *R. E. Lee*, 3:495.

108. September 22–23, 1864, Fisher's Hill: Lieutenant Colonel Alexander Swift "Sandie" Pendleton, CSA, fatally wounded; Sandie Pendleton treated by Federal surgeons; death of Sandie Pendleton; "To the war shall my powers be devoted . . ." Bean, *Stonewall's Man*, 143, 210–11. Freeman, *Lee's Lieutenants*, 3:584.

108. "I know the men of my old corps . . ." Lieutenant General Richard "Old Bald Head" Ewell. Bean, *Stonewall's Man*, 219.

108, 109. September 29–30, 1864, Petersburg front: Federal XVIII Corps crosses the James River; Fort Harrison falls to Federals; army cheers General Lee, but two Confederate assaults fail to retake Fort Harrison; Federal and Confederate trenches only one mile apart. Dowdey, *Lee*, 505. Frassanito, *Grant and Lee*, 312. Freeman, *Lee's Lieutenants*, 3:590–91. Freeman, *R. E. Lee*, 3:501–04.

CHAPTER THIRTEEN

110. Fall, 1864, Petersburg: Fifty thousand Confederates in trenches; General Lee had lost four generals between July 30 and October 1. Freeman, *Lee's Lieutenants*, 3:594. Freeman, *R. E. Lee*, 3:497.

110. "The men at home . . . bringing out all our arms-bearing men." General Lee letter to President Davis, undated, October, 1864. Ibid., 3:506–07. Not noted in *Wartime Papers*.

110, 111. October 7, 1864: Failed attempt by General Lee to retake Fort Harrison; death of General Gregg. Ibid., 3:507–09.

111. October 19, 1864: Lieutenant General Longstreet returns to First Corps; General Anderson given command of new Fourth Corps. Dowdey, *Lee*, 511. Freeman, *R. E. Lee*, 3:510–11. Thomas, *Robert E. Lee*, 346.

111, 112. October 19, 1864: General Early's Second Corps nearly destroyed at Cedar Creek in the Valley; Federal surgeons cannot save mortally wounded Confederate General Stephen Ramseur. Dowdey, *Lee*, 511. Freeman, *Lee's Lieutenants*, 3:599–610. Freeman, *R. E. Lee*, 3:512.

112. October 24, 1864, Lexington, Virginia: Burial of Sandie Pendleton. Bean, *Stonewall's Man*, 207, 215–17.

112, 113. October 27, 1864, Petersburg: Massive, two-pronged assault by General Grant; heavy fighting along James River, at Burgess Mill, and along Southside Railroad; Confederate cavalry commander, General Hampton, has one son killed and another wounded; General Lee condolence letter to General Hampton, October 29, 1864, "I grieve with you . . ." Dowdey, *Lee*, 512–13. Freeman, *Lee's Lieutenants*, 3:615–16. Freeman, *R. E. Lee*, 3:513-514 (Note 136, General Lee's letter). Lee's condolence letter to Wade Hampton is not in *The Wartime Papers*.

113. Confederate humor in the Petersburg trenches: "rat holes" and "Lee's Miserables." Freeman, *Lee's Lieutenants*, 3:619. Freeman, *R. E. Lee*, 3:515–16.

113. "Grant will get every man . . . a great calamity . . ." General Lee letter to Jefferson Davis, November 2, 1864. Dowdey and Manarin, *The Wartime Papers*, 868.

113. November 4, 1864, Lexington, Virginia: Kate Corbin Pendleton gives birth to Sandie's son. Bean, *Stonewall's Man*, 224, 229.

113. "Never neglect the means . . ." General Lee letter to daughter Mildred, November 6, 1864. Lee Jr., *Recollections and Letters*, 139.

114. November 25, 1864, Petersburg: General Lee moves headquarters. Freeman, *R. E. Lee*, 3:525.

114. November 30–December 5, 1864, Petersburg: General Lee's force increases to 61,000 and General Grant adds VI Corps to his strength. Ibid., 3:518, 520.

114. "I am afraid you will ruin my character . . ." General Lee's cheery letter to son Custis, December 13, 1864. Dowdey and Manarin, *The Wartime Papers*, 876.

114. December 14, 1864, Petersburg: General Lee recalls Grimes's division; Grimes's and Judge Evans's divisions to Second Corps under the new command of General Gordon. Dowdey, *Lee*, 516. Freeman, *R. E. Lee*, 3:522.

115. December 19–22, 1864: Nashville and Savannah fall to Federals; Confederate Navy shares salt pork ration with Petersburg troops. Ibid., 3:522–23, 535.

115. Christmas, 1864, Petersburg: Confederate, starvation food ration. Freeman, *Lee's Lieutenants*, 3:620–21.

115. New Year's Day, 1865, Petersburg: 51,776 effective Confederates face 134,278 Federals. Ibid., 3:618.

115. January, 1865, Petersburg: Confederate defensive position thirty-five miles long. Freeman, *R. E. Lee*, 3:533.

115. "We have but two days' supplies . . ." General Lee letter to War Secretary Seddon, January 11, 1865. Dowdey and Manarin, *The Wartime Papers*, 881.

115. January 15, 1865: Fall of Wilmington, North Carolina. Dowdey, *Lee*, 519. Freeman, *R. E. Lee*, 3:533.

115. "Considering the relation of master and slave . . . greater calamity to both." General Lee letter to Andrew Hunter, January 11, 1865. Horn, *The Man Who Would Not Be Washington*, 217. Nolan, *Lee Considered*, 21. Thomas, *Robert E. Lee*, 347.

116. "In this enlightened age . . ." General Lee letter to Mrs. Lee, December 27, 1856. Dowdey, *Lee*, 108. J. William Jones, *Life and Letters*, 82. Fitzhugh Lee, *General Lee*, 69.

116. "If I had the ability . . ." General Lee letter to Jefferson Davis, January 19, 1865. Dowdey and Manarin, *The Wartime Papers*, 884–85.

116. January 19, 1865, Petersburg: Major General Wade Hampton, CSA, detached to South Carolina. Freeman, *Lee's Lieutenants*, 3:639.

116. "There is suffering for want of food . . ." General Lee letter to War Secretary Seddon, January 27, 1865. Dowdey and Manarin, *The Wartime Papers*, 886.

116. February 5–8, 1865, Petersburg: Three-day skirmish at Hatcher's Run. Freeman, *R. E. Lee*, 3:535–36.

116, 117. Dog "Sallie" of the 11th Pennsylvania Infantry, killed at Hatcher's Run. *Civil War Times Illustrated, Gettysburg!*. Harrisburg, PA: Historic Times, Inc., 1985.

Page "i" inside front cover frontispiece. Internet images of the 11th Pennsylvania Infantry monument now standing at Gettysburg say it all, without a single word. And, actually standing at that monument says even more, if one has been blessed by the devotion of a dog. (Literary critics and professors of English prose properly brand the foregoing sentence as an unforgivable "author intrusion." They must be forgiven, because probably they have not shared their beds with a dog nor had their faces licked by a purebred wolf.)

117. January 19–February 6, 1865, Hatcher's Run: Marriage and death of Confederate Brigadier General John Pegram, 32. Freeman, *Lee's Lieutenants*, 3:629. Thomas, *Robert E. Lee*, 348.

CHAPTER FOURTEEN

118. February 6, 1865, Richmond: Confederate Secretary of War, James Seddon, described as a "galvanized corpse . . ." John B. Jones, *A Rebel War Clerk's Diary*, 1:380 (journal entry of July 16, 1863).

118. John Breckinridge succeeds James Seddon as Confederate secretary of war. Burke Davis, *The Long Surrender*, 70. Freeman, *R. E. Lee*, 4:11. General Breckinridge's relationship to Mrs. Lincoln. Justin G. Turner and Linda Levitt Turner, *Mary Todd Lincoln: Her Life and Letters*. New York: Alfred Knopf (1972), 82 (Note 8).

118. February 6, 1865: General Robert E. Lee becomes Confederate general-in-chief. Dowdey, *Lee*, 519–20. Freeman, *Lee's Lieutenants*, 3:634–35. Freeman, *R. E. Lee*, 3:534.

118. "Some of the men have been without meat . . . calamity befalls us." General Lee letter to retiring War Secretary Seddon, February 8, 1865. Dowdey and Manarin, *The Wartime Papers*, 890.

118. February 10, 1865: President Jefferson Davis proposes arming slaves to defend the South. Ballard, *A Long Shadow: Jefferson Davis*, 13.

119. "I fear it may be necessary . . ." General Lee letter to War Secretary Breckinridge, February 19, 1865. Dowdey and Manarin, *The Wartime Papers*, 905. Freeman, *R. E. Lee*, 4:4. John B. Jones, *A Rebel War Clerk's Diary*, 355. Dowdey and Manarin's transcript of this memorandum contains the word "all" in "all our cities." But Dr. Freeman omits the more urgent "all" in his transcript.

119. February 20, 1865, Richmond: The Confederate House of Representatives passes the Davis proposal to arm slaves. Ballard, *A Long Shadow: Jefferson Davis*, 13.

119. February 20, 1865, Petersburg: "They are trying to corner this old army . . . to die game," Lieutenant Colonel Walter Taylor. Anderson and Anderson, *The Generals*, 421. Freeman, *Lee's Lieutenants*, 3:644. Freeman, *R. E. Lee*, 4:4 (Note 12).

119. "Should it be necessary to abandon . . . fearful condition." General Lee letter to Mrs. Lee, February 21, 1865. Dowdey and Manarin, *The Wartime Papers*, 907.

119, 120. February 24, 1865, Petersburg: Four hundred desertions in twelve days from Army of Northern Virginia; "It seems that the men are influenced . . . to take care of themselves." General Lee letter to War Secretary Breckinridge. Ibid., 910.

120. February 26–28, 1865: General Lee goes to Richmond for war council; Confederate force in Petersburg trenches of 50,000 men faces 160,000 Federals; Freeman, *R. E. Lee*, 4:6 (Note 25).

120. March 2, 1865: Shenandoah Valley, the Army of Northern Virginia's Second Corps destroyed. Dowdey, *Lee*, 524–25. Freeman, *Lee's Lieutenants*, 3:635–36. Freeman, *R. E. Lee*, 4:7.

120, 121. March 4, 1865: General Lee holds midnight conference with General John Gordon; 65,000 surviving Confederates on all fronts face 280,000 Federals; on Petersburg front, only 35,000 effective Confederates hold off General Grant's force of 150,000 Federals; General Lee leaves for Richmond. Dowdey, *Lee*, 525–26. Freeman, *R. E. Lee*, 4:7-8.

121. March 4–5, 1865: General Lee in Richmond for war council with Jefferson Davis; General Lee worships at St. Paul's Episcopal Church, visits Mrs. Lee and his daughters. Dowdey, *Lee*, 527. Freeman, *R. E. Lee*, 4:9–10.

121. "I have been up to see the Congress . . . my army is starving." General Lee letter to son Custis, undated, March, 1865. Freeman, *R. E. Lee*, 3:538. Pryor, *Reading the Man*, 393. Thomas, *Robert E. Lee*, 348. Not transcribed in *Wartime Papers*.

121. March 8, 1865: Confederate Senate passes measure to arm slaves in defense of South. Ballard, *A Long Shadow: Jefferson Davis*, 13.

121. "Unless the men and animals can be subsisted . . . " General Lee letter to War Secretary Breckinridge, March 9, 1865. Dowdey and Manarin, *The Wartime Papers*, 913. Freeman, *R. E. Lee*, 3:536–37.

121. "Those owners who are willing to furnish . . ." General Lee letter to Jefferson Davis, March 10, 1865 (punctuation changed). Dowdey and Manarin, *The Wartime Papers*, 914.

121. March 13, 1865, Richmond: President Jefferson Davis signs into law the Confederate statute that authorizes the arming of slaves. Freeman, *R. E. Lee*, 3:544. General Lee objects to omission of provision granting emancipation to slaves who serve in the Confederate military. Thomas, *Robert E. Lee*, 349.

122. March 11–23, 1865, Petersburg: General Lee ponders and accepts a last desperate Confederate attack against Lieutenant General Grant's siege. Freeman, *R. E. Lee*, 4:11–13.

122. March 19, 1865: General Sheridan's Federal cavalry adds 13,000 men to Grant's siege of Petersburg front. Freeman, *Lee's Lieutenants*, 3:656.

122. February–March, 1865: General Lee loses nearly 10 percent of his army to desertion. Ibid., 3:624, 628. Freeman, *R. E. Lee*, 3:541.

122. March 20, 1865, Petersburg: Exhausted and ill Lieutenant General A. P. Hill. Freeman, *Lee's Lieutenants*, 3:677. Robertson, *General A. P. Hill*, 310–13.

122, 123. March 22, 1865, Petersburg: General Lee plans breakout thrust to join General Joe Johnston's force in the Carolinas. Freeman, *R. E. Lee*, 4:5–6.

123. Generals Lee and John Gordon plan breakout assault for March 25, with General Gordon given command of Second Corps remnant. Freeman, *Lee's Lieutenants*, 3:645–46. Freeman, *R. E. Lee*, 4:12, 14, 16.

123, 124. March 25, 1865, Petersburg: Breakout assault against Federals fails; General Lee loses 5,000 men. Dowdey, *Lee*, 530–32. Freeman, *Lee's Lieutenants*, 3:647–51. Freeman, *R. E. Lee*, 4:17–19.

124. March 27, 1865, Petersburg: General Lee has only 36,000 effectives on Petersburg-Richmond front. Freeman, *Lee's Lieutenants*, 3:652. Freeman, *R. E. Lee*, 4:20–21.

124. March 27, 1865, Petersburg: General Orders Number 8—deserters to be executed. Dowdey and Manarin, *The Wartime Papers*, 918.

124, 125. March 27, 1865: General Lee holds twenty-seven-mile-long position with 1,140 men per mile; First, Second, and Fourth Confederate corps are shorthanded and hungry. Freeman, *R. E. Lee*, 4:23–25.

125. March 28, 1865, Richmond: Davis family prepares to evacuate; Confederate State Department ships archives to North Carolina. Ballard, *A Long Shadow: Jefferson Davis*, 42. Burke Davis, *The Long Surrender*, 15, 29.

125. "To no one, General, . . ." General Lee letter to General-in-Chief Winfield Scott, April 20, 1861. Dowdey and Manarin, *The Wartime Papers*, 8. "He appears the bold . . ." General Lee letter to Mrs. Lee, March 28, 1865. Ibid., 918–19. Freeman, *Lee's Lieutenants*, 3:527.

125, 126. March 29, 1865: Three Confederate cavalry divisions engage Federal infantry and cavalry assault west of Petersburg. Freeman, *Lee's Lieutenants*, 3:657. Freeman, *R. E. Lee*, 4:28–29.

126. March 29, 1865, Richmond: The wife and children of Jefferson Davis evacuate Richmond. Anderson and Anderson, *The Generals*, 426. Ballard, *A Long Shadow: Jefferson Davis*, 25. Burke Davis, *The Long Surrender*, 14.

126. March 30, 1865: General Lee's breakout shift of forces southeast toward Five Forks. Freeman, *R. E. Lee*, 4:30–32.

126, 127. March 31, 1865, Five Forks: 10,600 Confederates face 53,700 Federals; by shifting troops westward, only 27,000 Confederates now hold Petersburg line; General Lee attacks Federal V Corps with half a Confederate division along Hatcher's Run; Yankees crumble until reinforcements arrive. Dowdey, *Lee*, 533–35. Freeman, *Lee's Lieutenants*, 3:660. Freeman, *R. E. Lee*, 4:33–35.

CHAPTER FIFTEEN

128. April 1, 1865, Petersburg: General Lee plans Petersburg evacuation. "This, in my opinion . . ." General Lee memo to Jefferson Davis. Dowdey and Manarin, *The Wartime Papers*, 922. Freeman, *R. E. Lee*, 4:36.

128. April 1, 1865, Petersburg: Divisions of Generals Heth and Wilcox and survivors of Second Corps hold Confederate Petersburg line; divisions of Field and Kershaw hold the north bank of the James River. Freeman, *Lee's Lieutenants*, 3:675.

128. "Hold Five Forks at all hazards . . ." General Lee letter or cable to Major General Pickett, April 1, 1865. Freeman, *R. E. Lee*, 4:36.

128, 129. April 1, 1865, Hatcher's Run: Lieutenant General A. P. Hill returns from sick leave to lead Third Corps. Ibid., 4:37.

129. Major General George Pickett gets nomination to West Point only through the efforts of his uncle Andrew Johnston and Illinois lawyer, Abraham Lincoln. Dowdey, *Death of a Nation*, 266. During the mid-1840s, Johnston and Lincoln traded poetry. *The Collected Works of Abraham Lincoln*. 9 vols. Edited by Roy P. Basler. New Brunswick, NJ: Rutgers University Press, 1953, 1:366, 377.

129. April 1, 1865: Confederate Generals Pickett and Fitz Lee ride to join General Tom Rosser for "shad bake" on Nottoway River near Five Forks; General Sher-

idan's 30,000 Federals assault 6,000 Confederates at Five Forks; Pickett's division destroyed; Colonel Willie Pegram dies of wounds. Dowdey, *Lee*, 536–38. Freeman, *Lee's Lieutenants*, 3:665–74. Freeman, *R. E. Lee*, 4:39.

130. April 1, 1865, evening: Confederate line at Petersburg manned by 16,000 men along twenty-mile front as General Lee shifts forces westward after Five Forks disaster. Ibid., 4:41, 43.

130. April 1, 1865, Petersburg: Lieutenant General A. P. Hill weakening after sixteen hours in the saddle. Robertson, *General A. P. Hill*, 313.

130, 131. April 2, 1865, Petersburg: All-night Federal cannonade; Federals assault west end of Confederate line; Lieutenant General A. P. Hill killed in action. Dowdey, *Lee*, 539–42. Freeman, *Lee's Lieutenants*, 3:677–79. Freeman, *R. E. Lee*, 4:44–45, 47 (Note 20). Robertson, *General A. P. Hill*, 314–15, 318–19.

131, 132. April 2, 1865, Petersburg: General Lee's line is collapsing; General Grant's forces block Confederate retreat westward. "I see no prospect of doing more …". General Lee letter or cable to War Secretary Breckinridge, 10:30 a.m., April 2, 1865. Ballard, *A Long Shadow: Jefferson Davis*, 35. Burke Davis, *The Long Surrender*, 19. Dowdey, *Lee*, 544. Dowdey and Manarin, *The Wartime Papers*, 924–25. Freeman, *R. E. Lee*, 4:48–49.

132. "I think absolutely necessary that we should abandon …" General Lee letter or cable to Jefferson Davis, 11:00 a.m., April 2, 1865; Confederate defensive positions along Petersburg front collapsing. Ballard, *A Long Shadow: Jefferson Davis*, 36. Burke Davis, *The Long Surrender*, 22. Dowdey and Manarin, *The Wartime Papers*, 925–26.

132. April 2, 1865, Petersburg: General Lee resolves to march his shrinking force toward Amelia Courthouse. Freeman, *Lee's Lieutenants*, 3:680–81.

132. April 2, 1865, Richmond: Confederate government plans evening evacuation. Ballard, *A Long Shadow: Jefferson Davis*, 41. Burke Davis, *The Long Surrender*, 24.

132, 133. April 2, 1865, 1:00 p.m.: Federal artillery aimed directly at General Lee. Freeman, *R. E. Lee*, 4:50–51.

133. April 2, 1865, Petersburg: Six hundred Confederate infantry hold off three Federal divisions at Fort Gregg to give General Lee time to plan full retreat from Petersburg. Freeman, *Lee's Lieutenants*, 3:682. Freeman, *R. E. Lee*, 4:51–52.

133. April 2, 1865, Petersburg: General Lee consolidates his forces and plans evening retreat. First, Second, and Third Corps to move northward to cross Appomattox River; Fourth Corps will retreat on south side of river. Confederate retreat begins at 8:00 p.m. Freeman, *Lee's Lieutenants*, 3:683–84. Freeman, *R. E. Lee*, 4:53–54.

133. April 2, 1865, Petersburg: Lieutenant Colonel Walter Taylor enjoys twenty-four-hour leave to get married in Richmond. Ibid., 4:56. Taylor, *General Lee*, 276–77.

134. April 2, 1865, evening: Wife and children of Jefferson Davis arrive in Charlotte, North Carolina. Burke Davis, *The Long Surrender*, 28.

134. April 2, 1865, Petersburg: Nighttime evacuation of Petersburg line; only 29,000 Confederate survivors pursued by five Federal corps. Freeman, *R. E. Lee*, 4:58–59.

134. April 2, 1865, Richmond: Preparing to leave Richmond, President Davis sends his favorite chair to crippled Mrs. Lee. Anderson and Anderson, *The Generals*, 431. Burke Davis, *The Long Surrender*, 28.

134. April 2–3, 1865, Richmond: Jefferson Davis and his Cabinet board train; Lieutenant General Ewell's troops burn Richmond's cotton and tobacco warehouses and pour

barrels of whiskey into streets before evacuating Richmond with the capital's home guard troops to join General Lee's retreat; civilian mobs drink liquor from gutters; fires rampage, narrowly missing house of Mrs. Lee and three daughters. Anderson and Anderson, *The Generals*, 431. Ballard, *A Long Shadow: Jefferson Davis*, 46–48. Burke Davis, *The Long Surrender*, 31, 34–35, 40.

135. April 3, 1865: Retreating Army of Northern Virginia and pursuing Army of the Potomac suffered 10,000 casualties in last four days; General Lee races General Grant to Amelia Courthouse; Federals have shorter route to both Amelia and Lee's rendezvous point with Joe Johnston; as General Ewell's force evacuates Richmond, Federal troops enter the capital city. Dowdey, *Lee*, 550–51. Frassanito, *Grant and Lee*, 334, 388. Freeman, *R. E. Lee*, 4:59, 123.

135. April 3 or 4, 1865, Richmond: Lee daughter Agnes visits Yankee Major General Godfrey Weitzel in command of Federal occupation forces; Agnes fears for Mrs. Lee amid fires and mobs; General Weitzel graciously dispatches honor guard to Lee home and stations ambulance outside. Coulling, *The Lee Girls*, 147. Burke Davis, *The Long Surrender*, 40–41.

CHAPTER SIXTEEN

136. April 3, 1865: Confederate First and Second Corps march toward Bevill's Bridge; diversion at Goode's Bridge. Freeman, *R. E. Lee*, 4:63–64.

136. April 3, 1865: Jefferson Davis and Cabinet reach Danville, Virginia. Ballard, *A Long Shadow: Jefferson Davis*, 53, 55. Burke Davis, *The Long Surrender*, 52.

137. "I must therefore appeal to your generosity . . ." General Lee begs for food and forage at Amelia Courthouse, April 4, 1865. General Lee's plea for food to Richmond from Jetersville, Virginia, probably not telegraphed. Dowdey, *Lee*, 548–49. Freeman, *Lee's Lieutenants*, 3:690 (Note 66). Freeman, *R. E. Lee*, 4:66–67 (Note 35).

137. April 4–5, 1865: Jefferson Davis and his Cabinet convene at Danville, Virginia; Davis proclamation, "Let us but will it . . ."; proclamation composed by CSA Secretary of State Judah Benjamin. Ballard, *A Long Shadow: Jefferson Davis*, 56–57. Burke Davis, *The Long Surrender*, 53–54. Evans, *Judah P. Benjamin*, 299.

137, 138. April 4, 1864, Richmond: Abraham Lincoln visits captured Richmond. Burke Davis, *The Long Surrender*, 55. Frassanito, *Grant and Lee*, 289.

138. April 5, 1865: General Lee's troops starving at Amelia Courthouse; Army of Northern Virginia finds only artillery ammunition instead of food. Freeman, *Lee's Lieutenants*, 3:691. Freeman, *R. E. Lee*, 4:72.

138. April 5, 1865: General Ewell's troops arrive at Amelia Courthouse; Confederate retreat from Petersburg bound for Jetersville. Dowdey, *Lee*, 551. Freeman, *Lee's Lieutenants*, 3:691–92.

139. April 5, 1865: Rooney Lee's cavalry troop engages three corps of Federals between Amelia Courthouse and Jetersville; General Lee changes retreat destination to Lynchburg; Federal General Phil Sheridan's cavalry captures 20,000 Confederate rations. Dowdey, *Lee*, 553. Freeman, *Lee's Lieutenants*, 3:693–94. Freeman, *R. E. Lee*, 4:72–76.

139. April 5–6, 1864, sixty miles west of Petersburg: Forced march by Confederates, concentrating on both sides of Appomattox River near Farmville; heavy loss of stragglers;

starving Confederates eat captured farm animals raw. Dowdey, *Lee*, 554–55. Freeman, *Lee's Lieutenants*, 3:696. Freeman, *R. E. Lee*, 4:77–81.

140. April 6, 1865, Rice Station: Disastrous separation of retreating Confederates when General Ewell takes unexpected detour that General Anderson follows, creating two gaps in Confederate line unknown to General Lee. Federals assault two divided units of Lee's army. By evening, Fourth Corps and Ewell's Richmond home guard with supply wagons destroyed, with loss of nearly eight thousand Confederates in an afternoon. Dowdey, *Lee*, 556–58. Freeman, *Lee's Lieutenants*, 3:700–11. Freeman, *R. E. Lee*, 4:82, 88–93.

141. "My God! Has this army dissolved?" General Lee to General Mahone, April 6, as Army of Northern Virginia troops flee double Federal assault. Ibid., 4:84. Thomas, *Robert E. Lee*, 359.

142. April 6, 1865, Sayler's Creek: General Mahone rallies fleeing Confederates and General Lee holds up the red battle flag of the disintegrating Army of Northern Virginia; dirty-faced survivor cries, "Where's the man who won't follow Uncle Robert!" New Confederate line holds. Dowdey, *Lee*, 560. Freeman, *R. E. Lee*, 4:83–86.

142, 143, 144. April 6–7, 1865: Confederate effectives down to 15,000 to face 80,000 Federals. First and Second Corps detached toward Farmville; Confederates find rations after five days without food; War Secretary Breckinridge confers with General Lee; Second Corps detached to burn bridge across the Appomattox to slow pursuing Federals; Federals put out fire and cross the river; engagement at Cumberland Church; most Confederates had been marching for eighteen hours, some having gone without sleep for forty hours. Confederate remnant nearly surrounded. Ballard, *A Long Shadow: Jefferson Davis*, 63. Dowdey, *Lee*, 561–67. Freeman, *Lee's Lieutenants*, 3:712, 715–16. Freeman, *R. E. Lee*, 4:87, 93–103.

Chapter Seventeen

145. April 7, 1865, Cumberland Church, Virginia, 9:30 p.m.: Robert E. Lee receives first note from Ulysses S. Grant delivered by Federal General Williams; Lieutenant General Longstreet: "Not yet." Dowdey, *Lee*, 567. Freeman, *Lee's Lieutenants*, 3:719. Freeman, *R. E. Lee*, 4:103–04. Thomas, *Robert E. Lee*, 359.

145. "I have read your note . . ." General Lee written reply to General Grant, April 7, 1865. Dowdey, *Lee*, 567–68. Dowdey and Manarin, *The Wartime Papers*, 931–32. Freeman, *R. E. Lee*, 4:105–06.

146. April 7–8, 1865: All-night march by Confederates racing Federals to Appomattox Station where General Lee hopes to find food sent from Lynchburg. Dowdey, *Lee*, 568. Freeman, *R. E. Lee*, 4:106–08.

147. April 8, 1865: Five Federal corps of infantry and Phil Sheridan's cavalry close in on Confederates; General Pendleton recommends surrender; General Lee determined to join General Johnston in North Carolina. Ibid., 4:109.

147. April 8, 1865: General Lee relieves Generals Pickett, Anderson, and Johnson of command; George Pickett: "That old man . . ." Dowdey, *Lee*, 564. Freeman, *Lee's Lieutenants*, 3:721. Freeman, *R. E. Lee*, 4:111–12. Piston, *Lee's Tarnished Lieutenant*, 62.

147. April 8, 1865, afternoon and evening: General Lee's survivors converge at Appomattox Courthouse; Federal campfires confirm Federals have blocked further retreat. Dowdey, *Lee*, 569. Freeman, *Lee's Lieutenants*, 3:723. Freeman, *R. E. Lee*, 4:113–14.

147, 148. April 8, 1865, Danville, Virginia: Lieutenant Wise advises Jefferson Davis that General Lee's destruction imminent. Ballard, *A Long Shadow: Jefferson Davis*, 64. Burke Davis, *The Long Surrender*, 57.

148. "Peace being my great desire . . ." Lieutenant General Grant's second note to General Lee, April 8, 1865. Dowdey, *Lee*, 570. Freeman, *R. E. Lee*, 4:112.

148. "To be frank . . ." General Lee written reply to General Grant, April 8, 1865. Dowdey, *Lee*, 570. Dowdey and Manarin, *The Wartime Papers*, 932. Freeman, *R. E. Lee*, 4:113.

148, 149. April 8, 1865, Appomattox Courthouse: Nighttime, Federal artillery barrage; General Lee's war council plans one final breakout offensive; Robert E. Lee gives General Fitzhugh Lee permission to be absent from any surrender; General Lee to General Gordon, "Tennessee." Dowdey, *Lee*, 571–72. Freeman, *Lee's Lieutenants*, 3:723–25. Freeman, *R. E. Lee*, 4:114–15, 118.

149, 150. April 8–9, 1865, midnight: Longstreet and First Corps deploy; General Lee dons elegant new uniform. Dowdey, *Lee*, 572. Freeman, *R. E. Lee*, 4:117–18.

150. April 9, 1865, dawn–8:30 a.m.: General Lee launches three-hour assault; attack confirms General Lee surrounded by Federal infantry; "How easily I could be rid of this . . ." General Lee to aide Charles Venable. Anderson and Anderson, *The Generals*, 445. Connelly, *The Marble Man*, 192. Dowdey, *Lee*, 573. Flood, *Lee: The Last Years*, 4. Freeman, *Lee's Lieutenants*, 3:728–29, 734. Freeman, *R. E. Lee*, 4:120–22. Thomas, *Robert E. Lee*, 362.

150, 151. April 9, 1865, Appomattox: General Robert E. Lee suspends his last assault; "There is nothing left for me . . ." General Lee to Lieutenant Colonel Venable. Anderson and Anderson, *The Generals*, 444. Dowdey, *Lee*, 573. Flood, *Lee: The Last Years*, 4. Freeman, *R. E. Lee*, 4:120–22.

Chapter Eighteen

152. April 8–9, 1865, Appomattox: General Grant's nighttime headache. Grant, *Memoirs and Selected Letters*, 730.

152. "That army has, by discipline alone . . ." General Hooker. McMurry, *Two Great Rebel Armies*, 104.

152, 153. April 9, 1865, Appomattox, mid-morning: Under a white flag, General Lee rides out to meet Lieutenant General Grant; Federal Lieutenant Colonel Whittier intercepts General Lee; General Grant's note declines meeting General Lee; General Lee drafts new note requesting interview to surrender. Ballard, *A Long Shadow: Jefferson Davis*, 62. Burke Davis, *The Long Surrender*, 59. Dowdey, *Lee*, 573–74. Dowdey and Manarin, *The Wartime Papers*, 932. Grant, *Memoirs and Selected Letters*, 727–31 (the series of written exchanges between Generals Grant and Lee, April 7–9). Freeman, *R. E. Lee*, 4:124–27.

153. General Lee sends a second copy of surrender note through the lines and another note requesting "a suspension of hostilities . . ." Dowdey and Manarin, *The Wartime Papers*, 933.

153. April 9, 1865, Appomattox, 11:00 a.m.: Courteous Federal officer asks General Lee to leave the open field when Federal assault imminent; Federal Major General Meade agrees to one-hour delay in attack; Federals and Confederates only one hundred yards apart in places; Federal Major General Sheridan agrees to temporary ceasefire; General

Lee retires to Lieutenant General Longstreet's position; temporary truce extended to 2:00 p.m. Dowdey, *Lee*, 575–76. Freeman, *R. E. Lee*, 4:127–29.

154, 155, 156. April 9, 1865, Appomattox: Federal Lieutenant Colonel Babcock delivers General Grant's written consent to meet with Robert E. Lee; General Lee, two aides, and Lieutenant Colonel Babcock arrive at McLean home close to 1:00 p.m.; Lieutenant General Grant arrives thirty minutes later; 3:30 p.m., McLean house scene of signing the document surrendering the Army of Northern Virginia; gracious gestures by Lieutenant General Grant. Dowdey, *Lee*, 576–81. Dowdey and Manarin, *The Wartime Papers*, 933–34. Flood, *Lee: The Last Years*, 10. Freeman, *R. E. Lee*, 4:130–42.

156. Robert E. Lee as a West Point cadet known as the "marble model." Freeman, *R. E. Lee*, 1:68. Miers, *Robert E. Lee*, 197.

156. "What General Lee's feelings were I do not know . . ." Grant, *Memoirs and Selected Letters*, 735.

156. General Grant and Federals doff hats in silent salute as Lee departs McLean house; General Lee's neck known to become red when he is under emotional stress. Connelly, *The Marble Man*, 189, 204. Dowdey, *Lee*, 442. Freeman, *R. E. Lee*, 2:488, 3:243, 4:143, 145. Flood, *Lee: The Last Years*, 10, 13. Miers, *Robert E. Lee*, 129. Taylor, *General Lee*, 156. Taylor, *Four Years*, 77. Thomas, *Robert E. Lee*, 366.

157. "the men . . . had fought so bravely . . ." Grant, *Memoirs and Selected Letters*, 689.

157. April 9, 1865, Appomattox: "Men, we have fought the war together . . ." General Lee greeted by his army's survivors; General Lee rides between cheering throng of his veterans. Dowdey, *Lee*, 581–82. Freeman, *R. E. Lee*, 4:144–47.

157. April 9, 1865: Army of Northern Virginia reduced to 7,892 effectives; another 20,000 infantry and cavalry trickle in before April 12. Dowdey, *Lee*, 585–86.

158. April 10, 1865, Appomattox: Generals Lee and Grant chat on horseback for half an hour. Grant remembers a "very pleasant conversation . . ." Grant, *Memoirs and Selected Letters*, 741–44. General Lee gives General Grant permission to allow his officers to visit old friends in the Army of Northern Virginia. Dowdey, *Lee*, 582–84. Flood, *Lee: The Last Years*, 21–22. Freeman, *R. E. Lee*, 4:148–51.

158. April 10, 1865, Appomattox: General Lee asks Lieutenant Colonel Charles Marshall to compose the first draft of his Farewell, which became General Orders Number 9. Katcher, *The Army of Robert E. Lee*, 56.

159. April 10, 1865, Appomattox: Federal Generals Seth Williams and George Gordon Meade share warm reunion with Robert E. Lee within Confederate lines. Flood, *Lee: The Last Years*, 23. Freeman, *R. E. Lee*, 4:152–53.

159. April 10, 1865, Danville, Virginia: Jefferson Davis advised of General Lee's surrender. Ballard, *A Long Shadow: Jefferson Davis*, 65. Burke Davis, *The Long Surrender*, 59.

159, 160. April 10, 1865, Appomattox, evening: Lieutenant Colonel Marshall presents to General Lee the first draft of Lee's Farewell Address to his army; no copies of General Orders Number 9 in General Lee's handwriting except for his signature. Farewell is read to each regiment of Southern survivors. Dowdey and Manarin, *The Wartime Papers*, 934–35. Flood, *Lee: The Last Years*, 23–24. Freeman, *R. E. Lee*, 4:154–55. That "Robert E. Lee" never in his life signed any letter or document except as "R. E. Lee": Pryor, *Reading the Man*, xi, 300.

160. April 10, 1865, Danville, Virginia: Jefferson Davis advised General Johnston to meet the fleeing government in Greensboro, North Carolina; Davis train heads south at midnight. Ballard, *A Long Shadow: Jefferson Davis*, 68. Burke Davis, *The Long Surrender*, 60–61.

160. "It is with pain . . ." General Lee letter or cable to Jefferson Davis, April 11, 1865. Dowdey and Manarin, *The Wartime Papers*, 935. Freeman, *R. E. Lee*, 4:156.

160, 161 April 11, 1985: Jefferson Davis and Cabinet arrive Greensboro, North Carolina; Mrs. Davis and children leave Charlotte, North Carolina; Greensboro cool toward fleeing CSA government. Ballard, *A Long Shadow: Jefferson Davis*, 74–77. Burke Davis, *The Long Surrender*, 62–64, 72.

161. April 12, 1865, Appomattox: The Army of Northern Virginia officially surrenders, stacking weapons and tattered battle flags before respectful Federal victors. Dowdey, *Lee*, 587. Freeman, *R. E. Lee*, 4:157.

161, 162. April 12, 1865, Greensboro, North Carolina: Tense meeting between Jefferson Davis and General Johnston; Johnston and Confederate Cabinet, with the exception of Judah Benjamin, recommend surrender. Ballard, *A Long Shadow: Jefferson Davis*, 78, 80. Burke Davis, *The Long Surrender*, 65–67.

162. April 12, 1865, Appomattox: General Lee leaves his army for the one-hundred-mile horseback ride home to Richmond; Federal honor guard. Freeman, *R. E. Lee*, 4:158.

162. General Lee suffered 121,000 casualties in thirty-four months of command. McWhiney and Jamieson, *Attack and Die*, 19.

CHAPTER NINETEEN

163. April 12–13, 1865: General Lee and Lieutenant General James Longstreet part forever on the road to Richmond on April 13. Anderson and Anderson, *The Generals*, 8. Freeman, *R. E. Lee*, 4:159, Note 35, suggesting that the primary historical sources are not unanimous that Lee and Longstreet met on the night of April 12 and parted forever the next day. Piston has their final farewell on the evening of April 12, *Lee's Tarnished Lieutenant*, 92, as does Wert, *General James Longstreet*, 404.

164. General Lee's heavy casualties among his generals and colonels. Freeman, *Lee's Lieutenants*, 3:743–44, 766.

164. General Lee's officer corps of professional soldiers with formal, military academy educations. McMurry, *Two Great Rebel Armies*, 99, 108.

165. April 13, 1865: General Lee bound for Richmond camps in Cumberland, Virginia; Traveller needs new horseshoes. Freeman, *R. E. Lee*, 4:160.

165. April 13, 1865, Greensboro, North Carolina: Jefferson Davis faces near unanimous consensus of his generals and Cabinet secretaries that a truce should be pursued; Davis proposes "peace" terms that Federals are not likely to accept; no mention of the future of slavery. Ballard, *A Long Shadow: Jefferson Davis*, 82–83. Burke Davis, *The Long Surrender*, 69-71.

165. Captain Robert E. Lee Jr. visits President Davis in North Carolina. Ballard, *A Long Shadow: Jefferson Davis*, 86. Burke Davis, *The Long Surrender*, 67.

166. April 14, 1865, Powhatan County, Virginia: General Robert E. Lee camps outside under canvas at his brother Carter's home. Flood, *Lee: The Last Years*, 35. Freeman, *R. E. Lee*, 4:160. Thomas, *Robert E. Lee*, 368.

166. April 14, 1865, Greensboro, North Carolina: Billy Porter, age three, watches Jefferson Davis. Burke Davis, *The Long Surrender*, 77–78.

166. April 14, 1865, Washington: President Lincoln examines a photograph of Robert E. Lee, saying, "It is a good face ..." Foote, *The Civil War*, 3:947. D. P. Kunhardt and P. B. Kunhardt, *Twenty Days* (New York: Castle Books, 1965), 19.

166. April 15, 1865, Greensboro, North Carolina: As President Lincoln lay dying, Jefferson Davis and his government leave on horseback with 1,300 Confederate cavalrymen; food riots with casualties in Greensboro. Ballard, *A Long Shadow: Jefferson Davis*, 88, 95. Burke Davis, *The Long Surrender*, 76–77, 79–81.

167. April 15, 1865, Richmond: General Lee and Major General Rooney Lee ride into Richmond where occupying Federals doff their hats in silent tribute. Dowdey, *Lee*, 590. Flood, *Lee: The Last Years*, 36, 39. Freeman, *R. E. Lee*, 4:160–63.

167. April 15, 1865, Richmond: Generals Robert and Rooney Lee arrive home on East Franklin Street; owner of rented house refuses to accept rent from the Lee family. Ibid., 4:207–08.

167. Mrs. Lee sends breakfast tray to the Federals guarding her home. Flood, *Lee: The Last Years*, 43.

167. Robert E. Lee's saber and inscriptions. Fitzhugh Lee, *General Lee*, 375 (footnote).

167, 168. April 15, 1865, nighttime: Jefferson Davis camps at Jamestown, North Carolina; Varina Davis and children at Woodward Baptist Church. Burke Davis, *The Long Surrender*, 74–75, 90.

168. April 16, 1865, Richmond: General Lee, Custis Lee, and Walter Taylor pose for photograph by Matthew Brady. Frassanito, *Grant and Lee*, 416.

168, 169. April 16–18, 1865, North Carolina: Jefferson Davis sent John Breckinridge to General Joe Johnston; Joe Johnston, CSA, meets General Sherman, USA, near Durham; Davis's "peace" proposal rejected until Generals Johnston and Sherman review it under the influence of Yankee whiskey. Ballard, *A Long Shadow: Jefferson Davis*, 93–98.

169. "It is sad news . . . I regret it deeply." Jefferson Davis, April 18, in Charlotte, North Carolina, on assassination of President Lincoln. The secondary authorities disagree on when Jefferson Davis learned of Lincoln assassination and the date of his comment. Ibid., 99, 102 (citing April 19). Burke Davis, *The Long Surrender*, 84–86 (citing April 20, 1865).

169. April 22, 1865, Charlotte, North Carolina: Jefferson Davis Cabinet meeting; Davis determination to keep fighting. Ballard, *A Long Shadow: Jefferson Davis*, 104–05.

169. April 23, 1865, Charlotte, North Carolina: Jefferson Davis goes to church. Burke Davis, *The Long Surrender*, 87.

169. "The cruel policy . . . never could win by their valor." Mrs. Lee letter to her cousin. MacDonald, *Mrs. Robert E. Lee*, 198.

169, 170. April 24–26, 1865: Confederate Attorney General resigns; Washington rejects the Davis truce proposal; General Joseph Johnston surrenders to William Tecumseh Sherman on April 26. Ballard, *A Long Shadow: Jefferson Davis*, 107–09. Burke Davis, *The Long Surrender*, 93–94. Dowdey, *Lee*, 593.

170, 171. April 26–May 2, 1865: Jefferson Davis last Cabinet meeting in Charlotte; Samuel Cooper resigns from CSA government; Davis on horseback leaves Charlotte;

George Trenholm resigns from CSA government; President Andrew Johnson puts bounty on Jefferson Davis; Jefferson Davis on horseback rides toward Georgia, night of May 2. Ballard, *A Long Shadow: Jefferson Davis*, 109–11, 117–18, 120–21, 127–28. Burke Davis, *The Long Surrender*, 96–97, 103, 106, 108–09, 114, 117, 121.

171. May 3, 1865: Jefferson Davis reaches Georgia; Judah P. Benjamin leaves CSA Cabinet to escape to Cuba; Jefferson Davis reaches Washington, Georgia; Executive Branch of the government of Confederate States disbands. Ballard, *A Long Shadow: Jefferson Davis*, 128–33; Burke Davis, *The Long Surrender*, 122, 125–26. Davis and Ballard agree that Judah Benjamin left Davis on May 3. Evans, *Judah P. Benjamin*, 311, citing April 24 as date Benjamin resigned.

172. May 4, 1865: Jefferson Davis leaves Washington, Georgia; General Richard Taylor surrenders his army, leaving no Confederate armies east of the Mississippi River. Burke Davis, *The Long Surrender*, 128. Dowdey, *Lee*, 594.

CHAPTER TWENTY

173. May 4–5, 1865: Jefferson Davis on horseback all night. Burke Davis, *The Long Surrender*, 137.

173. Fathers of Robert E. Lee and George Gordon Meade served George Washington. Fitzhugh Lee, *General Lee*, 258.

173. May 5, 1865, Richmond: Federal Major General George Gordon Meade pays his respects to Robert E. Lee; Lee rejects running for governor of Virginia; Lee's revered ancestors. Dowdey, *Lee*, 641–42. Flood, *Lee: The Last Years*, 52–53. Freeman, *R. E. Lee*, 4:195.

174. "I am looking for . . ." Robert E. Lee, undated. Flood, *Lee: The Last Years*, 60. Freeman, *R. E. Lee*, 4:197. MacDonald, *Mrs. Robert E. Lee*, 199.

174. "It would have the best possible effect . . ." Letter of Lieutenant General Ulysses S. Grant to Major General Henry Halleck, May 5, 1865. Dowdey, *Lee*, 641.

174, 175, 176. May 5–14, 1865: Jefferson Davis camps at Sandersville, Georgia; Mrs. Davis and her children attacked by Confederate looters; Jefferson and Varina Davis reunited at midnight at Dublin, Georgia; Davis family camps at Irwinville, Georgia; Davis family captured on the night of May 9–10; Yankees fire on each other in the dark; Federals ransack Davis family's belongings; Davis family taken to Macon, Georgia; pleasant meeting between Jefferson Davis and Federal Major General James Wilson at Macon. Ballard, *A Long Shadow: Jefferson Davis*, 136–39, 141–43, 150–52. Burke Davis, *The Long Surrender*, 131, 138–39, 141–47, 151. Dowdey, *Lee*, 594.

176. May 14–22, 1865: Davis family arrives Augusta, Georgia; "Tommy" Wilson sees President Davis under guard; Davis family taken to Savannah, Georgia, and then to Hampton Roads, Virginia; Jefferson Davis taken to Fort Monroe. Ballard, *A Long Shadow: Jefferson Davis*, 152–53. Burke Davis, *The Long Surrender*, 156, 174–77.

176. May 22, 1865: Jefferson Davis jailed at Fort Monroe; Davis in leg irons. Ballard, *A Long Shadow: Jefferson Davis*, 158–59. Burke Davis, *The Long Surrender*, 176–79.

176, 177. General Kirby Smith surrenders last CSA army, May 26; statistical and population figures of prewar North and South; Northern industrial superiority; Virginia's Civil War generals. McMurry, *Two Great Rebel Armies*, 19–26, 107, 111.

177. Army of Northern Virginia's 169 generals and 1,763 colonels; officers with military academy training: Katcher, *The Army of Robert E. Lee*, 48–52, 74.

178. Summary of casualties North and South; deaths among prisoners of war; homes, North and South, which had lost a soldier. Mitchell, *Civil War Soldiers*, 181. Robertson, *Soldiers*, 147, 190, 194, 203–06, 212.

178. Confederate outrage at white Union officers leading black troops, May, 1863; heavy Union casualties among Federal black troops. Ibid., 34–35.

178. Horses and mules killed in Civil War. *Equus* magazine, August 1988, 55.

178. May 28, 1865, Fort Monroe, Virginia: Leg irons removed from Jefferson Davis. Burke Davis, *The Long Surrender*, 181.

179. Physical ailments of Jefferson Davis; Davis's chronic insomnia treated with chloroform or castor oil and opium; Davis family of soldiers. Burke Davis, *The Long Surrender*, 7. Evans, *Judah P. Benjamin*, 127, 150–51. Woodworth, *Jefferson Davis*, 6, 15–16.

179. May 29, 1865: President Johnson's proclamation of amnesty; Robert E. Lee's exclusions from Federal amnesty; loyalty oath requirement. Dowdey, *Lee*, 642–43. Freeman, *R. E. Lee*, 4:200.

179. Lieutenant General Ulysses S. Grant petitions President Johnson to quash criminal indictments of Confederates paroled at Appomattox. Flood, *Lee: The Last Years*, 61–63.

179. Memorial Day, 1865: Southerners prohibited from honoring their dead; denial of Confederate burial on Antietam (Sharpsburg) battlefield. Burke Davis, *The Long Surrender*, 191–92.

180. June 7, 1865, Richmond: Robert E. Lee indicted for treason. Dowdey, *Lee*, 643. Freeman, *R. E. Lee*, 4:202 (Note 38).

180. June 13, 1865, Richmond: Robert E. Lee submits written request for presidential pardon; "I do not wish to avoid trial"; Lee request endorsed by Lieutenant General Grant. Dowdey, *Lee*, 643–44. Freeman, *R. E. Lee*, 4:204, 206–07.

180. June 17, 1865, Fort Monroe, Virginia: Jefferson Davis protests all-night lights and pacing guards. Burke Davis, *The Long Surrender*, 202.

180. "I shall avoid no prosecution . . . There is nothing that I want . . ." Robert E. Lee letter to Markie Williams, June 20, 1865 (syntax slightly changed for clarity). Craven, *To Markie*, 62–63. Pryor, *Reading the Man*, 433. Scott and Webb, *Who is Markie?*, 166.

180, 181. Martha "Markie" Williams and her brother Orton's wartime execution; Martha's connection to Ulysses S. Grant during Mexican War; Lee daughter Eleanor Agnes loved Orton. Anderson and Anderson, *The Generals*, 78. Connelly, *The Marble Man*, 174. Coulling, *The Lee Girls*, 37. Scott and Webb, *Who is Markie?*, xi. Execution of Orton Williams. Ibid., 151–52. Capt. (Brevet Major) Robert Lee retrieved sword belt of Markie's father who was killed at Monterey on September 21, 1846, and sent it to Markie that October. Lee/Markie correspondence dated 1846. Scott and Webb use 1847 for Lee's posting of the belt, but do note that the battle of Monterey was September, 1846. Even Markie appears to believe that her father died in 1847. Ibid., 42, 63, 64, 72 (Note 6). Orton Williams serving in 1859 with Capt. George Gordon Meade in Army Corps of Engineers. Ibid., 121.

181. Robert E. Lee's sire, Richard Lee, arrived in American Colonies in 1639; Robert Lee genealogy in depth: Freeman, *R. E. Lee*, 1:160. Fitzhugh Lee, *General Lee*, 12. Nagel, *The Lees of Virginia*, 7–8, 10, 14, 22, 39, 44, 79–80, 159, 161–62.

182. June 29, 1865, Richmond: Robert E. Lee accepts invitation to move with his family to Derwent cottage in Cumberland County, Virginia; Mrs. Elizabeth Cocke. Coulling, *The Lee Girls*, 152–53. Dowdey, *Lee*, 646–47. Flood, *Lee: The Last Years*, 70. Freeman, *R. E. Lee*, 4:209–11. MacDonald, *Mrs. Robert E. Lee*, 199.

182. Summer, 1865, Derwent: Lee daughter Agnes struck with typhoid; nursed by sister Mildred. Coulling, *The Lee Girls*, 154.

182. "I want that the world shall know . . ." Robert E. Lee's "circular letter" requesting Army of Northern Virginia histories, July 31, 1865. Dowdey, *Lee*, 650. Freeman, *R. E. Lee*, 4:213, 235–36. Also see the elegant volume, Douglas Southall Freeman, *The South to Posterity*, 41.

182. "My heart and thoughts will always be with this army." General Lee letter to Major General Jeb Stuart, December 9, 1863. Dowdey and Manarin, *The Wartime Papers*, 642. Freeman, *R. E. Lee*, 3:208.

183. "[T]he great mistake of my life . . ." Robert E. Lee, undated comment. Freeman, *R. E. Lee*, 4:278. This statement by Robert E. Lee is noted as a comment to Professor Milton W. Humphreys of Washington College, Lexington, VA, at Pryor, *Reading the Man*, 67, 502 (Note 54).

Chapter Twenty-One

184. August 4, 1865, Lexington, Virginia: Trustees of Washington College approve offering college presidency to Robert E. Lee; offer delivered by Judge Brockenbrough, wearing a borrowed suit. Dowdey, *Lee*, 654. Flood, *Lee: The Last Years*, 80. Freeman, *R. E. Lee*, 4:215.

184. Washington College history; Lexington, Virginia, looted by Federals. Coulling, *The Lee Girls*, 157. Freeman, *R. E. Lee*, 4:222. Fitzhugh Lee, *General Lee*, 385–86.

185. August 24, 1865: Robert E. Lee sends conditional acceptance letter to Washington College trustees; Lee declines to teach classes due to heart disease. Dowdey, *Lee*, 658. Flood, *Lee: The Last Years*, 84. Freeman, *R. E. Lee*, 4:217–18. Horn, *The Man Who Would Not Be Washington*, 228–31.

185. August 31, 1865: Judah P. Benjamin from England writes to Varina Davis; funds deposited to support Varina and Davis children; Davis children in Canada. Evans, *Judah P. Benjamin*, 349. Burke Davis, *The Long Surrender*, 206.

186. September 15–18, 1865: Robert E. Lee rides Traveller alone from Richmond to Lexington and Washington College; Lee women arrive three months later. Dowdey, *Lee*, 658. Flood, *Lee: The Last Years*, 88, 91. Freeman, *R. E. Lee*, 4:226–27. MacDonald, *Mrs. Robert E. Lee*, 207. For Lee daughter Mary Custis preserving her father's stars from his uniform, see Chapter 24 annotations.

186. Fort Monroe, Virginia: Mold grows on the shoes of Jefferson Davis; Federal General Miles moves Davis to drier cell. Burke Davis, *The Long Surrender*, 207.

186. October 2, 1865, Lexington, Virginia: Robert E. Lee becomes president of Washington College; Lee lives in hotel; Lee now has only 50 college students compared to commanding 91,000 men. Dowdey, *Lee*, 660. Flood, *Lee: The Last Years*, 99. Freeman, *R. E. Lee*, 4:223, 229–30, 233. Katcher, *The Army of Robert E. Lee*, 90.

186. "True patriotism sometimes requires . . . conform to the new order of things." Robert E. Lee letter to General P. T. Beauregard, CSA, October 3, 1865. J. William Jones, *Life and Letters*, 390 (syntax slightly changed for clarity). Pryor, *Reading the Man*, 457. Thomas, *Robert E. Lee*, 370.

186, 187. Fall, 1865: Robert E. Lee's daily routine at Washington College; late-afternoon rides on Traveller. Flood, *Lee: The Last Years*, 105, 109.

187. Washington College: Robert E. Lee calls students "yearlings" and "my boys"; audiences with president Lee for new students. Coulling, *The Lee Girls*, 166. Dowdey, *Lee*, 661, 665–66. Freeman, *R. E. Lee*, 4:275.

187. "We have but one rule . . ."; "I have a way of estimating . . ." College president Lee; Lee writes to parents. Ibid., 4:278, 280 (Note 31), 294. Horn, *The Man Who Would Not Be Washington*, 240. Thomas, *Robert E. Lee*, 397.

188. Late October, 1865, Lexington: Robert E. Lee's son Custis accepts teaching position at VMI, arrives Lexington, and moves into Lexington Hotel with his father. Coulling, *The Lee Girls*, 158–59. Flood, *Lee: The Last Years*, 109. Freeman, *R. E. Lee*, 4:242.

188. "I have known him well . . ." Lieutenant General Grant letter to President Johnson, November 7, 1865. Longstreet, *Lee and Longstreet*, 105–06.

188. December 2, 1865, Lexington: Mrs. Lee, Mildred, Mary Custis, and Rob join Robert E. Lee in Lexington; local ladies add curtains from Arlington. Coulling, *The Lee Girls*, 159. Dowdey, *Lee*, 666–67. Flood, *Lee: The Last Years*, 114–15. Freeman, *R. E. Lee*, 4:228, 242–43. Horn, *The Man Who Would Not Be Washington*, 233. MacDonald, *Mrs. Robert E. Lee*, 211. Scott and Webb, *Who is Markie?*, 166.

189. Lexington: Lees become friends with Margaret Preston; Robert E. Lee sleeps on old army cot; afternoon rides with Robert E. Lee on Traveller and Mildred on Lucy Long. Coulling, *The Lee Girls*, 162, 170. Flood, *Lee: The Last Years*, 134.

189. December, 1865: General Lee summoned to testify to Congress; "In looking back . . ." General Lee letter to Markie, December 20, 1865. Craven, *To Markie*, 66. Flood, *Lee: The Last Years*, 116.

189. January 11, 1866, Richmond: Robert E. Lee testifies before Virginia legislature. Freeman, *R. E. Lee*, 4:244–45.

189. Donations to Washington College because of President Lee's name; Cyrus McCormick, Thomas Scott, Samuel Tilden. Dowdey, *Lee*, 673. Freeman, *R. E. Lee*, 4:247.

190. Mrs. Lee, Lexington: Grace Episcopal Church Sewing Society. MacDonald, *Mrs. Robert E. Lee*, 223, 225.

190. "My interest and affection for you . . ."; "I do not consider my partnership . . ." Robert E. Lee letter to James Longstreet January 19, 1866, and Lee letter to Longstreet's business partner. Freeman, *R. E. Lee*, 4:159, 273. Longstreet, *Lee and Longstreet*, 80–82.

190. February 17, 1866: Robert E. Lee testifies before federal Congress; "The act of Virginia in withdrawing . . ."; Lee returns to Lexington February 20. Flood, *Lee: The Last Years*, 118–19, 124. Freeman, *R. E. Lee*, 4:250–51, 253, 256.

190. February, 1866: Lee family estate at Arlington home now has 16,000 Federal graves. Connelly, *The Marble Man*, 34. Horn, *The Man Who Would Not Be Washington*, 246. (Horn uses 1870 for this count of Federal graves at Arlington.)

191. "I am easily wearied now . . ."; "I am considered now such a monster that I hesitate . . ." Robert E. Lee letter to Martha "Markie" Williams, April 7, 1866. Craven, *To Markie*, 68, 70. Horn, *The Man Who Would Not Be Washington*, 236.

191. May 3, 1866, Fort Monroe, Virginia: Mrs. Jefferson Davis and baby Varina Anne visit Jefferson Davis. Burke Davis, *The Long Surrender*, 215.

191. Summer, 1866, Lexington, Virginia: Robert E. Lee's salary increased to $3,000; approval of new college chapel; Robert E. Lee donated $6,000 for the new chapel. Freeman, *R. E. Lee*, 4:248, 267.

191, 192. Summer and fall, 1866, Lexington, Virginia: College president Robert E. Lee selects site for new chapel and then designs it; Mrs. Lee suffers serious fall; Robert E. Lee rides Traveller twenty miles per day; Washington College enrollment continues to increase. Dowdey, *Lee*, 676–77. Freeman, *R. E. Lee*, 4:265, 270, 299, 307–08.

192. "If I were an artist like you." Robert E. Lee letter to Martha "Markie" Williams, December 22, 1866. Craven, *To Markie*, 73-74. Scott and Webb, *Who is Markie?*, 169. Robert E. Lee Jr., erroneously cites this letter to Markie as one to Lee daughter Agnes at Lee Jr., *Recollections and Letters*, 83. See also J. William Jones, *Life and Letters*, 191–92.

192. March 13, 1867: Federal Congress strips Virginia of all state sovereignty in First Reconstruction Act. Flood, *Lee: The Last Years*, 148. Freeman, *R. E. Lee*, 4:310–12.

192, 193. "The country that allows such scum . . ." Mrs. Lee letter, undated. MacDonald, *Mrs. Robert E. Lee*, 231.

193. May 13, 1867: Jefferson Davis released from two years imprisonment at Fort Monroe. Ballard, *A Long Shadow: Jefferson Davis*, 162. Burke Davis, *The Long Surrender*, 221–23.

193. Spring, 1867: Washington College trustees approve new home for Lee family. Freeman, *R. E. Lee*, 4:318.

193. July, 1867: Robert E. Lee takes Mrs. Lee to Greenbrier County, West Virginia, White Sulphur Springs health spa, "The Old White," for her crippling arthritis; General Lee's horse Traveller once named "Greenbrier." Traveller's purchase and prior names: Adams, *Traveller*, 22, 37. Freeman, *R. E. Lee*, 1:644–45.

193. July, 1867, The Old White, Greenbrier County, West Virginia: Southerners and Northerners rise in silent tribute to Robert E. Lee in the dining room; "Harrison Cottage" at The Greenbrier resort. Dowdey, *Lee*, 698. Flood, *Lee: The Last Years*, 160–62. Freeman, *R. E. Lee*, 4:323–26, 330.

CHAPTER TWENTY-TWO

194. September 1867: Robert E. Lee stricken ill on trip from The Old White back to Lexington. Dowdey, *Lee*, 697. Flood, *Lee: The Last Years*, 168. Freeman, *R. E. Lee*, 4:330–32.

194. September 17, 1867, Sharpsburg, Maryland: Federal General McClellan not invited to dedication of national cemetery on Antietam battlefield. Luvaas and Nelson, *Guide to the Battle of Antietam*, 252.

194. School year 1867–1868 begins at Washington College with four hundred students; president's salary increased. Dowdey, *Lee*, 705. Freeman, *R. E. Lee*, 4:344, 391.

194. Rooney begs his father to return to Petersburg to attend Rooney's remarriage. Flood, *Lee: The Last Years*, 168–69.

195. November 25–28, 1867, Richmond: Robert E. Lee testifies before federal grand jury; reunion with Jefferson Davis; Davis boards at Spotswood Hotel. Burke Davis, *The Long Surrender*, 234. Flood, *Lee: The Last Years*, 170–71. Frassanito, *Grant and Lee*, 396.

195. November 28, 1867, Petersburg, Virginia: Pensive Robert E. Lee enjoys warm welcome; "Dixie"; Rooney's wedding to Tabb Bolling; return to Richmond, November 30; December 7, Robert E. Lee returns to Lexington. Flood, *Lee: The Last Years*, 172. Freeman, *R. E. Lee*, 4:334–43.

196. Christmas, 1867, Lexington: MacDonald, *Mrs. Robert E. Lee*, 247.

196 "My interest in time . . ." Robert E. Lee letter to Martha Williams, January 1, 1868. Craven, *To Markie*, 78. "How are you progressing . . ." Ibid., 80. Scott and Webb, *Who is Markie?*, 43, 169. For mention of Martha Williams's formal art school training: Craven, *To Markie*, 57 (Note 2). Markie Williams studied painting and art in 1860 at the New York City, Cooper Union for the Advancement of Science and Art. Scott and Webb, *Who is Markie?*, 46. Interestingly, while Martha "Markie" Williams was at Cooper Union in 1860, presidential candidate Abraham Lincoln delivered his monumental "Cooper Union Address" on February 27, 1860, where Mr. Lincoln condemned the expansion of slavery into the western territories that were not yet states in the Union. Lincoln declared there: "Let us have faith that right makes might, and in that faith, let us, to the end, dare to do our duty as we understand it." Apparently, there is no historical record that suggests that Martha Williams attended Mr. Lincoln's speech. Likewise, there is no historical record that Cousin Markie ever finished a portrait of Traveller. Ibid. 169.

196. "[T]hough opposed to secession . . ." Robert E. Letter to Reverdy Johnson, February 25, 1868. Lee Jr., *Recollections and Letters*, 27.

196. "death in its silent, sure march . . ." Robert E. Lee letter to William F. Wickham, whose wife was the niece of Lee's mother, March 4, 1868. Freeman, *R. E. Lee*, 4:272.

196. "I find too late . . ." Robert E. Lee letter to General Richard "Baldy" Ewell, March 3, 1868. Connelly, *The Marble Man*, 218. J. William Jones, *Life and Letters*, 430.

196. May 1 and June 3, 1868, Richmond: Robert E. Lee summoned for grand jury testimony; both sessions canceled. Freeman, *R. E. Lee*, 4:363, 365.

197. "General [J. E. B.] Stuart was my ideal . . ." Robert E. Lee to General Hampton, June 14, 1868, when new chapel dedicated at Washington College. Ibid., 4:367.

197. July–August, 1868, Warm Springs spa: Lee daughter Mildred stricken with typhoid fever; Robert E. Lee at her bedside for full month; about August 14, Robert E. Lee on Traveller goes on alone to The Old White. Coulling, *The Lee Girls*, 173. Flood, *Lee: The Last Years*, 192–93.

197, 198. August 26, 1868, The Old White resort: Robert E. Lee signs "The White Sulphur Springs Letter"; "The Negroes have neither the intelligence nor the other qualifications . . ." Dowdey, *Lee*, 707–12. Flood, *Lee: The Last Years*, 195–97. Freeman, *R. E. Lee*, 4:373–77. Pryor, *Reading the Man*, 452-53. Thomas, *Robert E. Lee*, 390. The secondary historical sources disagree as to whether recovering Mildred accompanied her father on his second visit to The Old White spa.

198. "I have no fears that our dead . . ." Robert E. Lee letter to nephew, former major general Fitzhugh Lee, December 15, 1868. Fitzhugh Lee, *General Lee*, 388.

198. Christmas Amnesty, 1868: Dowdey, *Lee*, 714. Freeman, *R. E. Lee*, 4:381. "dirt, lice . . ." Robertson, *Soldiers*, 60.

199. Christmas, 1868, Lexington: Lee family together except for Rooney and Tabb. Freeman, *R. E. Lee*, 4:380.

199. February, 1869: Robert E. Lee's treason indictment quashed; Rooney and Tabb give birth to the second Robert E. Lee III. Flood, *Lee: The Last Years*, 201.

199. March 1–3, 1869: Mrs. Lee's formal petition to US Congress for the return of her precious family and George Washington artifacts seized with Arlington home is approved by President Johnson but is rejected by Congress. Dowdey, *Lee*, 714–15. Flood, *Lee: The Last Years*, 201–02. Freeman, *R. E. Lee*, 4:382–84.

199, 200. April 20–May 1, 1869: Robert E. Lee travels to Baltimore to discuss railroad spur to Lexington; Robert E. Lee and President Ulysses S. Grant meet for brief, sad reunion at the White House on May 1, 1869. Flood, *Lee: The Last Years*, 207, 209–10. Freeman, *R. E. Lee*, 4:395–403, 520–21.

200. Robert E. Lee forbids Washington College faculty from speaking ill of Lieutenant General Grant. Dowdey, *Lee*, 715. Flood, *Lee: The Last Years*, 188.

200. May 4–8, 1869: Robert E. Lee visits brother Sidney Smith Lee and former general Fitz Lee; Lee returns to Lexington, May 8. Dowdey, *Lee*, 716. Freeman, *R. E. Lee*, 4:403–05.

200, 201. May, 1869: Robert E. Lee returns to Fredericksburg; another visit with Lee brother Sidney Smith Lee. Ibid., 4:406–08.

201. May 31, 1869: Robert E. Lee returns to Lexington; at Lee's request, the new home for the college president has Traveller's stable attached to the house. Dowdey, *Lee*, 705, 717. Flood, *Lee: The Last Years*, 211–12. Freeman, *R. E. Lee*, 4:408.

201. "Forty years ago, I stood in this room . . ." Robert E. Lee's last pilgrimage to his boyhood home, July 24, 1869, after missing the funeral of his beloved brother, Sidney Smith Lee. Dowdey, *Lee*, 718. Freeman, *R. E. Lee*, 4:434. Lee Jr., *Recollections and Letters*, 363.

201. August, 1869: Robert E. Lee and son Rob visit Rooney Lee; Robert E. Lee and daughters Agnes and Mildred return to The Old White; Mrs. Lee goes to Rockbridge Baths spa; Lees return to Lexington at the end of August. Dowdey, *Lee*, 718–19. Flood, *Lee: The Last Years*, 214–16. Freeman, *R. E. Lee*, 4:435, 437.

202. Robert E. Lee agrees to sit for portrait by Swiss artist, Frank Buchser; portrait in Switzerland until returned to the United States in January, 1990. Flood, *Lee: The Last Years*, 217–22. Thomas, *Robert E. Lee*, 404, 447 (Note 4). Return of this portrait of Robert E. Lee to the United States is detailed in letter to this author, dated March 14, 1990, from Hon. Francois Barras, Cultural Affairs Office; Embassy of Switzerland; Washington, DC 20008.

202. October, 1869: Robert E. Lee suffers chest pain for a week; coronary angina pain lasts for three months. Dowdey, *Lee*, 719. Flood, *Lee: The Last Years*, 223.

202. Spring, 1870, Lexington, Virginia: Robert E. Lee's congestive heart failure worsening. Ibid., 227. Freeman, *R. E. Lee*, 4:440–41.

202. "I think if I am to accomplish it . . ." March 22, 1870, Robert E. Lee letter to son Rooney; Robert E. Lee's desire to visit the grave of his daughter, "Sweet Annie."

Flood, *Lee: The Last Years*, 228. Freeman, *R. E. Lee*, 4:442–43. Lee Jr., *Recollections and Letters*, 386.

203. March 24–25, 1870: Robert E. Lee and daughter Agnes arrive Lynchburg and Richmond; Robert E. Lee too weak to address the Virginia State Senate or to visit old friends. Flood, *Lee: The Last Years*, 229. Freeman, *R. E. Lee*, 4:444.

203. March 26, 1870, Richmond: Robert E. Lee examined by Richmond physicians. Ibid., 4:445.

203. March 28–29, 1870, Warrenton, North Carolina: Robert E. Lee and Agnes leave Richmond March 28 for Warrenton; Tuesday, March 29, visit to North Carolina grave of "Sweet Annie"; "Perfect and true . . . ," inscription on Annie's grave marker; "I hope you will always appear . . . ," Robert E. Lee letter to Annie, February 25, 1853; no photographs of Annie Lee; Agnes and her father leave flowers at Annie's grave and lock of Lee's hair for North Carolina hosts. Anderson and Anderson, *The Generals*, 274. Coulling, *The Lee Girls*, 17, 108–10, 173 (photo of Annie's North Carolina grave at Plate 16). Flood, *Lee: The Last Years*, 232–34. Freeman, *R. E. Lee*, 4:446–47. Lee Jr., *Recollections and Letters*, 15 (Lee's 1853 letter to Annie), 81. The authorities cited all agree that Robert E. Lee and Agnes visited Annie's grave on Tuesday, March 29, 1870, but they disagree on whether the Lees arrived at Warrenton late evening on March 28 or after midnight on March 29.

CHAPTER TWENTY-THREE

204. Private pilgrimage by Robert E. Lee and Agnes becomes triumphant Farewell Tour: train cheered Raleigh, Charlotte, and Columbia; Porter Alexander and Fitz Lee USMA cadets together; Lees arrive Augusta, Georgia, and seen by young Tommy Wilson. Flood, *Lee: The Last Years*, 237. Freeman, *R. E. Lee*, 4:447–49.

204. April 1, 1870, Savannah, Georgia: Largest crowd in city's history greets Lees; former generals Robert E. Lee and Joe Johnston photographed together. Flood, *Lee: The Last Years*, 240, 242. Freeman, *R. E. Lee*, 4:449–51.

205. April 12, 1870, Savannah, Georgia: Lees visit grave of Robert E. Lee's father; sketch of "Light Horse Harry" Lee; Light Horse Harry sends severed head to George Washington. Anderson and Anderson, *The Generals*, 10.

205. "I presume it is the last time . . ." Robert E. Lee letter to Mrs. Lee, April 18, 1870. Flood, *Lee: The Last Years*, 242–43. Freeman, *R. E. Lee*, 4:451–52. Lee Jr., *Recollections and Letters*, 398.

205. April 13–15, 1870, Jacksonville, Florida: CSA veterans greet Robert E. Lee only with reverent silence. Flood, *Lee: The Last Years*, 244. Freeman, *R. E. Lee*, 4:452–53.

205. April 16–19, 1870: Lees in Savannah, Georgia, for nine days; Washington College trustees approve annual pension for Mrs. Lee, April 19. Flood, *Lee: The Last Years*, 241.

205, 206. April 25–May 21, 1870: Lees leave Savannah for Charleston, South Carolina; Portsmouth, Virginia, Lees met by former aide, Walter Taylor; Lees visit Shirley Plantation; visit with Rooney Lee's family; visit with son Rob at Romancoke. Freeman, *R. E. Lee*, 4:453–61.

206. May 22–June 23, 1870: May 24, Robert E. Lee visits physicians in Richmond; May 28, Lees return to Lexington, VA; Robert E. Lee rejects college's pension for Mrs. Lee;

June 23, college president Lee hands out diplomas. Dowdey, *Lee*, 722–27. Flood, *Lee: The Last Years*, 248, 250; Freeman, *R. E. Lee*, 4:463–65, 468–69.

206, 207. July 1–25, 1870: Robert E. Lee submits to more medical examinations; visit to Alexandria, Virginia; visit to Ravensworth Plantation, where Lee's mother died. Ibid., 4:473–74, 477. Lee was too grief stricken to attend his mother's 1829 funeral. Horn, *The Man Who Would Not Be Washington*, 44. Pryor, *Reading the Man*, 72.

207. August 9, 1870: Robert E. Lee visits Hot Springs spa; railroad meeting in Staunton, Virginia; Lee returns to Lexington. Freeman, *R. E. Lee*, 4:479–80.

207. "May God help the suffering . . ." Robert E. Lee's last letter to Markie Williams, August 27, 1870. Craven, *To Markie*, 91. Scott and Webb, *Who is Markie?*, 172.

207, 208. September, 1870, Lexington, Virginia: Washington College's school year begins, September 15; Robert E. Lee attends faculty meeting, September 27; former General-in-Chief Robert E. Lee signs a photo for a student for the last time, September 28; rainy meeting at Grace Episcopal Church; Robert E. Lee suffers stroke at dinner table, September 28, 1870. Flood, *Lee: The Last Years*, 255–57. Freeman, *R. E. Lee*, 4:481, 484–89.

208. September 28, 1870, Lexington: Physician turns Lee dining room into a hospital room; Mildred holds her father's hand. Flood, *Lee: The Last Years*, 259.

208. October 10, 1870, Lexington: "The doctors think . . ." Mrs. Lee's desperate note to Francis Smith at VMI. MacDonald, *Mrs. Robert E. Lee*, 280.

208. October 11, 1870, Lexington: Robert E. Lee still bedridden; "Tell Hill he *must* come up."; Mother Lee, Custis, Mildred, and Agnes at the bedside; framed photo of General Lee falls from the wall; "Strike the tent!" Ibid., 282–83.

209. October 12, 1870: former major general and reverend William Pendleton, Sandie's father, prays. Robert Edward Lee is dead. Dowdey, *Lee*, 731–34. Flood, *Lee: The Last Years*, 261. Freeman, *R. E. Lee*, 4:490–92. MacDonald, *Mrs. Robert E. Lee*, 282. Although the apocryphal "last words" of General Lee are widely quoted, as are Stonewall Jackson's "Let us cross over the river and into the trees" (even Ernest Hemingway used Jackson's "famous last words" as the title for his novel, *Across the River and Into the Trees* [New York: Charles Scribner's Sons, 1950]), modern historians and neurologists must wonder if there was a course taught at West Point in the nineteenth century that was called, "Dying Well." Because Robert E. Lee rarely if ever spoke during his two-week-long last illness, which was most likely a stroke, it is now widely thought doubtful that he could have uttered his often-quoted "famous last words." See "Strike the Phrase, 'Strike the Tent'," *Civil War Times Illustrated*, September–October 1990, 47, 56, citing *Virginia Magazine of History and Biography*, April 1990. Excellent summary of improbability of General Lee's "famous last words": Pryor, *Reading the Man*, 615 (Note 15). Also rejecting the likelihood of Lee's last words: Thomas, *Robert E. Lee*, 412, 417. Jonathan Horn specifically cites Pryor on the "famous last words" credibility, but he does seem to state them as facts in his text proper. Horn, *The Man Who Would Not Be Washington*, 329 at Notes for text at 243.

CHAPTER TWENTY-FOUR

210. October 15, 1870, Lexington: Agnes dresses her father's body; Lee buried without shoes in college library; family finds Lee's US Army colonel's insignia. Coulling, *The Lee Girls*, 176–77. Freeman, *R. E. Lee*, 4:309, 493, 526–27.

210. Faithful warhorse Traveller dies from tetanus, summer, 1871. MacDonald, *Mrs. Robert E. Lee*, 177.

211. June, 1873: Mrs. Lee visits Arlington. Ibid., 295.

211, 212. "Were it not that I would not add . . ." Mrs. Lee's angry letter to Winfield Scott, 1861. Ibid., 151. "It never occurred to me . . ." Mrs. Lee's letter to General Sandford, May 30, 1861. Coulling, *The Lee Girls*, 88. "When you desire to return . . ." Federal Brigadier General Irwin McDowell's generous response to Mrs. Lee's letter to General Sandford. J. William Jones, *Life and Letters*, 142–43. Fitzhugh Lee, *General Lee*, 109. Edwin Stanton created Arlington National Cemetery in June, 1864. Pryor, *Reading the Man*, 313. The Federal quartermaster general insisted that the first Union graves at Arlington should completely encircle the house to render the Lees' return impossible: Horn, *The Man Who Would Not Be Washington*, 211.

212. October 15, 1873: Death of Eleanor Agnes Lee; "You must not forget me . . ." Coulling, *The Lee Girls*, 179. deButts, *Growing Up in the 1850s*, 112. MacDonald, *Mrs. Robert E. Lee*, 178.

212. November 5, 1873: Death of Mrs. Robert E. Lee. Coulling, *The Lee Girls*, 180.

212. Mildred Lee keeps house for brother Custis at Washington College. Ibid., 181, 184–85.

212. Lexington Sunday school founded by "Stonewall" Jackson: Bowers, *Stonewall Jackson*, 27, 33.

212. Memorial Day, 1885: General George McClellan returns to Antietam battlefield; Southern veterans parade in review. Douglas, *I Rode with Stonewall*, 174.

212, 213. July, 1885: Dying Ulysses S. Grant races death to complete his memoirs. "I felt like anything rather than rejoicing . . ." Grant, *Memoirs and Selected Letters*, 735.

213. July 1885: General Grant treated with morphine and brandy; "The fact is, I think I am a verb . . ." Ibid., 1120, 1159.

213. 1886, Richmond: Death of Stonewall Jackson's horse Fancy. Burke Davis, *They Called Him Stonewall*, 457.

213. Mary Custis Lee travels the world for nearly fifty years. Coulling, *The Lee Girls*, 187.

213. May 29, 1890, Richmond: "We wanted to sleep with the Old Man . . ." Douglas, *I Rode with Stonewall*, 229–30.

213, 214. February 19, 1891: Old Confederate Joe Johnston attends funeral of General Sherman; "If I were in his place . . ."; death of General Johnston. Foote, *The Civil War*, 3:996.

214. October 15, 1891: Death of Rooney Lee. Coulling, *The Lee Girls*, 190.

214. Lieutenant General A. P. "Little Powell" Hill, CSA, buried three times. Robertson, *General A. P. Hill*, 319–22, 324–25.

214. Aged General George McClellan speaks of A. P. Hill: "Fiction no doubt . . ." Douglas, *I Rode with Stonewall*, 175.

214. 1893: Oak tree sheared in half by Spotsylvania gunfire displayed in Chicago. Matter, *If It Takes All Summer*, 373, 417 (Note 4, Appendix C).

215. "When the smoke cleared away . . ." Lieutenant General James Longstreet on Gettysburg. Longstreet, *Lee and Longstreet*, 51–52 (with slight change in syntax for clarity).

215. "That day at Gettysburg . . ." Lieutenant General James Longstreet, CSA. *Battles and Leaders*, 3:345. Piston, *Lee's Tarnished Lieutenant*, 59.

215. St. Patrick's Day, 1892, Atlanta: Joyful, hearty reunion between old adversaries, Generals Daniel Sickles and James Longstreet. Longstreet, *Lee and Longstreet*, 19.

215. April, 1893, Gettysburg: James Longstreet's last pilgrimage to Gettysburg with former Union generals Sickles and Howard. Connelly, *The Marble Man*, 62–63.

216. January, 1904: Death of Lieutenant General James Longstreet. Longstreet, *Lee and Longstreet*, 20–21, 93, 217, 221–22, 228.

216. No statue honoring James Longstreet in Old South. Connelly, *The Marble Man*, 64. Piston, *Lee's Tarnished Lieutenant*, ix.

216. December, 1897: Mildred Lee moves out of president's house at Washington and Lee. Coulling, *The Lee Girls*, 193.

216. 1898: President William McKinley commissions Fitz Lee a Yankee general for Spanish-American War. Nagel, *The Lees of Virginia*, 296.

216. January, 1905: General Fitz Lee's last public appearance in Canton, Ohio. Gault, *Ohio at Vicksburg*, 338.

216. March, 1905: Death of Mildred Childe Lee. Coulling, *The Lee Girls*, 194.

217. 1913–1914: Robert E. Lee's parents reburied in college chapel crypt; death of Robert E. Lee Jr., Ibid., 191, 193. Freeman, *R. E. Lee*, 1:87.

217. 1917–1918: Mary Custis Lee returns to United States; entertained by President Wilson; returns to Lexington; death in November, 1918. Coulling, *The Lee Girls*, 195–97.

217. May 10, 1923: Death of Mrs. Jeb Stuart. Thomas, *Bold Dragoon*, 297.

217. July 3, 1938: President Franklin Roosevelt at seventy-fifth anniversary of the Battle of Gettysburg. McLaughlin, *Gettysburg*, 223.

217. December, 1959: Death of Walter Williams, CSA; launch of USS *Robert E. Lee* (SSBN 601). Burke Davis, *The Long Surrender*, 283. Launch date of the submarine *Robert E. Lee* (SSBN 601) generously provided to the author by Ms. Elizabeth A. Felicetti, Communication Services, General Dynamics Electric Boat Division, Groton, CT, October 21, 1990.

217, 218. 1957–1975: History of Robert E. Lee's October, 1865, loyalty oath, lost for 105 years; Robert E. Lee's full citizenship restored by Congress and President Gerald Ford, August, 1975. Flood, *Lee: The Last Years*, 276. Marjorie Hunter, "Citizenship Is Voted for Robert E. Lee," *New York Times*, July 23, 1975. Richard D. Lyons, "Amnesty Amendment May Be Attached to Resolution Restoring Lee's Citizenship," *New York Times*, May 12, 1974. Thomas, *Robert E. Lee*, 380–81.

218. 1988, Sharpsburg, Maryland: Soldiers' remains still found on Antietam battlefield. B. Drummond Ayres Jr., "Clues from Antietam Grave Offer Hope Soldier May Regain Identity," *New York Times*, August 19, 1988.

218. June, 1989, Richmond: Last seven daughters of Confederate veterans evicted. Nancy Cook, "Judge OKs Moving Confederate Women," Newport News, Virginia, *Daily Press*, June 6, 1989.

218. October, 1990: Death of last Confederate widow. *USA Today*, October 17, 1990. Two weeks after the death of Daisy Cave at age perhaps 105, Ms. Alberta Martin, eighty-three, came forward to say that she was the real Last Living Confederate Widow, having married a seventy-five-year-old veteran when she was twenty-one—a common Southern trend for young women to marry history, to carry the name. *USA Today*, October 22,

1990. Indeed, Lieutenant General James Longstreet's devoted widow and second wife, Helen, cited often here, was Old Pete's junior by forty-two years: Piston, *Lee's Tarnished Lieutenant*, 161.

218. September 29, 1994: Annie Lee reburied beside her parents and siblings in chapel crypt at Washington and Lee University. Parke Rouse, "W & L Is Resting Place for Lees," *Daily Press*, Newport News, Virginia, April 16, 1995.

218. 2002, Alexandria, Virginia: Two steamer trunks belonging to Mary Custis Lee found in bank. Linda Wheeler, "Mementos of Robert E. Lee's Daughter Found," *Washington Post*, December 1, 2002. Peter Carlson, "A Portrait in Letters: Mary Custis Lee's Two Trunks Full of Memorabilia Tell Much about a Famous Father," *Washington Post*, July 12, 2007. Pryor, *Reading the Man*, xxiii.

219. July, 2015, Columbia, South Carolina: The so-called Confederate flag removed from the capitol grounds was originally only the battle flag of the Army of Northern Virginia. Katcher, *The Army of Robert E. Lee*, 9.

219. "The sun of the morning was in our faces then . . ." Brigadier General Charles W. Miner at Vicksburg, Mississippi, May 22, 1905. Gault, *Ohio at Vicksburg*, 319, 366.

Selected Bibliography

Adams, Richard. *Traveller.* New York: Alfred A. Knopf, 1988.

Albright, Harry. *Gettysburg: Crisis in Command.* New York: Hippocrene, 1991.

Alexander, Edward Porter. *Fighting for the Confederacy.* Edited by Gary W. Gallagher. Chapel Hill: University of North Carolina Press, 1989. The original, 1,200-page, handwritten manuscript of this book remained unpublished for nearly eighty years. Thanks to the University of North Carolina, Brigadier General Alexander's reminiscences have finally seen the light of day. Porter Alexander's cannon attempted to "soften" Federal positions for the ninety minutes before Pickett's Charge at Gettysburg. General Alexander's memories can still make the reader smell the sulfur of black-powder clouds hanging over "those ghastly fields."

Anderson, Nancy S., and Dwight Anderson. *The Generals: Ulysses S. Grant and Robert E. Lee.* New York: Alfred A. Knopf, 1988.

Bailey, Ronald H. *The Bloodiest Day: The Battle of Antietam.* Alexandria, VA: Time-Life Books, 1984.

Ballard, Michael B. *A Long Shadow: Jefferson Davis and the Final Days of the Confederacy.* Jackson: University Press of Mississippi, 1986.

Battles and Leaders of the Civil War. Vol. 3. Secaucus, NJ: Book Sales, Inc., 1986.

Bean, W. G. *Stonewall's Man: Sandie Pendleton.* Wilmington, NC: Broadfoot Publishing Company, 1959, 1987.

Bowers, John. *Stonewall Jackson: Portrait of a Soldier.* New York: William Morrow, 1989.

Busey, John W., and David G. Martin. *Regimental Strengths and Losses at Gettysburg.* Hightstown, NJ: Longstreet House, 1986.

Catton, Bruce. *Gettysburg: The Final Fury.* Garden City, NY: Doubleday, 1974, 1990.

Clark, Champ. *Gettysburg: The Confederate High Tide.* Alexandria, VA: Time-Life Books, 1985.

Coddington, Edwin B. *The Gettysburg Campaign: A Study in Command.* New York: Charles Scribner's Sons, 1963, 1984.

Connelly, Thomas L. *The Marble Man: Robert E. Lee and His Image in American Society.* Baton Rouge: Louisiana State University Press, 1977. This fascinating study may be the first revisionist analysis of Douglas Southall Freeman's epic biography of Robert E. Lee.

Coulling, Mary P. *The Lee Girls.* Winston-Salem, NC: John F. Blair, 1987. This is a wonderful, one-of-a-kind treatment of the lives of Robert E. Lee's daughters.

Craven, Avery. *To Markie: The Letters of Robert E. Lee to Martha Custis Williams.* Cambridge: Harvard University Press, 1933. This slim, elegant volume introduced historians to Robert E. Lee's much loved cousin and confidante, Markie. The author is grateful to the Huntington Library, San Marino, CA, for the author's use of *"To Markie": The Letters of Robert E. Lee to Martha Custis Williams.* San Marino, CA: The Huntington Library (HM 8807-8845). Its 2007 companion volume, *Who is Markie?*, by Scott and Webb is noted below.

Davis, Burke. *Jeb Stuart: The Last Cavalier.* New York: Fairfax Press, 1957, 1988.

———. *The Long Surrender.* New York: Random House, 1985.

———. *They Called Him Stonewall: A Life of Lt. General T. J. Jackson, C.S.A.* New York: Fairfax Press, 1954, 1988.

Davis, William C., ed. *Touched By Fire: A Photographic Portrait of the Civil War.* 2 vols. Boston: Little, Brown, 1985–1986.

———. *The Image of War (1861–1865).* 6 vols. Garden City, NY: Doubleday, 1981–1984.

———. *Battle at Bull Run.* Garden City, NY: Doubleday, 1977.

———. *Jefferson Davis: The Man and His Hour.* New York: HarperCollins, 1991.

deButts, Mary Custis Lee. *Growing Up in the 1850s: The Journal of Agnes Lee.* Chapel Hill: University of North Carolina Press, 1984.

Douglas, Henry Kyd. *I Rode with Stonewall.* Simons Island, GA: Mockingbird Books, 1940, 1961, 1983.

Dowdey, Clifford. *Death of a Nation: The Story of Lee and His Men at Gettysburg.* New York: Alfred A. Knopf, 1958 (Butternut and Blue edition, 1988).

———. *Lee.* New York: Bonanza, 1965.

Dowdey, Clifford, and Louis H. Manarin, eds. *The Wartime Papers of Robert E. Lee.* New York: Da Capo Press, 1961, 1989. No Robert E. Lee collection is complete without this essential volume. Excerpts from Robert E. Lee letters and battlefield dispatches in *The Wartime Papers of Robert E. Lee,* edited by Clifford Dowdey and Louis H. Manarin, copyright © 1961 and renewed 1989 by the Commonwealth of Virginia, are reprinted with the permission of Little, Brown and Company. All rights reserved.

Drake, Samuel A. *The Battle of Gettysburg.* Wilmington, NC: Broadfoot Publishing Company, 1891, 1988.

Evans, Eli N. *Judah P. Benjamin: The Jewish Confederate.* New York: The Free Press, 1988.

Faust, Patricia L., ed. *Historical Times Illustrated Encyclopedia of the Civil War.* New York: Harper and Row, 1986.

Flood, Charles B. *Lee: The Last Years.* Boston: Houghton Mifflin, 1981. This wonderful study begins with the surrender of the Army of Northern Virginia. All research on Robert E. Lee's life after April 9, 1865, must start with Mr. Flood's compelling narrative.

Foote, Shelby. *The Civil War, A Narrative.* 3 vols. New York: Random House, 1958–1974. No footnotes or endnotes clutter this massive set of three thousand pages. The bibliography in each volume is a bare sketch. The "narrative" flows across the author's single-minded twenty-year research and composing campaign. This is truly elegant history, written with the pacing, eloquence, and passion that only a novelist could bring to bear on that terrible war.

Frassanito, William A. *Antietam: The Photographic Legacy of America's Bloodiest Day.* New York: Charles Scribner's Sons, 1978. Frassanito's three volumes are haunting and brilliantly staged, matching wartime photos with their modern views photographed from the Civil War photographer's actual position on the field.

———. *Gettysburg: A Journey in Time.* New York: Charles Scribner's Sons, 1975.

———. *Grant and Lee: The Virginia Campaigns 1864–1865.* New York: Charles Scribner's Sons, 1983.

Freeman, Douglas Southall. *Lee's Lieutenants.* 3 vols. New York: Charles Scribner's Sons, 1942–1944.

———. *R. E. Lee.* 4 vols. New York: Charles Scribner's Sons, 1934–1935, 1962–1963. With appropriate respect for and apologies to Professor Thomas Connelly and attorney Alan Nolan and their thoughtful criticism of *R. E. Lee*, all study of Robert E. Lee as man and soldier must begin always with Douglas Freeman's monumental achievement. Historian by education (history PhD, Johns Hopkins) and newspaper editor by trade, Dr. Freeman's father served for the entire war in the Army of Northern Virginia. A little bias in favor of General Lee may be excused. To question Freeman's objectivity when writing about General Lee is quite legitimate, and Connelly and Nolan manage to be revisionist historians with respect toward and gratitude for Dr. Freeman and his work. But a Robert E. Lee or general Civil War collection without all four volumes of the original *R. E. Lee* is not a real library. Various one-volume abridgements of the biography do not count.

———. *The South to Posterity.* New York: Charles Scribner's Sons, 1939, 1951. Wendell, NC: Broadfoot Bookmark edition, 1983.

Furgurson, Ernest B. *Chancellorsville 1863: The Soul of the Brave.* New York: Alfred A. Knopf, 1992.

Glatthaar, Joseph T. *Forged in Battle: The Civil War Alliance of Black Soldiers and White Officers.* New York: The Free Press, 1990.

Grant, Ulysses S. *Memoirs and Selected Letters: Personal Memoirs of U. S. Grant and Selected Letters 1839–1865.* New York: Literary Classics of the United States (Viking Press), 1990. This one-volume edition of what has been called the best military memoir in the English language is elegant. The original two-volume set was published and distributed by Mark Twain, a devoted friend of general of the army and former president Grant. General Grant died five days after completing his first draft of *Memoirs*.

Hattaway, Herman, and Archer Jones. *How the North Won.* Chicago: University of Illinois Press, 1983.

Hogan, Jr., David W. *The Overland Campaign, 4 May – 15 June 1864.* Washington, DC: US Army Center of Military History, Pub 75-12, 2014.

Horn, Jonathan. *The Man Who Would Not Be Washington: Robert E. Lee's Civil War and His Decision that Changed American History.* New York: Simon & Schuster, Inc., 2015.

Horn, Stanley F., ed. *The Robert E. Lee Reader.* New York: Konecky & Konecky (reprint), 1949 (Bobbs-Merrill Company).

Jones, John B. *A Rebel War Clerk's Diary.* 2 vols. Alexandria, VA: Time-Life Books, 1981. Facsimile of 1866 edition.

Jones, J. William. *Life and Letters of Robert Edward Lee*. Harrisonburg, VA: Sprinkle Publishers, 1986. Facsimile edition of Neale Publishers, 1906.

Katcher, Philip. *The Army of Robert E. Lee*. London: Arms and Armour Press, 1994.

Krick, Robert K. *Stonewall Jackson at Cedar Mountain*. Chapel Hill: University of North Carolina Press, 1990.

Lee, Fitzhugh. *General Lee*. Greenwich, CT: Fawcett Publications, 1961. An elegant facsimile edition of *General Lee* (first edition, 1894) was released in 1989 by the Broadfoot Publishing Company, Wilmington, North Carolina. This is an eminently readable biography of Robert E. Lee, Fitz Lee's uncle. During the Spanish-American War (1898–1904), President William McKinley appointed Fitz Lee, former major general in his uncle's Army of Northern Virginia, as a US Army major general of volunteers. In 1905, Fitzhugh Lee was buried wearing his US Army uniform. McKinley was the last Civil War veteran to become president.

Lee, Robert E., Jr. *Recollections and Letters of General Lee* (1904). Wilmington, NC: Broadfoot Publishing Company, 1988.

Longstreet, Helen D. *Lee and Longstreet at High Tide* (1904). Wilmington, NC: Broadfoot Publishing Company, 1989.

Luvaas, Jay. *The Military Legacy of the Civil War: The European Inheritance*. Chicago: University of Chicago Press, 1959. The noted titles of Professor Luvaas must be part of any Civil War library because of his brilliant research and his eloquent prose, and because he graduated from Allegheny College, grew up around the corner from West John Street in Meadville, Pennsylvania, and because his revered father, Professor of Music Morton Luvaas, is remembered with abiding love by so many of his Allegheny College students from the 1940s.

Luvaas, Jay, and Harold W. Nelson. *The US Army War College Guide to the Battle of Antietam*. Carlisle, PA: South Mountain Press, 1987.

———. *The US Army War College Guide to the Battles of Chancellorsville and Fredericksburg*. Carlisle, PA: South Mountain Press, 1988.

———. *The US Army War College Guide to the Battle of Gettysburg*. Carlisle, PA: South Mountain Press, 1986. These guides to "walking tours" of Civil War battlefields reflect almost eighty years of tradition at the US Army War College and the US Military Academy at West Point. Shortly after the Civil War, these tours were designed to teach army officers the vital importance of understanding the terrain of a battlefield. At West Point, Robert E. Lee was trained as a civil engineer more than as a battlefield tactician. This gave him a finely tuned eye for recognizing any field's "good ground," the control of which could decide the battle. Many times, Lee must have said to Jeb Stuart, "Find me the good ground." Likewise, Stonewall Jackson relied upon his famous "map maker," Jedediah Hotchkiss, a teacher and geologist by training, to find him the "good ground." These walking tours of Civil War battlefields stopped before World War II. Professor Luvaas revived the tours in 1982.

MacDonald, Rose M. *Mrs. Robert E. Lee*. Pikeville, MD: Robert B. Poisal Publisher, 1939, 1973.

Matter, William D. *If It Takes All Summer: The Battle of Spotsylvania*. Chapel Hill: University of North Carolina Press, 1988.

McLaughlin, Jack. *Gettysburg: The Long Encampment*. New York: Bonanza Books, 1963.

McMurry, Richard M. *Two Great Rebel Armies*. Chapel Hill: University of North Carolina, 1989.

McWhiney, Grady, and Perry D. Jamieson. *Attack and Die: Civil War Military Tactics and the Southern Heritage*. Tuscaloosa: University of Alabama Press, 1982.

Miers, Earl S. *Robert E. Lee*. New York: Harper and Row, Perennial Library, 1956.

Mitchell, Joseph B. *Decisive Battles of the Civil War*. New York: Fawcett Premier, Ballantine Edition, 1989.

Mitchell, Reid. *Civil War Soldiers*. New York: Viking Penguin, 1988.

Murfin, James V. *Battlefields of the Civil War*. New York: Crown Publishers, 1988.

Nagel, Paul C. *The Lees of Virginia*. New York: Oxford University Press, 1990.

Nevins, Allan. *The War for the Union: The Organized War 1863–1864*. New York: Charles Scribner's Sons, 1971.

Nofi, Albert A. *The Gettysburg Campaign, Revised Edition*. Conshohocken, PA: Combined Books, 1993.

Nolan, Alan T. *Lee Considered: General Robert E. Lee and Civil War History*. Chapel Hill: University of North Carolina, 1991.

The Official Military Atlas of the Civil War (1891–1895). Compiled by Captain Calvin D. Cowles. New York: Arno Press/Crown Publishers, Inc., 1978. This massive and magnificent collection of Civil War maps was prepared under the supervision of the nineteenth-century US secretaries of war to accompany *The Official Records of the Union and Confederate Armies, The War of the Rebellion*. See below, *War of the Rebellion: Master Edition*.

Pfanz, Harry W. *Gettysburg: The Second Day*. Chapel Hill: University of North Carolina, 1987.

Piston, William G. *Lee's Tarnished Lieutenant: James Longstreet and His Place in Southern History*. Athens: University of Georgia Press, 1987. Professor Piston's biography of James Longstreet is to Longstreet what Douglas Freeman is to Robert E. Lee. The same must be said of Jeffry D. Wert's biography of Lieutenant General Longstreet, noted below.

Priest, John M. *Antietam: The Soldiers' Battle*. Shippensburg, PA: White Mane Publishing, 1989.

Pryor, Elizabeth Brown. *Reading the Man: A Portrait of Robert E. Lee through his Private Letters*. New York: Penguin Books, 2007. This groundbreaking study may be the closest anyone gets to knowing what Robert E. Lee was thinking during his adult life. Elizabeth Pryor's 142 pages of exceptionally detailed endnotes is almost a second book for those of us who are compulsive footnote/endnote readers.

Rafuse, Ethan S. *Robert E. Lee and The Fall of the Confederacy, 1863-1865* (The American Crisis Series: Books on the Civil War Era). Lanham, MD: Rowman & Littlefield, 2009.

Robertson, James I., Jr. *General A. P. Hill: The Story of a Confederate Warrior*. New York: Random House, 1987. This is the definitive biography of "Little Powell" Hill.

———. *Soldiers Blue and Gray*. Columbia: University of South Carolina Press, 1988.

Scott, Frances, and Anne Cipriani Webb. *Who is Markie? The Life of Martha Custis Williams Carter, Cousin and Confidante of Robert E. Lee*. Westminster, MD: Heritage

Books, 2007. This is the first thorough biography of Robert Lee's cousin Markie. It is not likely to be equaled. The Avery Craven text noted above is its companion volume.

Sears, Stephen W. *Landscape Turned Red: The Battle of Antietam*. New Haven, CT: Ticknor and Fields, 1983.

———. *George B. McClellan: The Young Napoleon*. New Haven, CT: Ticknor and Fields, 1988.

Stackpole, Edward J. *Chancellorsville, Second Edition*. Harrisburg, PA: Stackpole Books, 1958, 1988.

———. *They Met at Gettysburg*. Harrisburg, PA: Stackpole Books, 1956, 1989.

Symonds, Craig L., and William J. Clipson. *A Battlefield Atlas of the Civil War*. Baltimore, MD: Nautical and Aviation Publishing Company, 1983.

Tanner, Robert G. *Stonewall in the Valley*. Garden City, NY: Doubleday, 1976.

Tapert, Annette. *The Brothers' War: Civil War Letters to Their Loved Ones from the Blue and Gray*. New York: Times Books, 1988.

Taylor, Walter H. *Four Years with General Lee*. New York: Bonanza, 1962.

———. *General Lee: His Campaigns in Virginia*. Facsimile edition by Dayton, OH: Morningside Bookshop, 1906, 1975.

The West Point Atlas of American Wars: 1689–1900. Vol. 1. General Vincent J. Esposito, ed. New York: Henry Holt and Company, 1995.

Thomas, Emory M. *Bold Dragoon: The Life of J. E. B. Stuart*. New York: Harper and Row, 1986.

———. *Robert E. Lee, A Biography*. New York: W. W. Norton and Company, 1995.

Trudeau, Noah Andre. *Bloody Roads South: The Wilderness to Cold Harbor, May–June 1864*. Boston: Little, Brown and Co., 1989.

Ward, Geoffrey C., Ric Burns, and Ken Burns. *The Civil War*. New York: Alfred A. Knopf, 1990.

War of the Rebellion: Master Edition. 2 DVDs. Tamarac, FL: THA New Media, LLC, 2011. This two-DVD set is a remarkable national treasure, containing all 128 volumes of the US War Department's *The War of the Rebellion: A Compilation of the Official Records of the Union and Confederate Armies (1880–1901)*. The printable PDF files are exact copies of the original series at 1 percent of the cost of reprints of the full series. This is simply a must for any Civil War library.

Wert, Jeffry D. *General James Longstreet*. New York: Simon & Schuster, 1993.

Wheeler, Richard. *Witness to Gettysburg*. New York: New American Library, 1987.

Who Was Who in the Civil War. John S. Bowman, ed. Avenel, NJ: Crescent Books (Brompton Books Corp.), 1994, 1995.

Woodworth, Steven E. *Jefferson Davis and His Generals*. Lawrence: University Press of Kansas, 1990.

INDEX

Abbeville, 171

Aiken's Landing, 108

Alexander, Edward Porter, 143, 204, 215

Alexandria, 207

Alsop farm, 32, 34, 37, 39

Amelia Courthouse, 132, 133, 135, 137, 138

Anderson, Richard "Dick," 15, 60; Bermuda Hundred and, 92; Early, J., and, 37; Ewell and, 141; First Corps and, 81, 140; Fourth Corps and, 111, 125, 133, 136, 138, 139–41, 146; Hancock and, 70; at Hanover Junction, 66–67; Lee, F., and, 32; Longstreet, J., and, 28; Old Cold Harbor and, 77, 78; promotion of, 84; relief of command of, 147; in Shenandoah Valley, 103; at Spotsylvania, 30–31, 33, 64–65; Warren and, 39

Andersonville, 178

angina, 3, 10, 202

Antietam Creek, 6, 21, 46, 53; Bloody Lane at, 35; Hill, A.

P., and, 33; McClellan and, 96, 212; Sedgwick at, 37; Sharpsburg cemetery at, 194, 218; Stuart, J., at, 56

Appomattox Courthouse, 147, 149, 154

Appomattox River, 110, 134, 135; Bevill's Bridge on, 136; High Bridge on, 143; Hill, A. P., and, 95; James River and, 146; Petersburg and, 87, 126; Sayler's Creek and, 141; Violet Bank on, 98

Appomattox Station, 146

Aquia Creek, 57–58

Arlington House, 181, 188, 199, 211–12

Army Corps of Engineers, 5, 37, 181, 182

Army of Northern Virginia, 1, 11, 14, 44, 46; Beauregard and, 71; dissolution of, 161; Hill, A. P., and, 97; history of, 182; as "Lee's Miserables," 113; Mother Lee and, 9; officers of, 164; Orange Turnpike and, 20; at Petersburg, 90, 98–99,

100; resignation from, 2–3; at Sayler's Creek, 142; surrender by, 145–56, 160; Virginia Militia into, 73. *See also* First Corps; Fourth Corps; Second Corps; Third Corps

Army of the Potomac, 7–8, 9, 30; at Cold Harbor, 79; in Hanovertown, 73; honor guard by, 172; James River and, 83, 93; Meade and, 16; at Rapidan River, 13; at Spotsylvania, 60; at "the Wilderness," 60

Ashland, 43

Atlee's Station, 74; Old Cold Harbor and, 77

Babcock, Orville, 154

Barlow, Francis, 49

Battle of Cedar Creek, 111

Battle of the Crater, 102

Beauregard, Pierre "Old Bory," 197; Army of Northern Virginia and, 71; Bermuda Hundred and, 76; Davis, Jefferson, and, 161; at Petersburg, 87, 90–95

Beaver Dam, 38, 48, 55

Belle Plain, 44, 67

Benedict House, 136

Benjamin, Judah, 125, 137, 162, 165, 171, 185

Bermuda Hundred, 90, 93, 96, 104; Anderson and, 92; Beauregard and, 76; Smith, W., and, 77

Bethesda, 77

Bethesda Church, 76

Bevill's Bridge, 136

blacks (Negroes), 107, 178; rights of, 198; in 29th US Colored Infantry, 102. *See also* slaves

Blandford Cemetery, 95

Block House Bridge, 39

"Bloody Angle," at "the Mule Shoe," 51–56

Bloody Lane, at Antietam Creek, 35

Bloody Run, at Gettysburg, 35

blue mass, 71

Bolling, Mary Tabb, 194

Boydton Plank Road, 110, 127

Brady, Matthew, 168

Breckinridge, John, 79; Hampton and, 170; as Secretary of War, 118, 119, 120, 132, 142, 165; in Shenandoah Valley, 86

Bremo Plantation, 102

Brewer, Charles, 45, 48, 55

Brockenbrough, John, 184

Brock Road, 25, 31, 32, 34, 37

Brompton Plantation, 75

Brown, Campbell, 16

Buchser, Frank, 202

Buckingham Courthouse, 163

Buckner, Simon Bolivar, 213

Bull Run, 18

Burgess Mill, 112, 128

burial, 210

burial truce, at Cold Harbor, 84–86
Burkeville, 135
Burnett farm, 79, 88
Burnside, Ambrose, 7, 16, 21, 27, 36; at Chesterfield Bridge, 68; Dimmock Line and, 93; at Fredericksburg, 201; at Guinea Station, 66; Hill, A. P., and, 70; at "the Mule Shoe," 61; at Petersburg, 92–93
Burt, Armistead, 171
Butler, Ben, 36, 72, 75, 76–77, 96
Butterfield, Daniel, 216
Byrd, Harry, 218

Cary, Hetty, 117
Cemetery Ridge, 20, 49, 129
Central Railroad, 68–69
Chaffin's Bluff, 93, 101, 104, 108–9
Chamberlain, Joshua, 161
Champ (horse), 7, 15, 131
Chancellorsville, 3, 6, 13, 16, 46, 53; Hooker and, 126, 152
Chandler, Mary, 65–66
Chandler, Tom, 65–66
Charles City Courthouse, 88
Charles City Road, 104
Charleston, 115, 205
Charlotte, 169
Chesterfield Bridge, 68, 69, 72
Chicamauga, 197
Chickahominy River, 44, 45, 76, 89

Christmas Amnesty, 198–99
Church Crossing, 129–30
Cincinnati (horse), 36, 158
citizenship, 217–18
City Point, 96, 103, 106–7, 137
Clark's Mountain, 12, 13
Clay house, 93
Cocke, Cary Charles, 102
Cocke, Elizabeth, 182
Cold Harbor, 72, 75, 82; Army of the Potomac at, 79; burial truce at, 84–86; Early, J., and, 88; Grant, U., and, 79, 82; Grant, U., movement from, 88–89; Lee, F., and, 76; trenches at, 79, 86
Columbia, 118, 204, 218
Compton, William, 50–51
Confederate flag, 218
Confederate Home for Women, 218
conscription law, 6
Cooke, Philip, 44
Cooper, Samuel, 170
Coward, Asbury, 14
Crawford (General), 68
Culpepper, 103
Cumberland Church, 143
Cumberland Island, 205
Custer, George Armstrong, 38, 45
Custis, Parke, 72–73

Dana, Charles, 29
Daniel, Junius, 51
Danville, 136, 138, 148, 160

Darbytown Road, 104
Davenport's Bridge, 38
Davis, George, 169
Davis, Jefferson, 2–3, 7, 10–11, 75; at Abbeville, 171; arming slaves by, 118–19, 121–22; in Charlotte, 169; conscription law by, 6; in Danville, 136, 148, 160; evacuation from Richmond by, 132, 134; at Fort Monroe, 180, 186; in Greensboro, 160–61, 165, 166; household goods auction by, 125; illnesses of, 179; imprisonment of, 191; Johnston, J., and, 161; Lincoln and, 138, 169, 171; at Petersburg, 105; Presidential Proclamation by, 137; release from prison, 193; on the run, 161–74; Stuart, J., and, 55, 59; surrender of, 175–76; treason indictment of, 195; truce by, 168–70
Davis, Joseph, 11–12
Davis, Varina, 12, 126, 171, 174, 179; stipend for, 185
Davis, Varina Anne, 126, 168, 175, 191
death, 209
Derwent, 182
desertions, 3; death penalty for, 124; in Petersburg, 109, 119–20, 122
Dimmock Line, 91, 93

Dinwiddie Courthouse, 126, 127, 128
Doles, George, 41
Douglas, Robert, 200
Douglas, Stephen, 79
Drewry's Bluff, 90, 92
dysentery, 69, 71, 73, 86, 88

Early, Jubal "Old Jube," 19, 25, 29; Anderson and, 37; at Cold Harbor, 88; Ewell and, 74; Gordon and, 50; Hill, A. P., and, 39; Hunter, D., and, 87; Pendleton, S., and, 108; promotion of, 84; Second Corps and, 87, 112; in Shenandoah Valley, 87–88, 97–98, 103, 111, 114, 120; at Spotsylvania, 35, 36; Third Corps and, 33
Early, Robert, 19
Edge Hill, 114, 130
11th Pennsylvania Infantry, 116
Ely's Ford, 13, 29
Evans, Clement, 114
Ewell, Richard "Baldy," 2, 5–7, 12, 15–16, 18–19, 21, 25, 29; Amelia Courthouse and, 138; Anderson and, 141; Early, J., and, 74; evacuation from Richmond by, 134; Fort Gilmore and, 109; Gordon and, 140; Hancock and, 70; illness of, 73, 74; Johnson, E., and, 47; Long, Armistead

L., and, 48; Pendleton,
S., and, 54; Richmond-
Fredericksburg-Potomac
Railroad and, 73; at Shady
Grove Church, 31; Sheridan
and, 139; at Spotsylvania,
33, 64–65; surrender of, 141;
wounding of, 63

Fancy (horse), 213
Farewell Address, 158, 159–60
Farmville, 139, 142, 143
Field, Charles, 15, 22, 25, 104,
128; Fort Harrison and, 111;
Heth and, 101
15th New Jersey Infantry, 53
5th Michigan Cavalry, 45
1st Virginia Infantry, 131
1st Wisconsin Cavalry, 175
First Corps, 6, 10–11, 15–16,
21–22, 25, 30–31, 34, 73;
Anderson of, 81, 140;
Kershaw of, 78; Longstreet,
J., of, 112, 125, 133, 136, 149;
at Spotsylvania, 35
First Reconstruction Act, 192
Fisher's Hill, 107
Fitzhugh, Maria, 200
Five Forks, 126, 127, 128, 129
Forge Bridge, 45
Fort Gilmore, 109
Fort Gregg, 132, 133
Fort Harrison, 108–11
Fort Monroe, 176, 180, 186
Fort Stedman, 123, 124

45th North Carolina Infantry, 166
48th Pennsylvania Infantry, 101
4th Michigan Cavalry, 175
Fourth Corps, 111, 125, 133, 136,
138, 139–41, 146
Fox, W. E., 67
Frayser's Farm, 92
Fredericksburg, 6, 27, 29, 31, 114;
Grant, U., at, 46, 47; hospital
at, 75; Lexington Episcopal
Church and, 200–201;
Marye's Heights and, 70;
Sheridan at, 38–39; Stuart, J.,
at, 56; The Sunken Road at, 35

Gaines Mill, 84
general amnesty, 174, 179
general-in-chief, 116, 118, 122–23
General Orders Number 8, 124
General Orders Number 9, 160
General Orders Number 15, 1
General Orders Number 44, 57
Germanna Ford, 13, 16, 29
Germanna Plank Road, 29
Gettysburg, 2, 6, 27, 53; Bloody
Run at, 35; Cemetery Ridge
at, 20, 129; Confederate
graves at, 198; Gordon at,
159; Hancock at, 49; Little
Round top at, 161; Longstreet,
J., at, 215; Pickett's Charge
at, 11, 20, 84, 143, 182; The
Slaughter Pen at, 35
Gettysburg Association, 198
Gibbons, John, 81

Goode's Bridge, 136–37

Gordon, John B., 19, 25–26, 29, 33, 41, 50–51, 59, 63; at Appomattox Courthouse, 147, 149; Barlow and, 49; Early, J., and, 50; Ewell and, 140; at Gettysburg, 159; Lee, Rooney, and, 140; at Lynchburg, 146; at "the Mule Shoe," 50; at Petersburg, 123–24; Richmond and, 120–21; of Second Corps, 114, 120, 123, 125, 128, 136, 149, 161; in Shenandoah Valley, 107; Sheridan and, 154; Union salute to, 161

Grace Episcopal Church, 207; Sewing Society, Mother Lee of, 190

Grant, Julia, 8

Grant, Ulysses S. (Hiram Ulysses), 7–10, 12–13, 16, 26–30; as "Butcher Grant," 61; Chickahominy River and, 89; Cold Harbor and, 79, 82, 88; death of, 212–13; at Fredericksburg, 46, 47; general amnesty from, 174; at Guinea Station, 66; Hays and, 20; Hill, A. P., and, 65, 67; horseback meeting with, 158; Jackson and, 65–66; James River and, 87, 90, 91; Jetersville and, 139; Lincoln and, 96;

Longstreet, J., and, 188; Mahone and, 145; Meade and, 70; "the Mule Shoe" and, 60–61; at North Anna River, 70; "On to Richmond" offensive of, 47; Overland Campaign by, 82, 96; pain train of, 29; at Petersburg, 96–97; as president, 200; at Quarles' Mill, 71–72; Rapidan River and, 82, 100; request for surrender from, 145; Richmond and, 36, 65, 72, 100, 112; saddle sores of, 36; Sedgwick and, 37; in Shenandoah Valley, 103; Smith, W., and, 77; at Spotsylvania, 29–30, 46, 47, 58, 61–64; at surrender, 154–56; surrender terms by, 145–54; Upton and, 42; as "Useless," 30; Washburne and, 43; White House Landing and, 73; Williams, M., and, 181

Greenbrier. See The Old White

Greene, Nathaniel, 205

Greensboro, 160–61, 165, 166

Gregg, John, 22, 111

Griffin, Charles, 16, 68

Grimes, Bryan, 114

Guinea Station, 64, 65, 66

Halleck, Henry, 43, 174

Hampton, Frank, 113

Hampton, Wade, 89, 116; Breckinridge and, 170; at chapel convocation, 196–97; City Point and, 106–7; Stuart, J., and, 103–4, 112; White House Landing and, 104

Hancock, Winfield, 16, 19, 25, 36; Johnson, E., and, 50; Meade and, 51; "the Mule Shoe" and, 49; at North Anna River, 70; at Petersburg, 92–93; Pickett's Charge and, 84; Shady Grove Road and, 39

Hanover Junction, 28, 38–39, 42, 64–67, 73

Hanovertown, 72, 73, 74

Harris, Nathaniel, 52

Harris Farm, 63–64

Hatcher's Run, 112, 116–17; Southside Railroad and, 124–26; Third Corps at, 116, 128–29

Haw's Shop, 73, 74

Hays, Alexander, 20

Heth, Henry, 20, 22, 39, 46, 101; at Burgess Mill, 128; at North Anna River, 67; at Shady Grove, 37–38

High Bridge, 143

Hill, Ambrose Powell "Little Powell," 6–7, 12, 14–16, 20–22, 25, 46, 60, 89; at Antietam Creek, 33; at

Appomattox River, 95; Army of Northern Virginia and, 97; Burnside and, 70; at Chaffin's Bluff, 93; death of, 131, 214; Early, J., and, 39; Grant, U., and, 65, 67; at Hatcher's Run, 116; illnesses of, 7, 21, 27, 33, 63–64, 97, 105, 122, 130; at Jericho Mill, 69; at Malvern Hill, 91, 92; McClellan and, 214; at Petersburg, 94, 97, 104, 130; at Spotsylvania, 64–65; of Third Corps, 73, 97, 106, 112, 128–29, 136

Hill, Baptist, 13

Hill, Dolly, 12, 106, 122, 131, 214

Hill, Lucy, 12

Hoke, Robert, 77, 90, 109, 111, 115

"Home, Sweet Home" (song), 42

Hood, John Bell, 21, 95, 115

Hooker, Joe "Fighting Joe," 7, 16, 27, 126, 152

Hot Springs resort, 207

Houston, M. H., 206

Houston, Sam, 3

Howard, Oliver O., 215

Huff, John, 45–46, 48, 74

Hughes' Shop, 74

Hunter, Andrew, 115

Hunter, David, 87, 97

Jackson, Thomas Jonathan "Stonewall," 2, 6, 14, 18–19, 27, 53, 163; Grant, U., and,

65–66; home of, 188; Second
Corps and, 97–98

James River, 36, 44; Appomattox
River and, 87, 146; Army
of the Potomac and, 83,
93; Bermuda Hundred and,
96; Grant, U., and, 87, 90,
91; Petersburg and, 88;
Richmond and, 75, 83, 94;
Rockett's Landing on, 137;
Wilcox Landing on,
89–90

Jenkins, Micah, 13–14, 23, 25

Jericho Mill, 67, 69, 71

Jerusalem Plank Road, 96, 97

Jetersville, 137, 138–39

Johnson, Andrew, 171; Christmas
Amnesty by, 198–99;
general amnesty by, 179;
Reconstruction and,
173–74

Johnson, Bushrod, 109, 121,
129–30, 147

Johnson, Edward "Allegheny,"
34, 35, 59; Barlow and, 49;
capture of, 50, 57; at "the
Mule Shoe," 47, 48

Johnson, Reverdy, 196

Johnston, Andrew, 129

Johnston, Joe, 56, 73, 122–23, 161,
168–70, 213–14

Joint Committee on
Reconstruction, 189

Jones, John Marshall "Rum," 18

Junkin, Elinor, 188

Keitt, Lawrence, 78

Kentucky (horse), 173

Kershaw, Joe, 15, 22, 32, 128;
at Bermuda Hundred, 93;
Blandford Cemetery and,
95; Hoke and, 77; Keitt
and, 78; at North Anna
River, 69; at Petersburg, 94;
in Shenandoah Valley, 103;
surrender of, 141

Laurel Hill, 32, 33–34, 39, 42

Lawton, Alexander, 3

Lee, Agnes, 9, 127, 135, 167,
201, 203–6; death of, 212;
at funeral, 210; Mother Lee
and, 212; typhoid fever of,
182

Lee, Anne Carter, 200, 210

Lee, Annie, 112, 203, 218

Lee, Charles Carter, 166

Lee, Charlotte, 3–4, 194

Lee, Custis (George Washington
Custis), 5, 114, 137; death
of, 217; surrender of, 141; at
Virginia Military Institute,
188–89

Lee, Fitzhugh "The Old Rebel,"
5, 32, 74, 149, 200, 216; at
Cold Harbor, 76; at Five
Forks, 126, 129; at Old Cold
Harbor, 77; at Petersburg,
122; in Shenandoah Valley,
103; Sheridan and, 77, 140;
Stuart, J., and, 42, 44, 45;

Virginia Central Railroad and, 89; wounding of, 107

Lee, Henry "Light Horse Harry," 173, 184, 205

Lee, Mary Custis, 9, 186, 211–12; death of, 217, 218–19; Stuart, J., and, 58; travels of, 213; typhoid fever of, 97; Wilson, T., and, 217

Lee, Mildred "Precious Life," 9, 98, 182, 189, 201; at death bed, 208–9; death of, 216; typhoid fever of, 197; at Washington College, 212

Lee, Richard, 181

Lee, Robert E. *See specific topics*

Lee, Robert E., III, 4, 199, 201

Lee, Robert E., IV, 218

Lee, Robert E., Jr., 73, 165

Lee, Rooney (William Henry Fitzhugh), 3–4, 9, 45, 126, 143, 167; at Chaffin's Bluff, 108; on Charles City Road, 104; death of, 214; Gordon and, 140; at Petersburg, 122; promotion of, 11; second marriage of, 194–95; Stuart, J., and, 44; at White House Landing, 73; at Wilcox Landing, 94

Lee, Sidney Smith, 9, 200, 201

"Lee's Miserables," 113

Lexington, 87, 97–98

Lexington Episcopal Church, 200–201

lieutenant general, 7

Lincoln, Abraham, 121; at City Point, 137; Davis, Jefferson, and, 169, 171; death of, 166, 168; Grant, U., and, 7, 8, 43, 96; McClellan and, 96; Pickett and, 129; in Richmond, 137–38

Little Round top, at Gettysburg, 161

"Load in Nine Times" drill, 40

Locust Grove, 15–16

Logan, John, 199

Long, Armistead L., 48, 174

Longstreet, James "Old Pete," "Old Warhorse," 6–8, 10–12, 15–16, 18, 21, 23, 190; Anderson and, 28; at Chicamauga, 197; death of, 216; at Farmville, 142, 143; of First Corps, 112, 125, 133, 136, 149; at Gettysburg, 215; Jenkins and, 14; at Petersburg, 111, 133; at Pickett's Charge, 215; presidential pardon for, 188; Southside Railroad and, 146; after surrender, 163; on surrender, 145, 149–50; Third Corps and, 133; at Turnbull House, 130; wounding of, 25, 27, 63, 73

Longstreet, Mary Dent, 8

The Lost Cause, 164, 215

Lynchburg, 87, 139, 146

Mahone, Billy, 23, 28, 39, 141–42; at Cold Harbor, 79; at Fort Gregg, 133; at Goode's Bridge, 137; Grant, U. and, 145; Harris and, 52; at High Bridge, 143; on Jerusalem Plank Road, 96; promotion of, 84; at wedding of Lee, Rooney, 195

malingerers, 5

Malvern Hill, 91, 92

Manassas, 53

Mangan, James, 53

Marshall, Charles, 3, 152–54, 158, 159–60

Marye, John, 75

Marye's Heights, 70

Massanutten Mountain, 107

Massaponax Baptist Church, 65

Mauck, John, 131

McClellan, George, 7, 44; at Antietam Creek, 96, 212; Hill, A. P., and, 214; Lincoln and, 96; Richmond and, 73–74; Sharpsburg cemetery and, 194; White House Landing and, 72

McCormick, Cyrus, 189

McDowell, Irvin, 211–12

McDowell, Irwin, 7

McIlwane, Robert, 133

McKinley, William, 216

McLean, Wilmer, 154, 156, 158

Meade, George Gordon "Old Snapping Turtle," 7, 9, 11, 12, 14, 27, 30; Army of the Potomac and, 16; delayed attack before surrender, 153–54; Fort Stedman and, 124; Grant, U., and, 70; Hancock and, 51; meeting with, 159, 173–74; at "the Mule Shoe," 61; at North Anna River, 70; at Petersburg, 93; at Quarles' Mill, 71–72; Sedgwick and, 33–34; Smith, W., and, 82; at Spotsylvania, 59, 62–63, 64; Warren and, 33–34, 39–40; Wise and, 99

Mechanicsville, 73

The Mess, 1, 9, 167

Mexico, 46, 52

Miles, Nelson, 176

Miner, Charles W., 219–20

Mitchell's Shop, 38

Mosby, John, 44, 147

Mother Lee, 1, 3, 37, 75, 84, 96, 102–3, 119; Army of Northern Virginia and, 9; at Bremo Plantation, 102; Davis, Jefferson, and, 134; death of, 212; of Grace Episcopal Church Sewing Society, 190; Lee, Agnes, and, 212; protection of by Union troops, 135; at Rockbridge Baths Spa, 201; socks by, 9, 50, 107; on starvation, 169; after surrender, 167; typhoid fever of, 97, 102;

Washington, G., and, 199, 211–12; at White Sulphur Springs health spa, 193, 197; Williams, M., and, 180–81

Mott, Gershom, 41

Mountain Road, 43, 44

Mount Carmel Church, 66

"the Mule Shoe": "Bloody Angle" at, 51–56; evacuation of, 56–57; Gordon at, 50; Grant, U., and, 60–61; Second Corps and, 35, 36, 39–42, 47–57; trenches at, 48, 57

Nashville, 115

Negroes. *See* blacks

New Market, 111

New Market Heights, 104

9th Vermont Infantry, 135

Noel's Station, 68

Norfolk, 206

North Anna River, 38, 65–73

Ny River, 63

oak tree, in Spotsylvania, 56, 58, 214

oath of allegiance, 218

O. Henry (Porter, Billy), 166

Old Church Road, 76

Old Cold Harbor, 77, 78

The Old White, 193, 194, 197–98, 201

138th Pennsylvania Infantry, 131

140th New York Infantry, 32

"On to Richmond" offensive, of Grant, U., 47

Orange Courthouse, 6, 12, 15

Orange Plank Road, 14, 15, 16, 20, 21, 23, 25, 31; Third Corps on, 33

Orange Turnpike, 14, 15, 19, 20

Ord, Edward O., 155

Overland Campaign, 82, 96

Ox Ford, 68

pain train, 29

Palmer, William Henry, 131

Pamunkey River, 72, 73, 74

Parker's Store, 15–16

Pegram, John, 114, 117, 118

Pegram, Willie, 129

Pender, Dorsey, 15

Pendleton, Alexander Swift, Jr., 113

Pendleton, Kate Corbin, 2, 5, 89, 108, 112, 113

Pendleton, Sandie, 2, 5–6, 17, 89; death of, 108, 112; Early, J., and, 108; Ewell and, 54; Jackson and, 163; son of, 113

Pendleton, William, 108, 147

Perrin, Abner, 52

Petersburg: Appomattox River and, 87, 126; Army of Northern Virginia and, 90, 98–99, 100; Beauregard and, 90–95; Davis, Jefferson, and, 105; desertions in,

109, 119–20, 122; explosion beneath, 101–2; Gordon and, 123–24; Grant, U., and, 96–97; Hill, A. P., and, 94, 97, 104, 130; James River and, 88; Kershaw and, 94; Lee, Rooney wedding in, 194–95; Longstreet, J., and, 111, 133; Meade and, 93; railroads at, 91; rat holes in, 113; rebuilding of, 195; Second Corps and, 114; Sheridan and, 122; siege of, 94, 98, 106–7, 124; starvation at, 105, 106–7, 109, 115; trenches in, 97, 98–99, 100, 105, 114; Wilcox and, 128; withdrawal from, 132–33

Pickett, George, 13, 64, 66, 69, 125, 141; Bermuda Hundred and, 93; Chaffin's Bluff and, 108; Dinwiddie Courthouse and, 128; Drewry's Bluff and, 92; Five Forks and, 126, 127, 129; Hatcher's Run and, 125; relief of command of, 147; Sayler's Creek and, 140

Pickett's Charge, 11, 20, 84, 143, 182, 215

poison fields. *See* Spotsylvania

Pope, John, 7

Po River, 35, 37, 39, 60

Porter, Billy (O. Henry), 166 portrait, 202

Port Royal, 65, 67, 72

Portsmouth, 205–6

presidential pardon, 180, 188

Preston, Margaret Junkin, 189

Pritchard, Ben, 175

the Punch Bowl, 58

Quarles' Mill, 71–72

railroads, 10, 28; Central Railroad, 68–69; Jetersville and, 138–39; at Petersburg, 91; Richmond-Danville Railroad, 138; Richmond-Fredericksburg-Potomac Railroad, 65, 71, 73; Valley Railroad, 207; Weldon Railroad, 96–97, 104–5. *See also* Southside Railroad; Virginia Central Railroad

Ramseur, Stephen Dodson, 51, 63, 76, 84, 111–12

Randolph, Edmund, 182

Rapidan River, 1, 6–7, 9–16, 27, 29, 36; Grant, U., and, 82, 100

Rappahannock River, 65

rat holes, in Petersburg, 113

Ravensworth Plantation, 200, 201, 207

Reagan, John, 170, 171, 172

Reams Station, 105

"Rebel Yell," 30–31

Reconstruction, 198; First Reconstruction Act, 192;

Johnson, A., and, 173–74; Joint Committee on Reconstruction, 189
Reynolds, John, 37
Rice, James, 39–40
Rice Station, 140
Richmond, 28, 47; Confederate Home for Women in, 218; evacuation of, 126, 132; Gordon and, 120–21; Grant, U., and, 36, 65, 72, 100, 112; James River and, 75, 83, 94; Lincoln in, 137–38; McClellan and, 73–74; Petersburg and, 87; postwar visit to, 206; return to after surrender, 162, 163–64, 167; Sheridan and, 42; Stuart, J., and, 59, 58
Richmond-Danville Railroad, 138
Richmond-Fredericksburg-Potomac Railroad, 65, 71, 73
Riddell's Shop, 90, 92
Rifle (horse), 18
Robert E. Lee (submarine), 217
Robinson, John, 32, 34
Rockbridge Baths Spa, 201
Rockett's Landing, 137
Rodes, Robert, 51, 52, 63, 114; death of, 107; Old Church Road and, 76; in Shenandoah Valley, 107
Roosevelt, Teddy, 216
Rosecrans, William, 197–98

Rosser, Tom, 126, 129
Ryan, George, 32

Sallie (dog), 116–17, 178
Sandford, Charles, 211
Saunders Field, 18, 19
Savannah, 115, 204
Sayler's Creek, 140, 141, 142, 147
Scott, Thomas, 189
Scott, Winfield, 7, 125
scurvy, 77, 87
Second Corps, 6, 15, 16, 21, 25, 29, 34, 63; desertions from, 122; Early, J., and, 87, 112; Gordon and, 120, 123, 125, 128, 136, 149, 161; Lexington and, 97–98; "the Mule Shoe" of, 35, 36, 39–42, 47–57; at Petersburg, 114; Rodes and, 114; in Shenandoah Valley, 97–98, 107–8; Union salute to, 161
Seddon, James, 5, 87, 107, 115, 118
Sedgwick, John "Uncle John," 16, 19, 30; at Antietam Creek, 37; death of, 37; Grant, U., and, 37; Meade and, 33–34; at Spotsylvania, 62; Stuart, J., and, 56
The Seven Days, 53, 73, 76, 84, 92
Seven Pines, 112
Shady Grove, 37–38
Shady Grove Church, 31, 33, 36

Shady Grove Road, 39

Shand farm, 93

Sharpsburg cemetery, 194, 218

Shenandoah Valley, 107–8; Breckinridge and, 86; Early, J., and, 87–88, 97–98, 103, 111, 114, 120; Grant, U., and, 103; Second Corps in, 97–98; Sheridan and, 120; Staunton in, 87; Washington College in, 87, 184–98

Sheridan, Phil, 8, 36; Dinwiddie Courthouse and, 126; Ewell and, 139; at Fredericksburg, 38; Gordon and, 154; Lee, F., and, 77, 140; on North Anna River, 73; on Pamunkey River, 72; at Petersburg, 122; Ramseur and, 112; in Shenandoah Valley, 107–8, 120; Stuart, J., and, 32–33, 38–39, 42–45; at surrender, 155; Virginia Central Railroad and, 87; White Oak Road and, 128

Sherman, William Tecumseh, 115, 118; death of, 213–14; Johnston, J., and, 168–70

Shippen estate, 98

Shirley Plantation, 206

Sickles, Daniel, 215, 216

The Slaughter Pen, at Gettysburg, 35

slaves, 115–16; arming of, 118–19, 121–22

Smith, Edward Kirby, 172, 176

Smith, Francis, 137, 208

Smith, William "Baldy," 72; Butler and, 75, 76–77; Dimmock Line and, 91; Grant, U., and, 77; Meade and, 82; Old Cold Harbor and, 78; at Petersburg, 92–93; White House Landing and, 75–76, 88

Snell Bridge, 60

soap, 103

socks, by Mother Lee, 9, 50, 107

Sorrel, Moxley, 23, 28

South Anna River, 43

Southern Christendom, conversion to, 1

Southside Railroad, 112; Amelia Courthouse and, 135; Farmville and, 139; Five Forks and, 128; Hatcher's Run and, 124–26; Longstreet, J., and, 146; Rice Station and, 140

Spotsylvania, 28, 35; Anderson at, 30–31, 33, 64–65; Army of the Potomac at, 60; Early, J., at, 36; Ewell at, 33, 64–65; Grant, U., and, 29–30, 46, 47, 58, 61–64; Hill, A. P., at, 64–65; Meade and, 59, 62–63, 64; oak tree in, 56, 58, 214; poison fields of, 36, 40, 42, 46; Sedgwick at, 62; Third Corps at, 36; trenches in, 39. See also "the Mule Shoe" starvation, 6, 10, 105, 106–7, 109, 115, 143; Mother Lee on, 169

Staunton, 87, 207

Stephens, Alexander, 176, 197

Steuart, George, 50

Stewart, John, 167

Stonewall Brigade, 9, 18, 41, 49–50

Stuart, Flora, 38, 48, 55–56; death of, 217

Stuart, James Ewell Brown "Jeb," 2, 6, 16, 18, 197; Custer and, 45; death of, 55–57; Hampton, W., and, 103–4, 112; Jackson and, 163; Lee, F., and, 32, 42, 44, 45; Lee, Mary Custis, and, 58; Lee, Rooney, and, 44; Richmond and, 58–59; Sheridan and, 32–33, 38–39, 42–45; wounding of, 45–46, 48, 55; at Yellow Tavern, 44

Stuart, Margaret, 10, 11

Sultana (steamboat), 178

Sumner, Edwin, 56

The Sunken Road, at Fredericksburg, 35

surrender, by Army of Northern Virginia, 145–56, 160

Sutherlin, William T., 136

Sweeney, Sam, 6

Sycamore Spring, 45

Taylor, Richard, 172

Taylor, Walter, 119, 133, 135, 152, 154, 206, 210

Taylor, Zachary, 181

Taylorsville, 42, 43, 71

Telegraph Road, 43, 44, 45, 66, 67

Third Battle of Winchester, 107

Third Corps, 6–7, 13, 15–16, 18–22, 27, 37, 46, 65; Early, J., and, 33; at Hatcher's Run, 116, 128–29; Hill, A. P., of, 73, 97, 106, 112, 128–29, 136; Longstreet, J., and, 133; on Orange Plank Road, 33; at Spotsylvania, 36

Tilden, Samuel, 190

Todd's Tavern, 13, 29, 31

Totopotomoy Creek, 75, 76

Traveller (horse), 6, 11, 22, 50–51, 141, 165, 186, 192; at Appomattox Courthouse, 149; cannon ball under, 52; death of, 210–10; at surrender, 156

treason indictment, 179–80; dismissal of, 199

treason indictment, of Davis, Jefferson, 195

trenches: at Cold Harbor, 79, 86; at Dimmock Line, 91; at "the Mule Shoe," 48, 57; in Petersburg, 97, 98–99, 100, 105, 114; in Spotsylvania, 39

Trenholm, George, 170

Tucker (Sergeant), 131, 154, 156

Turkey Hill, 78, 79, 80

Turnbull House, 130

Turnbull plantation, 114

12th New Hampshire Infantry, 81

26th Michigan Infantry, 49

29th US Colored Infantry, 102

typhoid fever, 97, 102, 182, 197

Upton, Emory, 40–42, 53

Valley Campaign, 53

Valley Railroad, 207

Venable, Charles, 22, 71, 131, 149, 210

Verdiersville, 15–16

Vicksburg, 7, 219

Violet Bank, 98

Virginia Central Railroad, 10, 28, 74; Custer and, 38; Lee, F., and, 89; Sheridan and, 87

Virginia Military Academy, 87, 97

Virginia Military Institute (VMI), 188–89, 208

Virginia Militia, 73

VMI. *See* Virginia Military Academy

Walker, James, 18–19

Warren, Gouverneur, 16, 32; Anderson and, 39; Meade and, 33–34, 39–40; on North Anna River, 68

Washburn, Cadwallader, 43

Washburn, Israel, 43

Washburne, Elihu, 43

Washington, George, 7, 72, 184, 199, 211–12

Washington, Martha, 72, 180–81

Washington College, 87, 184–98, 202, 206; chapel for, 191, 196–97, 207; Lee, Mildred, at, 212

Weitzel, Godfrey, 135

Weldon Railroad, 96–97, 104–5

Weyanoke, 90, 93

White House Landing, 72–73; Hampton, W., at, 104; Sheridan at, 122; Smith, W., at, 75–76, 88

White Oak Road, 126, 128

White Oak Swamp, 89, 96, 112

White Sulphur Springs health spa, 193, 197

Whittier, Charles, 152, 153

Widow Tapp, 20, 21

the Wigwam, 14

Wilcox, Cadmus, 15, 19–20, 21, 22; at Central Railroad, 68–69; at Cold Harbor, 79; Fort Gregg and, 133; at Noel's Station, 68; at North Anna River, 67; at Petersburg, 128; at Turkey Hill, 79

Wilcox Landing, 89–90, 94

the Wilderness, 13–30, 33, 41, 50; Army of the Potomac at, 60; Burnside at, 16, 21, 27; Early, J., at, 19; Hill, A., at, 14, 15, 16, 18, 20, 21–22, 25, 27; Meade and, 14, 16, 27, 30

Wilderness Tavern, 16

Williams, Martha Custis
  "Markie," 180–81, 191–92,
  196, 207
Williams, Orton, 181
Williams, Seth, 29, 50, 145, 155,
  159
Williams, Walter, 217
Wilmington, 115, 205

Wilson, James H., 175–76
Wilson, Thomas Woodrow, 176,
  217
Wise, Henry, 99
Wise, John, 147–48
Wright, Horatio, 37, 40, 68

Yellow Tavern, 43, 44